INTRODUCTION

to

CLASSIC

JAPANESE LITERATURE

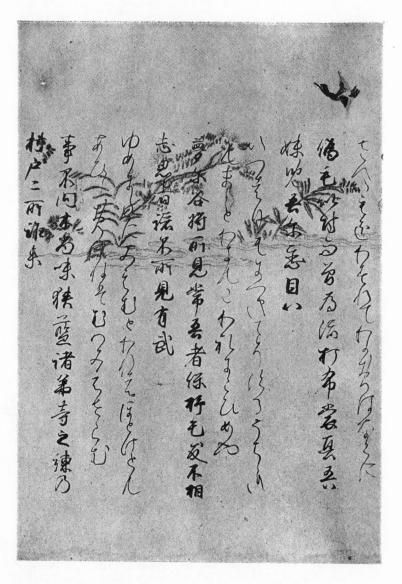

MANYÔSHÛ (ANTHOLOGY OF A MYRIAD LEAVES).

Manuscript copy (so-called Katsura Bon. Prince Katsura Scroll) made in the 10th century. Property of the Imperial Household.

INTRODUCTION

TO

CLASSIC JAPANESE LITERATURE

EDITED BY

THE KOKUSAI BUNKA SHINKOKAI

GREENWOOD PRESS, PUBLISHERS
WESTPORT, CONNECTICUT

Originally published in 1948
by Kokusai Bunka Shinkokai
(The Society for International Cultural Relations)

First Greenwood Reprinting 1970

Library of Congress Catalogue Card Number 72-98847

SBN 8371-3118-9

Printed in the United States of America

PREFACE

Historical background and tradition impress on a nation its own peculiar manner of observing and appreciating the culture which it has evolved. Yet while it is in literature that national peculiarities are expressed in their strongest form, the literature of any country, if it purports to achieve the real aim of literature, must go beyond the restricted limits of such peculiarities, and endeavour, by portraying the feelings and sentiments common to humanity, to demonstrate the essential universality of man. Thus only can a national literature, while maintaining its indigenous peculiarities and characteristics, fulfil its higher role as a component part of world literature.

Since the eighth century Japan has continued to produce a great variety of literary works, the pervading note of which has ranged from description of the trials and sufferings of mankind to a deep yearning after its common ideals. Yet withal the whole of this literature reflects the life of the nation and its sentiments, and it is the expression of these feelings of the nation that we feel will constitute a welcome and enlightening addition to the world's emotional literature.

The Japanese language is an insurmountable barrier to most to the appreciation of Japanese literature in the original, and so in the desire to make more widely known the beauty of a literature which most cannot savour at first hand, the Society published a collection of synopses of modern Japanese literature covering the period 1902-1935 in *Introduction to Contemporary Japanese Literature* (1939).

To that collection the present compilation is a companion volume with the aim of interpreting the spirit of the classics of old Japan by a series of synopses of literary masterpieces of the long period which preceded it, these two volumes then covering the whole field of Japanese literature.

Old Japan as it may be called covers the long period of thirteen centuries, during which the course of our history was a not uneventful one; successive political disputes and struggles, fluctuations of thought, trials of all kinds, terrible calamities were, as it were, steps by which the nation progressed to its ideals. Yet even in days of trials, the Japanese people never neglected their high spiritual aspirations or their passion for what is true, what is good, and what is beautiful. Nay, in the very midst of these sufferings, they produced in the realm of literature some of the most memorable of masterpieces. Japanese literature has thus in all ages reflected the progress, development, and whole consciousness of the people, and by a consideration of the classical Japanese literature the culture of old Japan can be appreciated and understood.

We hope therefore that this volume will meet a demand of those interested in Japanese culture in general; and we should be delighted furthermore, if some among these synopses arouse sufficient interest to call for a complete translation of the work here often inadequately summarized.

We wish to express our sincere thanks to the writers of the original synopses, Messrs Sen'ichi Hisamatsu, Yûkichi Takeda, Tetsuzô Tanikawa, Kikan Ikeda, Hisamoto Shimazu, Toyoichirô Nogami, Kiyoshi Hiraizumi, Yoshihidé Shida, Tsukuru Fujimura, Seiseien Ihara, Izumi Yanaghita, Hisao Honma, and Kôchi Doi, all of whom are noted in Japan as authoritative students of classical Japanese literature; to Messrs Kenji Hamada and Michitarô Shidehara who translated these synopses; to Messrs Hisamoto Shimazu, Sen'ichi Hisamatsu, and Toyoichirô Nogami who have given much valuable advice in the compilation; and to Messrs Wilfrid Whitehouse and Ernest Pickering, who have rendered many services with regard to the translation and revision.

November, 1940.

KOKUSAI BUNKA SHINKOKAI

CONTENTS

LIST OF ILLUSTRATIONS

AN OUTLINE OF JAPANESE LITERATURE

1. The Social and Historical Background

The earliest period of Japanese literature comprehends the ages from the foundation of the State to the era of the Taika Reformation (745 A. D.). Although no written literature existed before the first part of the eighth century, this earliest period is represented in the myths and legends included in the *Kojiki* (Records of Ancient Matters), the *Nihonshoki* (History-Book of Ancient Japan), and the *Fudoki* (Records of Local Surveys), and also in the collections of prayers in the *Norito* (Shinto Rituals) of the early tenth century, as well as in a number of ancient ballads. All this early traditional material, when arranged and recorded in writing, was, of course, treated according to the political ideas prevailing at the time.

Then come the two centuries lying between the Taika Reformation and the beginning, in 866 A.D., of that system of government which was characterized by the rule of the Sesshô (Regent) and the Kanpaku (Civil Dictator). This period, in which the chief political development was the emergence of a bureaucratic State with the Emperor as centre in place of the clan system of the first period, produced the *waka* poetry, which (together with its longer, shorter, and repetitive varieties, the *chôka, tanka* and *sedôka*) is to be found in the great anthology, the *Man'yôshû*, of the middle of the eighth century.

The next period also covers about two centuries to the introduction (in 1086) of the Insei system of government (the Rule of the Cloistered Emperors). This was the age of the manorial system, with the members of the Fujiwara family as the greatest manor holders. They secured to themselves the succession to the important offices of Sesshô and Kanpaku, as well as the privilege of selecting the succession of Empresses from within their family, and in so doing kept the management of affairs of State entirely in their own hands. The characteristic form of literature which was devel oped during this period of the dominance of the Fujiwara family was written, and could only have been written, by Court nobles, and almost deserves to be termed " Fujiwara literature."

The spirit animating this Court literature differed greatly from that of the preceding age. The inspiration of the earlier was *makoto* (sincerity) and was characterized by the naive expression of sensuous feelings, while the literature of the Fujiwara period was infused with a refined emotionalism, a pensiveness or sentimentality, called *mono no aware* (the sadness of things), which is most clearly revealed in the writings of the Court ladies, of which the most represent-ative is *Genji Monogatari*. In the sphere of *waka* poetry also, the *Kokinshû* anthology, compiled at a somewhat earlier date, shows the transition from " sincerity " to " sentimentality."

The manorial system collapsed of its own inherent weaknesses, and with its decline there began a period of dangerous rivalry be-tween the Court nobles, the chief manorial lords, and the newly rising force of the military class, the samurai, which led to the down-fall of the great Fujiwara family, and the Rule of the Cloistered Emperor.

There followed a century marked by the growth of a new feudal society built up on the collapse of the manorial system to culminate in the triumph of Minamoto Yoritomo, founder of the shogunate at Kamakura in 1192, the literature of the period clearly reflecting the confusion and disintegration of the traditional courtly literature. The *Shin-Kokinshû*, in particular, compiled a little later, after the establishment of the Kamakura shogunate, reflects this. The spirit that permeated the literature of this time, and which was to be carried still further in the ages that followed, was that of *yûgen* (lonesome beauty).

The centuries that succeeded the establishment of the Kamakura shogunate until Oda Nobunaga brought about the unification of the whole country on the downfall of Ashikaga Yoshiaki, the last Muro-machi shogun, in 1573, were filled with a succession of civil wars. Those were stirring times indeed in the history of Japan, marked by such events as the War of Shôkyû (1221), the Restoration of Imperial Rule (1333), the foundation of the Muromachi shogunate (1338), the long and indecisive Ônin War (1467-1499), and the long period of upheavals (1490-1600) known as the *Sengoku jidai*, the Age of

Wars. The more ancient feudal society, based on the manorial system, yielded to a much more completely feudalistic society, while there was growing up at the same time alongside the old agricultural economy a new economic order based on merchandise, the development of which was, however, greatly hindered by the decentralization of the administration. To achieve a greater centralization of power, national unity became an urgent necessity; this was for a brief period attained by the victory of Oda Nobunaga. The literature of this whole period reflects the prevailing confusion and disturbance. We see the final break-up of the literature of the Court nobles, which had begun at a much earlier date, while the impress of a newly rising social class is clearly visible in a certain touch of novelty in subjects and methods, as, for example, in the *gunki mono-gtari* (tales of wars), the *yôkyoku* (texts of the Noh plays), the *nô-kyôgen* (Noh comedies) and the *otogi-zôshi* (fairy tales).

Nevertheless, although the vigorous spirit of the newly-risen military class which was unmistakably setting its stamp on social and economic development was thus not without its influence on letters, literature was in the main still drawing its inspiration from the traditions of the " monarchic literature " of the Heian period. The samurai, despite their growing strength, had little direct influence on the literature; their very raison d'être and function in those troubled times prevented it. Also, the source of the power that the samurai wielded was from their land holdings, and for a long time had no connection with the new commercial economy. The Buddhist conception of life as transitory and uncertain which governs traditional literature and which is so dominant a characteristic of the literature of this time, was strongly reinforced by contemporary conditions which were such as to make the mutability and uncertainty of human affairs only too evident. Literature could hardly fail to express a pessimistic view of life, especially as the samurai, who were chief supporters of literature, were living and functioning amid conditions that both materially and spiritually accorded only too well with the earlier literary traditions. The *yôkyoku* (Noh texts) suggests this unmistakably, as does the *Hôjôki* (Notes of a Recluse) although its composition is a connecting link between the two last periods.

The three great men who brought about the unification of the

State in the sixteenth century were Oda Nobunaga, Toyotomi Hide-yoshi, and Tokugawa Iyeyasu, who became Shogun in 1603, thus initiating the succession of the Tokugawa shogunate which endured for two and a half centuries. This period falls into two parts with the Kyôho era (1716-1736), and the shogunate of Yoshimuré(1716-1745), the eighth of the line, marking the division. The earlier period saw the feudal system, which was the main strength of the Tokugawa shogun, reach the zenith of its power and development, while the latter half found feudalism on the defensive against the rising tide of capitalism. The most notable literary epoch in the earlier period synchronized with the Genroku era (1688-1704) and produced what is called the "Genroku literature," in which the influence of the newly-rich citizens began to show itself. The literature of the later period was oppressed and devitalized, and what was best in it was produced in the Tenmei era (1781-1789) and the Bunka and Bunsei eras (1804-1830), after which it fell lower and lower to the level of popular nonsense. As a broad generalization, the earlier literature had its centre in the Kyoto and Osaka districts while that of the Bunka and Bunsei eras was produced almost entirely in Edo. Still poor and unpromising though it was in the main, the literature of this period is memorable in that for the first time in Japanese literary history the work of the governed rather than the governing classes attained to prominence.

During the first half of the Tokugawa period the main inspiration of the literature was the demand for emancipation, for individual liberty and self-expression as opposed to the negation of human nature and the suppression of individuality which had been so clearly marked in Buddhist thought since the Kamakura and Muromachi periods. This revealed itself in literature as a liberalistic realism, which tried to see and describe things as they really are, free from the restraints of convention. An example of this is the revival of the spirit of "sincerity" (makoto) in the hairon (critical discussions of haikai poems). Thus a positive humanism of a Japanese character became a potent force in literature.

Yet this new spirit was restrained by the persistence of traditional ideas as, for example, in the appreciation and cultivation of "mellowness" (sabi, patina) in literature, as in the haikai (poetic epigrams) of Bashô's school, which had originated in the mediaeval spirit of *yûgen*, gracefulness. In the later period of decadence, literature descended to the level of an amusement and a pastime, and writers to that of farceurs. The phase of realism passed all too quickly, and literature was lost in productions of a banal and popular type.

The Tokugawa period, however, is marked by the appearance of a great variety of literary types, as the diffusion of education enlarged the circles of readers. In the second half of that period the demand was always for novelty, and whatever realism still remained was limited to works of an ephemeral and jocular character. The outstanding types of the earlier period were the *ukiyozôshi* (genre novels) of Ihara Saikaku, the *jôruri* (ballad-drama texts) of Chikamatsu Monzaemon and the *haikai* (poetic epigrams) of Matsuo Bashô. Of the various kinds of novels of the later period we may mention the *kibyôshi* (yellow-backs), so called from the colour of their covers, *sharebon* (jest-books) mainly concerned with life in the gay quarters, *kokkeibon* (books of humour), *ninjôbon* (books of love), *gôkan* (literally, " works bound together," each volume being a collection of several independent tales), and *yomihon* (reading books), the contents of which were considered of more importance than the illustrations, the *haikai* of Buson and Issa and various *haikai* derivatives, particularly the *senryû* (satirical epigrams), the *kyôka* (comic *waka* verse) and the *jôruri* of Takeda Izumo and Chikamatsu Hanji.

In the years following the Meiji Restoration of 1868 when the transfusion of ideas from the capitalistic society of Europe and America revivified feudalistic Japan, so that she became a modern state organically associated with the modern world, Japan was set free from her centuries of national isolation and became intimately linked up with the social and economic progress of the European Powers. The demand for liberty and the defence of popular rights, which sprang up immediately after the Meiji Restoration, developed on lines of individualism, liberalism and democracy, as the social system of Meiji Japan came to maturity.

This development is reflected in the literature, as writers came to stress more and more the independence of literature as an art and to assert the value of individuality, reversing completely the non-individualistic, anti-naturalistic and didactic trend apparent in the banal productions of the Edo period, especially as it approached its close. It was in Shôyô Tsubouchi's *Shôsetsu Shinzui* (Essentials of

Fictior), published in 1885, that the voice of the literature of the Japanese people first found full expression, completely liberated from the banal literature of the later feudal days.

After 1897 when such individualism had brought in the naturalism of Europe with its basis in scientific thought, a golden age of literature began. The intention of writers was to look on life in a strictly scientific way and, in accordance with the spirit of naturalism, to express the prevailing spirit of doubt and to present impartially the various problems which faced humanity rather than to treat of society as an organic whole, of men and women as members of society in specific cultural relations with one another. But many of the traditional elements still lingered and hampered novelists in their resolve to adopt fully the new scientific ideas and methods. The effect of this was that literary naturalism remained shallow and limited and had its interest focussed in the main on the dark and ugly aspects of life.

In the reaction that set in against this, attention came to be riveted upon aspects of individual psychology in relation to environment, while the art of composition became of supreme importance. More recently, writers have found that there are many important literary problems demanding serious reflection, such as the question of the autobiographical novel, the excessive introduction of self-consciousness, and also the relation of the art of literature to the propagation of political principles.

2. *The Earliest Literature* : *Norito, Myths and Legends*

Although the *Kojiki* was not compiled until 712 A.D., more than fifiy years after the Taika Reformation, the originals of most of the stories in it belong to a society much older, that existing even before the establishment of the ancient State. This mass of material had existed for long in a fluid state, out of it being built up an authoritative history of Japan whose compilation had been in hand since the reign of the Emperor Tenmu (673-686). In this process the tales were subjected to a process of change and elaboration to shape them to serve definite ends in the tendency towards national unification ; these myths thus being fixed under a definite political influence, they received the finishing touches in the early part of the eighth century to assume the form in which we find them in the *Kojiki* and, a little later, the *Nihonshoki*.

The ancient material in the *Kojiki* and *Nihonshoki* may be classified under the three heads of Ballads, Ritual Prayers and Myths. The ritual prayers, based upon the idea of word-mana, the magical power of the word, later crystallized into the *norito* recited at Shinto services or ceremonies, and in this form can be found in the *Engishiki*, the code compiled in the Engi era (901-922). During the age of the clan system, this idea of word-mana exercised a living and potent influence upon human society, leaving many traces in the myths and legends of the *Kojiki*. The belief in the magical power of the word is, for example, behind the story of the god Takagi-no Kami who, from the heavenly river-bank of Ameno Yasuno Kawara, shot back the arrow of the god Amewakahiko who had descended to Ashiwara no Nakatsu Kuni. Takagi-no Kami then accompanied the return of the arrow with words in which he showed his purpose to redress the wrong that had been done him. Another instance is to be found in the warning uttered by the Seagod to Yamahiko, when he granted him the two jewels, Shiomitsutama and Shiohirutama, and the idea is somewhat more developed in the account of the cession of the country by Ôkuninushi-no Mikoto. The ancient ballads also frequently reveal the influence of this ancient belief, in this respect anticipating the *norito*.

The myths and legends, such as stories of marriages between men and beasts, of a good man and his wicked elder brother, of the destruction of harmful monsters, of a visit to the dragon's palace, of the creation of the country, of the birth of gods and men, resemble those in the literature of other countries ; but they have all passed through the crucible of the Japanese spirit before assuming the form in which we now have them, their elaborations and modifications making patent the tendency towards national unification.

The *norito* exercised a strong influence on the later *chôka* (longer poems) and on other forms of poetry, although they themselves, becoming stereotyped in form, did not develop further. In the same way the myths and legends never reached a higher literary quality than in these days, although in later ages they underwent a considerable amount of development and elaboration.

3. Waka Verse

The ancient traditional ballads recorded in the *Kojiki* and *Nihonshoki* were also the source of *waka* verse and of the first written literature, in the *Man'yôshû*, the colossal anthology of poetry which is the main literary representative of the ancient State after the Taika Reformation, just as those other great collections of verse, the *Kokinshû* and *Shin-Kokinshû*, represent respectively the ages of prosperity and decline of the manorial system.

The ancient ballads were products of the communal spirit of the clans, and so lacked individuality. With the establishment of the ancient State, the lives of individuals took on a more personal character, and so the choice of subject for ballads ranged much more widely. This was encouraged by the popularization of new methods of writing, by the introduction of the Japanese syllabary (*kana*) in the primitive form known as *man'yôgana* (*Man'yôshû* style *kana*) where the Chinese ideographs were used with their phonetic value, and resulted in the establishment of *waka* poetry as an individualistic art, in the appearance of professional poets, and the minute differentiation of themes. We can see the development well illustrated in the *Man'-yôshû*, the poems of which cover a period of about four and a half centuries, during which the naive and sensuous expression of feeling that characterizes the earlier days gives place gradually to a subtle emotionalism, the contributions to this well-balanced collection covering also a wide social range, coming exclusively reither from one definite stratum of society, nor from those who led lives of poetic seclusion apart from human society.

Different conditions prevailed in the period in which the next great anthology, the *Kokinshû*, was written, for by then the composition of poetry had come to be confined mainly to the Court nobles, and the themes, the method of treatment, even the rhetoric, were much more narrowly conceived. Also the great store which the courtiers of the time set on *zaé* (wit) had considerable influence on the course of development of *waka*. Indeed so much were they concerned with achieving this that the verse of the period took on an exceedingly intellectual and artificial character, as is revealed in particular in the poems of the age of Ki-no Tsurayuki, the compiler of the *Kokinshû*.

The *Shin-Kokinshū*, produced by the nobles of the declining manorial age, was of a very different spirit. The poetical convention of dwelling always on the evanescence of life was by now firmly established, and so, in addition to the traditional pensiveness or sentimentalism (*mono no awaré*), value came to be laid on a personal and quiet emotionalism which reflected a pessimistic and solitude-loving temperament. So while the writers of the time took their poetic standards from the *Kokinshū*, expressive of the youth of their now declining society, they tended to express this new feeling very suggestively in the form of *yojô*, after-sensation.

Another new method of poetic composition, called *honkatori*, the following of ancient models, came into vogue. The purpose of this was to enrich the substance of a poem by making a phrase, quoted from or reminiscent of an older poem, the basis of a new feeling, or by converting the meaning of an older poem into a new channel. Yet, speaking generally, the *Shin-Kokinshū* followed the *Kokinshū* closely both in the selection of themes and its manner of treating them. The essential nature of the *waka* remained unaffected ; what had happened was that the artificial and intellectual approach was superseded by the sense of brooding loneliness.

The *Shin-Kokinshū* marks the end of *waka* poetry as Court literature. The mere fact that it was not the last of the *waka* anthologies but had many successors must not lead us to suppose that *waka* poetry still maintained its dominance. It was not a matter of chance that the *renga* (linked stanzas) and *haikai* (poetical epigrams) began to appear in opposition to the *waka* ; that form had come to take on the character of a classic of bygone days.

Certainly *waka* poetry survived and still survives after the lapse of many ages. But this is to be accounted for by the very nature of the form of poetry. The essence of *waka* is that it focusses itself on those aspects of nature and human affairs that remain comparatively unchanged with the passage of years—the beauty of the blossom and the pangs of love—treating them as things apart from the larger movements of life. Incapable though it is of touching on the complicated issues of changing societies, yet so long as natural beauty and human love endure, so also will endure that poetic form known as *waka*.

4. Tales (*Monogatari*)

The earliest extant work of this kind, *Taketori Monogatari* (The Old Bamboo-Cutter), belongs to the " monarchic age " of the Heian period. Taken together with *Isé Monogatari* (Tales of Isé), a work of a very different type, the *Taketori Monogatari* shows clearly how this branch of Japanese literature came into being.

The framework of the *waka* through which the Court nobles sought literary expression was too confining to picture within it the actual events of life. As aristocratic life became more firmly established, a more comprehensive and freer medium became necessary. *Takatori Monogatari* is an essay in this direction ; it is a strange blending of realistic description and supernatural legends, giving a picture of the aristocratic life of the times through the medium of familiar legendary material derived from the Buddhist scriptures. Its realism is evident in the way in which the old supernatural legends are adapted to actual contemporary events, and in the detailed description of contemporary conditions. Hitherto, the nobles had had no literary experience whatever of portraying their lives directly in prose ; it was natural to attempt it now through the medium of existing legends.

On the other hand, the *uta-monogatari* (poem-tales) developed out of the *koika* (*waka* love-letters). These poems invariably deal with some absolute phase of love in the abstract, considered apart from all circumstantial complications, and so no further development was possible in the direction of details. Accordingly, the first attempt to present the subject in a more circumstantial and concrete manner took the form of amplifying the *kotobagaki*, the prose notes to the *waka*, into stories explanatory of the circumstances of the exchange of these *koika* and of the emotion that was there crystallized into verse. A comparison of the prose parts of *Isé Monogatari* and the *kotobagaki* connected with poems on similar themes in the *Kokinshû* and other anthologies will illustrate this point. The exclamatory lyricism which characterizes the prose of *Isé Monogatari* is due to the fact that the *koika*, which form the essence of the work, were compositions of the age of Ariwara Narihira and the Rokkasen (the Six Master Poets), the chief contributors to the *Kokinshû*. The intellectual artificiality which distinguishes other poems in this anthology, for example, those of the compiler, Tsurayuki, is of a later age. It is the romantic and emotional spirit of the age of the Rokkasen that breathes in *Isé Monogatari*, and this work exercised far more influence on the later prose of the Court ladies than did *Tosa Nikki* (The Tosa Diary), that elegant prose production of Tsurayuki.

Heralded by *Taketori Monogatari* and *Isé Monogatari*, the novel entered on its golden age in the Fujiwara period. This was the time when the manorial culture had reached its zenith, and writers sought to describe with subtle, rich emotionalism the elegance of Court life at that period. The delicate feelings and sensibility of women writers came to be regarded as the most fitting vehicles for literary expression in such an emotionalized environment, and thus was ushered in a brilliant age of women's letters, unique in the history of Japanese literature.

The women writers of the Heian period devoted themselves to portraying the various phases of the elegant lives of Court nobles from the standpoint of *mono no awaré*, pensive sentimentalism. Their productions were subjective and uncritical. That is why the voluminous *Genji Monogatari* (The Tale of Genji) appears to be rather a connected series of short novels than one novel with a unifying theme or plot. *Tsutsumi Chûnagon Monogatari* (The Tales of Tsutsumi Chûnagon), although regarded as the forerunner of this kind of literature, cannot, properly speaking, be regarded as fulfilling the requirements either of a novel or of a collection of short stories. The static conditions of the manorial aristocratic society rendered the treatment of whole phases of it quite meaningless, and whatever character such a work has as a collection of short stories is due to its treatment of the decadent aspects only.

The circumstances amid which novel-writing came into being could not help retarding its development beyond a certain point. The same conditions operated when *Hamamatsu Chûnagon Monogatari* (The Tales of Hamamatsu Chûnagon) and *Sarashina Nikki* (The Sarashina Diary) were written; both these works are redolent of a dreamy romanticism. So also is *Eiga Monogatari* (The Tales of Glorious Days) which dwells on the palmy days of the then bygone manorial culture. Yet, withal, it was this manorial culture that produced the *monogatari*, and when the old manorial families, as represented by the Fujiwara family, came to ruin, no further development

[xiii]

in that particular type of story-telling was possible. The next stage accordingly was rather a distinct change than a development, as writers began to take as their subjects the changing experiences around them, battles, deeds of heroism and the life of the samurai in general. The literature based on aesthetic idealism, tradition and aristocratic culture gave place to battle-stories (*gunki-monogatari*), such as *Heiké Monogatari* (Tales of the Heiké). Yet the accounts of fighting that loom so large in these stories are not concerned so much with its significance and outcome, but are presented according to the aesthetic canons of the " monarchic age." Even the later stories of the Muromachi period known as *otogi-zôshi* (fairy tales), although they extended their scope so as to include other than nobles among their heroes and often employed colloquial expressions of the day, were yet inspired with much the same aims as the older Court literature, and presented love and hard-won happiness in the same vein of sentiment. However, an age that took the Court literature of the past as its ideal and yet lacked the social basis on which that literature had flourished, produced in *otogi-zôshi* works that for the most part were a distorting parody of the " monarchic " spirit. Still, if one thing more than another enabled both the *gunki-monogatari* and the *otogi-zôshi* to achieve some degree of realism, it was the strength of the Buddhist influence, together with the very nature of the material with which they dealt.

5. *Haikai* (*Poetic Epigrams*)

Although the forerunner of the *renga* (linked stanzas) was the *shôwa* (singing in dialogue), which originated from the most ancient ballad poetry, yet the mediaeval *renga* itself actually came into being in opposition to the *Kokinshû* and the *Kokinshû* spirit, which had become fixed in form and stereotyped in emotion. Unhampered as it was by the traditional aesthetic attitude towards the beauties of nature and the necessity of observing its many complicated poetical conventions, the mediaeval *renga* proved an excellent medium for the free treatment of the more familiar aspects of life. Yet the graceful beauty of the *waka* persisted to point another way, and the tendency in this direction was brought to fulfilment in the middle of the fifteenth century by Sôgi, whose work in particular shows that artistic finish characteristic of the mediaeval *waka* poetry. What saved the more familiar form of the *renga*, with its capacity for ranging among wider fields of beauty, was its transformation into the modern *haikai*, a development which may be said to have been initiated with the object of preventing the *renga* being re-absorbed into the more limited, though beautiful, *waka* form. This aim indeed may not have been fully conscious in the earlier writers of *haikai* such as Yamazaki Sôkan, Arakida Moritaké and Matsunaga Teitoku, but the modern significance of the *haikai* was clearly revealed by the Danrin-ha (the Danrin school), particularly by Ihara Saikaku, under the inspiration of Nishiyama Sôin.

By that time the actual life of the newly-risen merchant class was offering itself for treatment in literature. But this was, after all, too strong meat for the *haikai*; the *haikai*, despite its comparative freedom, had from its nature as a form of poetry its conventional restrictions which prevented its treating the life of the new social conditions which had to be met by means of the new novel form of the *ukiyo-zôshi* (genre novels), possessing much greater elasticity. *Haikai*, therefore, deprived by its limitations of the material that it was once supposed to be so well fitted to employ, had to shun the portrayal of typical aspects of modern life and turn once again, like the *waka* and the *renga*, to expressing the point of view of the recluse. Within that restricted sphere, however, it did make use of its greater elasticity to observe more varied aspects of nature and human life, and attain a stage of great profundity, particularly in the work of Bashô in which the *haikai* found its culmination. Since that time the history of the *haikai* has been a chequered one, but it has never been able to change its attitude towards the work-a-day world.

After Bashô, the *haikai* poets of note are Buson of the Tenmei era (1781-1789), who attained an exceedingly sensuous and highly coloured style, and Issa of the Bunka and Bunsei eras (1804-1830), whose work enjoyed a re-valuation in the Meiji era because of his distinctly individualistic style.

In more recent times, various types of humorous versification derived from the *haikai*, such as the *kamurikuzuké* and *maekuzuké*, have catered for a somewhat more popular demand. Of these developments the most noteworthy is the *senryû*, humorous and satirical epigrams, that form of seventeen-syllable verse which was originated in the Meiwa era (1764-1772) by Karai Senryû, a master of the *maekuzuké*. The *senryû* evokes the sense of humour by its suggestive treatment of the meaner side of city life, or by dealing with serious historical or traditional events and persons in a popular, light and epigrammatic manner. All such works as these, treating ironically and humorously some obscure corner of life or indulging in trifling fantasy, although they may not merit a place in the first rank of literature, were nevertheless exceedingly popular in their own day.

It deserves noting, moreover, that those *senryû* which deal with historical events accord perfectly in spirit with the *haibun*, prose in the *haikai* style, which was established long before by the school of Matsunaga Teitoku, and which, even after Bashô, has been regarded as a collateral product of *haikai* literatre.

6. *Drama and the Theatre*

The earliest theatrical performances were those of the *nôgaku* (Noh drama), and the *nô-kyôgen* (Noh farces). The libretto cf these plays is called *yôkyoku*, and is of the epic type. The general structure is something as follows : A priest on pilgrimage is the *waki*, the deuteragonist, who in the course of a journey arrives at a place of historic interest and learns from some villager of the legend connected with the place. During the night that he passes there, the ghost of one of the personages connected with the story appears to recount to him what happened there, as the *shité*, the protagonist of the drama, the two scenes that this recital occupies being termed the *maé-shité* (first scene) and the *nochi-shité* (after scene).

It is customary to classify the *yôkyoku* according to their position in the normal Noh programme as *ichibanmemono, nibanmemono, sanbanmemono, yobanmémono* or *gobanmémono* (plays cf the first, second third, fourth or fifth group), or else according to the theme of these five groups as 1. *shin* (deities), 2. *nan* (men), 3. *nyo* (women), 4. *kyô* (lunatics) and 5. *ki* (demons). Of these, the plays of the first group are more of a ceremonial, or memorial character, the themes being supernatural and derived from the classics or other ancient material;

the second, also called *ashuramono* (warrior-plays), are concerned with battle scenes and the deeds of warriors, usually narrated by a ghost, but these accounts of conflicts are not given with realistic detail, but are treated in the manner of the *gunkimono*, the tales of battle, of the old aristocratic literature.

It is the third group treating of women that best exprsses the spirit of *yûgen* (grace), derived from *mono no aware* (sentimentalism), which is the ideal of Noh.   This group is almost entirely based upon incidents in *Genji Monogatari, Isé Monogatari*, and other " monarchic " tales, or else upon " monarchic " episodes in the *gunkimono*, not upon actual phases of life typical of the age in which the Noh drama was produced.   The life of the time is most frequently touched on in the fourth group.   Usually in regard to those legal conflicts arising out of the aggressive acts of feudal lords which were a feature of the period following the break-down of the decentralized method of government, they treat, for example, of the tragic fate of a wife because of the institution of a lawsuit in the absence of her husband, the embarrassments suffered by truly loyal subjects, the wrongs wrought by wicked retainers, family disagreements or difficulties, vendettas and feuds, and the domestic tragedies arising from the prevalence at that time of the kidnapping and sale of children.

In their manner of treatment of such subjects the *yôkyoku* are not dissimilar to the *otogi-zôshi*, except that they were much more strongly influenced by the aristocratic literature so that even the treatment of new subjects was along classical lines, whereas the *otogi-zôshi* were much more in accord with the taste of the common people.

The fifth group is a collection of supernatural pieces, in which ogres, demons and the like play a great part.

The *kyôgen* (Comic interlude), performed as interludes between the Noh plays, have a plot developed by means of conversation between the characters and are purely dramatic.   Most of them satirize corrupt priests and ignorant daimyo, being significant of their age in thus reflecting the contemporary tendency for the lower classes to assert themselves.   But their satire is confined within very narrow limits ; they lack the true critical insight into life and the vigorous rebuke of error that are essential to real satire, and aim little higher than raising a laugh.

Neither the Noh nor the *kyôgen* appealed originally to the popular taste. The popular drama that arose in modern times, in the age of the rise to importance of the citizens, took the form of the *kabuki* and the puppet-show. The *kabuki* had its origin in Shinto performances and attained to its significance and position as modern drama by its presentation of the free and unfettered life of the rising citizen class. The puppet-drama came into being as a combination of three different elements, performances of instrumental music, especially on the *samisen*, puppet-shows and epic literature, chiefly the *otogi-zôshi*. The text used in the puppet-drama is known as *jôruri*. In its earliest days, however, it had no special text of its own but made use of the *otogi-zôshi*, the *mai no hon* (the text of the *kôwaka* dance) and the *yôkyoku* of the Noh drama, the ancient *jôruri* thus belonging to the sphere of epic literature. It was the genius of Chikamatsu Monzaemon that gave the *jôruri* their special character with his *sewamono* (mundane plays) dealing with the life of the citizens.

The modern drama, including both *kabuki* and *jôruri*, reached its highest development in the late 17th and the early 18th centuries, and then, with the decline of the merchant classes, began to degenerate. Its output was greatly reduced, although there was some improvement in technique. Of these forms of the popular drama the *kabuki* is likely to outlast the puppet theatre.

In the Meiji era, the *kabuki* gave rise to two new developments more adapted to modern tastes, the *shinpa-geki*, the "new school" of drama, and the *shin-kabuki*, the new *kabuki*. By this time the drama of Europe was being introduced and popularized in translations, and from this the newest drama form, the *shingeki*, arose. This deals mainly with the life of modern intellectual circles in Japan, but since this appeals to a very limited audience, the demand is continually being put foward for a more truly national drama that shall have a much wider appeal, something intermediate between the "new" drama and the older forms. The difficulty is, and so far it has proved insuperable, that a real dramatic movement can hardly arise which is capable of appealing to an audience composed of people of so greatly differing backgrounds.

7. *The Modern Novel*

Though the modern novel is generally held to have its origin in that miscellaneous group of writings of the Tokugawa period known as *kana-zôshi* (books in *kana*), the novel of significance dated from 1682 with the appearance of Saikaku's *Kôshoku Ichidai Otoko* (The Life of a Satyr). It is worth noting that this work, which has as its theme typical phases of the life of the merchant class, owed a great deal, as did also the same author's subsequent works, to the topographies, the stories and anecdotes about popular actors, and other miscellaneous books dealing with the practical side of life, that were so popular at that time. The aim of all these books was simply to give the rising citizen class of that time just what it wanted. Both the materials and the mode of expression were fresh and suitable to the new public, and free from the restraints of traditional literature. The intention was to present new aspects of life from a new angle, and Saikaku thus succeeded in accomplishing what the *haikai* had failed to do.

But, after Saikaku, these mundane stories (*ukiyo-zôshi*), like the other literary works amid which they had arisen, failed to maintain their realistic attitude to life and were reduced to that class of ephemeral productions, known from the name of their publisher as *Hachimonjiya-bon* (Hachimonjiya's editions). At last, the diffusion of popular education in the age of Edo culture brought in a flood of novel literature. There were those aiming at low humour, like the *kibyôshi* (yellow backs) and the *kokkeibon* (books of humour), those picturing the pleasure-seeking side of life with a delicate realistic touch, such as the *sharebon* (jest books), and those that stimulated the reader with artificial conceptions and sensational scenes with the professed object of Confucian exhortation, such as the *yomihon* (reading books).

Even in modern times, respect for the traditions of the "monarchic" aristocratic literature still persisted, the merchant class showing a tendency to despise their own productions as *tengôgaki* 1njb(esque). This tendency increased so much that the citizen-authors, unable to take themselves seriously, cheapened themselves as writers of trivial nonsense. This point is of importance in achieving a proper understanding of the development of the later novel.

8. Modern Literature

With the Meiji era began the period of enlightenment whose aim was adjustment to the new social system transplanted from Europe and America. The literature of those early Meiji days was full of the spirit of romanticism expressive of the ardent temper of the new Japan. But this literature, despite its enthusiasm, had not yet developed any intellectual capacity for the concrete observation of reality. To this was due the prosperity of the *shintaishi* (new style poetry) which was concerned almost entirely with the expression of abstract feelings.

Romanticism soon gave place to naturalism. In this period the novel was the dominant form of literary production, being regarded as the form most suitable for coping with the realities of modern Japan, but the age-long tradition of the country still cramped the growth of the scientific spirit, from which naturalism cannot be dissociated, since its first essential is a strong critical intelligence. Even up to the present this grave weakness of Japanese literature still persists. It was this defect that, in the first place, led to the movement towards naturalism, and then just as surely to its stagnation. Even those branches of literature that began in reaction against naturalism also labour under the same defect.

This lack of deep, critical thought, and of those long, coherent novels which can only originate in profound thought and critical acumen, is a characteristic of Japanese literature throughout its long history. The unique position which modern Japanese short stories or novelettes are said to hold in the world is one of the secondary effects of this characteristic. In the absence of scientific spirit and critical judgement, the result is an over-emphasis upon form and technique in all forms of art, not excluding literature. We must recognize the patent fact that it is in technique rather than thought that both the aritists and writers of Japan excel. It is due to the traditional dislike of the scientific spirit that the importance of the thought-content in literary works, studies and criticism is not even today understood—nay, rather disregrded as not falling within the scope of literature—whereas all that pertains to technique is widely discussed. This weakness had meant a serious narrowing in the choice of themes and encouraged a flood of personal mis-

cellanea. The world of petty passion and trifling subjective meander-
ings that constitutes the favourite theme for Japanese writers has
its source in the view that the one thing that matters is to picture
any kind of subject skilfully.

KOJIKI and NIHONSHOKI*

(Records of Ancient Matters and History-Book of Ancient Japan)

Kojiki and *Nihonshoki* are the earliest extant histories of Japan. *Kojiki* (Records of Ancient Matters) consists of three books, and *Nihonshoki* (History-Book of Ancient Japan) of thirty. As both were compiled for the purpose of presenting the history of the Japanese race and explaining the formation of the Japanese State and the essence of the national polity, they are of high significance to Japan and her people ; no study of the ancient history of Japan is possible unless it is based upon the accounts given in these two books. Both begin with an account of the creation of the world, *Kojiki* ending with a record of the reign of the Empress Suiko, the thirty-third sovereign (592–628), while *Nihonshoki* extends as far as the eleventh year of the reign of the forty-first ruler (697), the Empress Jitô (687–702).

Both commence with stories of the activities of the Shinto deities from the creation of the world prior to the formation of the Japanese State. Then comes an account of the formation of the State and of the achievements of the first Emperor, Jinmu Tennô (d. 585 B. C.), and his successors. Thus the contents of both fall naturally into two parts, one dealing with the world of deities and the founding of the State, the other giving the history of the reigns of successive Emperors with a wealth of valuable records.

The part dealing with the Age of the Gods, the richest of all Japanese myths in literary value, is focussed on the important matter of the origin of the Empire. In their accounts of the preliminary events, the creative act and its terrestrial consequences, *Kojiki* and *Nihonshoki* differ only in minor details.

Let us now give an outline of the divine story, dividing it somewhat arbitrarily into five sections, and drawing mainly on *Kojiki*.

---

* Also known as *Nihongi* ; cf. W. G. Aston : Nihongi, subtitled " Chronicles of Japan from the Earliest Times to A. D. 697."

Section One deals with the beginning of the world. Various deities appear, notably the Reed Sprout deity and the Mud deity, who are responsible for the creation of the world and its gradual development. Then comes the important pair, Izanagi and Izanami, whose names explain their functions as the deities invoking all things into existence. They descend from heaven to Ukihashi (the Floating Bridge), the connecting link between heaven and earth and stir up the sea with their halberds, creating the Isle of Onogoro with the drops of water that fall from the tips of their weapons. Thither descend Izanagi and Izanami ; they marry and beget the Japanese Archipelago (Ôya-shima) with its mountains, rivers, trees and stones. Finally, Izanami is delivered of the Deity of Fire, in the process of which she is burnt to death, and is transported to Yomi no Kuni, the Land of the Dead. Overwhelmed with grief Izanagi follows her to the nether world, from which however she never returns. Izanagi returns alone and proceeds to purify himself of the infernal impurities. Out of this purificatory process arise the three noble deities, Amaterasu Ômikami, Tsukuyomi-no Mikoto and Susanoö-no Mikoto.

Section Two treats of the festival in Heaven (Takamagahara) and of Susanoö's slaying of the Eight-forked Serpent (Yamata no Orochi). It is here that Amaterasu is given reverence as the divine ancestress, not only of the Imperial Family but also of the whole Japanese people, and is presented as possessing the properties of the Solar deity. Tsukuyomi-no Mikoto is the Moon-god, and Susanoö-no Mikoto, the impetuous Hero-god, is the deity of the storm. The story tells how Susanoö-no Mikoto ascended to Heaven to take leave on his departure for the land he was to rule. Amaterasu, however, was surprised at his threatening looks and, suspecting him of no good intent, armed herself to receive him. Each appealed in the name of justice to the verdict of the Solemn Oath (Seiyaku), to decide on the sincerity of each other's intentions. But when the oaths proved the innocence of Susanoö-no Mikoto, he became inflated with victory and behaved outrageously so that Amaterasu, disgusted with his conduct, shut herself up in a cave, thus depriving the world of light. At last she was induced to reappear when the other deities, in their anxiety to appease her, made a mirror and a string of curved jewels, which they hung on branches placed in front of the cave, and held a high festival.

Susanoö-no Mikoto was expelled to Izumo province where he killed the Eight-forked Serpent which was ravaging the countryside, and from the middle tail of the serpent he acquired the famous sword known as Kusanagi no Tsurugi (Grass-mowing Sword), which was later used by Yamatotakeru-no Mikoto to save himself from the prairie fire which had been started by his enemy.

This passage is of great importance because it contains the story of the origin of the Three Sacred Treasures of Japan (Sanshu no Shinki), the Mirror, the Curved Jewels and the Sword, which are handed down generation after generation from one Emperor to another to confirm their enthronement. It is also notable as giving the story of the origin of the main Shinto festival.

Section Three deals with the state of the Japanese Archipelago at the time when the foundations of the national polity were being prepared. The Japanese Islands were first inhabited by a number of tribes of aborigines. Among these the most powerful local hero was Ôkuninushi-no Mikoto, a descendant of Susanoö-no Mikoto, whose chief seat was Izumo province. It was in this territory, facing the Japan Sea, that culture made an early appearance, and methods of medical treatment there date far back into remote antiquity. Here also was produced some literature of importance, mainly in the form of ballads and congratulatory writings called *yogoto*. Accordingly, *Kojiki* gives highly elaborate accounts of Ôkuninushi-no Mikoto, his conquest of the land, his marriage and so forth.

Section Four deals with the firm establishment of Japanese sovereignty. It contains the proclamation made by Amaterasu Ômikami in Heaven when she established her dominion : " Coeval with heaven and earth, this country shall be ruled by my descendants." It tells how she sent down her son Oshihomimi-no Mikoto, who, finding the country still disturbed and unruly, returned to Heaven. Thereupon, a valiant deity was again dispatched to conquer the land, who forced Ôkuninushi-no Mikoto into surrendering his dominions. With the way thus prepared, Ninigi-no Mikoto, the son of Oshihomimi-no Mikoto, attended by a train of ancestral deities of various families, descended to the summit of Mount Takachiho in

Tsukushi (Kyushu). This section is of great value for its accounts of the firm establishment of the monarchy and its essential prerogatives.

Section Five is concerned with the deeds of Ninigi-no Mikoto, the grandson of Amaterasu Ōmikami, after his descent to earth. During his lifetime and for the two following generations, the Imperial Court was settled in Kyushu, in the south-west of the Japanese Archipelago. Among the stories dealing with these days, that of the visit of Hikohohodemi-no Mikoto to the Palace of the Sea-god is written in an easy and attractive style.

These myths, derived almost entirely from *Kojiki*, correspond so closely to those contained in *Nihonshoki* as to form a unified story centring on the foundation of the Japanese State. Their importance lies in their value as a record of the origins of the nation, as expressive of the Shinto spirit, and also as indicating the fundamental character of the national polity.

Such is the great importance attached to these myths in the past, as also in the present, and it may be in the future. Moreover, the very literary quality of these stories is derived from their mythological character. Take, for instance, the story of how the two deities, Izanagi and Izanami, created the Island of Onogoro, and, later, the whole Japanese Archipelago. These myths, designed on a truly grand scale, have all the characteristics of sea myths, bearing witness to their transmission from those ancient times when the core of the Japanese race inhabited the maritime districts. Although *Kojiki* and *Nihonshoki* were not compiled in book form until long after the central government had migrated to the inland province of Yamato, their contents reveal their earlier maritime origin.

Further, the entire works breathe a spirit grand and sublime, derived from the fact that they centre round the magnificent historical fact of the foundation of the nation, and are redolent of a definite religious attitude towards life. Also, in the course of the stories, the temper of the Japanese people reveals itself, bright and cheerful, yet distinctly ethical.

In the accounts of the first and subsequent Emperors, each reign is dealt with separately in paragraphs of varying length. These accounts tell the history of the growth and fulfilment of the Japanese Empire, whose formation has already been shown as the culminating point of the stories of the deities. They are full of interesting stories on such subjects as the overcoming of the numerous difficulties encountered in the task of bringing order to the uncivilized districts, and the establishment of the characteristic Japanese culture, as it came into contact with, assimilated and absorbed the culture of the continent.

Nihonshoki gives definite dates for the reigns of the first Emperor, Jinmu Tennô, and his successors. The year of the enthronement of the Emperor Jinmu (660 B. C.), after his conquest of Japan Proper, is reckoned as the first year of the Japanese era. In the history of the first Emperor, and also of subsequent Emperors, there are stories calculated to encourage the spirit of the Japanese warriors. It is told how the Emperor Jinmu himself sailed eastward along the Inland Sea (Seto Naikai) and, after severe trials, suppressed powerful clans in Yamato. Then there is the famous story of the heroic Yamato-takeru-no Mikoto (A. D. 84–113), son of the twelfth Emperor, Keikô Tennô, who subjugated the wild Kumaso race in the west and various powerful rebels in the east, and who, on his way to Kyoto, contracted a serious illness on Mount Ibuki in central Japan which proved fatal before he could reach his destination.

Then, in both *Kojiki* and *Nihonshoki*, there are stories in an elegant literary style, with poems interspersed, of the doings of the fifteenth Emperor, Ôjin Tennô, the sixteenth Emperor, Nintoku Tennô, and the twenty-first Emperor, Yûryaku Tennô ; both also recount at length the exploits of the Empress Jingû Kôgô, consort of the fourteenth Emperor, Chûai Tennô, on her expedition to Korea, which refer to contemporary relations with the continent. The numerous old ballads in these works dealing as they do with diverse aspects of life—military affairs, marriage, feasting and festive occasions—form a literary treasure-house.

The first compilation of a national history can be traced to Prince Shôtoku (573–621) in collaboration with several others. This was compiled in A. D. 620, the twenty-eighth year of the reign of the Empress Suiko (592–628), but unfortunately it has been lost. The long-felt need for a history becoming acute by the time of the fortieth Emperor, Tenmu Tennô (672–686), the plans for compiling both *Kojiki* and *Nihonshoki* date from his reign. The Emperor made a selection of authentic historical traditions, up to that time orally transmitted, and brought them to the notice of Hiyeda-no Aré, who was to put them into book form, but never succeeded in doing so. According to tradition this Aré was a sagacious chamberlain in the service of the Imperial Court, but opinions are still divided as to whether Aré was a man or a woman. Later, on the eighteenth of September in the fourth year of the Wadô era (711), in the reign of the Empress Genmei (707–715), one of great scholars of the day, Ô-no Yasumaro (d. 723), was ordered to record the traditions, which had been arranged by Hiyeda-no Aré, in book form. This was done, and *Kojiki* was completed on the twenty-eighth of January of the following year.

The other compilation of ancient history, *Nihonshoki*, was started by Kawashima-no Ôji (d. 691) and others, at the command of the Emperor Tenmu, and was brought to completion by Toneri Shinnô (676–735), son of that Emperor, and his collaborators in May, 720, the fourth year of the Yôrô era, during the reign of the Empress Genshô (715–724). These dates show that both works were completed soon after the Imperial capital had been settled at Nara.

That time is significantly marked by the perfecting of the national organization, the great development of various branches of culture, the improvement of the condition of the people in face of considerable difficulties, by the firm establishment of the national consciousness, and by the extension of our foreign relations due to increasing intercourse with continental peoples.

Thus, Japanese history, which from antiquity had been transmitted orally, was finally compiled in book form soon after the introduction of Chinese ideographs had taught the Japanese the art of writing.

The preface to *Kojiki* is important because it shows clearly the intentions of our ancestors in compiling both that book and *Nihonshoki* and the significance which they attached to their history. The preface regards history both as the elucidation of the facts of past ages and also as affording a standard for life in the present. The history of Japan is to be studied not only as a record of past events but also as prescribing the essential qualities of the modern state. In this faith *Kojiki* was orally transmitted from antiquity and afterwards compiled in book form. *Nihonshoki*, which lacks a preface, was brought to completion in the same period and by the same means, and so may naturally be regarded as embodying the same purpose.

Kojiki, although written exclusively in Chinese ideographs, contains much of the ancient language of Japan and is all in a style capable of being read in the Japanese way. This style was elaborated by Ô-no Yasumaro, the compiler, whose great achievement it was to devise various ways of making the inconvenient Chinese ideographs serve his purpose. *Nihonshoki*, on the other hand, is in Chinese. Other differences between these two works are that while *Kojiki* gives only one version of the stories of the deities of the Divine Age, *Nihonshoki* mentions several additional stories beside the main one, and gives more detailed accounts especially of our relationships with Korea and China ; *Nihonshoki* to some extent shows the influence of Chinese thought, as, for instance, with regard to the account of the creation of the universe, which was quite conceivably adopted in those days as offering a sort of scientific theory ; *Kojiki* is clearly intended for the exclusive use of the Japanese themselves, while *Nihonshoki* possesses greater international significance.

FUDOKI

(Records of Local Surveys)

Very different in character from *Kojiki* and *Nihonshoki* are the other ancient documents of about the same period, the eighth century A. D., called *Fudoki*. These were topographical surveys compiled in various parts of the country by order of the Central Government, giving records of local conditions.

The Nara period, to which these records belong, was marked by a great development of Japanese culture, due to cultural importations from the continent, which being eagerly absorbed stimulated the traditional culture to a fuller manifestation. Under the influence of this spirit, the Central Government ordered the compilation of these *Fudoki*, conceivably with the object of strengthening the relations between the centre and the local districts by gaining a clearer knowledge of provincial conditions, and also of raising the standard of living generally by making provisions appropriate to the needs of the various localities. That the compilation of these local records was regarded as essential is another indication of the great interest shown in the Nara period in the ancient history of the country.

It was in the sixth year of the Wadô era (713), in the reign of the Empress Genmei (707–715), that an Imperial decree was issued to the local authorities ordering the compilation of *Fudoki*. The edict prescribed that all the names of places, the districts and the villages within their jurisdiction should be set down clearly in written characters; that they should give detailed lists of the products of their provinces, of plants and trees, minerals, birds and beasts, fish and insects; and that the comparative fertility of the various districts, the derivations of the names of mountains, rivers and plains, as well as old tales and strange customs remembered by old people, should all be recorded and forwarded to the Central Government. Thus were the *Fudoki* drawn up and presented by the local authorities in compliance with the Imperial command.

KOJIKI (RECORDS OF ANCIENT MATTERS). Manuscript copy made in the Kamakura Period (13-14th century), owned by the Yoshida family, Kyoto.

HIZEN FUDOKI (RECORDS OF LOCAL SURVEYS OF HIZEN PROVINCE). Manuscript copy in the Kamakura Period (13-14th centnry), owned by Mr. Inokuma, Kyoto.

HARIMA FUDOKI (RECORDS OF LOCAL SURVEYS OF HARIMA PROVINCE). Manuscript copy in the late 12th century, owned by the Sanjyonishi family, Tokyo.

NIHONSHOKI (HISTORY-BOOK OF ANCIENT JAPAN). Manuscript copy in 1326, owned by Shōkōkan Library, Mito.

It is highly probable that a large number of these records were compiled throughout the country, but the only ones extant are the *Fudoki* of Izumo province, and, in an abridged form, those of Harima, Hitachi, Hizen and Bungo provinces. Nevertheless, the large number of topographical references in works of the thirteenth century leads one to suppose that many other *Fudoki* survived until that century.

Of high literary value is that section of the *Fudoki* which records the tales told by the village elders, stories of both mythological and historic times, vividly picturing the spiritual life of the ancient Japanese people. The records lack the historical unity of *Kojiki* and *Nihonshoki*, yet they sometimes preserve better the original form of the stories. Sometimes, also, one of the tales will be seen to have been current in several districts and so recorded in several *Fudoki*. Such tales have a special significance in that they often supplement the stories in *Kojiki* and *Nihonshoki*.

The *Fudoki* of Izumo province was finished on the thirtieth day of the second month of the fifth year of the Tenpyô era (733) in the reign of the Emperor Shômu (724–749). It bears the names of Izumo-no Hiroshima and Miyaké-no Kanatari as compilers. Izumo-no Hiroshima was the head of a powerful family in Izumo province, over a part of which he ruled. No other *Fudoki* give the names of the editors, but it can be surmised that they were all compiled by such local officials. Izumo is situated in the south-western part of Japan Proper, facing the Japan Sea, and now forms part of Shimané prefecture. It had long been settled by Japanese stock of Izumo descent and had been prosperous from earliest times. It had a rich and distinctive mythology, which is recorded in the *Izumo Fudoki*, especially in stories of Ôkuninushi-no Mikoto, to whom is attributed the creation and establishment of the world, and of other deities descended from him.

These tales derive many of the place names from events and objects connected with the deities who settled there. Particularly striking is the *Kunibiki* (land-pulling) myth of Yatsukamizu Omizuno-no Mikoto, who with a spade cut off a slice of territory from Silla, the ancient Korean kingdom, and pulled it with ropes to Izumo in order to increase the size of that province. This story is remarkable for boldness of imagination, beauty of literary style, its preservation of archaic words, and the simple artlessness which, because of the early origins of Izumo province, it shares with the other Izumo myths.

From this *Fudoki*, as the only one preserved in complete form, we can estimate the nature of the *Fudoki* generally. The value of the material derived from these sources consists not only in the significance of these old men's tales, but in the topographical information which was the main reason for the compilation of the *Fudoki*. Detailed accounts of the villages, the fertility of the various districts, the characteristics of the mountains and rivers, the local products, the shrines and temples, are given for each of the ten districts into which the province was divided at that time by means of the main roads, enabling us to obtain an idea of the general condition of Izumo province up to and during the eighth century.

The province of Harima faces the Seto Naikai, or Inland Sea, and now forms part of Hyôgo prefecture. The *Fudoki* of this province, together with those of three other provinces, Hitachi, Hizen and Bungo, has been transmitted only in an abridged form, probably because the scholars of the succeeding age, being more interested in the old tales, mainly concerned themselves with handing down this part of the *Fudoki*. In consequence, there is very little of that topographical information which forms such an important section of the *Izumo Fudoki*, even its introductory part having been lost. Its compiler and the date of compilation are therefore unknown, but it is believed to have been written within two or three years of the issue of the Imperial edict for its compilation.

Owing to its geographical position, the province of Harima had been, from antiquity, an important centre of communications. The mountains on its northern border separated it from the powerful province of Izumo whose deities are said to have paid frequent visits to Harima. On the south it faced the sea, so that influential voyagers from the south and west frequently called there, while it received constant stimulus from the central province of Yamato, a short distance to the east. It is natural that this convergence of influences should be clearly reflected in the tales belonging to this province, as, for instance, in the myth narrating the struggle between Ôkuni-nushi-no Mikoto of Izumo, and Amé-no Hihoko-no Mikoto from the west, for possession of the land, a notable description of a struggle for power between ancient rivals.

The *Fudoki* of Harima also contains a number of other myths of

Ôkuninushi-no Mikoto whose competition in endurance with Sukuna-hikona-no Mikoto affords a delightful example of the ancient Japanese conception of honour. The Harima records are also of interest because of the numerous tales dealing with cultivation and myths concerning the divine ancestor of mankind.

The province of Hitachi in the east, now part of Ibaraki prefecture, situated as it is far from the important central districts, was naturally slower in development. This fact is shown in its *Fudoki*, the significant features of which are its reflection of the spirit of the first settlers who colonized the land, and the traditions regarding its wells and springs. It affords us then a truly living picture of the development of Japan as we read of the hardships experienced by our ancestors in transforming bogs and moorlands into fertile ricefields and in destroying the almost inexhaustible hordes of snakes. Even when read simply as stories, the tales in the *Fudoki* are remarkable, as a brief illustration will show.

Ômikami paid a visit to Mt Fuji, but, as this happened to be on the sacred night when the first fruits of the harvest were solemnly offered to the deities, she was refused admittance. Very different, however, was the reception given her at Mt Tsukuba in Hitachi; although a similar festival was taking place there, she was specially admitted and hospitably entertained. Therefore Mt Fuji is continually covered with frost and snow, making it inhospitable and inaccessible to climbers, while Mt Tsukuba is visited by happy crowds in spring and autumn.

Another tale gives the origin of the name, Otomé no Matsubara, Maiden Pine Wood. Once upon a time a young man and a maiden used to meet in this wood to exchange poems, but one morning the dawn surprised them there and, ashamed of being seen, they transformed themselves into pine trees. Such tales as these are written in an elegant style, and are interspersed with ballads.

The name of the compiler and the date of the *Hitachi Fudoki* are unknown, but Fujiwara-no Umakai, who was lord of this province in the early Nara period and was well versed in Chinese Han poetry, is said to have had some part in its compilation. Another name mentioned in connection with it is that of Takahashi-no Mushimaro, his subordinate, whose compositions in the *Man'yôshû* include several poems on themes similar to those in this *Fudoki*.

In contrast to the three *Fudoki* already discussed, those of the provinces of Hizen and Bungo, which are apparently of a somewhat later date, are fuller in their accounts of the relations of the provinces with the Central Government. This is perhaps due to the fact that these two provinces, being situated in northern Kyushu, were the first channels of the new alien culture.

Of the lost *Fudoki*, a large number of fragments survive as quotations in later works. One of the most notable of these is the tale of Urashima of the province of Tango (now part of Kyoto prefecture). Once upon a time there lived in Tango a fisherman named Urashima who caught a five-coloured tortoise in the sea. This tortoise was actually the sea-god's daughter and, turning itself into a woman, she took Urashima with her to the Sea-god's palace. At length Urashima began to yearn for his native land, but when he returned he was astounded to find that three hundred years had elapsed. This typical Japanese tale of the marriage of a human with a deity has been re-told in many forms and is universally known among the children of the present day.

Equally memorable is another provincial tale, that of the Manai Spring of Hiji. Long ago eight heavenly maidens came down to earth and were bathing in this spring, when an old couple hid the garments of one of them. Unable to return to heaven with the others, she had to stay behind to live as their daughter. She was skilled in brewing saké and so brought wealth and prosperity to the family, but after a while she was turned adrift and thereafter wandered about in tears, a homeless exile.

These two stories are accounts of intercommunication with strange countries of a world created by the imagination of the ancients. The tale of the deer of Yumeno (Field of Dreams) which survives as a fragment from the *Fudoki* of Settsu province depicts the manners of the early Japanese and their affection for animals. An indication of its literary quality is given in its derivation of the name " Yumeno " from the deer's dream. The number of tales about deer in the various records show how common these animals must have been in antiquity. There are still other tales of high literary value. Further, the inscription on a monument at a hot-spring in Iyo province (now Dôgo in Ehimé prefecture), erected by Prince Shôtoku (573–621), which survives in a fragmentary *Fudoki* of Iyo province, is valuable as an example of the earliest writing in Japan still extant.

These records being compiled in many different places, by different compilers with different standpoints and cultural attainments, their styles of writing are also diverse. In the *Fudoki* of Izumo, written for the most part in the Chinese Han style, the famous story of the " Land-pulling " preserves the archaic Japanese. Such portions must have been transcribed direct from oral tradition. The *Fudoki* of Harima is in Japanese style, very suitable for the narration of myths. *Hitachi Fudoki*, on the other hand, is beautifully written in pure Chinese style, and even the songs of Ōmikami are translated into Chinese poetry. The original Japanese form is retained, however, in the majority of other poems, and the notes occasionally preserve archaic native words. The *Fudoki* of Hizen and Bungo are both in Chinese style.

There is a similar lack of stylistic unity in the other fragmentary *Fudoki*. They are frequently diversified with ballads and folk-songs, which occupy a special place in the history of Japanese literature. The *Fudoki* are a treasure-house for students of provincial conditions in ancient Japan. The production of Japanese classics, not only by the Central Court but also by such provincials as the compilers of the *Fudoki*, bears witness to the wide diffusion of culture in those early days.

MAN'YÔSHÛ

(Anthology of a Myriad Leaves)

Man'yôshû is the fountain-head of Japanese poetry; the poems contained therein are cries from the hearts of the ancient Japanese as well as manifestations of their lyrical art. With that great historical work *Kojiki* (Records of Ancient Matters), this collection of poems gives a wonderful revelation of the fundamentals of the Japanese spirit. A comparatively modern author, Kamo-no Mabuchi (1697–1769), summed up the essence of *Man'yôshû* in the words "manly style" (masuraoburi). By this phrase he seems to have referred to the strong feeling in the poems, a feeling flowering directly out of sincere emotion. In other words, sincerity and strength of emotion combined with simplicity of utterance distinguish *Man'yôshû*, and indeed ancient Japanese literature as a whole, from such later collections of verse as *Kokinshû* (An Anthology of Poems, Ancient and Modern), and *Shin-Kokinshû* (A New Anthology of Poems, Ancient and Modern).

The twenty books of *Man'yôshû* preserve about 4,500 poems, dating from the time of the Emperor Nintoku (313–399) to that of the Emperor Junnin (758–764) of the later Nara period. Of these poems, the lyrics so far outnumber the others that *Man'yôshû* is regarded as essentially a lyric anthology, but epics, scenic descriptions and reflective poems are also represented.

Besides this variety of outlook, there is a variety of verse-form. The three main types are *chôka*, *tanka* and *sedôka*. The *chôka*, the form used for the longer poems, consists of alternate lines (*ku*) of five and seven syllables, with a final line of seven syllables. To each *chôka* is appended the *hanka* (envoy), one or more poems of thirty-one syllables, which repeat, summarize or supplement the main poem.

There are 262 *chôka* in *Man'yôshû*, varying considerably as to the number of lines from as few as nine to as many as one hundred and forty-nine. It has been suggested that these should be distinguished as the *dai* (great) *chôka*; the *chû* (medium) *chôka*; and the *Shô* (small) *chôka*. The poems of this style deal mainly with descriptions of scenery or impressions.

The *tanka* consists of thirty-one syllables, written in five lines—five, seven, five, seven, seven syllables. According to the reckoning adopted in *Man'yôshû Kogi* (Ancient Meanings of the Man'yôshû) the collection includes 4,173 *tanka*, which thus far outnumber the *chôka* and the *sedôka*.

The *sedôka* consists of thirty-eight syllables which are written in six lines—five, seven, seven, five, seven, seven. Sixty-one poems in this form are included, all in the earlier part of the collection. Owing to a lack of unity and the overmuch repetition involved, the popularity of this form soon waned.

But no matter how varied and complicated the subject-matter and the poetic form may be, they are permeated and vitalized by the lyric spirit. In order to trace the development of the lyric spirit, the Man'yôshû Age, as it may well be called, can be divided into four periods, beginning with the reign of the Emperor Jomei (629–641), in which a comparatively large number of the poems included in this anthology were produced. The time prior to the Emperor Jomei from the reign of the Emperor Nintoku may be called the Age of the Kiki (The Age of *Kojiki* and *Nihonshoki*), since most of the poems of this period consist of ballads found in these two history-books.

Lyrics belonging to the first period of the Man'yôshû Age, from the reign of the Emperor Jomei to that of the Emperor Tenmu (673–686), are artless and simple. The characteristics of that period are best revealed in Book XIII, although one ought also to include the *azuma'uta* (poems dealing with the Eastern Provinces) in Book XIV. For although some of these *azuma'uta* were composed at a later date, they ought to be classed with the simple lyrics because of their provincial origin, most of them having been composed by the easterners themselves. The poems of this period, although unpolished in technique, are characterized by power of imagination ; they are songs of innocence. In spite of the fact that poets of renown are few, the period has given us a number of moving poems. Artlessness is the keynote of the following example :—

> My poor chapped hands,
> Chapped with hulling of rice !

> To-night once again
> My young lord of the mansion,
> Sighing, will take them in his.
> *from Book XIV.*

The second period (687–707), covering the reigns of the Empress Jitô and the Emperor Monmu, who lived in the Fujiwara no Miya (Fujiwara Palace) in Yamato province, saw the consummation of Man'yôshû lyricism. In the poems of this period, racial characteristics gave way to expression of the poet's individuality. Outstanding among the poets of the period is Kakinomoto-no Hitomaro.

In comparison with his predecessors, Hitomaro chose themes of a far wider range, while in technique of expression he attained far greater perfection. His quality is epic as well as lyric, including within the scope of his verse the Shinto deities and national ideas as well as personal emotions. This can be traced to his connection with the Imperial Court, but it also shows how he rose above simple lyricism to observation of the broader aspects of life.

Hitomaro's chief excellence may be said to have been in the technique of expression, for he handled freely all the forms of verse, *chôka*, *tanka* and *sedôka*, and the poetic devices of Man'yôshû poetry —the *makurakotoba* (pillow words of five syllables), the *jo* (pillow words of more than five syllables) and the *tsuiku* (antithesis). No matter what his subjects, they sparkle with life, and become rhythmical and melodious under his touch.

The following poem of his contains in the original most lively and subtle euphonies which cannot be reproduced in translation :—

> The bamboo-grass blades
> Fret and rustle so loudly
> From yonder hill-side—
> But of her only I think
> Whom I have left behind me.
> *from Book II.*

In contrast to such lyrics his poems praising the Emperor, or reverencing the Emperor as a living Divinity, or expressing his devotion to the State, all reveal a strong and noble spirit, as for instance :—

Beholding these straits,
Of our Sovran's Court the gate,
Thoughts unbidden rise
Of the Age of mighty Gods
Who did these islands create.
from Book III.

The tendency which pervades Hitomaro's work forms the main current of the second period.

The third period covers the early years of the Nara period (708–748), the reigns of the Empresses Genmei and Genshô and the Emperor Shômu. The representative poets of this period are Yamabé-no Akahito, Ôtomo-no Tabito, Yamanoé-no Okura and Takahashi-no Mushimaro, who may be said to have followed the lines laid down by Hitomaro, only, as it were, differentiating more fully the various types he had initiated.

Yamabé-no Akahito is believed to have flourished in the early Nara period, a little later than Kakinomoto-no Hitomaro. He is notable for his profound observation of nature and the skill with which he expresses it. *Man'yôshû* contains thirteen *chôka* and thirty-six *tanka* from his hand, of which Nature is for the most part the theme. He gazes at Mt Fuji, visits the grave of Mama-no Tekona in Shimôsa province, goes to the hot-springs of Iyo province in Shikoku, or makes a journey to Kii province, and wherever he travels he loves nature and sings of its beauties. His *chôka*, though they do something more than give realistic pictures of nature, containing, as they do, creative elements, do not attain to the level of Hitomaro's work in the same form, but his *tanka*, partly perhaps because the form does not permit the use of antitheses or the introduction of extraneous ideas, appear to penetrate to the very essence of nature. This is the effect largely of his whole-hearted concentration upon and affection for it. Further, his nature poems are for the most part characterized by a pictorial and ichnographical quality and an elegance of taste, sometimes reflecting the quiet voice of nature itself :—

In the tops of trees
On Yoshino's Mt Kisa,
Hark, the voice of birds
Shattering the quietude
With multitudinous song!
from Book VI.

[17]

Unlike Akahito, Ôtomo-no Tabito and Yamanoé-no Okura, each in his own way, sang of life. Ôtomo-no Tabito came of noble family, and, after residing at Tsukushi as head of the local government (Dazai-no Gonnosochi), went up to the Capital as Chief Councillor of State (Dainagon). Sometimes he was depressed with thoughts of the fleeting nature of the present life as is shown in one of his many poems in praise of saké :—

> Instead of fruitless
> Thought on unavailing things,
> Far better seems it
> One cup of new wine to drink—
> And drive such vain thoughts away.
>
> *from Book III.*

Yet such pessimistic reflections on the uncertainty of human life had little influence on the sunny nature of Tabito. He concerned himself little about the future, but approached life with warm and optimistic feelings, and found great joy in his wife's love and the affection of his colleagues. As regards the form of his verse, he chiefly composed *tanka*, and his aptitude for Chinese Han literature made him a skilful writer of Chinese prose and verse.

Yamanoé-no Okura used to exchange poems with Tabito when they lived in the same district of Tsukushi (northern Kyushu), and he also concerned himself with life generally rather than with nature. He went over to China while still in his early manhood, and, while he was to some degree versed in Chinese Han literature, he was more strongly influenced by Confucianism. Consequently he had a deep affection for, and attachment to, reality. The probabilities are that he did not, like Tabito, come of a good family, and he was less inclined to society. Most of his poems which were composed after maturity deal with the pains of illness and poverty. This tendency is remarkably illustrated in his poem called " Catechism of Poverty " (*Hinkyû Mondô*). From some of his poems, we receive a strong and sometimes pathetic impression because of his love for his children and his search for the brighter side of life, as in the following :—

> I must be leaving,
> For now my little children
> For me are crying ;
> And for me will be waiting

The children's mother also.

from Book III.

His tender love finds expression in the poem written on the occasion of the death of his son, Furuhi :—

Dying so early,
My son will not know the way.
Angel of the Shades,
To you I give this present—
On your back please bear him there.

from Book V.

These lines are a *hanka* (envoy) to a *chôka* written on that sad occasion. Nevertheless, in the Confucian spirit he resigned himself to suffering the slings and arrows of outrageous fortune, and at least made an effort to perpetuate his name in this transient world. Although Confucianism was the main influence in his life, he still hailed Japan as the country blessed with the " word-spirit " (*kototama*), and ennobled by the rule of the gods.

Takahashi-no Mushimaro, the fourth of the poets mentioned as representative of this third period, is notable for his epics on traditional subjects. Only one poem in *Man'yôshû* is actually ascribed to him, but all the poems in the anthology bearing the note " From the Poetical Works of Mushimaro " are believed to be by him. In these he proves himself an excellent epic poet, especially in dealing with the traditions of Mama-no Tekona and Urashima, which he develops with skill and felicity.

Another distinguished representative of the third period is the poetess, Sakanoé-no Iratsumé, a younger sister of Ôtomo-no Tabito. Of all the poetesses in *Man'yôshû* she left the largest body of work, remarkable for its variety, its scenic descriptions, its reflective pieces and its lyrics. Unlike other poetesses, who for the most part sing lyrically of true love in a naive and simple manner, Iratsumé is significant for her breadth of vision. In contrasting the third period with the second, as represented by Hitomaro, who combined all sorts of tendencies in himself, we may say that this period is conspicuous for the gradual deepening of individual tendencies and the consequent development along varied lines.

Finally, the poems of the fourth period, extending from the

last days of the Emperor Shômu, through the reign of the Empress Kôken, to the year 759 in the reign of the Emperor Junnin, are remarkable for the paucity of new elements introduced; the poems of this period for the most part only bring together and reproduce all the elements previously initiated. Yet they do this in so striking a fashion that we may call this the Golden Age of *Man'yôshû*. On purely poetic grounds, we may regard Ôtomo-no Yakamochi as representative of the period, for, although his poems show no great originality, he played an important part in the compilation of *Man'-yôshû*. Moreover, more is known of his life than the lives of other Man'yôshû poets. He also wrote a greater number of poems, both comprehensive in theme and varied in thought, which it is possible to arrange chronologically, so that we are able to follow his artistic development.

As the son of Ôtomo-no Tabito and nephew of Sakanoé-no Iratsumé, he was fortunate in his birth, and from an early age had every opportunity for composing verse. We may divide his literary career into five periods. The first covers his boyhood, before he began to write, when he was under the care of his father Tabito, the poet. In the second period, as a youth, he served at the Imperial Court, falling in love many times, among others with Kasa-no Iratsumé and Sakanoé-no Ôiratsumé, and writing a number of poems dealing with these love affairs. The work of the Yakamochi of this period is characterized by a direct and pure, though somewhat thin and sentimental, expression of yearning, much like that of the poetesses of *Man'yôshû*.

His third period begins with his arrival at his post as Governor of the province of Etchû at the age of twenty-eight or so, and practically covers his term of office in this northern province. During this time he rid himself of his youthful emotionalism and devoted himself chiefly to the composition of *chôka* on various themes. These are merely descriptive and are devoid of any unifying lyrical spirit. If we except the passionate elegy inspired by the death of his younger brother Fumimochi, which took place shortly after his arrival in Etchû, we may say that his poems lack individuality, being merely imitative of Okura even to the vocabulary. This period may be regarded as one of personal trials and introspection. Only in the following period did Yakamochi gradually develop a style of his own. There is still some imitation of the ancients even in the next period, but the following instance shows that he had developed some individuality in his observation of nature :—

> Over the moorland
> The mists of spring are trailing;
>   And sad is my heart.
> Then in the evening twilight
> A warbler begins to sing.
>   *from Book XIX.*

As his outlook on life set and hardened, his poems took on a somewhat more philosophical cast. Like Okura, his outlook on life is realistic; both endeavoured to immortalize their names by great achievements, the main difference between them being that while Okura was individualistic in his aim, Yakamochi, as becomes the head of the aristocratic clan of Ôtomo, is disposed to magnify the renown of his family rather than confine himself to seeking his own personal fame alone. This engendered in him a spirit of loyalty, as the following poem suggests :—

> Men of this great clan,
> Which through all the wide land bears
>   An illustrious name,
> In service of your Sovran
> Quit you like Ôtomo men.
>   *from Book XX.*

In this period he was back in the Capital as an official in the War Department, where he showed a strong sympathy for those guards (*sakimori*) who had to leave for Tsukushi in the service of the Emperor. He felt their pangs on parting from mothers, wives and children as if they were his own. Such warmth and breadth of sympathy seems to have turned him from poetic composition to practical activities, bringing his poetic career to an end in 759. His last period, or the twenty-five years or so before his death in 785, may be regarded as poetically his dark days, when he sacrificed the work of composition on the altar of family duty. Taken as a whole, his poetry marks the transition from the style of *Man'yôshû* to that of *Kokinshû*, and may be said to foreshadow the qualities of the later poetry.

The fourth period of *Man'yôshû* produced poets, and poetesses like Chigami-no Otomé and Kasa-no Iratsumé, who sang of pure and simple emotion, but occasionally they wrote poems social in tone and sometimes expressing emotions other than their own, which lack such purity of feeling.

In spite of the continuous development shown to have taken place during these four periods, we should do well to regard *Man'yôshû* as the clear expression of pure feeling derived from vigorous character. This essential spirit of *Man'yôshû* has continued to flow through the long history of Japanese poetry. In such later poets of Man'-yôshû style as Minamoto-no Sanetomo, Kamo-no Mabuchi and Masaoka Shiki, we can see a return to the spirit of that anthology, the foundation of their art.

A few words should be said about the compilation of *Man'yôshû*. From ancient times there has been a divergence of opinion as to the editorship. Some hold that it was compiled by Tachibana-no Moroé in obedience to an Imperial command ; others, that it was a private compilation by Ôtomo-no Yakamochi and others. The more cogent of these theories is that which favours its being a private compilation by Ôtomo-no Yakamochi. In any case, it is now beyond dispute that Yakamochi is at least chiefly responsible for the arrangement of *Man'yôshû*. Yet it ought to be added that Yakamochi did not, in the first instance, compile the whole anthology single-handed. His work was to rearrange preceding compilations and materials, and even after his time the order of the work was frequently revised ; it was probably soon after 759 that Yakamochi drafted the compilation, but the work did not take its present form until the early years of the Heian period.

From this it naturally follows that there is little uniformity in structure in the twenty books of *Man'yôshû*. First, let us glance at the nature of each book. The excellent order of the poems of Book I and II leads us to suppose that they were compiled by Imperial command ; Book V appears to be Okura's copy of his poems dealing with his environment ; Books XVII—XX, inclusive, are apparently Yakamochi's diary in verse ; Book XIV is noteworthy for its *azuma' uta* (poems of the Eastern Provinces). But Yakamochi compiled a greater number of books than any other poet (Books III, IV, VI, VIII, XVII, XVIII, XIX, and XX) besides assisting in the compilation of the anthology as a whole.

Secondly, *Man'yôshû* may be classified either, as regards form, into *chôka*, *tanka* and *sedôka*, or on the basis of directness or indirectness of expression, into *seijutsu-shincho* (direct expression of personal thoughts) and *kibutsu-chinshi* (indirect expression of one's thoughts through another medium). The most characteristic classification is that into *zôka* (miscellaneous poems), *sômonka* (exchange songs, that is love-letters in verse) and *banka* (elegies), but this classification includes among the *zôka* too large a number and too large a variety of poems.

Thirdly, in contrast with later anthologies written in the Japanese syllabary (*kana*), *Man'yôshû* is written entirely in Chinese ideographs. Two methods of use of these should, however, be distinguished: in one they are read phonetically, disregarding the significance of the characters (*on*), and in another the significance of the characters is rendered by the equivalent Japanese word (*kun*). So one Chinese character is used in one of the two ways, either phonetically (*man'yô-gana*) or as an ideograph properly so called. Chinese characters are, of course, used in other ways, but these afford the two chief points of contrast; broadly speaking, though throughout the whole anthology we find the two styles in indiscriminate use, the books differ in the respective emphasis they lay on each. The *on* style is chiefly employed in Books V, XIV, XV, XVII, XVIII, XIX and XX, and the *kun* style in the rest.

A fourth point is that *Man'yôshû* is not intended to be a comprehensive collection of poems, but is rather a selection compiled by Imperial command according to no fixed standard (in contrast to the later anthologies), and therefore expressive of no strongly critical spirit on the part of the compilers. Therefore, *Man'yôshû* is sadly lacking in uniformity in the structure of its twenty books, in the classification of its poems and in the use of ideographs. Nevertheless, throughout we find a natural, or, at any rate, unrestrained, lyricism. Accordingly, any definite intention of unifying the entire *Man'yôshû* being lacking, each of the poems appears to be floating naturally in its own individual and quiet way, over this vast ocean of verse.

KOKIN WAKASHÛ or KOKINSHÛ

(An Anthology of Poems, Ancient and Modern)

Together with *Man'yôshû* and *Shin-Kokinshû*, *Kokinshû* (An Anthology of Poems, Ancient and Modern) occupies a notable position among the collections of Japanese poetry. It contains representative poetry of the early Heian period when elegance had superseded the earlier virility that had reached its consummation in *Man'yôshû*, a further development, that of mediaeval symbolism, being perfected in the later collection called *Shin-Kokinshû* (A New Anthology of Poems, Ancient and Modern).

The view of poetry given in the Prefaces to *Kokinshû* may be claimed as foreshadowing Japanese literary criticism. The origin of such criticism at that moment was due first of all to the introduction of Chinese prosody and to the publication of Kûkai's *Bunkyô Hifuron*, on Chinese rhetoric with copious quotations, which inspired the study of Japanese prosody. The development of a critical consciousness was aided at this moment by the newly-introduced *uta-awasé*, poetical contests, which necessarily evoked discussion on the merits and demerits of the poems, and also by the publication of numerous anthologies. And, to some degree, of course, this newly-developed critical spirit was the gradual outcome of a deepening literary consciousness.

The Prefaces to *Kokinshû* form two essays on the essence, origin, classification and historical conception of Japanese poetry. It would be too much to say that the interpretation of poetry by bringing its spirit in relation to the diction originated with these Prefaces, but they certainly did summarize the issue in plain and simple language, and that is the reason for its long continuance as the central problem of Japanese prosody.

The classification of the poems in the main text into *zôka* (miscellaneous poems), *sômonka* (exchange songs) and *banka* (elegies) follows that of *Man'yôshû*, and sets an example to later anthologies.

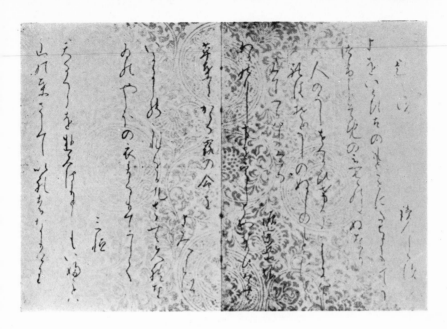

KOKIN WAKASHŪ (ANTHOLOGY OF POEMS, ANCIENT AND MODERN). Manuscript copy in 1120. The oldest complete text in existence. Owner: Mitsui family, Tokyo.

KI-NO TSURAYUKI
(d. 946)
From "Portraits of the Thirty-Six Poetical Geniuses of Old Japan", ascribed to Fujiwara-no Nobuzane (13th century), known as Satake Bon, Marquis Satake Scroll.

In the matter of poetical development, *Kokinshû* falls roughly into three stages. The first is that of the anonymous pieces; the second, the poems of the Rokkasen, the Six Master Poets; and the third, poems of the time of Ki-no Tsurayuki, Ôshikôchi-no Mitsuné and others who collaborated in compiling the anthology. The third stage may be regarded as the main period of *Kokinshû*, with the first and second stages as periods of transition from *Man'yôshû* to *Kokinshû*. In the matter of form, pauses after the second and the fourth lines predominate. Here is an example :—

Five syllables	Ko-no sa-to ni In this remote spot
Seven syllables	Ta-bi-né shi-nu be-shi, Am I forced to stay the night;
Five syllables	Sa-ku-ra-ba-na For cherry blossoms,
Seven syllables	Chi-ri no ma-ga-i ni Falling, bewildering me,
Seven syllables	I-e-ji wa-su-re-té. Make me forget my way home.

Anon. from Book II.

The anonymous poems are mostly of this kind, a comparatively large number of them being in the *Man'yôshû* style ending in the *shûshikei*, the terminating forms, of verbs. One may take these poems as marking the early stages of the transition from *Man'yôshû* to *Kokinshû*.

Outstanding in the next period are the poems by the Rokkasen, the Six Poetical Geniuses. This name was derived from Tsurayuki's Prefaces to the Anthology concerning the six master poets, Ariwara-no Narihira, Ono-no Komachi, Sôjô Henjô, Ôtomo-no Kuronushi, Fun'ya-no Yasuhidé and Kisen Hôshi. From a technical point of view their works are of greater interest than those of the age of Tsurayuki; they have rid themselves of primitive naïveté, and are strongly characterized by the artificiality of the Heian period, which however is made to harmonize well with the emotional content of the poem. We shall deal briefly with the main characteristics of Narihira, Komachi and Henjô, the most notable of the Six.

Ariwara-no Narihira, with other poets of the Heian period such as Izumi Shikibu and Saigyô, was a virile singer of his sincere feelings.   He differs from the other poets of the Age of the Rokkasen in that his mode of expression tends to be naive rather than intellectual.   His poems are sometimes marked by an unrestrained emotionalism, expressed plainly yet with conscious technique.   To cite one instance from *Kokinshû* :—

> Although for long years
> Have I clearly perceived what
> Is man's final fate,
> How could I have foreseen that
> It would fall on me so soon!
> *from Book XVI.*

This poem shows a boundless sentiment expressed in the plainest style.   The next example which reveals a pure and simple heart subtly employs a certain degree of artifice in order to express the intensity of emotion :—

> Would that it were that
> In this world was no hour of
> Inevitable parting
> For those who wish a thousand
> Years of life for their parents.
> *from Book XVII.*

Below are two poems by Ariwara-no Narihira :—

> The moon I see is
> Not the moon of other days ;
> The spring that is come
> Is not as that other spring ;
> Only I remain unchanged.
> *from Book XV.*

> I wonder whether
> To believe or not believe :
> But now starts to fall
> More heavily the rain that
> Shall test the depth of your love.
> *from Book XIV.*

In these two poems traces of artificiality can be found in the repetition of the words "spring" and "believe." Tsurayuki's criticism was that these words are too limiting to be expressive of rich emotion. He was probably intending to point out the poverty of expression, but the present writer thinks that Narihira used such repetition on set purpose. For, unlike *Man'yôshû*, these poems make use of conscious artistry. Yet the fact that they can be criticized by Tsurayuki as being too compressed, too limiting, shows that in this respect they differ from the pure emotion of Tsurayuki himself.

Sôjô Henjô, unlike Ariwara-no Narihira, was straightforward and serene in character ; his poems are not passionate, but unconventional and realistic. For instance :—

> O Lotus flowers !
> Your stainless hearts keep you pure
> In muddy waters :
> Why cheat us into taking
> Dew-drops on your leaves for gems ?
> *from Book III.*

In this poem the use of the colloquial word "cheat" (*azamuku*) reflects the unconventional bent of the poet.

> O maiden-flower,
> Attracted solely by your name,
> I have plucked a spray.
> Do not whisper it abroad
> That loving you did I fall.
> *from Book IV.*

His love of the maiden-flower (*ominaeshi*) the priestly Henjô playfully counts a fall from ideals of celibacy ; the poem reveals how capable he is of giving spontaneous expression to a delicate emotion, and is a good example of his artistic mentality.

The poems of Ono-no Komachi, eulogized by Tsurayuki as harmonizing most perfectly spirit and diction, also strike the elegant note characteristic of a poetess, showing purity of feeling.

> Long continuing rain
> The beauty of the flowers
> Has painfully marred ;
> So has age stolen on me,
> As I brooded pensively.
> *from Book II.*

Ever since that time
When I did dream of the one
I love so dearly,
Have I come to a belief
In that which I see in dreams.
from Book XII.

There is no unnatural artificiality in these poems, but a spontaneity with no conscious effort at artistic expresssion. Yet when Komachi, in her poems, compares herself to flowers or expresses her feeling by means of a dream, she is showing more artificiality than can be found in *Man'yôshû*. Moreover, her technique is not the slave of her intellect, and conceivably it is in this that the superiority lies of the Age of the Rokkasen.

However, Tsurayuki's attitude to poetry in the Prefaces shows a disposition to attach importance to conscious artistry, apparently as the fundamental principle of poetry. This he reveals also in his own work, as indeed it is revealed as the outstanding feature of all the poets of the third period of *Kokinshû*.

A few examples of his work are given below :—

When mists are trailing
And the trees begin to bud,
Then the Spring snow falls
As if blossoms are drifting
Over a flowerless village !
from Book I.

In the fragrant Spring
Even on Mount Darkness
On a moonless night,
By their fragrance we perceive
The plum blossom's presence there.
from Book I.

His artistic skill is seen in his comparison of the snow to flowers and in his making the blossoms almost visible by their fragrance. He also wrote a number of poems touched with intellectual wit, while the following shows his capacity for expressing a spontaneous emotion when he so chooses :—

On a winter night
In the chill river breezes,

Plovers are keening,
When, my heart filled with yearning,
I set out to come to you.

from Book IV.

Other poets contemporary with Tsurayuki are Ôshikôchi-no Mitsuné and Ki-no Tomonori. Mitsuné writes:—

When the night was cold,
Brushing off an early frost
    Settling white and hoar,
Oft did I, a traveller,
Lay myself down on the grass.

from Book IX.

And Tomonori :—

On such a spring day,
So calm and quiet, and blessed
    With gentlest sunshine,
Why should the blossoms now fall
And scatter so restlessly ?

from Book II.

Both these poems give a direct expression to the charms of nature, but it must be admitted that on the whole Mitsuné and Tomonori give evidence rather of an intellectual and witty technique similar to that of Tsurayuki. This then is the leading characteristic of Tsurayuki's generation, the third period of *Kokinshû.* Despite its differences from the first period, that of the anonymous poems, and even from the second, of the Six Master Poets, this period of Tsurayuki forms the centre of *Kokinshû* as a whole and represents its essential qualities.

Kokinshû is of interest from the point of view of wit. Its emotional poems, however, show a certain shallowness and artificiality, although, here and there, one finds poems which give the impression of coming directly from the heart. Granted the artificiality, yet one cannot deny the presence of a genuine emotion.

Further, in contrast to the naïveté and often roughness of *Man'-yôshû, Kokinshû* lays stress on smoothness, and that not only in words but also in whole phrases. This is indeed a strong point of the anthology. The following poem by Fujiwara-no Toshiyuki reveals how a strong emotion can be smoothness itself:—

> Autumn is coming!
> Though its approach is hardly
> Yet to be perceived,
> Its coming can be felt now
> In the coolness of the wind.
> *from Book IV.*

For this reason, this poem is regarded as the best in *Kokinshû*.

Despite its being open to the charge of artificiality, *Kokinshû* as a whole is full of a genuine poetic quality, heart-felt emotion and facility of expression. Undoubtedly, the great importance attached to intellectual artifice is responsible for the weak point of these poems of the Heian period, namely, their lack of individuality, yet the smoothness of the versification is, as Kagawa Kageki, a critic of the later Tokugawa period, insists, a very real merit indeed. The high position held by the school of *Kokinshû* (Kokin-ha) in the development of Japanese poetry is testimony enough of the significance of this collection.

Kokinshû in twenty books was compiled in the fifth year of the Engi era (A.D. 905) by Ki-no Tsurayuki, Ki-no Tomonori, Ôshikôchi-no Mitsuné and Mibu-no Tadaminé, in obedience to the order of the Emperor Daigo. It consists of 1,100 poems in all and was intended as a successor to *Man'yôshû*. It therefore contains recent pieces as well as older poems not included in *Man'yôshû*, while several poems are included in both anthologies.

The twenty books are divided as follows: "Spring" (two parts), "Summer," "Autumn" (two parts), "Winter," "Congratulatory Poems," "Partings," "Travels," "Word-plays," "Love Poems" (five parts), "Elegies," "Miscellaneous Pieces" (two parts), "Pieces in Various Forms" and "Pieces Recited at the Imperial Bureau of Poetry." The majority of the poems are *tanka*, but "Pieces in Various Forms" contains several *chôka* and *sedôka* and a few *haikaika*, a humorous variety of *tanka*.

There are two Prefaces, one written in Japanese (*kana*), and the other in Chinese. It has not been definitely decided which of these was the orignal.

TAKETORI MONOGATARI

(The Old Bamboo-Cutter)

Taketori Monogatari (or, more accurately, *Taketori no Okina Mono-gatari*), sometimes known as *Kaguya Himé Monogatari*, appeared in the early Heian period, the ninth century. The author is unknown and it is ascribed, though with no certain evidence, to the period of the Engi era (901–922). The word *monogatari* means tale or novel; and *Taketori Monogatari* has long been regarded as the earliest *monogatari* written in *kana*. It is referred to in that famous classic, *Genji Monotagari*, as " *Taketori no Okina*, the forerunner of the *mono-gatari* literature." It is one of the historic sources of the Japanese novel and affords valuable evidence regarding this form of literature in the early days of Japanese culture.

" Once upon a time, there was an old bamboo-cutter, who went out every day on to the hills and moors to cut bamboo for use for various purposes. His name was Sanuki-no Miyatsukomaro." These opening sentences make it quite clear that the work is intended as a tale ; both in form and content, it resembles a nursery tale, as one would naturally expect in such a primitive form of fiction.

One day, when he went out to cut bamboo as usual, the old man found a bamboo with a shining stem. In amazement he drew near, and saw seated in the hollow of the bamboo a beautiful baby girl, only a few inches in height. The astonished old man carried her home with great delight to his wife who brought her up with loving care, but so small and delicate was she that she had to be kept in a tiny basket. Wonderful to relate, thenceforth the old man frequently found pieces of gold in the bamboo which he cut down, and gradually acquired a fortune. Meanwhile the child grew so rapidly that in three months she was already of normal height for a woman and most beautiful, so that the house was always filled with the radiance of her beauty.

The maiden was named Nayotaké-no Kaguya Himé, the Shining Princess of the Slender Bamboo, and those who heard of her haunted the old man's house night and day, in the hope of obtaining a glimpse at least of her wonderful beauty, but all in vain. Of all these visitors her most devoted admirers were Prince Ishitsukuri, Prince Kuramochi, the Minister of the Right, Abé-no Miushi, the Chief Councillor of State, Ôtomo-no Miyuki, and the Second Councillor of State, Isonokami-no Maro.

Moved by their devotion Kaguya Himé decided to test their fidelity, promising to marry the most worthy of the five. Accordingly, they assembled together one day at her house, where she demanded from each one a particular thing, promising to marry that one who succeeded in bringing what she asked.

Prince Ishitsukuri was asked to fetch from India " Buddha's stone begging-bowl"; Prince Kuramochi, " a branch of the tree with root of silver, stem of gold and fruit of precious jewels which grows on Hôrai-san (the Elysian Mountain)"; Abé-no Miushi, " a Chinese robe made of the fur of fire-rats (*hinezumi*)"; Ôtomo-no Miyuki, " a five-coloured jewel from a dragon's head "; and Isonokami-no Maro, " the cowrie-shell charm of a swallow." The five admirers, eager to win Kaguya Himé at any cost, cudgelled their brains as to how they could obtain the articles demanded of them.

Prince Ishitsukuri, finding it utterly impossible to find Buddha's stone begging-bowl, even if he went the long journey to India, told Kaguya Himé that he was leaving for India, but in fact he merely went into hiding. Three years later he respectfully presented to Kaguya Himé the sooty bowl from in front of an old image of Buddha in a mountain temple, elaborately enclosed in a bag of brocade. " Here is what you desire," he said. But she knew in a moment that the bowl was a counterfeit, for it hardly emitted as much light as a firefly. So she threw it away outside in front of the gate ; the Prince's trick had failed.

Prince Kuramochi, just as wily, told Kaguya Himé that he was going to Hôrai-san to fetch the branch of gems, and pretended to sail away from Naniwa. But three days later he returned, and ordered skilful artisans to make a branch of gems behind closed doors. When the work was finished, he pretended he had brought it back from Hôrai-san. As he showed it to her, he told a plausible story of all the troubles and hardships he had suffered on his travels. The old couple were completely deceived; and the Lady was grieved to think that she had been vanquished and would have to marry him. Then just at that moment the jewellers turned up to demand their unpaid wages from the prince! Thus was his deceit immediately unmasked and, covered with shame, he beat a hasty retreat.

The third admirer, Abé-no Miushi, who was a member of a wealthy, powerful family, ordered a Chinese acquaintance to obtain a robe of *hinezumi* fur. On receiving it, he joyfully presented it to the Lady. It was a splendid treasure, with the rich fur gleaming like gold on a dark blue ground. But the Lady knew that if it were a robe of genuine fire-rat fur it would not burn; so as a test she threw it on the fire. To Miushi's dismay, the flames licked it up and quickly reduced it to ashes.

The fourth suitor, Ôtomo-no Miyuki, called his servants together and said, " I will grant any request to the man who will bring me a five-coloured jewel from a dragon's head." With strict orders not to return without it, he sent them off in various directions. Astounded at their master's unreasonable command, the servants took the travelling expenses allotted to them and went where their fancy led them. Not one of them made any search for the jewel. Ignorant of this, Miyuki waited long and vainly for their return. At last, angered at their failure, he determined to go on the quest himself, and accordingly embarked at Naniwa. But he had not gone far before he encountered a terrible gale, from which he barely succeeded in escaping with his life. Then, at last, he perceived his folly, and gave up all idea of winning Kaguya Himé.

Isonokami-no Maro, the fifth admirer, set out to seek for the cowrie-shell charm of a swallow. He got into a basket and had it pulled up by a rope to a swallow's nest under the ridge of the roof of a granary. Feeling something solid and flat in the nest, he joyfully decided that he had found the thing he was looking for. So he had the basket let down in a great hurry. But just then the rope broke, and he and the basket fell plump to the ground, where he lay senseless. When he recovered, all his hopes were dashed. For it was no cowrie but a swallow's droppings that he held tightly grasped in his hand!

Reports of the great beauty of the Lady had meanwhile reached the ears of the Mikado. Under the pretence of hunting in that neighbourhood, he paid a visit to the house of old Taketori-no

Okina, where he marvelled at her dazzling loveliness. After this, the sovereign wrote frequent letters to her.

Three years passed. From the beginning of the spring, Kaguya Himé had gone out alone more and more often to weep at the sight of the moon sailing serenely across the sky. Then in the month of August, as the night of the full moon drew near, she cried even more bitterly.

The old man anxiously asked what was troubling her. "I am not really a girl of this world. I belong to the city of the moon. I was born in the temporary form of a human being, but now the time has come for me to return. On the night of the full moon, the people of the moon will come to take me away. That is why I have been so sad." So answering she burst into tears, and the old man, in his misery, could only weep with her.

When the matter was brought to the knowledge of the Mikado, it caused him great anxiety, and he determined to prevent the ascension of the Lady at any cost. So, on the night when the moon would be at the full, the sovereign stationed a guard of two thousand warriors around the house; while the old wife, holding Kaguya Himé in her arms, entered an inner chamber and shut the door, determined to keep strict watch and to ward off any heavenly visitants.

Before long, heaven and earth were filled with a sudden light. On the wings of the clouds a group of angels floated gently to the ground, with a beautifully decorated flying chariot in their midst. The guards, who had been impatiently awaiting the advent of the heavenly visitors in the full determination of beating them back, lost their heads completely at this sight. They had not even the strength to raise their bows and arrows, but could do nothing except look on with vacant eyes.

One of the heavenly messengers went up to the old man, who was lying on the ground as if senseless, and said, "It was as a reward for your virtue that I have left Kaguya Himé in your charge for a space. But the time has now come for you to give her up to me. Kaguya Himé! Come forth at once!"

As he spoke, the tightly closed door of the Lady's room opened noiselessly, and she stepped out. She came to the weeping couple and thanked them for all their care of her, and tried to console them. As a token of her gratitude she left them the garment she was wearing, while to the sovereign she sent a farewell letter thanking him for his benevolent intentions.

Also she left for him a poem :—

> And now as I go,
> In this Heavenly Garment
> Of feathers robed,
> Happy memories of you
> Do I longingly recall.

And as a parting gift, she gave him some drops of the elixir of immortality. Then in her robe of feathers she stepped into the waiting chariot, but slowly and reluctantly, and attended by hundreds of angels ascended to the moon, leaving the people on earth as if in a trance. When the old couple came to themselves they shed bitter tears, beside themselves with grief. The sovereign receiving the farewell letter and the elixir sang in sorrow :—

> My tears of grief flow,
> When I think that never shall
> I see her again ;
> Then how worthless to me now
> Is this elixir of life !

So he had the elixir burnt on the top of that mountain in Suruga province whose peak reaches nearest to heaven. Thus it came to be called Mt Fuji (' Undying ')—and " it is said," the story concludes, " that the smoke from the fire which was then lit still rises up into the clouds from the summit of that mountain."

Such is the outline of the story. Because of its tenderness and its simplicity as of a nursery tale, combined with a wealth of fantasy sustained throughout, it has always made a strong appeal to readers. Actually the plot and theme are derived from old Chinese traditions and the Buddhist scriptures, but its chief interest and value as a work of art lie in the ease and skill in which the author retells them in his own words, and the beauty with which they are developed as part of the life of the age in which the tale was written. The women of the Heian period, full of lofty ideals and proudly exacting respect for their superior position, are clearly reflected in Kaguya Himé with her unreasonable demands on her admirers, while the five devoted admirers illustrate the aristocractic life of the time enlivened by amorous dalliance.

The author intends to give an ironically humorous expression to the tragedy arising from the clash between the real and the ideal. Kaguya Himé, who maintained a calm and dignified idealistic attitude towards any kind of human love, in the end was able to find her ideal expressed for the first time on earth in the benevolence of the sovereign. Nevertheless, even this was earthly love and a human affection ; while, for her, love was a heavenly conception eternally sacred. Hence in this story we have an exaggerated picture of the boundless ideals and fancies of the women of the Heian period, together with a reflection of one beautiful phase in the Japanese character, profound reverence for the Royal Family.

Furthermore, the heroine's life in the house of the humble old couple, so different from that aristocratic court life which is the subject of nearly all the stories of the Heian period, is of interest in that it reveals the lingering old world naïveté of the early novel. In addition to the freshness of the theme and the interest of the plot, blending supernatural fantasy and realism, the language in which it is told gives life and character to the tale ; the pleasant, crisp, unaffectedly simple style, and the humour, exactly fitting the subject-matter, give the whole work an added lustre. It should be noted also how each of the separate tales ends with a play on words, a characteristic of the *rakugo* (comic stories) of modern Japan. In *Taketori Monogatari* they are employed to account for, in a humorously playful manner, the derivation of place-names and proverbial sayings. Again, the structure of the work, consisting as it does of independent short tales each ending with a lyric (*waka*), shows a close relationship with the contemporary *uta-monogatari* (" poem tale," a sequence of short tales interspersed with poems).

It belongs to the " contest for a wife " class of story, embellished with the current Chinese conceptions of fairies and of Buddhism, which heighten the colour of the legendary and fantastic atmosphere. In particular, its resemblance to a children's story, so marked in the earlier part, justifies us in regarding it as an artistic nursery tale.

GENJI MONOGATARI

(The Tale of Genji)

Genji Monogatari is the oldest and greatest of Japanese novels. It was written soon after the year 1000—over nine hundred years ago—by Murasaki Shikibu, the famous authoress of the Heian period. This lengthy work—it consists of fifty-four chapters or rather books—and *Man'yôshû* are the two highest peaks in the whole range of our literature, the two finest artistic achievements of Japan.

Genji Monogatari is a biographical novel dealing with the life and loves of one Hikaru Genji, a young noble of the Heian period, unparalleled for elegance and talent. Its fifty-four books, all gracefully entitled, from the first, the Book of "Kiritsubo," to the last, the Book of "Yumé no Ukihashi," can be divided roughly into two parts. The first forty-one tell of Hikaru Genji and his loves, while the last books centre upon his son, Kaoru.

Kiritsubo (The Lady of the Paulownia Hall): This first book relates how Kiritsubo-no Kôi, a young lady of the court, beautiful, tender and delicate, enjoyed the love of Kiritsubo-no Mikado, but suffered from the envy and jealousy of his many other loves. Yet she considered herself the most fortunate woman in the world, for it was on her that the sovereign lavished his fondest affections, and by him she was the mother of a baby prince. Then one summer's day, when the prince was but two years old, her delicate eyelids closed for ever, like the fleeting paulownia flowers falling in the garden. The grief of the sovereign and of her son was inexpressible. For a time even the sighing of the wind in the trees and the complaining murmurs of the crickets moved them to tears.

The years passed swiftly until the motherless young prince had attained his sixth year. He bore the honorific title of Hikaru Kimi (Radiant Prince), his radiant beauty and his intelligence winning the admiration of all and the high favour of his Royal father. Never-

〔 37 〕

theless, the sovereign was anxious about the future of his young son, if he should remain unsupported by family connections; so he granted him the family name of Genji, although by this he was lowered to the status of a subject. Then, one spring, when Genji was eleven years old, Aoi-no Ué, the daughter of the Minister of the Left, was chosen as his bride. She was four years older than he, and he could not help feeling there was something lacking, and therefore distasteful, in her; well-born and graceful she certainly was, but she was too conventional to be natural and charming of manner. And for the most part he was too intent on entering into the gay life at Court to visit her.

Meanwhile, Fujitsubo Nyôgo had entered the service of the Court, and as she bore a remarkable resemblance to the dead Kiritsubo-no Kôi, her presence gradually assuaged the sovereign's grief for his lost favourite. Fujitsubo, admired of all, took the place of Kiritsubo and was called Kagayaku Hi-no Miya, the Shining Sun Princess. The young Genji, told that she was the living image of the mother he had lost at the age of two, felt an innocent longing for her, desiring always only to be near her.

Hahakigi (The Broom-Tree): One night during the early summer rains, Genji and three friends, including his most intimate friend, Tô-no Chûjô, were together in the room allotted to Genji at Court. They entered on a discussion which lasted the whole night through regarding various types of women. Each gave his own views, and in the course of the talk each confessed the mistakes they had made in love adventures. But in the end they all agreed that it was very difficult to single out any one woman who would make an ideal partner for life. One wife was good, but so jealous that she bit her husband's finger in her rage; another was brilliant and refined, but fickle; another was too timid and quiet; yet another was far too learned. This discussion on women, known as " Amayo no Shinasadamé " (" The Appraisement of Women on a Rainy Night "), is interesting as revealing the authoress's ideas about women and wives.

Utsusemi (The Cicada's Discarded Mantle): About that time chance brought to Genji's notice a middle-class lady named Utsusemi, stepmother of the Lord of Kii. He frequently visited this lady, who looked so delicate and frail but whose flexible character was as unbreakable as a slender bamboo. She was too chaste to yield to his affections easily, and her coolness drove him to an impatience hitherto outside his experience. She showed herself grateful for his kindnesses, but firmly refused his advances. Ah, she would declare, how sad it was to be reminded always that she was no longer entitled to the love of such a man!

One evening when Genji had driven up to Utsusemi's dwelling he found that, as usual, she had concealed herself to avoid him. Sad at heart, he took up the gauze mantle she had abandoned in her flight and carried it home.

Yûgao (Lady Moonflower): One evening in late summer, Genji discovered the dwelling of the beautiful lady, Yûgao; it lay in a lonely spot on the highway, enclosed by a tiny fence entwined with moonflowers. Her case was pitiable, for she had been a love of Tô-no Chûjô, Genji's bosom friend, but, unable to endure the merciless treatment of Tô-no Chûjô's lawful wife, she had hidden herself away. Genji was captivated by the slender loveliness of the quiet and gentle lady, and visited her frequently with his face heavily veiled, and without telling her his name. The more he saw of her, the more he pined for her, until he found himself impatiently awaiting the evening as soon as they had parted in the morning.

The lady also was enchanted with Genji's ardent love-making, and so, although sometimes each felt uneasy about the other's identity, they at last were deeply in love.

On the night of the Harvest full-moon, the bright moonlight shone into her humble cottage where Genji was passing the night. In these unfamiliar surroundings with the lady, clad in white, close to him, completely absorbed and exquisitely lovely, Genji felt enchanted even by the distant sound of the fulling of cloth and the cry of the wild geese on the wing. Desirous of seeking a still quieter place where they could talk together, he led her away to a house standing alone. Long deserted, high-grown weeds and a wild, rank growth of trees surrounded it and a grim atmosphere of desolation lay over it. There, at midnight, a strange phantasm appeared at their bedside, and bereft his beloved Yûgao of her life. Rokujô-no Miyasudokoro, one of Genji's loves, crazed with jealousy, had sent her wraith to wreak her vengeance on her supplanter. As a result of this sudden tragic event, Genji long lay languishing and suffering on a sick-bed.

On recovering, he took Ukon, Yûgao's waiting-maid, to his own house, and from her learnt for the first time of the identity of his dead love. She also told him of the infant daughter whom Yûgao had borne to Tô-no Chûjô, but although he sought everywhere for her it was in vain.

Wakamurasaki (Young Purple Grass): One day when Genji had called on a priest in Kitayama to ask him to perform incantations to restore him to health, in a cottage at the foot of that mountain, he chanced upon Wakamurasaki, a lovely young girl who bore a great resemblance to Fujitsubo Nyôgo, his stepmother to whom he was so constant in his affections. Eagerly desiring to educate her according to his own views of what an ideal wife should be, he entreated for her and took her away, to ponder day and night over the education of the beautiful girl, who came to love Genji like a father. She proved to be the niece of Fujitsubo Nyôgo and was afterwards to become Murasaki-no Ué, Genji's lawful wife.

Suetsumuhana (Safflower): Suetsumuhana was a young lady who after the death of her father Hitachi-no Miya led a lonely life, with a *koto* (harp) as her sole companion. Genji chanced to hear of her and used to visit her, but for some time had no opportunity of seeing her features clearly. Then, one snowy morning he had a glimpse of her face. He was astounded to see a broad bulging forehead, a long, pale face, and a huge pendulous nose. He left the lady as soon as he could and flew back home. But thinking over the matter he realized what a miserable life she must lead, lonely and so hideous. Out of pity he took her under his protection, while at home Wakamurasaki pleased and delighted him with her growing beauty and charm.

Momiji no Ga (The Maple Banquet): In mid-autumn one year when the trees were a brocade of autumn tints, a banquet was given. A beautiful boat, containing musicians, floated on a pond in the shade of the rocks, overhung with maples in their dark crimson foliage. Sweet music falling continually upon their ears, all were entranced by the view of the graceful figure of Genji as he danced the *Seigaiha* (one of the *Bugaku*, ancient court dances) among the falling leaves gleaming like a brocade, his dancing figure sharply and beautifully defined against the glow of the evening sun.

Hana no En (The Cherry-Blossom Party): One genial day in late

March, the cherry-viewing feast was held in the Court Hall known as Naden or Shishinden. All day long, the merry twittering birds had flown about under the full-blown cherry blossoms and basked in the warm spring sun. But, with the coming of night, the merry-making came at last to an end, and the sounds of music were heard no more. Attracted by the bright moonlight, Genji left the convivial scene and stepped out into the corridor. There by chance he met and entered into friendly conversation with Oborozukiyo, a gay young woman and the younger sister of Kokiden Nyôgo, who had long hated Genji.

Aoi (Lady Geranium): Following the abdication of Kiritsubo-no Mikado and the accession of Suzaku-no Mikado, the cheerful festival of the Kamo shrine was celebrated. The thoroughfares of the capital were lined with gorgeously decorated carriages filled with spectators whose rich garments rivalled the flowers in gay beauty and added colour to the grand ceremony, among them the handsome figure of Genji standing out conspicuously. In the tumult among the carriages to secure good places, Rokujô-no Miyasudokoro, one of Genji's mistresses, suffered the public shame of having her carriage wrecked by the followers of Genji's lawful wife, Aoi-no Ué, who was also among the spectators. Furious with rage and jealousy, the wraith of Miyasudokoro used to visit and torment Aoi-no Ué, and finally frightened her to death.

Genji's feeling of bitter loneliness on the Lady Aoi's death seemed intensified by the melancholy breeze of autumn.

Sakaki (The Sacred Tree) and *Hana Chiru Sato* (The Village of Falling Flowers): After many days of anguish and agony, Miyasudokoro, who had suffered terrors in nightmares since her wraith had killed Aoi-no Ué, made up her mind to leave the capital where Genji was living, and to go to Isé. It was a desolate autumn evening when the two met with sad hearts for the final parting. That winter the ex-sovereign Kiritsubo died, the Genji family thus being suddenly deprived of their support, so that they were forced to live obscurely in a very different style from formerly. Kokiden Nyôgo, the Queen Dowager and mother of Suzaku-no Mikado, seized this opportunity to oppress Genji more and more. He had paid a secret visit to Oborozukiyo, Kokiden's younger sister who was then in Court service, but this unfortunately becoming known, the angry Queen

Dowager determined to take vengeance on Genji in every way possible. It was not long before Fujitsubo, second dowager of the abdicated sovereign and Genji's beloved stepmother, was forced to become a nun. For Genji the New Year, usually so gay and bright, brought with it an atmosphere of unsurpassed gloom and loneliness. No friends came to visit him: his residence was deserted.

In the desolate spring, Genji, overcome with ennui, decided to call on his love, Hanachirusato, whom he had not seen for a long time. It was a quiet night, and the cry of the cuckoos, as they flew in quest of the scent of the mandarin-orange flowers, echoed clearly across the sky.

Suma (Exile at Suma) and *Akashi* (Akashi): The contrast between his increasing adversity and his previous good fortune made it impossible for Genji to suffer patiently any longer the hatred of Kokiden, and he determined to leave the capital and retire to Suma, by the sea. It would be too cruel, he thought, to take his wife, Murasaki-no Ué, to the desolation of a seashore for ever pounded by the raging surf. Yet it was only with the utmost reluctance that he decided that he must leave her behind, for since the death of Aoi-no Ué he had given his whole heart to Murasaki. In these unfamiliar surroundings on the seashore at Suma, he experienced the utmost loneliness day and night and was for ever pining for the capital.

Summer passed, and then Suma was swept by the cold desolate wind of autumn. So overcome was he with sadness that the *koto* which he played to divert his mind moved him rather to tears.

Genji's attendants could not restrain their grief at the sight of the distress of their master, who had now greeted two springs in exile. One day a violent storm arose on that coast, and earthshaking claps of thunder struck terror into all their hearts. The rough weather continued for several days before it died down.

As Genji was lying half asleep, his dead father, Kiritsubo In, appeared and warned him to leave that place immediately. Genji marvelled at the vision, and yet next morning, as if in fulfilment of the warning, a small boat reached the shore, rowed by a lay-brother, Akashi Nyûdô, in order to take him away. The priest had also had a revelation, and his purpose was to take Genji to his house at Akashi.

This Akashi Nyûdô had an only daughter of surpassing beauty

and culture, named Akashi-no Ué, of whom he was inordinately proud. Her meeting with Genji took place in a tranquil atmosphere amid the soughing of the wind in the pine trees and the strident music of crickets. So intense was the silence that when the fringe of the curtain brushed against the *koto* which she had been playing, it sounded like a faint note of music. Nature smiled on the love of Akashi and Genji, seeming to declare that this had not happened by mere chance but had been fated to occur. Thenceforth, despite its loneliness, Genji's life was pleasanter than before.

In the autumn of the same year, news of Royal pardon suddenly arrived from Kyoto, and, quite unexpectedly, he was able to start on his happy return journey to the capital. But for Akashi-no Ué it was inexpressibly sad thus to part from him. The *koto*, whose music had become so dear to them, he left with her as a memento until their next meeting, and then sailed away from the shores of Akashi where he had lived so long.

In the capital the people greeted him with cheers, while the joy of Murasaki-no Ué, her long loneliness and her hardships forgotten, was beyond compare.

Miotsukushi (The Flood Gauge): In March of the following year, Akashi-no Ué gave birth to a daughter. This was unexpected news for Genji but it brought him great joy. He hoped that some day the child might perhaps rise to the position of Queen, and he hastened to summon her to the capital where he could oversee her upbringing. He thought of entrusting the baby to Murasaki-no Ué's care.

In the autumn when Genji made a pilgrimage to the Sumiyoshi shrine, Akashi-no Ué was there at the same time. Perhaps she had planned this encounter. But her heart was filled with sorrow when she could only look on from a distant boat at Genji's stately procession parading along the sea-shore. Then, grieving that they should be separated by the humbleness of her birth, she turned back.

Yomogyû (The Mugwort): Genji had left many to grieve and long for him in the capital during his exile at Suma. Of these, Suetsumuhana had led a completely solitary life, becoming ever more wretched and poverty-stricken since her parting from him. Her residence became more and more dilapidated, while the garden lapsed into a grisly home for foxes. Nevertheless, in face of all advice, she refused to leave the place. All alone, her one solace being the reading of old romances, she lived on there, confident that some day Genji would come again.

One day, as if her yearning for him had brought it about, he chanced to pass in front of her house. Suddenly reminded of his completely forgotten love, he stepped inside. The lady was delighted to see him and brought out from the bottom of a chest where it had lain so long her choicest attire, and in these musty-smelling and now unfashionable robes hastened to welcome him. Thenceforth she renewed her happy life under Genji's protection as before.

Sekiya (The Barrier) and *Eawasé* (The Picture Contest): The ill-starred Utsusemi too came in for a share of Genji's attention. At that time the sovereign was very fond of picture games, and so these were all the vogue at the Court. A number of excellent pictures, both old and recently painted, would be collected secretly, and then on a certain day the courtiers, divided into two groups, right and left, would hold a picture contest in the presence of the sovereign. It would be difficult to say which afforded the most attractive sight, the dazzlingly beautiful pictures themselves, or the elegantly dressed figures of the courtiers engaged in eager competition.

Matsukazé (The Wind among the Pines) and *Usugumo* (A Wreath of Cloud): After frequent invitations from Genji, Akashi-no Ué at last came up to the capital with her little daughter, but reluctantly. In order to avoid too open a life in any well-known district, she decided to reside for a while in the village of Ôi on the outskirts of the city. Out of respect to Murasaki-no Ué, Genji could not visit her very often there, and she used to seek diversion in her loneliness by playing the *koto* which he had given her. Genji was as eager as ever to adopt her daughter in order to have her brought up under Murasaki-no Ué's care but hesitated to broach the question. But Akashi-no Ué, divining his wish, pathetically resolved for the sake of the child's future to let her go as the adopted daughter of Murasaki-no Ué.

It was a morning of heavy snow. The sight of Akashi-no Ué, so reluctant to part with her child, whom, innocently smiling, she took up in her arms, moved Genji to tears in spite of himself. So the lovely little thing was taken away to Murasaki's home. She had no child of her own, and so she fondled the darling just as if she had been her own daughter and kept her constantly by her side. That spring, Genji's sorrow was increased by the death of the nun, Fujitsubo Nyoin. Despite the gladness of the season, he saw everything through a thick veil of gloom and loneliness. Even the sight of the cherry blossom in the garden only reminded him of the dead Fujitsubo, so that he could not restrain his tears.

Asagao (Lady Morning Glory): Genji began to pay attentions to a young lady called Asagao, who whether she fully realized the significance of his advances or not met them with a stubborn refusal. She bloomed indeed like a morning glory, entwined on a fence and rejecting the drops of dew. One cold winter day Genji paid her a visit, but as usual he had to return in vain.

The moonlight shed beauty on the tiny snowflakes still falling on the garden, already deeply blanketed in snow, while the frozen pond glistened like a mirror. Genji and Murasaki-no Ué looked out into the garden as though they would never tire of gazing at the scene. The dresses of the little lasses who trotted about in the garden making snowballs glittered with the variegated beauty of scattered flowers against the silvery snow. In quiet tones, they recalled to each other familiar stories of their past until the night was far advanced.

Otomé (A Maiden): Yûgiri, the son of Genji's dead wife, Aoi-no Ué, was growing up quickly and was pursuing his studies at the academy which he had entered on his father's advice. His innate intelligence responded quickly to instruction, and his genius, superior even to his father's, developed to the admiration of his professors. Before anyone knew, he had fallen in love with his cousin, Kumoi-no Kari, who had been brought by Genji to the same residence for her education. All the world smiled upon the lovers, so bound up in each other, except the girl's father, Tô-no Chûjô, who was now the Lord Keeper of the Privy Seal. He was furious, for he had been hoping that she would enter the Court and that one day might even be selected as Queen, and so he ruthlessly separated them.

The building of Rokujôin, Genji's new residence, which had been under construction for some time, was at last finished. There Murasaki-no Ué and others of Genji's principal loves were to live, each in her own special dwelling, within the same grounds. They were all splendid, gorgeous structures, each arranged in accordance with the tastes of its mistress, and were agreeable at all seasons, in a setting where nature was at its most glorious.

Tamakazura (The Lady Tamakazura) : Meanwhile, Tamakazura was growing up in Kyushu. She was the only child of Yûgao, the never-forgotten love of Genji's youth, who had died on that dreadful night in the desolate house. After her mother's death Tamakazura had been taken to Kyushu by her nurse, whose husband had a post there. Her noble beauty, unusual in such a remote spot, soon came to be talked about, so that her foster-mother was sorely troubled by the court paid to her by powerful local lords. To escape beyond their influence she secretly brought her charge, now nineteen years of age, to the capital.

The nurse had intended that the girl should see only her real father, the Lord Keeper of the Privy Seal, but on her way to the Hasé temple which she visited to pray for the girl's welfare, she happened to encounter Ukon, once maid-in-waiting to the dead Yûgao and now in the service of Genji, from whom she learnt how Genji was also searching for Tamakazura. Genji, having thus found her, adopted her as his daughter, and she started to enjoy a life of very different style from before.

Hatsuné (The Song of Early Birds) and *Kochô* (Butterflies) : On a bright, auspicious day of the New Year, the blades of grass and the tree-tops were glittering amid the snow as if to celebrate the zenith of Genji's prosperity. The palace of Murasaki-no Ué, with its delicate fragrance of plum blossoms, was like an earthly paradise. So the early spring sped by, until one day in mid-spring a musical entertainment was held on the little lake in Murasaki-no Ué's garden. There all sorts of blossoming flowers vied with each other in beauty, a picturesque background for the water-fête.

Hotaru (Fireflies) and *Tokonatsu* (Bed of Carnations) : In Genji's residence Lady Tamakazura grew up remarkably graceful and re-fined. Her gentle, innocent face was uncannily like that of the dead Yûgao and strangely disturbed even Genji's heart at times. A number of young nobles who had heard of her paid her court, but Genji had resolved to marry her to his younger brother, Hotaru-no Miya. One night when Hotaru-no Miya called on her, Genji surprised them by liberating some fireflies so that his brother might see her better in the dark.

[46]

Meanwhile Genji continued to take the deepest interest in the growing Akashi, taking great pains in her upbringing. The Lord Keeper of the Privy Seal, who was in complete ignorance of the fact that Genji had adopted his daughter Tamakazura, suffered great embarrassment and ridicule when a garrulous and uncultured young country girl, named Ômi-no Kimi, introduced herself as his daughter.

Kagaribi (Watchfires) and *Nowaki* (The Hurricane) : Tamakazura suffered great perplexity because, although she was anxious to see her real father, the Lord Keeper of the Privy Seal, she could not broach the subject out of regard for Genji, her foster-father. He loved her fervently, and frequently came to see her to talk over old memories or to give her lessons in playing the *koto*.

One evening, when all the garden was gay with the full-blown flowers of autumn, a violent gale sprang up suddenly, playing havoc with the trees and plants in Genji's garden. His son, Yûgiri, visiting him to express his sympathy, had then for the first time a glimpse of his father's lovers.

Miyuki (Imperial Progress), *Fujibakama* (Blue Trousers) and *Makibashira* (Lady Makibashira): In December of that year, when the snow was lightly falling, the sovereign accompanied by a long and splendid train went out to Ôharano.

Genji's intention was to marry his son, Yûgiri, to Kumoi-no Kari, whom he so dearly loved, but the Lord Keeper of the Privy Seal, having his mind fixed on his daughter entering Court service, obstinately refused to fall in with Genji's proposal. Meanwhile, by a sport of chance, Tamakazura, to her sorrow, found herself on intimate terms with Higekuro-no Taishô, the General of the Black Beard, whom at heart she detested.

Umegaé (Spray of Plum Blossom) and *Fuji no Uraba* (Under the Wistaria) : Lady Akashi was finally chosen to be Queen, and Genji with all his household was active in preparation for this event. The Rokujôin, now radiant with red plum blossoms, was blessed with the advent of still greater glory.

At last the obstinate Lord Keeper agreed to the marriage of Kumoi-no Kari and Yûgiri, inviting Yûgiri to a wistaria party where he made the proposal. The rapture of Kumoi-no Kari when so unexpectedly she was allowed to meet her beloved Yûgiri that night was beyond words. The two lovers, their long cherished

〔47〕

desire fulfilled, were wrapped up in each other, and the Lord Keeper, too, joyfully recognized Yûgiri's fine character.

About the same time Akashi-no Ué was overjoyed, hardly able to convince herself that she was not dreaming, when she saw her daughter enter the Court with so much glory and distinction. After her arrival there, the sovereign graciously paid a visit to the Rokujô-in, where a party to view the autumn colours had been arranged, thus bestowing the greatest honour upon Genji.

Wakana (Young Herbs), *Kashiwagi* (Lord Oak) and *Yokobué* (The Flute): In the autumn of the following year Genji's thirty-ninth birthday was celebrated in splendid style. At the earnest request of the ex-sovereign Suzaku, the elder brother of the reigning sovereign, who was then seriously ill, Genji agreed to take under his protection his princess, Nyosan-no Miya.

The New Year came round again, and then the spring. One beautiful day, a game of football (*kemari*) was played in Genji's garden, when an elegant spectacle was provided by Hotaru-no Miya, Genji's younger brother, and Yûgiri, his son, as together with his intimate friend Kashiwagi, son of the ex-Lord Keeper, they moved about amid the falling cherry blossoms. It was then that Kashiwagi caught a glimpse of Nyosan-no Miya through the accidental lifting of a rattan blind. He was deeply stirred, but the love that followed caused him so much anguish that he died. About the same time Nyosan-no Miya gave birth to a boy who was named Kaoru, in whom Genji traced so striking a resemblance to Kashiwagi as to arouse his suspicions.

Yûgiri called one day to inquire after the health of Ochiba-no Miya who, since the death of her husband Kashiwagi, had led a retired and solitary life. But he found himself going far beyond the sympathy of a family friend over her loss, and before he knew it he had fallen in love with her. One autumn evening he visited her and together they sat and gazed at the evening glow of the autumn flowers vying with each other in beauty, absorbed in quiet reminiscences of the dead husband and friend. Then, as a gentle breeze stirred and a line of wild geese swept across the sky encircling the serenely rising moon, they both experienced the gnawing loneliness of autumn. They found relief as Yûgiri played the Chinese tune, *Sôburen*, which expresses a wife's pining for her husband, on the te (*biwa*), while Ochiba-no Miya accompanied him on the *koto*.

Yûgiri returned home with the flute that the dead Kashiwagi had loved and which Ochiba-no Miya had given him as a souvenir, but the gentle complaints of his wife, Kumoi-no Kari, whose heart was troubled, covered him with shamed embarrassment.

As the boy Kaoru grew up his resemblance to Kashiwagi became more striking, and Yûgiri felt sure that the great anguish of the dead Kashiwagi had some connection with the birth of Kaoru.

Suzumushi (The Ball-Cricket) and *Yûgiri* (Lord Evening Mist) : The season when the lotus flowers cast their cool shadows on the water had passed.   It was the night of the harvest moon, and in the dwelling of Nyosan-no Miya, in the grounds of his own residence, Genji celebrated the autumn *suzumushi* festival to the accompaniment of soft music.

Yûgiri's affection for Ochiba-no Miya, meanwhile, was gradually increasing ; he visited her frequently until imperceptibly he found himself completely enthralled by her.   This made his wife, Kumoi-no Kari, jealous ; they had loved each other from childhood, but now they quarrelled incessantly, until finally she left him and returned to her own family with her children.   Yûgiri made all sorts of apologies to her but in vain ; she refused to return to him.

Minori (The Law) and *Maboroshi* (Illusion) :   Murasaki-no Ué, who had been ill for some time but had seemed to be recovering, suffered a relapse, and, in spite of all Genji's devoted care, her beautiful life came to an end.   The face of his beloved wife, indistinct to his eyes as if it were a thin wisp of vapour, haunted him continually, and he felt all the time as if he were moving in a dream.   What joy, or hope, or pleasure could the future hold for him ?   There was nothing more to do but pray that he soon would follow her and attain the same state of Buddhahood.   Flowery spring came round and summer with the cuckoo's song, then cool autumn glowing with the fireflies and winter hushed under its veil of snow.   Yet the beauty of the passing seasons held no interest for Genji, now that he had lost Murasaki-no Ué.   Unable to conquer his grief and losing all desire to live longer, he had a premonition that he would breathe his last before the following spring.   So he took all the treasured letters of Murasaki-no Ué out of his handbox, and committed them to the flames.

Kumogakuré (The Light behind the Clouds or the Death of Genji) :

Only the title of this book survives. There is no text. Doubtless the intention was thus to symbolize the death of the hero, Genji.

Niô-no Miya (Prince Fragrance), *Kôbai* (The Red Plum Blossoms and *Takegawa* (The Bamboo River): Genji had passed away like the light of heaven obscured by clouds; his equals, if at all, were Niô-no Miya and Kaoru, the sons of the sovereign's consort, Akashi, and Nyosan-no Miya. Both were handsome young men, especially Kaoru, who seemed to give out a fragrance as he moved, although Niô-no Miya competed with him by always suffusing his dress with fine incense. Yet while Kaoru was of a calm, gentle and serious nature and was in a constant agony of spirit from his feeling that somehow he was predestined to sorrow, Niô-no Miya was of a confident, gay and buoyant disposition. Still they always remained good friends.

Hashi Himé (Maiden of Uji Bridge), *Shii ga Moto* (The Buddhist Prince) and *Agemaki* (The Hair Knot): At Uji, two princesses, Ôigimi and Naka-no Kimi, lived with their father, Hachi-no Miya, the eighth son of Kiritsubo-no Mikado. Kaoru was their sole visitor who, admiring the noble faith of Hachi-no Miya, came occasionally to benefit from his conversation. But before he knew how it had happened, he had fallen deeply in love with the gentle Ôigimi, the elder sister. Further, to his surprise, he unexpectedly obtained a clue to the circumstances of his birth from an aged maid in the service of the princesses, who cleared up the mystery regarding his relationship to Kashiwagi by telling him of a letter sent by Kashiwagi from his death-bed to Nyosan-no Miya, showing that he was really the father of Kaoru. The young man, brooding over the unhappy story of his origin, became even more depressed and disheartened. Still, he could not help feeling great sympathy with Hachi-no Miya in his distress at the sad lot of his motherless daughters whose ripening beauty was left to waste itself in a lonely mountain village, and at Hachi-no Miya's request undertook protection of the two sisters.

In late autumn Hachi-no Miya fell ill and died and his daughters were left alone in the world. Their sole friend was Kaoru. They appealed to him, and he arrived to console the poor, lonely princesses, braving the cold blasts blowing over the mountain-passes, and the country-paths almost impassable with snow-drifts. Kaoru was still deeply in love with Ôigimi, despite the fact that out of diffidence

TAKEGAWA (THE BAMBOO RIVER)

HASHI HIMÉ (MAIDEN OF UJI BRIDGE)

From Genji Monogatari Emaki (scroll-painting illustrating the Tale of Genji). Made in the 12th century. Owner: Reimei-kai, Tokyo.

she avoided his insinuations of love. Kaoru's plan was to wed Naka-no Kimi to his friend Niô-no Miya, but Ôigimi wished her to marry Kaoru in her stead. Kaoru, however, refused to be moved, and one day brought Niô-no Miya to see the sisters in their mountain villa at Uji. He quickly became intimate with Naka-no Kimi and they lived happily together. Kaoru, finding it still impossible to persuade Ôigimi to marry him, fell into deeper and deeper distress of mind which so troubled the sensitive Ôigimi that she suddenly fell ill and at last died. The sorrow of Kaoru at this final blighting of his hopes was piteous to see; he refused to leave the house at Uji, and passed his days and nights absorbed in fond memories of his lost love.

Sawarabi (Young Fern), *Yadorigi* (Mistletoe) and *Azumaya* (The Summer-House): Soon afterwards Naka-no Kimi left Uji for the residence of Niô-no Miya, and Kaoru felt lost now that he had to leave the mountain villa which had become so dear to him.

Naka-no Kimi, after a brief period of happiness, was soon to taste sorrow also. In accordance with an earlier arrangement, Niô-no Miya had to take Yûgiri's daughter as his wife, but still he continued to show warm affection for Naka-no Kimi.

One day Kaoru heard from Naka-no Kimi of her young half-sister Ukifuné, who was the living image of the dead Ôigimi. He was eager to meet her, and so, after a long interval, he again visited the mountain villa at Uji, so fragrant with sweet memories of the past. There, by chance, he caught a glimpse of Ukifuné, who was staying for the night at the villa on her way home from a visit to the Hasé temple, and he felt in his heart the dawning of love.

Ukifuné was a daughter of Hachi-no Miya, but had been brought up by her stepfather, Hitachi-no Suké. Her mother, however, had quarrelled with her husband over Ukifuné's marriage, and had committed the girl to the care of her half-sister, Naka-no Kimi.

Kaoru sought out Ukifuné in her temporary home at Sanjô in Kyoto, and later took her to the villa at Uji, where he lavished his whole-hearted love on this substitute in his affections for Ôigimi.

Ukifuné (Lady Drifting-Boat): Niô-no Miya soon heard that Ukifuné was living under Kaoru's protection at Uji, and out of curiosity went alone to see her. There he was greeted by all the unsuspecting attendants who believed it was their master Kaoru

who had unexpectedly arrived. Ukifuné could not help bein
attracted by the ardour of the gay, young Niô-no Miya, even thoug
she still desired the continuance of Kaoru's affection. Torn betwee
her two lovers, she suffered anguish. When she again saw Kaor
who, in ignorance of her dilemma, was as affectionate as ever, sh
despised herself for her infidelity and was overcome with bitte
regrets. And when Kaoru beheld his Ukifuné, gazing intently u
with tears in her eyes at the evening moon as slender as her ow
beautiful arched eyebrow, he was reminded vividly of his lost Ôigin
and felt himself still more deeply in love with her.

Niô-no Miya, agitated by thoughts of her, could remain awa
from her no longer, and so came in secret to her at Uji. He carrie
the frightened girl in his arms to a boat and took her to a cottag
across the River Uji where they could talk all day long undisturbec
Ukifuné realized that she was gradually coming to love Niô-no Miya
Meanwhile Kaoru, all unsuspecting, was making arrangements t
take her to his own home as soon as possible; and Niô-no Miy
was anxious to forestall him by carrying her away first. In thi
predicament the distressed girl suffered torments until she reache
the decision to drown herself in the Uji. Borne on the wind th
sound of the lapping water reached her heart as if inviting the wear
Ukifuné to the peace of death.

Kagerô (Ephemera): One night Ukifuné suddenly disappeared
At her home at Uji everything was in utter confusion as they sough
for her high and low. She was finally given up for dead, and he
mother arranged for a funeral service to be held. The sad new
caused Kaoru to grieve bitterly over the mutability of life, whil
Niô, no less sad, passed the empty days in tears.

Tenarai (Penmanship): While on his way home from a pilgrimag
to Hasé, Yogawa Sôzu, a high priest from Mount Hiyei stopped at
temple at Uji to visit his sick and aged mother. In the shade of th
trees on the mountain behind the temple he found a young lady lyin
as if dead. With great difficulty he managed to bring her back t
life, and then his younger sister, a nun, believing that this was perhap
her recently dead daughter who had returned again to this world
gave her every attention. It was arranged that the young girl wh
had so narrowly escaped death should forsake the world to live
life of retirement in a hermitage at Ono. She refused to confes

her identity, but she was, of course, the beautiful Ukifuné who had attempted to drown herself. Now realizing how evil was her fate, she set herself free from all earthly desires and, having cut off her long black hair, took the veil in order to enter on single-hearted service of Buddha.

Yumé no Ukihashi (The Floating Bridge of Dreams) : Since the dreadful event of the River Uji, Kaoru had inclined more towards religion. One day on his way to Mt Hiyei, he visited Yogawa Sôzu, and heard of a lady living in seclusion in a hermitage at Ono. Suspecting that she might be Ukifuné, he sent her a letter by her younger brother, Kogimi.

Opposite a green, thickly-wooded mountain, the young nun of Ono sat watching the fireflies sparkling in the pellucid stream like memories of the past, when she was told of the approach of a procession with torches flickering along the valley. Kaoru's messenger arrived, and she was persuaded at last to read the affectionate letter Kaoru had sent by her brother, though she felt that nothing he could say could affect her. But as she read, her heart choked with those earthly desires from which she had determined to free herself, and she hung her head in shame. Kogimi importuned for a reply, but she could not bring herself to write one. Nor would she see him, and so Kogimi, unable to extract a word in response, went sadly away. Kaoru, disheartened at his frustrated hopes, tried in vain to understand Ukifuné's incomprehensible purpose in thus deserting him.

Such in outline is *Genji Monogatari*. It can be seen that it consists almost entirely of an account of the philanderings and love affairs of Hikaru Genji, the beau ideal of the Heian period. It is a picture of a life in quest of love, and thus expresses the ideals and outlook of the authoress herself in relation to the Court life of that time.

As a novel, it is amatory, idealistic, realistic, psychological, and intellectual; it is expressive of the personal life of the writer and of phases of the social life of the time. It consists of poems, narrative and dialogue, with incidental criticism on art, education and life, all completely fused into a unit breathing the fragrance of artistic creation. The characters and events are works of imagination in an atmosphere of beautiful fantasy but they are based on various aspects of the life of the Heian period, especially of the life at Court. In other words, the work is designed as an appreciation of life through blending of the realism of the novel and the fantasy of romance.

The authoress, Murasaki Shikibu, was a shrewd and sympathetic observer of people and events. Gifted with truly remarkable power of observation, she shows penetrating insight into complicated and subtle psychological situations. Her power of characterization is also remarkable ; she is able to give distinct individuality to character that in less skilful hands might have been taken as the same type. The work contains over four hundred characters, of whom more than thirty are of the first importance, and the idiosyncrasies of these are vividly and consistently sketched. Each character is distinct and individual. Each nuance of thought is depicted with the subtle skill of genius. It is the skilful and distinctive treatment of such varied themes as Genji's affection for Yûgao, the anguish of Utsusemi, the conflicting emotions of Akashi-no Ué, the forlorn agony of Kaoru and Ukifuné's hopeless distress that constitutes the chief value of *Genji Monogatari*. It may with some justice be urged that the character of Hikaru Genji is over-idealized, but Tô-no Chûjô and Kaoru stand out clearly as individuals, while each one of that bevy of charming ladies, Fujitsubo, Murasaki-no Ué, Utsusemi, Yûgao, Rokujô-no Miyasudokoro, Akashi and Ukifuné, is a distinct personality, and the varied circumstances of their relations with Genji and others are described with real psychological skill and great delicacy.

In addition, the characters in the book are the more convincing because of the realistic presentation of the background of their social environment. The relations of Genji and the other nobles with the heroines of the various books give us a real lifelike picture of the amorous and aesthetic life of the aristocrats in the golden age of the Fujiwara family. In an atmosphere redolent of peace the charming pageantry of the age with its elegant pastimes and solemn daily functions, musical entertainments, poetizing, Shinto festival and Buddhist masses is given in full detail, realistic if also beautified and idealized. Yet the book also portrays dark and ugly aspects of the period, the powerful using their influence mainly in struggles for the favours of women, the fawning upon power of a frivolous society, the effect of religious superstition, the mutual contentions, jealousies and enmities among the ladies of the Court. *Genji Monogatari* does not hesitate to reflect the life of the time from all the angles from which the writer had observed it.

The authoress also proves her outstanding mastery in her descriptions of nature. With keen sensitiveness and delicate observation, and above all with a trained aesthetic sense of beauty, she produces brilliant descriptions of natural scenery which she blends perfectly, in one incident after another, with the psychological moods of the characters. She is not content simply to describe the charms of the different seasons, but they are skilfully harmonized with the feelings of the characters, as in the description of the death of Kiritsubo-no Kôi amid the melancholy of autumn, and Genji looking up at the harvest moon during his exile at Suma; while the garden of Rokujôin, where each of Genji's favoured loves had her residence, is modelled according to the chief attractions of the four seasons, in consonance with the tastes and temperaments of the ladies who lived there. Throughout there is maintained a harmony between the authoress's observation of nature and the mood of the character.

This distinctive characteristic of associating nature with human affairs adds to the beauty and lyricism of the novel. The style is ornate, romantic and allusive, admirably adapted to portray the elegant figures of the characters in an impressive and clear-cut manner. There may be at times a certain amount of digression and verbosity, but on the whole the story makes continual and steady progress throughout in concise and pregnant phraseology, rendering it the finest of the writings in *kana* in its maturity.

The intention of the writer in her account of Hikaru Genji and his experiences in love is to bring under review various aspects of real life. The characters express their opinions on life in general and discuss education and the arts, and on occasion the authoress scathingly criticizes their views. The work is illuminated with her own brilliant discussions of various questions, her poignant understanding of women and her lofty ideals regarding art. Despite all its amours, *Genji Monogatari* is far from being only a love story; rather it completely realizes the ambition of the authoress in her view that a novel could be of greater value than a history.

Genji Monogatari does leave something to be desired in that its scope, limited as it is to the aristocratic Court life, is too narrow. Other defects which may be laid to its charge are the too delicate and enchanting emotionalism, the effeminacy, the lack of incident in the development of the plot, and the lack of variety in taste and style. Yet these criticisms do not affect the significance of the work as a whole.

It was inevitable that to some degree *Genji Monogatari* should have been influenced by the literature that had preceded it. Its narrative style is characteristic of the *monogatari* such as *Isé Monogatari* and *Taketori Monogatari*. Nor is it only in form, but also in subject-matter, plot and characters, that the work owes much to these earlier works, yet all that the authoress received from them was transformed in her hands. Its impress on the future was greater than the impress it had taken from the past. It influenced all subsequent novels, even producing a host of imitations, a flattering proof of its greatness. Also, not only has it had a tremendous influence on the development of literature in Japan, as in novels, and in the " Genji pieces " of the Noh theatre, the Kabuki drama and the ballads, but also it has permeated and affected the whole sphere of Japanese life. This nine-hundred-year-old novel is a monument not only in the literary history of Japan but of the whole world, a cultural heritage commanding universal admiration.

The authoress, Murasaki Shikibu, was a daughter of Fujiwara Tametoki, and from an early age evinced rare literary talent. It was the period of most fruitful production of literature by the ladies of the Court, the most outstanding figure being Sei Shônagon, the authoress of *Makura-no-Sôshi*. Or rather it was that such accomplished ladies who could express themselves so admirably in verse and prose were in great demand for service in the Court. Thus Sei Shônagon entered the service of the Empress Sadako, consort of the Emperor Ichijô, and it was in rivalry with her that Murasaki Shikibu was brought to attend on the second consort, Jôtô-Mon'in Shôshi, and give her instruction in literary accomplishments.

Early left a widow, Murasaki Shikibu had devoted herself to the upbringing of her fatherless daughter and to the writing of this novel in whatever leisure she had from her duties, first as the mistress of a house and then as a lady of the Court. Her ardent enthusiasm for writing is shown by her constant and devoted application to this long work. A comparison of the thoughts expressed by the characters in the novel with her diary, *Murasaki Shikibu Nikki*, in which her own thoughts and doings are recorded, provides convincing evidence that she must have started the novel in the early stages of her lonely widowhood.

It has been shown fairly convincingly that *Genji Monogatari* had at least been partially written by the year 1008 (the fifth year of the Kankô era) and was completed probably in 1021 (the first year of the Chian era). There is an extremely beautiful tradition regarding its composition. Murasaki Shikibu, having been ordered by Jôtô-Mon'in to write a novel, withdrew to Ishiyama-dera, a temple in Ômi province, to seek inspiration by prayer. There the full moon of the fifteenth day of the eighth month reflected in the waters of Lake Biwa brought to her the idea she wanted which she at once wrote down on the back of the Buddhist scriptures on the desk; and thus the two books of Suma and Akashi were the earliest to be written. Even to this day in the Ishiyama temple is preserved intact the Genji no Ma (Room of Genji) in which the authoress is said to have written the book, and even the inkslab which she used. These relics show how preciously the traditional associations surrounding the birth of *Genji Monogatari* have been preserved by later generations.

ISÉ MONOGATARI

(Tales of Isé)

Isé Monogatari, one of the earliest of the *monogatari*, or tales, still extant, is typical of the primitive literary form of the *monogatari* and deservedly takes a high place in the history of Japanese literature not only because of the great influence it has had on the course of the development of the literature but also because of its own value as a work of art.

The ancient *monogatari* can be divided into two types according to their construction, *denki-monogatari*, romances, and *uta-monogatari*, a sequence of tales interspersed with poems. The romances consist of stories, epic, supernatural or fanciful in character, transmitted orally in a somewhat fluid state from one generation to another until finally recorded and preserved in writing.

The *uta-monogatari* have their origin in *kashû*, anthologies and collections of poems. We see in them how poetical collections took on the form of a tale or rather a collection of tales. Their development was partly due to the consummation of Japanese poetry in the early Heian period (ninth century) and partly to the use from this time of the syllabary (*kana*), especially in the cursive form (*hiragana*), in writing Japanese. Prior to this period, the national language had had to be written in Chinese ideographs (*kanji*), in which it was difficult to give an accurate transliteration. The use of the *kana* overcame this difficulty and facilitated literary creation. The writing of lyrics (*waka*) was of great importance among the contemporary nobility as the almost invariable means of expression of their innermost thoughts, and was regarded as an indispensable social accomplishment.

An *uta-monogatari* is a brief story in *kana* based on the *kotobagaki*, the introductory note to each lyric (*waka*) in an anthology, recording the circumstances of its composition. The story may include several *waka* with their *kotobagaki*, connecting them together with a lot in the style of the *monogatari*. *Isé Monogatari* and *Yamato Monogatari* are both collections of stories made up in this way. Neither has a consistent plot throughout, but is rather a collection of short, unconnected stories, which might have been founded upon fact or had some relation with real events, or might be entirely fictitious.

Isé Monogatari consists of about a hundred and twenty-five short stories, the number varying in the different texts, each containing one or more poems preceded and followed by explanations in the style either of the *kotobagaki* of the *waka* or of the *monogatari*. It is impossible for such a story to depict life on any large scale, or to deal with complicated events. Its main quality is to depict some incident or aspect of life in a terse, direct and succinct form. On this account, we may regard *Isé Monogatari* as the earliest collection of short stories in our country.

Each story begins with the set phrase " Once upon a time there was a man " and relates a love adventure or an incident in the emotional life of this " man." Though each of these stories is independent and unrelated to the rest, yet the collection can be regarded as dealing mainly with the life of the same hero from his coming of age to his death.

The " man," or hero, of *Isé Monogatari* has from ancient times been identified with Ariwara-no Narihira (825–880), the fifth son of Prince Abo, and grandson of the Emperor Heijô, his mother, Princess Ito, being the daughter of the Emperor Kanmu. He was renowned for the number of his love adventures, but was also a man of great learning and talent ; he ranked as one of the Rokkasen, or Six Poetical Geniuses of the Heian period.

Most of the stories of *Isé Monogatari* describe various love affairs such as might befall such a sensitive man, but sometimes the themes are not of an amorous character but are concerned with travelling, hunting, mother love, etc.

Opinion is divided on the question of the authorship of *Isé Monogatari* in its present form. Some have held that Narihira was both hero and author ; others have inclined to the more probable view that it was written by Isé, a celebrated poetess of a later generation, the fact that it contains poems and tales by writers of a later period effectively disposing of the view that as it stands it was written by Narihira himself.

It is probable that the work derived from an anthology of Narihira's poems, supplemented and then transformed into a *monogatari*. The original work being a collection of separate and unconnected poems with explanations, it would be an easy matter to make adaptations, to lengthen the explanations into short tales and fit them into a connected series. The present work may then be the result of the adaptions and retouching by several hands.

Typical of the stories in the volume is the following :—

A man and a woman had grown up together, as children playing round the old well together. When they grew up, he wished to marry her and she was also in love with him, though they were both shy of expressing their feelings, as their parents did not encourage the match. At last, however, by the exchange of love-poems with reminiscences of their childhood, they came to accord.

But, in the course of his travels the man fell in love with another girl who lived in a village beyond Mt Tatsuta. One evening he dressed himself to go out intending to visit her. But he had noticed that his former love had shown no jealousy though she had known where he was going, and that this night she had paid special attention to her toilet. The man suspected from this that she also had a new lover. So he hid himself in the shade of some bushes in the garden to watch her movements. She looked up at the darkening sky, and then murmured mournfully :—

> Mount Tatsuta Pass
> Is lonely and desolate
> Even in day-time ;
> How then can my dear one cross
> At midnight, safely, alone !

The tender love of his wife touched him so deeply that he never again visited the girl beyond the mountain.

Isé Monogatari is a collection of such fragmentary tales. Written as early as *Taketori Monogatari* it has had a far greater influence on the literature. Indeed, although artistically inferior, it had an even greater influence than *Genji Monogatari*. All the *monogatari* of the Heian period, despite differences in plots and themes, can be regarded as extensions, adaptions, imitations and developments of *Isé Monogatari*. And few works of later ages entirely escaped its influence, while many rewritings and adaptions of the work itself have been produced. Further, the poems, especially those exchanged between lovers and friends, were taken as models during the middle Heian period and later, and have always been highly esteemed by poets and students of Japanese prosody.

Criticism of the morality of *Isé Monogatari* must, of course, be based on reference to the social conventions of the times. The pervading atmosphere of the book is one of love affairs. In the care-free lives of the court nobles, love affairs played a most important part, the sole complication in their lives ; and these liaisons began, progressed and ended to the accompaniment of the exchange of poems. Proposals of marriage were made by the presentation of poems, and etiquette demanded that the lady should at least reply in verse, whether she accepted the proposal or not. The morals of the time permitted polygamy, a husband usually living apart from his wife, whom he visited by night. This encouraged the frequent exchange of poems between them, so that the possession of poetical gifts was much more vital than we to-day can easily imagine. The writing of *waka* was a social accomplishment as well as a form of art.

Isé Monogatari, giving as it does in its innumerable stories pictures of love in many various phases accompanied by beautiful love lyrics, is indispensable for reference in the study of contemporary ideas on love and the relation of the sexes.

TSUTSUMI CHÛNAGON MONOGATARI

(The Tales of Tsutsumi Chûnagon)

Tsutsumi Chûnagon Monogatari dates from towards the end of the Heian period. As we have seen, the literary form known as *monogatari* sprang from two sources, *uta-monogatari*, tales interspersed with poems, of which *Isé Monogatari* affords so important an example and the *denki-monogatari*, romances, such as *Taketori Monogatari*. These two influences blended in *Genji Monogatari*. This famous work naturally produced a crop of imitators, but, at the same time a fresh development appeared ; out of the pursuit of grotesque plots and sensuous details was born a type of literary work resembling the modern short story. Of this type, *Tsutsumi Chûnagon Monogatari*, a collection of ten short stories, is the most noteworthy.

Half of these ten stories revolve around a love theme—" The Shôshô who plucked a Spray of Blossoming Cherry," " Good Matches," " Eyebrow Paint," " The Gon-Chûnagon who failed to cross the Slope of Meeting " and " The Shôshô who stayed in spite of themselves "—while " The Lady who loved Caterpillars," " By the Way," " The Game of Shells," " Court Ladies as Flowers " and " Nonsense " deal with individual themes. " The Lady who loved Caterpillars " tells, as its title implies, of a lady who slighted butterflies but loved green caterpillars ; " By the Way " is a realistic sketch of court ladies telling of remarkable incidents ; the long letter which forms " Nonsense " is a story of an old priest ; " The Game of Shells " is mainly devoted to an account of this game, but has a pretty heroine ; and " Court Ladies as Flowers," although centred upon young ladies, shows what a prominent part the love of flowers played in the life of the Heian period. Yet, while half of the stories in *Tsutsumi Chûnagon Monogatari* deal directly with amorous affairs, they are nevertheless handled paradoxically or at least from an unusual angle.

Thus " The Shôshô who plucked a Spray of Blossoming Cherry " humorously depicts a failure in love, for the Shôshô found that the lady whom he had kidnapped was the chaperon, the aunt of the girl with whom he was in love, a quite different ending from the usual sort of story where the lady is won after various complications. In " Eyebrow Paint " a lyrical love affair is rendered absurd by the dénouement, in which the heroine smears her face with eyebrow paint in mistake for powder. The contretemps in " The Shôshô who stayed in spite of themselves " arises from two Captains of the Guards (*Shôshô*) who loved two sisters eloping each with the wrong sister. In each of these stories then the author expresses his own peculiar attitude to love, or gives an unusual turn to the development of the plot. The tales may be open to criticism as novels, but they should rather be regarded as examples of that type of short story in which the effect is produced by emphasis upon one detail.

The stories in *Tsutsumi Chûnagon Monogatari* therefore deserve to be praised for their technique, their intellectual and constructive quality. The plot of each is carefully worked out in a way that leaves no feeling of unreality or of something lacking. The story about the two Shôshô and their mixed-up mistresses gives little attention to character-study or the background, but the way in which the two couples come to make their mistakes is so accounted for as not to impair the artistic truth of the tale. Structurally, the tale bears some resemblance to *Torikaebaya Monogatari*, but the plot is simpler, and the mistake of identity is due to accident, while in *Torikaebaya Monogatari* the characterization plays the most important part in the confusion.

In the matter of construction, each of these stories has a real beginning and a real ending. In the beginnings, especially, the development of an artistic consciousness is as clearly marked in this collection as in the novel, *Sagoromo Monogatari*. It is the beginning of a story that suggests the point of view embodied, and generally in *Tsutsumi Chûnagon Monogatari* the attitude is realistic. Thus " The Shôshô who plucked a Spray of Blossoming Cherry " is written from the point of view of one who saw the house concerned one morning when returning from his mistress's dwelling. " By the Way " is in idea and treatment a realistic sketch. But perhaps best of all in this respect are " The Game of Shells " and " Court Ladies as Flowers," which are told most vivaciously by a man who approaches the matter from the point of view of a realistically-minded spectator. The epistolary style of "Nonsense," written in the first person, proves most effective. Although letters are frequent in *Ochikubo Monogatari*, this story, consisting of a single long letter, strikes a distinctly individual note.

The endings, too, of the tales in this collection are often most original, as, for example, in "Eyebrow Paint" and "The Shôshô who plucked a Spray of Blossoming Cherry." There may be something rather artificial in this type of dénouement, but nevertheless when this type of ending is not too abruptly introduced but is softened by some of the tranquillity found in *Genji Monogatari*, it contributes greatly to the development of plot construction.

Most of the stories in this collection are more concerned with plot and effect than anything else, but "The Lady who loved Caterpillars" deserves to be mentioned for its treatment of character. Yet even this tale is written from the author's paradoxical point of view, in a spirit of contrariety to ordinary human sentiments and emotions. In *Genji Monogatari* and other tales, we find eccentric characters, especially humorous ones, but rarely do we find one quite so distinctly individualized as is this lady with her love for caterpillars.

The tales which make the greatest impression either for the effect they produce or for their background are "By the Way" and "The Gon-Chûnagon who failed to cross the Slope of Meeting." Neither of these is worthy of special notice in the matter of plot or character drawing, but they make a strong impression on the reader. It might be said that in each case the effect is produced by laying emphasis on one of the elements that go to make up a novel.

To conclude, *Tsutsumi Chûnagon Monogatari* was probably written at a time when the main current of Heian literature, with its *mono no aware*, its sense of the "sadness of things," its melancholy and pensive mood, had almost reached the limit of its development. There was a tendency to return to a more careless naïveté, and this collection of short stories is significant as evidence of this trend.

Neither the author nor the derivation of the title are authenticated. The leading critics hold that the work was attributed to Tsutsumi Chûnagon by error, and that it was given his name solely because it contains poems resembling those written by a certain Tsutsumi

Chûnagon Kanesuké of the Heian period.   As to date there is general agreement that, at the earliest, it must have been composed in the later Heian period, while some, from the evidence of the vocabulary, would attribute it to the early Kamakura period.   We have no external evidence for attributing all of its ten stories to a single author, and it has been maintained that it is a collection of tales by several authors.   We can only conclude from the internal evidence of the stories themselves that their style, their wealth of keen observation, and their original effects give good grounds for attributing the whole work, if not to a single author, at least to a group of authors very much of a single mind.

———————

KAGERÔ NIKKI

(An Ephemeral Life-Story)

Kagerô Nikki, written towards the end of the tenth century, is a woman's confession describing her emotional life.

It has been told how in the early days of the Heian period (794–1191) the *hiragana*, the syllabary, gradually superseded the *kanji*, Chinese ideographs, so inconvenient for transcribing accurately the Japanese language. To a very great extent this change in writing is responsible for the ensuing stream of poetical collections, tales, diaries, travel books and fugitive essays, freely written in *hiragana*.

Of such literary works, the diaries, travel books and essays have as their pioneer *Tosa Nikki*, a travel diary written in the years 934 and 935 by Ki-no Tsurayuki, one of the compilers of *Kokinshû*.

Kagerô Nikki was completed about forty years after *Tosa Nikki*. Although called a *nikki* (diary), it does not necessarily give day-to-day accounts, and may more properly be styled an autobiographical novel than a diary. The writer was a woman ; the work has a high value in the history of Japanese literature as the precursor of that literature produced by the ladies of the Court which is such a prominent feature of the Heian period.

Who then is this wonderful pioneer in the production of literature by the Heian Court ladies ? Notwithstanding the efforts of scholars her name as well as the dates of her birth and death remain a mystery, The utmost information we can obtain about her we must glean· from *Kagerô Nikki* itself and a few other fragmentary references.

From another source we learn that her father was Fujiwara Tomoyasu (d. 977), who held the post of governor in several provinces and was the father of two other daughters and two sons. Her younger brother was the celebrated poet, Fujiwara Nagayoshi, and her younger sister married Sugawara Takasué, their daughter becoming the author of *Sarashina Nikki*, the latest glory of the women's literature of the Heian period.

Her attendance with her brother Nagayoshi at the Court functions of *uta-awasé* (social competitions in the improvisation of Japanese poems) affords early proof of her literary talent. She was also beautiful, as is clear from another reference to her as " one of the great beauties of Japan."

Leaving the date of her birth and the events of her childhood wrapped in mystery, *Kagerô Nikki* takes us at a bound into her maidenhood by starting with her account, in the year 954, of her awakening to love. We may assume she was then about twenty. The object of her affections was Fujiwara Kaneié, an elegant, young noble of twenty-five and the son of Fujiwara Morosuké, the Udaijin, Minister of the Right.

According to contemporary custom, the daughters of nobles were kept in seclusion at home, so that their love life depended entirely on their lovers' visits to them there and on the exchange of love-letters in prose and verse. Nor was it very different after marriage, for it was not usual for husbands and wives to live together, but rather for the men to visit and lodge in the homes of the women. Consequently, if the visits of their husbands or lovers became less frequent, or the number of their letters fell off, the womenfolk felt acute distress, for it meant that love was on the wane.

In the approved style, Kaneié began to write and to visit the girl. The opening pages of *Kagerô Nikki* present a charming picture of the authoress, joyful, lovely and girlish, as with a fluttering heart she consulted her attendant ; she had just received the first affectionate letter from this stranger named Kaneié. Might she answer, or would it be better not ? Finally, on the other's advice, she does reply. Letters were exchanged, Kaneié visited her, and the two plighted their troth.

At the end of August of the next year she was the happy mother of a boy who was given the name of Michitsuna. " Kaneié is even more affectionate to me now," she comments.

The great happiness of her first love and her first child could not, however, last long. She soon begins to feel that Kaneié's love has waned since she became a mother.

" In September, while he was out, I was astounded to find a letter from him to another woman. Intending at least to show him that I knew all about it, I added in verse : ' That you should write to another woman! Do you intend to call on me no more?' Oh, how uneasy I felt then. . . "

The promise of bliss was thus cruelly cut short. At the end of October, Kaneié stayed away for three consecutive nights. When, at last, he came to see her, he very soon made excuse to leave. Anxious to know what was happening, she set a man to watch him, and her suspicions were confirmed. He went to the house of another woman and stayed there. " It was just as I had feared. I was so grieved that I could not express myself! " she frankly avows. Kaneié, just like most of the nobles of his time, had already paid visits to several other women ; he came to see her less and less.

The New Year came. Early in March, we find her sadly writing, " Decorating the room with peach blossoms, I waited for him, but in vain." By that time Kaneié was visiting the other woman openly. This made her intolerably sad. " Night after night I have slept alone. Despite all the comfort that surrounds me, I cannot help feeling miserable at his fickleness," she laments ; and again, " It has rained for such a long time. Gazing outside, I murmur to myself :—

> This long spell of rain
> Has ruined the tender plants
> In my flower garden ;
> Day after day passed longing
> Has robbed me of my beauty."

Another year passed. Her heart was consumed with jealousy on hearing that this other woman was the mother of Kaneié's child. She quarrelled incessantly with him, she refused to make his robes, and threw them back at him.

So time went on. In 958, she heard that the woman of whom she was so jealous had lost Kaneié's affection after the birth of the child, and this brought her a curious satisfaction. She wrote, " In my envy of her, I used to hope she would love long enough to know anguish of heart more poignant than mine. I wonder how she feels now. She must be more disconsolate than I can imagine, and I feel greatly relieved."

Her only son, Michitsuna, was now four years old, and was the sole solace of her dreary life. The innocent Michitsuna had a habit of lisping, " I shall soon be back," whenever he went out to play. This happened to be the phrase used by his father whenever he left her to visit the other woman, and it made her heart ache to hear the child's innocent mimicry.

There is no entry in *Kagerô Nikki* referring to the next three years. Michitsuna was growing up, and she and Kaneié had become still further estranged. Their relationship was constantly on the verge of rupture, but it still remained unbroken in 966, when Michitsuna was twelve years of age. However, their married life no longer yielded either of them any happiness. "Michitsuna, far from unpleasant in appearance, is now twelve. Day and night I spend in endless regrets that we no longer live as man and wife. All my hopes are now pinned on Michitsuna alone."

As the years passed the bitterness between them only deepened. Yet despite her hatred for Kaneié, whose visits now were very rare, she still could not shake off all lingering traces of affection. Thus did the two conflicting feelings continue to struggle in her heart, so that, with all her hatred of his inconstancy, she felt happy on the extremely rare occasions when he chose to visit her. But as she saw Kaneié's affection for her steadily grow less, enmity, anger and hatred became more intense.

Finally she abandoned herself to despair, undecided whether to die or to become a nun. To gain some respite from this gnawing pain of introspection, she occasionally went on pilgrimages to temples. On one occasion she shut herself up in a temple in the recesses of a mountain, and committed herself to Buddha's mercy. Yet she could never bring herself to renounce the world entirely ; her affection for her beloved son, Michitsuna, caused her to bring her confinement in the temple to an end.

She had failed in her appeal to her husband's love ; she had failed also in throwing herself on the mercy of Buddha. The only way left was to devote herself to her young son, and seek consolation in the beauties of nature. So she gazes at the hoar frost, finds poetry in the growing grass of spring, is attracted by the sight of a mountain village on her way to a temple, and listens eagerly to the shrill chirrups of the cicadas. How she gave herself to the search for satisfaction in the beauties of nature is richly revealed in her accounts of those days.

Meanwhile, Michitsuna was growing up ; she records her joy at his victory in an archery contest at Court, and her profound pleasure and pride when she saw his dignified behaviour among the young nobles on the occasion of a festival.

And so *Kagerô Nikki* comes to an end. The last year mentioned is 974, when Michitsuna was a young man of twenty. The records of the last five years are given in considerable detail, and are written in a very serious style, greatly heightening the effect of her spiritual confessions.

Of her life after the diary closes nothing is reliably known, but it is believed that she died on or about the second of May, 996, at the age of sixty or thereabouts.

Thus *Kagerô Nikki*, opening so confidently with a woman's joy at the dawning of love, presents autobiographically in a concise style the various emotions bound up with a life of love—the struggle between her attachment to, and her hatred for, the man she loved, following on the breakdown of her married life, her jealousy of her successful rival in love, her satisfaction at the latter's broken heart. It also touches briefly on other affections, love for the beauties of nature and of a mother for her child, which she turned to in the hope of freeing herself from the heavy blow of her disillusionment. Not only is it, as we have said, the precursor of the literature produced by the Court ladies of the Heian period, but, in itself, it possesses a rare charm that appeals to us most powerfully.

———————

MURASAKI SHIKIBU NIKKI

(The Diary of Murasaki Shikibu)

The diary written by Murasaki Shikibu, the authoress of *Genji Monogatari*, covers the period following the death of her husband, Fujiwara Nobutaka, when she was in attendance on Jôtô-Mon'in Shôshi, the Chûgû, second consort, of the Emperor Ichijô. This diary is more than a chronological record of her own private life, for it gives an account of the various Court ceremonies centring on the birth of the second son of the Emperor Ichijô, later the Emperor Go-Ichijô, with her comments on circumstances before and after that event, and upon the personalities of other ladies of the Court, as well as passing thoughts and impressions.

The beginning of the work is taken up with an account of the special prayers offered in September of the year 1008 at the residence of Fujiwara Michinaga, the father of the queen, for the intention of the queen and the expected Imperial child. Then follow descriptions of the events connected with the birth, and the ceremonies in celebration of it. The diary describes the festivities of New Year and ends with the ceremonies in celebration of the fiftieth day after the birth of the third son.

Makura-no-Sôshi of Sei Shônagon also contains detailed descriptions of similar Court ceremonies and public affairs, but Murasaki Shikibu's attitude is much more objective; even while she is expressing her opinions, she keeps her own personality and prejudices modestly in the background. The fact that both these authoresses are writing on this same subject of Court life brings out more clearly the differences in their characters.

The opening pages show us the authoress in attendance on her mistress, Jôtô-Mon'in, at Tsuchimikado, the residence of her father, Michinaga, to which the Imperial consort had returned for the birth. This portion is famous for the beauty of its narrative style, as polished and typical as anything else in the book, blending most harmoniously descriptions of nature with the movement of human affairs.

" With the coming of autumn, the beautiful garden of Tsuchi-mikado attained its greatest charm. The leaves on the thick clumps of trees grouped around the pond were turning, and the autumn flowers bloomed riotously by the side of flowing streamlets, a scene which enhanced the effect of the daily chanting of the sutras which echoed plaintively under the clear autumn sky. Through the night the murmur of flowing waters now more audible mingled with the chanting and fell softly on the ear. The queen tried to divert her mind from her weary agony by listening to her ladies-in-waiting who sought to make the long evening pass more comfortably for her by talking on one topic after another." The authoress wondered at herself as she took part in this scene, for it had been to forget her own weariness of the world that she had entered the service of this Imperial mistress. Full of admiration for her mistress's noble courage, she was able for a while to dismiss from her mind all the sorrows and pains of her own life.

It was probably only in the course of this autumn that she had entered into Court service, and this passage describes her first re-actions. She gradually became accustomed to her duties, and the happiness of such a service she always felt most keenly because of her admiration for the dignified beauty of Jôtô-Mon'in ; the pleasure of waiting upon such a mistress made the lady forget her own bereave-ment.

For the birth of the child Jôtô-Mon'in entered the maternity room, which was crowded by her excited attendants. Then there was the terrible presence of evil spirits taking advantage of her confinement, and their wailing could be heard above the murmuring voices of the priests as they sought to exorcise them. But, surrounded by the anxious care of her family and attendants, she did not suffer greatly ; and so, to the delight of all, a prince was born.

The Bathing Ceremony was punctiliously carried out in a splendid fashion, while the Third Night ceremony and the festival on the fifth night were picturesque in the extreme. The garden was as bright as day with huge bonfires glowing red in the bright moonlight, while all the attendants were smiling gaily in their joy and the ladies-in-waiting had put on their brighest robes. After the solemn cere-mony of congratulation, a banquet was held at which Lord Michinaga, looking supremely happy, joked continuously. On the seventh day the Emperor held an official ceremony in celebration of the prince's birth, and a few days later honoured Michinaga's residence with a visit. Ah, meditates the diarist, how heartily would Jôtô-Mon'in have enjoyed the sight of her father's house, so richly decorated in honour of the occasion, if only she had not been on a bed of suffering !

But the effect of all the rejoicings and gorgeous ceremonial on Murasaki Shikibu herself was only to trouble her spirit and intensify her craving for the Religious Life. Despite her conviction that it was useless to repine over things that could not be helped and would soon be forgotten, and that it was sinful to be discontented, she could not bring herself to a cheerful frame of mind.

This passage reveals the conflict ever going on within her heart, the conflict between her desire to free herself from the sorrow of her husband's death by entering the service of Buddha, and the necessity of remaining in the world to bring up her fatherless child as well as to continue her service to Jôtô-Mon'in. Her mental conflict formed a bitter contrast to the gaiety of her own outward appearance and the brilliancy of her environment.

On the day when they received the visit of the Emperor, the air was filled with sweet music from the boats floating on the pond, the bow of one decorated with a carved dragon, and the other with a carved heron. In the presence-chamber, a throne was provided for the Emperor, and the gay dresses of the Court ladies ranged on seats below summoned up visions of angel visitants to earth. Then, in a pause of breathless expectation, Lord Michinaga brought the infant prince into the Imperial presence and handed him to Jôtô-Mon'in. A more impressive and august sight could not be imagined. As the dusk of evening gathered, the music sounded more and more melodious, and one festive dance after another was performed in celebration of the matchless honour bestowed on Michinaga's family.

In this passage there are also given many details of the dresses worn by the Court ladies, bringing vividly before us the contemporary modes and fashions. Only on the *emaki*, picture scrolls, could anything so artistic be seen as the beauty of the colours and patterns of the ladies' under-kimono (*kasané*), the styles of their hair-dressing, and their own graceful forms.

One thing we can see clearly from this diary is the extraordinary power and position of Michinaga, the most important figure of his day and then at the height of his prosperity. In this and other respects this diary, although chiefly concerned with the personal experiences of a Court lady, offers materials essential to our knowledge of the manners and customs as well as the history of the time, giving, as it does, detailed pictures of inside facts and internal conditions such as are rarely touched on in ordinary works of history.

The ceremony in celebration of the fiftieth day after the child's birth was held on the first day of the eleventh month. The assembled company sat in rows, so richly and elaborately dressed that they resembled rather the figures of a painting. Lady Michinaga presented the most wonderful picture of all, in her magnificent dress of beautiful red, bearing the child in her arms. All were in a state of joyful excitement, and the great Lord Michinaga, with his friends, was partaking generously of the festive saké and whispering jokes to the ladies-in-waiting. Lord Kintô, who was Saemon-no Kami, Left Commander of the Imperial Palace Guards, came along to where the court ladies were sitting and said to one of them, " The Lady Murasaki is in service here, isn't she? " referring to the diarist who was beginning to be called by this name after the Lady Wakamurasaki, one of the many heroines of *Genji Monogatari*. " How could there be a Lady Murasaki here," the authoress pondered, " when there is no one worthy of the name of Radiant Genji ? "

This little episode is important as helping to fix the date of *Genji Monogatari*, for it shows that this novel was by that time well-known in Court circles. What also makes this whole passage additionally valuable is that not only is the ceremony of the fiftieth day so graphically described, but also the boundless joy of Michinaga at the child's birth, which fitted in so well with his ambitions.

Having been granted a short holiday, the authoress went to the house of her parents. As she stood in the garden of her old home, a clump of trees, heavily covered with snow and not in itself particularly attractive, reminded her of that time, just after the death of her husband, when she had passed day after day sunk in deep and hopeless melancholy. Yet, in those former days, whenever the unceasing changes of nature in the seasons, the colours of the flowers and the songs of the birds, the sky, the moon, and the frost and snow, had filled her with depressing thoughts about her own fate, she had been able to derive comfort by unburdening herself to friends of like disposition. But her thoughtless entry into the very different life of the Court, so far from affording any consolation, seemed only to have robbed her of any tranquillity she might have had and to have increased the agony in her heart. Novels could not divert her as they had formerly done, nor was she disposed to take the risk of writing to her former friends who, she thought, would despise her as a worldling who had entered Court service in pursuit of a gay life. Thus it was that, on her occasional visits to her old home, she felt like a lonely visitant to a strange world.

The inner distress of the authoress is poignantly revealed in this passage. Since her gay court life, intended to assuage, had only intensified, her anguish, she now confesses the sorrow experienced from the frustration of her deepest desire.

The grand ceremonial dances of November, the Gosechi no Mai, are next graphically described. The four dancing girls, as they proceeded to the Imperial Palace in their choicest attire, looked dazzlingly beautiful in the light of the torches held on high. And the dresses of the court ladies who sat in rows to watch the performance were as beautiful, each one different in colour and design. Then the special festival of the Kamo shrine following the Gosechi no Mai is described in detail.

In a passage said to be part of a letter written to her daughter or an intimate friend, Murasaki Shikibu gives the names of many of her fellow ladies-in-waiting at the Court, with little character sketches. Saishô-no Kimi was lovely and indefinably dignified, both charming and gay, sagacious and talented. Ko Shôshô was childlike and innocent, but too tender and timid. Miya-no Naishi was gay and amiable, full of wisdom, bright and frank. Among these ladies are presumably the models of the female characters of *Genji Monogatari*.

It is interesting to read the authoress's criticisms of the diarist Izumi Shikibu as being richly endowed with artistic talents and the writer of rather witty poems, but whose weak point was insincerity, and of the authoress of *Makura-no-Sôshi*, Sei Shônagon, who was haughty and affectedly prim, and whose intelligence and learning were not fully mature, in spite of her pretensions and her vanity shown in her frequent use of difficult Chinese ideographs. People who are always making efforts to appear more able than others necessarily become so affected that this shows as a defect, the diarist comments.

This passage bears eloquent witness to the hostility and antipathy entertained by Murasaki Shikibu for Sei Shônagon, who was in the service of the Empress Sadako, and whose character was the very opposite of her own. While Murasaki Shikibu was really learned, but so introspective and meditative as to pretend to be totally ignorant, Sei Shônagon took every opportunity to display her learning, and felt very proud to be able to compete with men in literary pursuits and defeat them in a striking manner. Here lies the fundamental difference in the characters of these two famous authoresses.

Murasaki Shikibu relates how she sought distraction from her loneliness in playing the *koto* or in reading in the seclusion of her dark and antiquated room. One day when she was reading an old book of classical *monogatari*, all riddled with bookworms, she heard the ill-natured comments of some of the other ladies-in-waiting on women concerning themselves with difficult Chinese writings. She did not trouble to defend herself against them, for she believed that she had a right to follow her own taste ; she herself felt that ostentatious sutra-chanting and rosary-rattling before others was not fitting. " Still I kept my thoughts to myself while I was in service, not seeing the good of explaining my ideas to those who do not understand and who criticise with an air of superiority." She felt that no one understood her really.

After she had been some time in Court service she was told : " You are quite different from what we had been led to expect. We heard that you were so unsociable and prim that you would make us ashamed of being with you ; that you devoted yourself to reading and poetical composition, pretending elegance, and that you would oppose and despise us—that altogether you were an odious woman. But now we have met you, we find you incredibly modest, quite the opposite of what we had expected."

The Lady Murasaki was ashamed of her retiring disposition, which caused her to be slighted. She observes that if one is modest, gentle and tranquil, one makes an agreeable impression on others, and appears more graceful. Pretentious people, because of their self-conceit, may indeed attract the attention of others in everything they do, but careful observation surely reveals something discordant in their speech and behaviour and indicative of their weakness. And, in any case, it is wrong to abuse others heartlessly, or to laugh at their blunders, no matter how serious. It is indeed the height of graciousness to pass quietly over anything disagreeable that may occur.

A Court lady named Saemon-no Naishi chanced to overhear the Emperor say, when praising the learning of *Genji Monogatari*, "The authoress must surely have studied *Nihongi*. She is certainly a genius." Forthwith Saemon-no Naishi spread a report among the courtiers that Murasaki Shikibu was a woman of profound learning and gave her the droll nickname of "Nihongi no Tsuboné," the "Court lady of *Nihongi*." Just think, Saemon-no Naishi said to everyone, this Murasaki Shikibu who pretends to be so illiterate even in the presence of her maids is really quite a scholar! To Murasaki Shikibu herself the cream of the jest was that the malicious gossip did not know how thoroughly her victim detested her.

Yet the fact remains that when Murasaki Shikibu was young and her elder brother, Nobunori, was studying the Chinese chronicles, *Shih Chi*, with his father, she mastered it more quickly than he could, causing her scholarly father to sigh and say, "What a pity she is not a boy!" But afterwards, "when I was told that it was not good even for men to be proud of their learning, I would not even write so much as a figure in Chinese characters, pretending utter ignorance. I was ashamed of that learning of which Saemon-no Naishi accused me of being conceited about; I even feigned inability to read the characters on the screens." Jôtô-Mon'in had entreated Murasaki Shikibu to read to her from *Po Lo-t'ien*. She had done so but had concealed this fact as far as possible from the courtiers. "How good it is that Saemon-no Naishi has not found this out yet! How she would gossip if she knew!" This passage shows the quality of the authoress's nature, modest even to the point of wishing to be unnoticed, and yet with a sound idea of her own ability.

Lord Michinaga saw Jôtô-Mon'in's copy of *Genji Monogatari* and in his usual jesting way wrote a poem suggesting that the authoress of the adventures of the amorous Hikaru Genji must have

〔 77 〕

had numerous lovers. Murasaki Shikibu replied, expressing her dislike of being spoken about in this way. " That night," she continues, " I was awakened from my sleep by some one tapping on the door, and I sat up all the rest of the night trembling with fear. The following morning a poem was brought to me, saying :—

> All night did I knock—
> The noise of my knocking drowned
> The water-rail's call.
> Weary, lamenting, I stood
> All night without the closed door.

To this I replied :—

> Would it not have been
> A thing to be regretted
> For ever after,
> If the door had been opened—
> At the water-rail's bidding ? "

This incident is the climax of the work. The implication is that it was Lord Michinaga who visited the lady's room, and this rejection of his lordship's advances confirms her reputation as a faithful widow.

SARASHINA NIKKI

(The Sarashina Diary)

Genji Monogatari, early accepted as an outstanding work and a model for all future novelists, was bound to exert a marked influence upon subsequent literature. The first and most conspicuous of all writers to come under its enchantment was the authoress of *Sarashina Nikki*.

This lady, a daughter of Sugawara Takasué, was born about 1008, just at the time when a portion of *Genji Monogatari* had become known to the public and had attracted great attention among the nobility. She came of famous literary descent, her father being descended in the fifth generation from Sugawara Michizané, revered by our people as the god of literature, while her mother was the younger sister of the authoress of *Kagerô Nikki*, a masterpiece significant as the precursor of the " literary diaries by Heian Court ladies." Her uncle was the poet Fujiwara-no Nagayoshi, and her stepmother, by whom she was brought up, was the poetess Kazusa-no Tayû. In such surroundings as these there would be encouragement for the steady development of literary talent. Nevertheless, as with most of our classical writers, little is known of the course of her life.

A doubtful tradition attributes to her various other works, *Hamamatsu Chûnagon Monogatari, Yowa no Nezamé*, and certain lost *monogatari*, such as *Mizukara Kuyuru* and *Asakura*. But the only work whose composition can with certainty be attributed to her is *Sarashina Nikki*.

This work deals with the outstanding events in her life between, roughly, 1020, when she was twelve, and 1059, the title it bears being generally supposed to be derived from the meaning of a poem quoted in the text. Her father was a local official in the province of Kazusa, to the east of the present city of Tokyo, a remote district, hundreds of miles from the capital. The young girl had a great love for reading stories, but in such a remote, uncultured place it was impossible for her to find any tale to which her highly emotional nature could respond. So intent was she on finding satisfaction that she made herself an image of Buddha before which she would prostrate herself in prayer for her speedy return to the capital and for the coming of the time when she should find all the reading she desired. It was when she was in her thirteenth year that her heart's desire was gratified and she was taken to the capital by her father on the expiration of his term of office.

The girl, unusually susceptible and romantic, was naturally overjoyed at her return to the capital. She describes in detail in her diary the events of this long journey from the province of Kazusa to the city of Kyoto. It was on this journey that she heard the traditions connected with the temple of Chikushi-ji in Musashi province (now in the city of Tokyo) and also of the river Fuji, south of Mount Fuji, which greatly impressed her. Further, she tells how at the foot of Ashigara-yama, she chanced upon three dancers one dark night, whose beautiful figures and voices and graceful dances so attracted her that she would never forget them. Then she had an experience which might have been part of a fairy tale, when she spent a night at an inn in Futamura-yama, a mountain in Mikawa province to the east of the present city of Nagoya, and her sleep was continually interrupted by the thumping of ripe persimmons on the roof as they fell from the overhanging trees.

Three months after leaving Kazusa province she arrived at Kyoto on the second day of the ninth month. At once she coaxed her mother to procure for her the books of tales she desired, and pored over them day and night. But even these romances could scarcely console her in the grief she felt when she learned that, in the spring of that year, two ladies whom she loved and admired had been carried off by the plague which had stricken Kyoto. These ladies were her own nurse and the daughter of the poet Fujiwara-no Yukinari.

Soon afterwards she withdrew with her mother to the retirement of Uzumasa-dera that she might entreat Buddha for an opportunity to obtain a copy of *Genji Monogatari*. It came as a miraculous response, so she believed, when her aunt presented her with *Genji Monogatari* in fifty volumes in a special chest. Her delight in such a wonderful present was unbounded, and she shut herself up in an empty room to read it all by herself; she was as thrilled, she declares, as if she had been selected as Queen.

[80]

Then she had a strange dream in which a priest bade her devote herself with all speed to the service of Buddha. But religion could find little place in the mind of a girl so completely engrossed in romantic literature; she lived her life in the pages of *Genji Monogatari*, yearning with her whole heart to be such a lady as Yûgao, the ill-starred beauty beloved of Genji, or one such as Ukifuné, the lovelorn beauty who, despite the deep love felt for her by Kaoru, the hero of the latter part of the tale, gave up all hopes of love and retired to a convent. Then, each springtime, when the flowers bloomed and then fell, she grieved over the thought of her dead nurse and the daughter of Fujiwara-no Yukinari.

In May or thereabouts, when she had been reading a book far into the night, a strange cat came into the room. She petted it to encourage it to stay and consulted her elder sister about keeping it. Then her sister had a remarkable dream in which this cat said, "I am the reincarnation of the daughter of Fujiwara-no Yukinari. I have come here because your younger sister is so kind and grieves for me continually." So after this the girls loved the cat all the more, and seemed to see in it some resemblance to the dead Lady, but unfortunately it was later burned to death in a fire.

In May of the following year the elder sister died after giving birth to a child, and that death brought the authoress the deepest sorrow she had ever known. In those days the religious impulse often drove even young girls to enter the religious life. But pious ideas of that sort never occurred to the diarist whose aspirations for a life of seclusion were more romantic in the flower of her maidenhood; just as much as in her younger days, she still pined for a life of romantic loneliness, such as that led by Ukifuné awaiting her lover in a remote mountain village, feasting her eyes the while on the cherry blossoms, the summer moon, the autumn tints, and the snow; she was confident that, sooner or later, her dreams of such a life would be realized.

At the age of twenty-seven or so, she presented a mirror to Hasé-dera, a temple to the south-east of the city of Nara. On his return, the priest whom she had sent to the temple as a messenger told her that he had had there a dream in which her future life was fore-shadowed. In his dream a noble lady had appeared showing him the mirror which had been presented. He looked into it and saw the reflection of a woman in tears, while the back of the mirror showed a beautiful palace, probably symbolizing a happy life amid blooming flowers and singing birds.

In the summer of her thirty-third year, on outside advice, she entered the service of a certain dignitary. Until then she had secluded herself almost entirely in order to devote herself to romantic literature. Her new acquaintance with actual life and its petty jealousies and ignoble struggles for power was a turning point in her career. For the first time she was able to judge how far her previous dreams differed from reality. Realizing now that in this world there were none such as Prince Genji and Ukifuné, the beloved of Prince Kaoru, his son, she gradually came to think more seriously about matters of religion.

Not long after her mind had thus been turned from romance to reality, she married Tachibana-no Toshimichi, being at about her thirty-sixth year of age. In the following year she had a son, who was named Nakatoshi. At that time her religious feelings were growing stronger; she often went into retreat at temples and shrines, and her dreams, which were frequent, now had a definitely religious character.

Her religious faith enabled her to face life calmly. Her sole desires were to see her son grow up and her husband successful, but the calm of her life was suddenly shattered by her husband's sudden death. It was when she was forty-nine that he set out for a new post in Shinano, among the Japanese Alps, but in the following April he returned to Kyoto to die there quite unexpectedly in the autumn. As she beheld her son Nakatoshi, clad in sombre mourning dress, performing the funeral ceremonies for his dead father, she was overcome with poignant memories of them both, father and son, in their bright, splendid dresses, on their way to Shinano only a year before. She felt that this great grief had been foreshadowed by the dream of her messenger when long before she had made the gift of a mirror to the temple at Hasé. Yet, no matter how much she pondered, she could not imagine what was foretold by the scene of the tranquil palace the messenger had seen on the reverse of the mirror in the same dream.

She lived on for several years after this bereavement, but her heart was oppressed with sorrow, misfortune and loneliness. The only thing to which she could turn for consolation was a dream of Buddha which she had in the late autumn of 1055. The dream alone gave her courage to live, convincing her of her salvation through Buddha.

Sarashina Nikki ends with the accounts of the events of the year 1059, when the authoress was fifty-one years old, and the work was probably written at that time.

The diarist gives accounts of eleven dreams: two of others, the other nine her own; these dreams, accepted by her as religious inspirations, are inseparable from her spiritual life. In girlhood her dreams are indicative of the authoress engrossed in romantic literature. She believed, in those days, that she could live in the world of the heroines of romance. As she grew older, her dreams took on an increasingly religious character as she came into contact with the cold world of reality and learnt that the world she had built up out of her reading was but a fantasy. Nevertheless, the romantic and emotional temperament which had been nourished on fancy could never bring itself to face the sufferings of the real world.

So she turned to her dreams, giving them first her belief, and then finding in them her main refuge. The serenity of mind she had once derived from literature she now achieved by relying on her dreams. In her dream-world she found the aesthetic beauty and the ideals that she failed to find in the world of reality; the world of dreams meant more to her than the world of truth.

It was not by chance that such a romantic spirit was cherished by the authoress of *Sarashina Nikki*. The golden age of aristocratic culture in the second half of the tenth and the first half of the eleventh century was in itself a " romantic age." The most direct expression of this feeling is given in the poetical works and diary (*Izumi Shikibu Nikki*) of Izumi Shikibu, the most impassioned and most gifted lyric poetess of the whole Heian period. This lyric poetess sought beauty in love itself, while Murasaki Shikibu sought it in human beings and wrote the masterpiece, *Genji Monogatari*, as a result. And the authoress of *Sarashina Nikki*, for her part, turned to dreams and visions. Thus the romanticism of the Heian period culminates in her, and the romanticism which she brought to such a pitch has since only degenerated into visionary absurdity.

MAKURA-NO-SÔSHI

(The Pillow Book of Sei Shônagon)

The culture of the mid-Heian period, the early eleventh century, attained its highest development under the Emperor Ichijô. During the two preceding centuries Chinese culture had exerted an overwhelmingly strong influence, but gradually this had been superseded by a more Japanese spirit, culminating in the grace and refinement so characteristic of the Heian period.

The Court, with its artistic atmosphere, was the cultural centre of the aristocrats, the leadership of this aristocratic society being in the hands of the great Fujiwara family who had secured a grip on the reins of power by allowing their daughters to enter the Court as consorts of the Emperor, for this brought them the honour due to fathers and relations of an Empress.

The outstanding feature of Heian culture and social life was the literary activity of a group of literary ladies in Court service. They came for the most part of aristocratic or semi-aristocratic stock, their outstanding representatives being, in poetry (*waka*), Izumi Shikibu and Akazomé Emon; in novels (*monogatari*), Murasaki Shikibu; and in occasional, fugitive essays (*zuihitsu*), Sei Shônagon. Of these four, Sei Shônagon shares with Murasaki Shikibu, authoress of *Genji Monogatari*, a fame so brilliant as to be almost unparalleled in the history of our literature. Nearly one thousand years have elapsed since she wrote *Makura-no-Sôshi* which gave her immortality, and her fame is still undimmed. But, as with most of the other authoresses, little is known of the details of her life. The Kiyohara family to which she belonged is descended from the Emperor Tenmu. Sei Shônagon was not her real name, but a popular designation, such as it was the custom then to employ. The " Sei " of Sei Shônagon is another reading for the " Kiyo " of her family name of Kiyohara, while " Shônagon " is a government official title, her designation as Sei Shônagon probably being due to her father or to a brother holding the title of Shônagon.

PART OF A SCROLL ILLUSTRATING THE MAKURA-NO-SŌSHI (THE PILLOW BOOK OF SEI-SHŌNAGON). Made in the mid-14th century. Property of the Asano family. Hiroshima.

MANUSCRIPT COPY OF MAKURA-NO-SŌSHI. Made in the 13th century. Owner: Maëda family, Kanazawa.

Her great-grandfather, Fukayabu, is notable as one of the poets of *Kokin Wakashû*, the first *chokusenshû*, collection of poems compiled as a national undertaking under Imperial command. Her father, Motosuké, was the most celebrated poet of his day, one of the five compilers of *Gosen Wakashû*, the second *chokusenshû*, and a learned commentator on the text of *Man'yôshû*, our earliest lyrical anthology. She was born, then, of a semi-aristocratic family of the rank which local governors were selected, while her father was a scholar and poet, and her uncle a student at the Daigakuryô, the government university, chiefly devoted to the study of the Chinese classics.

As a poet she was not remarkable. Her gifts were of too intellectual a quality for her to take naturally to the composition of the short lyric (*waka*) of thirty-one syllables. This must have been a disappointment for her when we consider that she came of a family famous for poetry, and also that the composition of *waka* was then regarded as the highest social accomplishment. Her genius lay rather with prose, to which however she gave so remarkable a poetic quality that her *Makura-no-Sôshi* consists of a succession of prose-poems as beautiful as a string of jewels.

Opinions differ regarding the time when she entered the service of the Empress Teishi, consort of the Emperor Ichijô, but in all probability her appointment dates from some time in the winter of 991, when she was no longer a girl. She stood high in the favour of the Empress, whom she served devotedly. Before entering Court service, the apt and spontaneous manner in which she had quoted passages from the Buddhist scriptures during a conversation with one of the nobles at a Buddhist gathering aroused the admiration of those who heard her, and afterwards she became very popular in Court circles because of her wit and her exhaustive knowledge of Chinese literature, shining like a star among the ladies of the Court. There were many well-known writers then at Court, among whom two young nobles, Fujiwara Tadanobu and Fujiwara Yukinari, were on very friendly terms with her.

She took a genuine pride in being in the service of the brilliant Empress. An eloquent witness to this is that, despite her distinctly egotistic nature and her burning ambition to be first in everything she undertook, she was genuinely content to receive even the humblest favours from her Imperial mistress.

In 995 Fujiwara Michitaka, the father of the Empress, died and the reins of government passed into the hands of Michinaga, his uncle and also his political adversary. In the following year, the dead Michitaka's two brothers, Korechika and Takaié, were implicated in a political intrigue and fell into disgrace. Since Sei Shônagon was related to Michinaga, she also suffered through the slanderous tongues of his rivals. Yet the confidence placed in her by the Empress remained unchanged, and, until the Empress's death in December, 1000, at the early age of twenty-four, she was faithfully attended by Sei Shônagon.

Probably Sei Shônagon did not long remain at Court after this, but of her subsequent doings nothing certain is known. Apparently she passed her declining years in retirement in a suburb of Kyoto as a nun, living on the memories of her glorious past, though one tradition says that she had to wander in poverty and exile from province to province. In any event the date of her death is unknown. She was as unfortunate in her end as was her ill-fated mistress, the Empress.

Makura-no-Sôshi, in which she lives for us, is the oldest example we possess of that literary form known as *zuihitsu*, occasional, fugitive essays. From its closing lines we learn that Sei Shônagon wrote the book on paper granted to her by the Empress.

Makura-no-Sôshi is the name given to the book by later generations. " Makura-no-sôshi " was at one time used as the general name for any such memorandum book, and during the Kamakura period (the twelfth century) the usual title of this book was *Sei Shônagon ga Makura-no-Sôshi* (Sei Shônagon's Pillow Book—The Commonplace Book of Sei Shônagon).

A number of texts of *Makura-no-Sôshi* are in existence, all probably later revisions, this work being regarded as the most difficult of the classics from the point of view of textual criticism. The common edition contains over three hundred essays, long and short, which may be brought under the following four classifications :

1. Essays on various subjects.
2. Essays expressing various emotions.
3. Stray notes.
4. Autobiograpical details and poems.

In the editions in common use these four types are not collected together into separate sections, as they are in some texts, which, according to the most recent authoritative opinion, are most faithful to the original form of *Makura-no-Sôshi*.

Under the first classification, we find collections of essays under separate headings such as "Mountains," in which the authoress treats, say, of Ogura-yama, Kasé-yama, Mikasa-yama, and other mountains, with frequent penetrating comments. The subjects of the essays of this section are as various as amusements, tastes, costumes, utensils, and natural objects treated as poetic themes. In such an essay as "Flowering Trees" the authoress reveals her own personal and poetic appreciation of the lovely pink of the pear blossom, which was not usually admired by the general public, while when writing on "Insects" she includes a pathetic tradition of the basketworms that utter their brief chirp when the winds of autumn blow.

Undoubtedly this part of the book owes much to such an encyclopaedia as *Wamyôruijûshô* and the classified anthology, *Kokinshû*, which were then widely read. Indeed, in those days, when the poetic art of Japan was developing under Chinese influence or was consciously aiming at new literary standards, it is only natural that the authoress of such a collection of essays should have been influenced to no small degree by reference books on poetry. Yet it was her own creative genius that enabled her to express the themes she treated in such artistic prose. Her book is the first application of such a form of literature, and this fact gives it the greatest importance.

The second classification, where the form is rather like that of the first, brings together various types of human feelings under about ten headings, such as "The Lovely," "The Hateful," with concrete examples of each feeling, covering the whole range from beauty to ugliness. Thus, under the heading of "The Lovely," the authoress mentions such things as the picture of a baby's face drawn on a melon (*uri*), and the sight of little chickens running after the mother hen, in this way finding universal beauty in individual examples. To illustrate what she regards as "The Hateful" she cites visitors continuing an interminable conversation with a host who has urgent business demanding his attention, and the faint buzzing of mosquitoes in one's ears when one is sleepy. Under the heading of "Things

Apparently Distant yet Really Near," this writer of a thousand years ago mentions "the relations between men and women," a comment which brings a fresh smile to our lips even today.

There is no doubting the rare eloquence with which human feelings are described. Are we to regard this as a revelation of the genius, the aesthetic ideas of the mid-Heian period? In any case, it is quite incorrect to hold, as it is by some, that the literary form she adopted had already been used in Chinese literature and was used by her as a model. Moreover, although the poetical works of her friend Izumi Shikibu are composed partly in the same style, yet *Makura-no-Sôshi* is written with more minute powers of observation and more delicate sensibility, and must be accounted a masterpiece rare in literature.

The essays falling under the third classification, namely, stray notes on nature and life, well merit the name of *zuihitsu*, fugitive essays. They contain a wealth of exquisite poetic prose describing such things as the moist charm of an autumn morning after the rain, or a garden in the morning after the autumn winds have swept across it, with which descriptions character-sketches are interspersed.

One may say that her view of life is somewhat lacking in depth and penetration, yet it has much in common with ours of much later and very different age. Can we help feeling the appeal of such a passage as "When one is crossing a ford in a carriage by moonlight, it is fascinating to watch the spattering drops of water, flashing like broken crystals, at the tread of the oxen"?

Under the fourth classification, autobiographical, we have accounts of her life before, but chiefly after, entering the service of the Court, where she won the applause of the courtiers by her wit and her knowledge of Chinese literature. They were probably completed after her retirement. She touches but rarely on the misfortunes of the Empress, still less on the events which cast a shadow over her own name, but rather dwells on the brighter aspects of her life. On this account one is bound to agree with the verdict of Murasaki Shikibu, her great contemporary, who speaks of her as a proud woman. These two great writers have much in common, for Murasaki Shikibu not only has a similar outlook on life in her works, but she too was harrassed by many of life's anxieties which she bore without a murmur. That both these women writers were well acquainted with suffering is clear, and yet neither cf them consciously records the fact. The interesting problem of why they should have shrunk from doing so is, however, one that cannot absorb our attention here. This section also contains a small number of her poems along with some by other poets which appealed to her.

In the descriptions based on the authoress's keen sensibility and careful observation there is a quality that lifts *Makura-no-Sôshi* outside the limits of its own age ; that indeed is the special distinction of the work. Yet it would be no injustice to the writer to point out that there are certain features which stamp her as a child of her own age ; despite the novel descriptive style of the work to which we pay our greatest tribute, the aspects of Nature observed hardly ever stray beyond the limits of the contemporary *waka*.

Accordingly, the main characteristics to be noted in this work are the cool, delicate power of observation and the keen, subtle sensibility, which in combination reveal the intensely emotional likes and dislikes of the writer. Hence also the rich associations, the realism and the artistic treatment of the themes. *Makura-no-Sôshi* is not introspective so much as sensuous and original ; it is not passionate, but rather objective. These are features that would give an exceedingly individual and distinctive form to any literary work.

As is well known, the mid-Heian period is distinguished by the high achievements of the " literature of the Court ladies," and this is doubtless the reason why the prevailing literary idea, which permeates all the works of that time, can be summed up in the phrase *mono no awaré*, pensiveness or compassionateness. *Makura-no-Sôshi* is no exception to this but is, besides, sensuous and realistic, and, in a word, it opens up a world of positive delight in things and occurrences of everyday life. This mental outlook is notable for the part it played in the poetic reform that was developed in the later Heian period.

ÔKAGAMI

(The Great Mirror)

In the late Heian period there was a reaction in favour of the gaiety of the past and a lively determination to found a new culture giving full expression to that traditional aspect. Outstanding among the literary productions which resulted was the historical novel. The themes of such novels were drawn from authentic records, the historical facts being unified by the addition of a plot and so transformed into *monogatari*. Of this form of literary art *Eiga Monogatari* and *Ôkagami* may be taken as representative. Both deal with the palmy days of the Fujiwara family, and are centred on Fujiwara Michinaga, the most commanding figure of that period.

Ôkagami gives a historical background to its narrative by opening with a brief record of the genealogy and deeds of the Imperial Family during the fourteen reigns from the Emperor Montoku to the Emperor Go-Ichijô (851–1036), and follows this with biographies of the leading dignitaries of the Fujiwara family from Fujiwara Fuyutsugu to the great Michinaga.

The structure of the narrative is interesting, aiming as it does at creating a feeling of objective historical reality. It is presented in the form of a conversation between three persons, two of whom are portrayed as being old enough to have been personally acquainted with the period described. Accordingly, we are introduced to the venerable figure of Ôyaké-no Yotsugi, who has reached the ripe age of 150 years, and is attending "Bodaikô," an assembly for the reading of the Saddharma Pundarika Sutra, held at the Urin-in temple of Kitayama in Kyoto in the summer of 1025. He enters into conversation about old times with another ancient, Natsuyama-no Shigeki 140 years old. A youthful samurai is present and listens eagerly hanging on the old men's words and urging them to tell still more. Thus encouraged, old Ôyaké-no Yotsugi goes beyond the story told in the historical records to give the inner history of the events

terest being added to the narrative by the young man's occasional
uestions and criticisms. This attempt at achieving authenticity by
sing the form of a conversation between appropriately created
maginary persons is quite a new device, and distinguishes this tale
om its predecessors.

The intention in summarizing the deeds and genealogy of the
ourteen Emperors between the fifty-fifth Emperor, Montoku Tennô,
nd the sixty-eighth Emperor, Go-Ichijô Tennô, the then ruler, is to
ring home to the reader the remote origin of the glory of Fujiwara
Michinaga, and also to furnish some preliminary knowledge of the
'ujiwara family. This introduction is done with great care and
kill.

The biographies of distinguished members of the family which
ollow include Fujiwara Fuyutsugu, the maternal grandfather of the
Imperor Montoku ; Nagara, Yoshifusa and Yoshisuké, the first,
econd and third sons of Fuyutsugu, and Mototsuné and Tokihira,
on and grandson of Nagara. This is also much more than a
mere biographical resumé, for it deals with certain important
istorical events, and also gives a minute analysis, criticism and
xplanation of lesser known matters together with details of the
lispositions, habits and behaviour of the persons concerned.

During the period of power of Fujiwara Tokihira, Sadaijin
Minister of the Left) during the reign of the Emperor Daigo, the
amous scholar Sugawara Michizané was driven into exile. Michi-
ané was the Udaijin (Minister of the Right), and a man of great
ntegrity and loyalty. In respect of character, knowledge and ideas
e was far superior to his colleague Tokihira, who was also much
is junior in years. But Tokihira, jealous of Michizané's greater
bility and influence which stood in the way of his own ambitions,
ntrigued against him, until finally the aged scholar was exiled by
he Emperor to Dazaifu of Kyushu on a false charge.

Although condemned to undeserved exile, Michizané did not
orget the favours he had received from the Emperor in the past,
nd his unwavering loyalty to the end has made a deep impression
on the Japanese people for all time. Michizané died before the
ccusations against him were proved false, but when proof of his
nrivalled loyalty and integrity finally reached the ears of the
Imperor, he issued an Imperial order deifying him as Kitano Tenman

Tenjin. Tokihira died soon afterwards, probably as a result of his evil doing.

The work goes on to give accounts of the powerful Tadahira in all his glory as the Dajôdaijin (President of the Council), of the courteous Saneyori, of the deeds of Yoritada, a thrifty person, a type rare among the nobles of the Heian period, while many anecdotes are told of Kintô, who was skilled in poetical composition and famed in later ages as poet and prosodist. We see how with the passage of time supremacy at Court passed increasingly into the hands of the Fujiwara family, who then began incessant struggles for power among themselves, domestic feuds which reveal the ugly side of human nature.

There are many fascinating stories of Michitaka, the eldest son of Kaneié, the Dajôdaijin, who held the posts of Kanpaku (Civil Dictator) and Naidaijin (Lord Keeper of the Privy Seal). Michitaka was by no means lacking in character and personality, but he invited failure through his habit of heavy drinking. Handsome himself, he had an equally handsome son in Korechika. But Korechika lacked energy, and thus the important office of Kanpaku passed from his father to Michikané and then to Michinaga, his uncles. In the end, he was exiled to Kyushu, because of some accidental blasphemy against the ex-Emperor Kazan, but on the birth of an Imperial Prince he was pardoned and recalled. Yet further rash acts brought him into continual trouble, and his reputation and fortunes, in consequence, declined, while his rival, Michinaga, waxed steadily in influence, winning that public confidence so necessary for his later success.

Another contrast to Korechika is furnished by his younger brother Takeié, who was a fine, energetic and strong character, as is clear from the fact that occasionally even Michinaga had to yield the palm to him. He too enjoyed great public confidence, but ultimately was no match for the rising fortunes of Michinaga and came to an unfortunate end.

This brings us to stories about the life of Michinaga, Dajôdaijin, which form the centre of the whole work. His connections were most propitious for a great career. He was the fifth son of Kaneié, uncle of the ex-Emperors Ichijô and Sanjô, and also grandfather of the then Emperor Go-Ichijô and the Crown Prince, who was later the Emperor Go-Suzaku. He rose to the highest possible rank attainable by a subject, living in the greatest magnificence. Undoubtedly his own personality and ability contributed much to his extraordinary prosperity, but he also owed a large debt to his remarkable good fortune.

His power was greatly furthered and strengthened by his being blessed with many sons and daughters. By his lawful wife, Rinshi, he had four daughters and two sons. All his daughters became the wives of Emperors, the first becoming the consort of the Emperor Ichijô, the second of the Emperor Sanjô, the third of the reigning Emperor Go-Ichijô, whilst the fourth married the Crown Prince who afterwards ascended the throne as the Emperor Go-Suzaku. One of his two sons became Kanpaku (Civil Dictator) and Sadaijin (Minister of the Left), the other Naidaijin (Lord Keeper of the Privy Seal). Michinaga had a great affection for his wife ; it can surely be said that she, as his wife and as the mother of such sons and daughters, was the most fortunate lady in Japan.

By his concubine Meishi, also, Michinaga had six children, two daughters and four sons, all of whom enjoyed remarkable prosperity. Then, to the astonishment of all the members of his family, Michinaga suddenly decided at the age of fifty-four to enter the priesthood. But at the time of the story (1025), when he was sixty years of age, he was still holding the reins of government and controlling the family fortunes, and actually continued to do so until death took him away two years later.

He also possessed great literary endowments in addition to his political genius, thus revealing himself as a typical nobleman of the Heian period, cultivating the emotional side of his life. Or we may say that contemporary fashion, by attaching such great importance to the accomplishment of writing poems (*waka*), afforded him a splendid opportunity of showing his talent in that direction and so of proving himself an ideal character.

The author of *Ōkagami* gives the highest praise to Michinaga's occasional poetical compositions. Further, he tells us how, from his youth up, Michinaga possessed nerves of steel, enabling him always to maintain a calm and dignified bearing that overawed all those about him. The following anecdote is given as illustrative of his character. Once, his father, Kaneié, in envy of the fame of that versatile genius,

Kintô, the son of Yoritada, exclaimed in the presence of his three sons with a regretful sigh, "What a pity that all three of you together seem to be no match for even the shadow of Kintô!" This stimulated Michinaga, so it is said, to the grandiloquent reply, "It will not be long before I surpass not only Kintô's shadow, but the best he can do." And he kept his word.

There is another revealing incident. One gloomy wet night when the ex-Emperor Kazan was talking to a group of young nobles among whom was Michinaga, the conversation turned to ghost stories. Then the ex-Emperor jokingly asked if any of them had the courage to go alone on such a night to a place reputed to be haunted. While the rest remained silent, Michinaga made the prompt answer, "I will go wherever Your Majesty chooses to send me." Thereupon, the ex-Emperor, delighted with the success of his joke, named three places, all of which were said to be haunted, for Michinaga and his two brothers to visit. The two brothers, Michitaka and Michikané, set out trembling and pale with fear, and turned back halfway; Michinaga alone went boldly to the place allotted to him and calmly left a token of his visit behind.

While Michinaga was still a youth a physiognomist foretold great things for him, prophesying that he would hold the reins of government. So it would seem that he was destined by nature to achieve the highest good fortune. Typical though he was of his age, he cannot lightly be dismissed as an effeminate politician of the Heian period. He was no mere gently-mannered courtier like so many of his contemporaries, but a great man, with an appearance both charming and commanding; *Ôkagami* eulogizes him as a man of courageous character, one versed in the military arts as well as in the elegant accomplishments of the court.

Then, as an illustration of the great extent of Michinaga's glory, the ancient narrator goes on to tell of the building of the great Hôjô temple, and the grand Buddhist service held in honour of its completion. The temple was of such magnificence as to seem a veritable paradise on earth, far superior even to the Hall of the Great Buddha at Nara, while the splendid appearance made by the Fujiwara family on that day beggared all description. There is no limit to the narrator's praise of Michinaga; he holds that his powerful personality brought peace and tranquillity to the nation, due entirely to the special protection vouchsafed to him by the deities. In a transport of joy, the old man declares that he is fortunate indeed to have been born in such a period.

At this, the other old man, his companion, breaks in with a prediction of misfortune. "This very year," he declares, "there is every possibility of many natural convulsions and the outbreak of some grave disaster," by this hinting at the destiny of the Fujiwara family—in other words, Michinaga, having attained the zenith of his glory, was on the brink of a fall. Owing to the feuds between various members of his family and the death of others, the second old man feels that Michinaga would soon find himself on the slippery descent to ruin.

The first ancient, however, will have none of such gloomy prognostications, and confines himself exclusively to emphasizing Michinaga's prosperity, probably unique in the history of Japan. This conflict of opinion in their stories reflects the purpose of the author. It was at this point in their conversation that the sermon in the Urinin temple began, and the young samurai lost sight of them in the crowd. He was anxious to hear more of the stories now that such an interesting point had been reached, and is left greatly regretting his loss. In this way Ôkagami comes to an end.

Thus does the book reveal to us the inside history of the rise of the Fujiwara family culminating in Michinaga. It lays bare the internal condition of the aristocratic society of the time, with those in authority constantly engaged in secret political intrigues. We see the darker side of that society, outwardly so care-free and tranquil, and in many episodes and examples the author reveals the actual state of affairs and the motives at work to a degree altogether beyond the scope of superficial histories.

By means of the fictitious characters of the two ancient cronies, who recount the past, and the young samurai, who represents the contemporary point of view, the author gives us a new type of historical novel, wherein the characteristic features of Japanese life are revealed in contrast, for example, to such a work as Eiga Monogatari which is devoted rather to historical detail.

The author's unqualified praise, through the medium of old Ôyaké, of Michinaga as the ideal type of man and minister not only bears witness to Michinaga's real greatness, but also expresses the attitude of contemporary society rejoicing in the peace and prosperity that accompanied the rise of the Fujiwara family. Yet the fact that the author is living in a period of transition where new ideas are developing out of or conflicting with the old is well brought out by the contrast between the old man's blind worship and the calmly critical mind of the young samurai.

The literary value of *Ōkagami* is due to its excellent and skilful conception, whereby it retains a consistent unity of idea amid its elaborate character-drawing and occasional dramatic incidents. Touches of humour and satire appear here and there, and it possesses both the pithy and concise style and the characteristic elegancies of the traditional *monogatari*. This work may be regarded as the precursor of the *gunkimono* (tales of war) which constitute the literary contribution of the following period.

Nothing is clearly known as to the authorship of this work, and not one of the theories put forward obtains anything like general support. Nor is the date to be definitely fixed, although it is put at about 1100. Michinaga was at the zenith of his power in 1025, and the book itself suggests that it must have been written somewhere between fifty and eighty years after that date.

———

KONJAKU MONOGATARI

(Tales of Long Ago)

Konjaku Monogatari, also known as *Konjaku Monogatarishû*, is a voluminous collection containing over one thousand tales and traditions, Indian, Chinese and Japanese, compiled in the closing years of the Heian period, about 1050. One of the greatest collections of traditional material in the world, it may be compared with the Indian *Jataka*, stories of the early life of Buddha, and also with the nursery tales that form the *Pancatantra*. Although in form it owes a great deal to such works as *Isé Monogatari*, *Yamato Monogatari* and others of that type, yet in descriptive style and mode of expression it breaks away from the conventions of the lyrical tales of the Heian period and to some extent anticipates the literary tendencies of the succeeding age, having in this respect much in common with *Ôkagami*, a historical novel of about the same date.

The work consists of thirty-one books and is divided into three parts, covering India, China and Japan. Not counting the three books which have been lost, the Indian section (Books I to V) includes 187 tales, the Chinese section (Books VI to X) 180 tales, and the Japanese section (Books XI to XXXI) 736 tales.

Although the work is so voluminous and its contents most varied, each of these three divisions has its own characteristics. The Indian section is concerned with the career and personal doings of Buddha, tales of his disciples, of birds and beasts, of karma, of the Buddhist Nirvana and of Buddha after his entrance there, and of Buddhist benefits, miracles and folklore. The Chinese section tells of the introduction of Buddhism into China, of the virtue of the sutras, of dutiful sons, and of historical traditions and secular stories. The Japanese section contains tales and traditions concerning the propagation of Buddhism in Japan, the erection of temples and pagodas, the virtue of the sutras, priests, conversion to Buddhism, miracles, karma, the various arts, brave deeds, inevitable retribution,

[97]

demons and goblins, popular superstitions, practical jokes, thieves, and birds and beasts. Obviously, therefore, the work contains a wealth of exceedingly valuable material for the study of contemporary culture and the folklore of these three countries.

Many of the tales are derived from various sutras and from earlier collections, histories and literary works, while others, dealing with popular customs and everyday life, have probably been taken from oral tradition and local report. The title is derived from the fact that each tale begins with the words "Ima wa mukashi" (long ago), *kon* and *jaku* being the alternative readings of the characters *ima* and *mukashi*. Outlines of some of the more famous tales are quoted below in order to give a general idea of the work as a whole.

The Indian section, treating of the life of Buddha from birth to his entry into Nirvana with many stories of his early sayings and doings, may be regarded as a life of Buddha in the form of myth. This section contains some famous tales, of which the two cited below are examples.

THE TALE OF THE THREE ANIMALS WHO PRACTISED BUDDHIST
AUSTERITIES, AND OF THE SELF-SACRIFICE OF THE HARE

Long ago, three animals in India, a hare, a fox and a monkey, devoutly practised Buddhist austerities, believing that they had been born as animals because of their sins of cruelty and avarice in a previous existence, and resolving to sacrifice themselves for the good of others in order to be reborn in a higher sphere in a future life. Hearing of this, Śakra devānām Indra, the Protector of Buddhism, descended from heaven in order to test their sincerity, appealing to their pity by appearing in the form of an old man. They showed the greatest eagerness in offering him hospitality; the monkey climbed trees to obtain fruit and brought corn from a neighbouring farm, while the fox gathered various Buddhist offerings for his support. There was no doubt about the sincerity of these two. The hare alone failed to find any food in spite of all the efforts it made, and was rebuked for this by the fox, the monkey and the old man. Thereupon the hare flung itself into the fire to provide food for the old man. The deity was so much moved by the hare's devotion that he introduced into the moon the figure of the brave hare plunging into the fire, so that all the ages to come should be reminded of its example, and whenever people looked up at the moon they would be reminded of the sacrifice of the hare. Here Buddhist teaching is illustrated by means of animals.

THE TALE OF THE TORTOISE WHO FORGOT THE CRANE'S WARNING

Long ago, India suffered a severe drought. A tortoise, on the verge of death because the pond in which it lived was dried up, appealed for help to a crane. " I will take you to a place where there is water," the crane replied. " I will hold a piece of wood in my beak and you must cling to it with your teeth. You must not open your mouth until we reach our destination. Now, be careful, for I know how talkative you are." The crane flew away with the tortoise, but on the way the tortoise was attracted by the unfamiliar scenes and, without thinking, it opened its mouth to say, " Where are we ? " As it did so, it fell headlong to the ground, smashed its shell and died. The results of chattering may be fatal.

This allegorical tale is also included in Aesop's *Fables* and the *Pancatantra*, showing the connection between India and Greece. Another example which is also found in the *Pancatantra* is that of the monkey deprived of its liver whilst still alive. This tale has also been introduced into China, and contains points of interest for the study of comparative folklore.

In the Chinese section, the most famous tales on Buddhism are those of Dharma journeying to China for the propagation of Buddhism, and of Hsüan Tsang, the Chinese priest who endured many hardships to reach India for the practice of Buddhist austerities. The tales relating to Buddhist doctrines are chiefly concerned with karma and with metempsychosis which is called, in Sanskrit, samsara, and, in Japanese, *rinné*. The rest of the section consists chiefly of traditions dealing with that exaggerated sense of filial duty which is one of the leading thoughts of the Orient. Here are two stories of that type.

THE TALE OF KUO-CHÜ WHO WON A GOLDEN KETTLE BY HIS FILIAL PIETY TO HIS MOTHER

Long ago, a man named Kuo-chü lived in China who was always dutiful towards his mother, despite his extreme poverty. After the birth of a son, food was so short that, in order to have enough to support his mother, he determined to bury his little son alive in the mountains. But, as he began to dig the hole, he found a gold kettle and became rich. His filial purpose must have reached the ears of Heaven.

THE TALE OF MÊNG-TSUNG'S FILIAL PIETY TOWARDS HIS OLD MOTHER WHICH ENABLED HIM TO OBTAIN BAMBOO SHOOTS IN WINTER

Long ago, Mêng-tsung who lived in China was so devoted to his mother that, even in the midst of winter, he went out into his garden to try to find bamboo shoots, to which she was extremely partial. And he found them, for Heaven sent him these bamboo shoots as a reward for his filial piety.

These two tales are representative of the stories on filial duties, in which Chinese tradition is peculiarly rich. Most of such tales deal with filial piety towards mothers, which shows the great importance attached to affection for mothers by the Chinese.

The Japanese section, which forms the chief part of the work, contains numerous stories of the greatest interest, those especially which deal with secular matters forming a treasure-house of folklore. There are stories of craftsmanship, of brave deeds, of superstitions, of practical jokes and human sympathy, all of which are characteristically Japanese, in the sense that they reflect the history, the times and the spirit of our people.

The Buddhist tales in this section show the transformation which the Indian tales underwent after their introduction into Japan, and also the conditions under which the Buddhist faith and teachings spread most vigorously throughout the nation.

THE TALE OF KUMÉ-NO SENNIN WHO
FOUNDED KUMÉ-DERA

Long ago, a very holy man named Kumé-no Sennin lived in the Ryûmon-ji temple in Yamato province. By virtue of his supernatural powers he was able to fly through the air, but one day his eye was attracted by the white legs of a woman, who was busy washing by the side of the river with her skirts tucked up. His magical power immediately failed him and he fell to earth, where he took the woman to wife. Afterwards, he turned again to Buddhism and undertook a course of severe Buddhist austerities, and by virtue of supernatural art, was able to erect the temple of Kumé-dera, which gained the support of numerous pious men.

This tale is a transformation of the story of the Hermit I-chüeh included in the Chinese section. There are also numerous tales of miracles wrought by Jizô (Kshitigarbha, the Bodhisattva who is the guardian deity of children) and Kannon (Avalokitêsvara, the Goddess of Mercy) which reveal the outlook of the people at that time and their ardent faith in these two deities.

The most interesting tales in the Japanese section, however, are those dealing with popular customs, with demons and the forces of evil. For here is to be found a great quantity of material for the study of Japanese traditions.

THE TALE OF A HUNTER OF MIMASAKA PROVINCE WHOSE
CUNNING THWARTED A SACRIFICE TO AN EVIL DEITY

Long ago, there dwelt in the province of Mimasaka an evil deity whose true form was that of a monkey. To this deity the village people were accustomed to offer one of their maidens each year as a victim. One year it was the turn of a certain beautiful maiden who was the apple of her parents' eye. But just when they were hopelessly abandoning themselves to grief, a travelling hunter appeared with his dogs. On being told of the situation he determined to slay the detestable monkey god and win the girl for his wife. So he took the place of the girl in the box, in which the victim was always placed, with his ferocious dogs on each side of him, and thus awaited the appearance of the god. Then, when the monkey opened the lid the two dogs jumped out and savaged him until he died. Thus was the evil deity which had so long troubled the village destroyed and the people freed from all anxiety.

This tale of the killing of the monkey god belongs to an interesting type of legend which can be found throughout the world.

In addition to the legends about supernatural monsters and demons, this section also contains strange stories of marriages between men and beasts, of which the most striking are those of a snake seducing a girl and of the marriage between a woman and a dog at Kitayama. The tale of a dog suckling a foundling at Datchimon is a rare example in the tradition of men being fostered by beasts. Among the demon stories there is the tale of a young man who was swallowed at a single mouthful by a demon who had taken on the guise of a woman, and also of a husband whose wife was swallowed by a demon.

This section also contains many traditional superstitions regarding such things as the *tengu* (long-nosed goblins), the heretical devils who obstruct the teaching of Buddhism. Other stories deal with heroes who kill such monsters. The number of tales that refer to the subjugation of robbers demands attention, for this shows how common such robbers were in those days. There is also a story of Minamoto-no Yorimitsu killing a mysterious fox that appeared in the snow; but the most famous story of that type tells of how the intrepid hero Fujiwara Yasumasa caught the robber Hakamadaré.

THE TALE OF HOW THE COURTIER YASUMASA DEFIED THE ROBBER HAKAMADARÉ

Long ago, there was a wicked robber named Hakamadaré who terrified all the country round about. On one occasion in the dead of night, he lay in wait along the road intending to rob wayfarers who came that way. Along came a fine-looking samurai, walking serenely in the moonlight, playing a tune on his flute. On first catching sight of this harmless-looking passer-by, the robber prepared to rush out on him, but the indefinable dignity of the samurai's presence made im hesitate and cower back. Then, screwing up all his courage, Hakamadaré at last came out and hurried after the samurai. He had almost reached him, when the samurai, calmly and without any sign of fear, suddenly thundered over his shoulder the one word, " Bah ! " It was too much for Hakamadaré, who fell down prostrate, quite overcome. Thereupon the samurai took him home, admonished him for his evil ways, and sent him off laden with gifts. The samurai was none other than the hero Fujiwara Yasumasa.

Among the many stories dealing with contests in skill the most famous is :

THE CONTEST IN ART BETWEEN KUDARA-NO KAWANARI AND HIDA-NO TAKUMI

Long ago, there lived Kudara-no Kawanari, an excellent painter, and Hida-no Takumi, a renowned architect, who, although on the best of terms, maintained a good-humoured rivalry. On one occasion Takumi said in a jesting sort of way, " Please come and see the six-feet-square Buddhist chapel that I've just built. I should like you to decorate it with mural paintings."

Off went Kawanari to visit the hall, and essayed to enter it. But the moment he put foot on the threshold of the southern doorway, the door shut with a bang, and a door on the west side flew open. So he went to that door, but that also, in the same way, shut tight. In turn he went round to the eastern and again to the southern door, but the same thing happened there, and he could not get in. Then he saw that Takumi, who had been watching him, was shaking his sides with laughter. Realizing then that a trick had been played on him, Kawanari set to work to turn the tables. After a while, he invited the architect to his house. But what a horrible sight met his eyes ! There in the room lay a huge, swollen black corpse, filling the place with evil odours. It was too dreadful. Takumi jumped out of the room in horror and surprise, while the artist smiled with pleasure at his fear. For when, later, Takumi made a careful examination of the dreadful object, he found it was only a picture painted by Kawanari.

Numerous stories telling how angels descended to earth attracted by the power of music, or of gods deeply moved by poetry (*waka*), reflect the popularity of those arts in the Heian period. Among the tales of place-names associated with ancient poems there is an interesting tradition about Mt Obasuté.

THE TALE OF OBASUTÉ-YAMA IN SHINANO PROVINCE

Long ago, there lived at Sarashina in Shinano province a man who was as kind and devoted to his old aunt as if she were his mother. But his wife hated the aunt, and, by means of her slanderous tongue, persuaded him to expose her on some remote mountain. So one night with very great reluctance he took his aunt upon his back and climbed a high mountain, where he put her down and left her weeping. But he could not sleep that night for sorrow, and then, as he was thinking of his old aunt in her suffering, the moon rose bright above the mountain ridge. The sight was too much for him.

> Inconsolable
> Grew my heart as I looked up
>   At the moon shining
> Above Mt Obasuté
> In lonely Sarashina.

Such was the poem he wrote, and then he hastened to the mountain and brought his aunt back to the house. Hence the origin of the name Obasuté-yama, the Mountain of the Forsaken Aunt.

The origin of this story is to be found in the Indian story of a country where, it is said, the abandonment of the aged was the custom. The Indian original has become associated with the place-name of Obasuté and this old poem has become linked with the Japanese version of the story. In this and other stories *Konjaku* clearly shows how the same tale is transformed in different countries and in different ages, and is also evidence of how the thought of the Heian period was permeated with Indian and Chinese ideas. For this reason the work is a landmark in our cultural history and of the greatest importance for the comparative study of folk stories.

Konjaku Monogatari has been traditionally attributed to Minamoto-no Takakuni, a noble who held the offices of Dainagon (Chief

State Councillor) and Kôgôgû Daibu (High Steward to the Empress). Later in life he entered the priesthood, and it was then, it is said, that he edited this large collection of tales. But some scholars hold that the work was compiled later.

In style it is entirely different from other *monogatari* of the time. As one might expect, it contains many Buddhist and Chinese terms, but throughout it is characterized by Japanese expressions both naive and concise. While *Konjaku Monogatari* may not rank high as literature, its value as a great collection of ancient tales cannot well be over-estimated. It is a wonderful source for the study of manners, customs and culture, as well as of literary origins and traditions. It was, moreover, the first of a series of such collections, long and short, produced during the mediaeval times, and belongs to the same group as *Uji Shûi Monogatari*.

SHIN-KOKINSHÛ

(A New Anthology of Poems, Ancient and Modern)

Shin-Kokinshû of the early Kamakura period is the last of the *Hachi-daishû*, the Eight Anthologies compiled by Imperial Command, and with *Man'yôshû* and *Kokinshû* forms the three most highly esteemed of all Japanese anthologies.

In *Kokinshû* we find, for a brief period, perfect expression given to poetic thought, but the *Shin-Kokinshû* is based rather on what we must call the after-taste, the lingering emotion evoked by the poem and borne in the heart long after it is heard no more. Poems in the style of *Kokinshû* ceased to be produced, and instead we find that, as in the poems of Soné Yoshitada and of Minamoto-no Tsunenobu and his son Toshiyori, great stress was laid upon freedom of diction and vivid description of scenery. Most of the works produced in the later Heian period followed this " new tendency," though the traditional school of poetry was strongly supported by Fujiwara-no Kintô and Fujiwara-no Mototoshi. Then, later, appeared Fujiwara-no Shunzei, an admirer both of the poems of the new school produced by Tsunenobu and Toshiyori and also of the works of Kintô and Mototoshi, who, by harmonizing these two schools, produced what is called the *yûgen-tai* (" lonesome " style), such as is found in the poems compiled by him in *Senzai Wakashû*.

Shunzei's ideal was to return as completely as possible to *Kokin-shû* with an acceptance of the various poetical changes since *Man'yôshû*. It was with this in mind that he compiled *Koraifûtaishô*, in which he included poems from the time of *Man'yôshû* up to his own time. The poetry of the " lonesome " style which he advocated valued highly the evocation of mood or emotion, an after-taste, and he seems to have attached the greatest importance to the feeling of tranquillity, the harmonizing of sublimity and charm, produced by a poem.

The effect of after-taste was elevated into a first principle by Shunzei's son, Teika, who was mainly responsible for the compilation of *Shin-Kokinshû*. This after-taste was for Teika the very soul of poetry, and so he was led to favour poetry of what was called the *yûshin-tai* (" emotionalistic " style). Although such poetry, in its symbolistic aim, is similar to the emotionalism of Shunzei, it lays stress on sensuousness, and *Shin-Kokinshû* is therefore characterized by its sensuous and rather florid expression, forming a contrast to the quiet beauty of *Senzai Wakashû*, or *Senzaishû* as it is often called.

In addition to Teika, there were four others who took part in the compilation of *Shin-Kokinshû*, Fujiwara-no Iyetaka, Fujiwara-no Masatsuné, Minamoto-no Michitomo and Fujiwara-no Ariié. Being compiled by these people at the encouragement of the ex-Emperor Go-Toba, the anthology is not limited to poems in the style of Teika, but contains many examples in the " loi esome " style inherited from *Senzaishû* which reveal a quiet emotionalism. Indeed, we may say that two streams of poetry flow through *Shin-Kokinshû*, in the florid pieces of the Teika school and in the more tranquil poems of the school of Shunzei. Yet they have this in common : they both have a symbolistic aim in virtue of the stress they lay on achieving the indescribable after-taste.

To attain its symbolism *Shin-Kokinshû* has its own peculiar technique of expression. In the first place, we find a symbolism resulting from the words themselves and their combinations. This method of achieving emotion is a striking characteristic of the poems in this anthology, where the verbal combinations result in symbolic expressions, rather than logical. For instance :—

> Thinking of my love
> Lonely in the Capital,
> I turned and looked back
> To see above the mountains
> The slender moon hanging low.

The exquisite touch of lonesomeness in the original can scarcely be felt in so inadequate a translation as this. Such a use of verbal combinations to produce an emotional rather than an intellectual effect was frequently resorted to later in the *yôkyoku*, the texts of the Noh plays, and in the *jôruri*, the dramatic ballads.

In the second place, *Shin-Kokinshû* is characterized by the special use of *kugiré* (pauses) and *taigen-domé* (noun-endings), the pauses at the end of the first and third lines, and the noun-ending at the end of the fifth line. Although there are naturally many poems that do not follow this plan strictly, this technique is definitely part of the symbolistic method of *Shin-Kokinshû*.

> Though anxious to halt
> My steed awhile and to brush
> From my sleeves the snow,
> Still could I find no shelter,
> One snowy eve in Sano.

Here there is a pause at the end of the third line and the noun-ending at the end of the last. Actually, when there are pauses at the end of both the first and the third lines, this indicates that the second and third lines are combined so as to give what is called *shichigo-chô* (seven-five metrical scheme), which is more characteristic of a flowery style than the *goshichi-chô*, with lines of five and seven syllables. The use of the noun-ending at the end of the fifth line is intended to interrupt the emotion and so evoke the desired after-taste. Poems with such noun-endings in *Shin-Kokinshû* number 456, or about one fourth of the total, which, according to *Yakumomishô*, is 1978. It is interesting to find that such noun-endings occur most frequently in pieces dealing with nature scenes included in the divisions of " Spring," " Summer," " Autumn " and " Winter." They amount to one third of the whole of those poems, while only about one fourth of the lyrics have noun-endings.

Another of the technical usages of *Shin-Kokinshû* is *honkatori* (imitations of originals), the employment of materials and forms of expression from previous poems. The degree to which this practice of *honkatori* was allowed varied considerably in the practice of different writers. Teika himself, in *Kindai Shûka*, lays it down that the literal imitation of ancient poems is permissible for the first two lines, but not for the second and third, nor for the fourth and fifth. Again, in *Maigetsushô*, he says that such imitation is absolutely inadmissible for the third line. In any case, in the use of *honkatori*, diction is as important as the subject-matter. Teika holds that it does not matter if the subject-matter and the diction be antiquated, so long as they are employed with a freshness of spirit, thus granting that for his diction and subject-matter a poet may make use of ancient

1odels. Of Teika himself it would be true to say that he breathed
ew life into whatever ancient expressions and subjects he adopted.
'his is the distinguishing featuie not only cf his work but of *Shin-*
okinshû as a whole, which is notable for its style and spirit as well
s its themes.

We shall now mention some of the poets represented most con-
picuously in this anthology. There are Saigyô, with ninety-four
oems, Jiyen with ninety-one, Yoshitsuné seventy-nine, Shunzei
eventy-two, Princess Shikishi forty-nine, Teika forty-six, Iyetaka
riy- wo, Jakuren thirty-five, the ex-Emperor Go-Toba thirty-four,
nd Ki-no Tsurayuki thirty-two. These names are representative of
1e two streams which flow through *Shin-Kokinshû*, Saigyô and Shunzei
eing typical of the older school, while most of the others belong to
1e same school as the compilers of the anthology.

The works of Fujiwara-no Teika form the key-note of *Shin-*
okinshû. They consist mainly of emotionalistic pieces in a gay,
laborate style such as have already been described. Fujiwara
yetaka, the devoted adherent of the ex-Emperor Go-Toba, whom
e served in his exile on the island of Oki, followed rather the school
f Shunzei, writing poems in the " lonescme " style, yet he lightened
hunzei's quietism with his limpid style. The following well reveals
is poetical vein :—

> How brightly the moon
> Now shines upon Lake Nio !
> The sight of the waves,
> Crested with white like flowers,
> Tells us that Autumn is come.

A very individual type of poetry was produced by the priest
'yen, of the Tendai sect of Buddhism, in which he was for a long
ime Abbot. There is not so keen an expression of emotion in his
vork which derives its character from its style and unworldly outlook.
'oshitsuné who, like Iyetaka, wrote poems in the "lonescme" style
vas a distinguished statesman who died comparatively young. Despite
he fact that he never attained the limpidity of Iyetaka and that his
vork lacks something in polish, he must still be ranked among the
eading poets.

The ex-Emperor Go-Toba gave every encouragement to the com-

pilation of *Shin-Kokinshû*, and personally scrutinized the pieces recommended by the compilers. Later, however, after his retirement to
Oki, he excluded hundreds of pieces from that anthology and made
his own compilation which is known as *Okibon Shin-Kokinshû*, the
Oki Text of the Shin-Kokinshû. He himself was of the "lonesome"
school of Shunzei, but his work took on a particularly sublime and
impressive character from the influence of his circumstances.

The anthology also contains the work of several women poets,
notably the Princess Shikishi who bodies forth a deep emotion
in the most delicate expressions and touches perfection in the "lonesome" style. Another was Shunzei's own daughter who, for the
most part, followed the style of Teika with its after-taste and sensuousness.

Shin-Kokinshû is the natural consummation of *Kokinshû*. It too
its stand on that tradition and drew inspiration from the spirit of
early mediaeval times to create a new style of poetry. It is, as it
were, the terminating point of the changes since *Man'yôshû*, to which
it offers so sharp a contrast. Later developments added the naive
realism of *Man'yôshû* to bring the *Shin-Kokinshû* style to perfection
as shown in *Gyokuyôshû* and *Fûgashû*. *Shin-Kokinshû* was not, indeed
the sole poetic influence in mediaeval times, when its elaborateness
had to contend with the simple beauty preferred by many. Yet it
had a strong following, and Shôtetsu (1380–1458) had a very
high opinion of Teika and the sensuousness of *Shin-Kokinshû*. In
more modern times, Kada Azumamaro and Motoöri Norinaga were
great admirers of *Shin-Kokinshû* and, under its influence, established
a school of poetry most influential from the "manneristic" standpoint. After the Meiji era there was a return to *Man'yôshû*, but recently *Shin-Kokinshû* has again found increased favour.

Shin-Kokinshû consists of twenty books with introductions in
kana and Chinese characters. It originated in an order of the ex-
Emperor Go-Toba, issued on the third day of the eleventh month
1201. Shami Jakuren and five others were ordered to undertake
the work of compilation, but Shami Jakuren died before the work
was half done, and eventually the work of compilation was completed by Minamoto-no Michitomo, Fujiwara-no Ariié, Fujiwara-no
Teika, Fujiwara-no Iyetaka and Fujiwara-no Masatsuné. The date

its first drafting is tentatively ascribed to the second month,
05, although frequent revisions followed until it took its present
ape in 1210 or thereabouts.   Later still the ex-Emperor Go-Toba,
hile in Oki, excluded about 380 pieces and compiled the *Oki-
n* text.

SANKA WAKASHÛ

(The Poetical Works of Saigyô)

Sanka Wakashû, or *Sankashû*, is the name given to the collecte
works of Saigyô, the nature-poet of the closing years of the Heia
period. His poetry on the whole inclines to the *yûgen-tai*, the " lor e
some " style; that is to say, it evokes a quietistic charm throug
the use of symbolic expressions. In this respect it resembles th
work of Fujiwara-no Shunzei, but whereas Shunzei achieved this styl
of poetic composition by means of meditation, Saigyô attained it e
perientially, by immersing himself in the varying moods of rature.

Saigyô's style is extremely simple, and his poems clearly expres
his attitude towards life and nature, and also reflect its variou
changes. We shall see that he began with a strong feeling abou
the uncertainty of life, regarding life as something from which h
must manage to extricate himself; as, for instance, in

> My only desire
> To find where to lie and die—
> Sad, indeed, my lot,
> Passing as pass the dew-drops
> On the grass by the roadside.

> Oh how plaintively
> Sounds the distant, casual,
> Tolling of a bell,
> Deepening the desolation
> Of my sad meditation!

These present his sense of life's mutability. So he stepped aside
from the main current of life to throw himself into the heart o
rature. His love of rature was single-minded. On viewing the
cherry blossom, glowing in full bloom on the mountains of Yoshino
his spirit escaped from his body to occupy itself solely with the beaut
before him. While impatiently awaiting the coming of the cherry

blossom, his whole mind was preoccupied in wondering on which peak it would bloom. Occasionally he would reflect objectively on his own state of mind and ask himself, as he was immersed in the beauty of the cherry blossoms, why such a deep love for them still persisted in his heart when, as he had thought, he had lost hope in everything.

Thus was Saigyô's love for the cherry blossoms, and nature generally, single-minded and sincere. If we ask what phase of nature it was that led him to seek union with the heart of nature, the answer is that it was the gentleness and tranquillity of nature, such as lurk in the depths of the cherry blossoms in their prime. Or again, we have the following :—

> From a rift cloven
> Through the mists that lie veiling
> The mountains dimly seen,
> There comes faintly to my ear
> The sad belling of a deer.

Here the cry of the deer faintly caught amid the mists lying over the dim mountains is felt to be the quiet voice of nature itself.

Yet although Saigyô's heart was so deeply attuned to nature and in harmony with its tender moods and its quiet voice, he sometimes reveals a hankering after actual life and an affection for this world, which he regarded with nature as his criterion. In this he resembles Kamo-no Chômei, who retired from the world to Hino-yama. Saigyô gives, as it were, his view of the world as seen from a mountain top, as in this, one of his most famous poems :—

> Here beside this swamp
> Where snipe dart up and take wing,
> On an autumn eve,
> Touched, would feel sad
> Even the dullest of souls !

Saigyô is here clearly touched with human feeling as he records his conviction that no man could be so coarse as not to be influenced by the quiet atmosphere of nature in which he finds himself.

Even though he felt himself at one with nature, Saigyô could never entirely free himself from the life of man, and this discord between his earnest wooing of nature and his frequent backward glances to the life of men suggests perhaps that he had not attained complete Buddhist enlightenment. Certainly, in contrast with the earlier Akahito, and the later Bashô, two other great lovers of nature who were suffused with its spirit, there is more of human weakness in Saigyô. Nevertheless, he marks an advance on Akahito, who was content to observe nature as it was, whereas Saigyô takes the love of nature a stage further by seeking for its essence. Moreover—and in this he differs from Shunzei—he based his life upon this essential nature in which he immersed himself. That gives a peculiar quality to Saigyô's humanistic tendency.

> Would that I were to die
> Underneath a cherry-tree
> In fullest blossom
> Upon the fifteenth day of
> This month of February!

This poem is characteristic, and the state of mind revealed lasted to the end of his days. His whole disposition was to spend himself in meditating on life and nature, and then to die under a cherry-tree on the fifteenth of the second month, the anniversary of the death of Buddha. From the time of his entry into the life of a priest, when he was twenty-three, until death fifty years later, in the spring of 1190 at the age of seventy-three, he lived in constant communion with nature.

The poet's real name was Satô Norikiyo, his name in religion being En'i or Saigyô. He was born in 1118 and entered the Court service as one of the military guards. Then, in 1140, at the age of twenty-three, he gave up both his official position and his wife to live the life of a priest at Saga. In 1146, when he was about twenty-nine, he made a journey on foot to the Ninna-ji temple, and then on to Kii province and the eastern districts. Ten years later, on the death of the ex-Emperor Toba, Saigyô was one of the party responsible for translating his remains to the Anrakuju-in temple. He seems to have spent many years in seclusion on the religious mountain of Kôya-san, but in 1167, when about fifty years old, he contemplated making a journey to Shikoku, and in the following year undertook a pilgrimage to the Shiraminé shrine in Sanuki province. He ap-years also to have made a tour of the Tsukushi province. In 1184, when he was sixty-seven, he contributed some of his poems to *Senzaishû*, which was then being compiled by Shunzei. Two years later he undertook a journey to Ôu in the north-east, and on his way thither visited Yoritomo at Kamakura and Hidehira at Hiraizumi. He died in 1190.

When, as a young samurai, he had entered the service of the ex-Emperor Toba Jôkô, he had received many favours; but once he had become a bonze he gave up everything to live the life of an itinerant priest with nature as his sole companion. He would seem to have pondered deeply and often over the events of the changing world; this brought him nothing but agony from which he emerged to find peace in harmony with the life of nature.

He was, indeed, far from being a feeble character. His appearance was potent enough to overawe the sage Mongaku, whilst, in the presence of the mighty Yoritomo, he conducted himself with dauntless courage. In any case it must have taken a very stout heart to follow so sincerely as he did the course dictated by his convictions. His very poems ran contrary to the accepted fashion, and it was just because they were the creation of such a temperament as his that their characteristic style found acceptance. His life was in harmony with his art, and the deep affection for Saigyô as a man contributes not a little to the favour and esteem with which his work is regarded.

Sanka Wakashû is also known as *Sankashû* and *Saigyô Hôshi Kashû* Poetical Works of the Priest Saigyô). Its date is uncertain, and there is also divergence of opinion as to whether or not he made the compilation himself. Even if he did compile it in its original form, there is no doubt that it was enlarged afterwards by the inclusion both of draft poems in his own handwriting and of those dictated to his disciples and friends.

There are various texts, differing in the number of poems included. *Sankashû* contains just over 1,570 poems. Besides these many other poems survive in *Ihon Sankashû* (Variant of the Sankashû) and *Saigyô Shônin Kashû* (Poetical Works of the Sage Saigyô), so that altogether his surviving poems may number more than two thousand.

KINKAI WAKASHÙ

(The Poetical Works of Sanetomo)

Kinkai Wakashû is the title given to the poetical works of Mina
moto-no Sanetomo who, because he marks a return to the style o
Man'yôshû, holds a peculiar position in the history of poetry. A new
poetic fashion was set by the compilation of *Kokinshû* in the Heian
period, a development which was continued in the verse of *Senzaish*
and *Shin-Kokinshû*, to culminate in the *yûgen* (lonesome) and *yûshi*
(emotionalistic) styles, the course of this evolution being represented
by the work of such poets as Saigyô, Shunzei and Teika.

Minamoto-no Sanetomo objected to both the "lonesome" and
the "emotionalistic" styles on the ground that the poetry of these
two schools had developed a tendency to art for art's sake, more o
less diverging from reality. It was in reaction to this trend that
Sanetomo took up an attitude which may be described as one o
"art for life's sake," deriving his inspiration from the ancient
Man'yôshû, which, as a samurai, he admired for its artless and virile
qualities. It may be that Sanetomo's youth and the fact that he
had little or no association with the dominant poetic schools o
his day enabled him the more directly to enter into the heart o
Man'yôshû and return to the spirit of the ancient days. A few quota
tions may help us to trace his mental development.

Such a verse as the following shows that a realization of the
uncertainty of life is the starting-point of his poetry :—

> Though he has nothing
> Of the appearance of death,
> To my great sorrow
> I know with each passing day
> More feeble will he become.

This poem refers to an aged priest of over ninety years of age who
was failing, although in the poet's opinion he was not yet at death's
door. The very manner of the poem reflects the old man's gradual

and continuous sinking. The mutability of life has often been the theme of poetry already in *Man'yôshû*, but with Sanetomo, as we see in his *Kinkai Wakashû*, the feeling is much more poignant. Here the spirit of the times, or, it may be, Sanetomo's own individuality differs from the more unaffected spirit of *Man'yôshû*. With this difference of outlook he sang much in the same way as the poets of *Man'yôshû* of a limitless affection for the State and its gods. One of the most outstanding examples is :—

> Should the day come
> When the mountains are torn up
> And the seas run dry,
> Even then my loyalty
> To the Emperor I vow.

In thus simply and frankly yet vigorously pledging his loyalty to the Emperor, come what may, the author of *Kinkai Wakashû* has much in common with the Man'yôshû poets.

Sanetomo also pondered deeply over human life and gave expression to its various aspects. Already we have quoted the poem showing his deep concern for old age, but he has an equal sympathy with childhood, especially with a parent's love for a child and a child's helpless yearning for his mother.

> How pitiful this !
> A sight to make unending
> Tears stream down the cheeks !
> An orphan child is seeking
> For his lost mother in vain.

From the *kotobagaki* (the introductory note) we learn that this poem was inspired by the actual sight of a little orphan by the roadside, tearfully seeking his lost mother. Quite naturally the poet's tears mingle with those of the child. This poem quickening our human sympathies has no equivalent for poignancy in the whole of the *Hachidaishû* (The Eight Anthologies).

Another instance is :—

> Among the dumb beasts
> Which we see all around us,
> Even among them

Do parents love their younglings.
How touching it all is!

The introductory note gives the subject of this poem as "A Merciful Heart." Evidently it was a *daiyei*, a composition written upon a pre-arranged subject, but the poet's very choice of the existence of parental love among the beasts of the field, which is responsible for the strong impression it makes on us, is convincing evidence of the breadth and depth of his love for all living things. In the original the impression is certainly helped by the skilful use he makes of such particles as *sura* or *dani* (even) and *kanaya* (how), but the essential thing is the spirit of sympathy that shines through it. The poet's love for the State is combined with a love for all that is comprised therein, all human beings and every living thing, and he observed and expressed all the various phases of life around, escaping, however, anything in the nature of either intellectualism or subjectivity.

As he looked out from the summit of Mount Hakoné, he was impressed by the grandeur of Nature suddenly presented to his eyes, and he wrote :—

> As I came over
> The pass of Mount Hakoné,
> My eye was caught by
> The waves washing an islet,
> Oh, off the Izu Province!

The phrase "Oh, off the Izu Province" does reveal something of an exclamatory temperament, but all the same the poem as a whole shows a pure reaction to the beauty of nature; certainly there is no petty emotionalism or intellectuality. A further instance is :—

> Oh, raging billows
> That dash from the great ocean
> Up on to the beach,
> With a tumult of cleaving,
> Breaking, splitting, scattering.

This is a pure, objective expression of the grandeur of nature. Above all, the onomatopoeia of the phrase, *wareté kudaketé saketé chiru kamo* (cleaving, breaking, splitting and scattering) shows how the diction of *Man'yôshû* which was his inspiration had been fused into the poet's own mode of expression. This poem does indeed suggest the employment of a more conscious technique than in the preceding poem, yet there is no denying the correct and vigorous grasp of the particular aspect of nature he describes.

Thus, in the observation both of life and nature, he succeeded in comprehending the mood of *Man'yôshû*, and also, as regards the method of expression, he adopts the diction and at times the very tone of that anthology. In such respects his work is in full accord with *Man'yôshû*. Yet it should be hardly necessary to point out that, although Sanetomo's poems on the whole deal with ideas and feelings similar to those of the ancient anthology, yet they lack its virility and clarity and show much of the sombreness and weakness which mark the spirit of his time. The expression of idealistic feelings is much commoner than in *Man'yôshû*, and, for the most part, these are manifestations of the poet's own personality, based indeed on the spirit of the great anthology of the Nara period, but expressive of his own sorrowful reactions to the pain of life.

He can be best understood and appreciated if it be remembered that he had no intention of composing outstanding masterpieces or of attempting to gain any reputation as a poet. His life was short—he was only twenty-eight when he died—and, in spite, or even because, of his high rank, it was spent in unrest and anguish. When he turned to the world of ancient poetry it was as a way of life, and the inspiration he derived was crystallized in *Kinkai Wakashû*, a sigh, so to speak, from the very depths of his heart. His case was not unlike that of Saigyô, who sought release by leading a wandering life in touch with nature, and also produced poetry that flowed from his heart with spontaneous emotion. Different though these two poets were in their attitude to poetry, they both emerged from the agitation of thought that prevailed from the end of the Heian to the beginning of the Kamakura period, and both of them expressed themselves, each in his own way, in all sincerity. An immortal place in the history of *waka* poetry has been accorded to *Sanka Wakashû* of Saigyô, and *Kinkai Wakashû* of Sanetomo deserves scarcely less.

Minamoto-no Sanetomo was a son of the great Yoritomo, by his wife Masako, and was born on the ninth day of the eighth month, 1192. His child-name was Senman. After the death of Yoritomo, the first Shogun of the line, the office passed to his elder brother Yoriié and after him to Sanetomo, who thus became third Shogun. In December, 1204, he married a daughter of Bômon Nobukiyo, a Kyoto court-noble, an indication of Sanetomo's interest in the Kyoto culture. Soon afterwards, in the spring of 1205, still only a youth, he composed twelve poems. It was just after this that he had an opportunity of reading *Kokinshû* and *Shin-Kokinshû*. This led him to send to Teika thirty compositions in verse written after 1206 for his criticism. On returning the poems, Teika sent at the same time his *Kindai Shûka* which he wrote for Sanetomo, together with a copy of *Man'yôshû*. Sanetomo, thus coming into contact for the first time with this anthology, determined to rid himself of current fashions and follow *Man'yôshû* style. He then devoted himself to the pursuit of his new poetic inspiration as a relief from sad reflections on his own unfortunate position due to the oppression of the Hôjô family. About the same time, a Chinese official of the Sung dynasty, named Ch'en Ho-ching, came to Kamakura for an audience with Sanetomo. He declared that Sanetomo in a previous existence had been the Superior of the monastery on Mount Ts'ung Chao Yu. Sanetomo himself had a dream of similar import and was so much affected that he bade Ch'en build him a ship in the Chinese T'ang style as he contemplated a voyage to China, but this voyage was never made.

Sanetomo was appointed Sadaishô (General of the Left) in 1218, and in the sixth month of that year he paid a visit to the Tsurugaoka Hachiman-gû shrine at Kamakura to celebrate his inauguration to that office. On the second day of the twelfth month he was appointed Udaijin (Minister of the Right), and it was while paying a nocturnal pilgrimage to the same shrine on the twenty-seventh day of the first month, 1219, in connection with this appointment that he was assassinated, the assassin Kugyô having hid himself behind the great gingko tree and stabbing Sanetomo as he was descending the stone steps.

Sanetomo's extreme sensitiveness enabled him to develop his own characteristic style of poetry at a very early age. Although belonging to a dominant samurai family he was naturally an aesthete inspired with high ideals and greatly interested in the culture of Kyoto. Inevitably his poetic and cultural aspirations came into onflict with his situation as a samurai, and therein lies his tragedy. Nevertheless, the success he achieved as a poet and the accomplishment of no small body of good work must have afforded him some onsolation in the incessant conflict between the ideal and the real.

Kinkai Wakashû, or *Kinkaishû*, which contains Minamoto-no ane.omo's poetical works, is also called *Kamakura Udaijin Kashû* (The Poetical Works of the Minister of the Right at Kamakura). It divided into Spring, Summer, Autumn, Winter and Miscellaneous, nd, according to the Jôkyô ext, contains 719 pieces; while a re- ently discovered text, an heirloom in the Te.ka family, contains ten ieces more.

This latter text bears the date in Teika's own hand of " the Eight- enth Day of the Twelfth Month in the Third Year of the Kenryaku .ra " (1213). When Sanetomo died in 1219 he was twenty-eight ears old, and so, if *Kinkai Wakashû* was finished by the date given y Teika, he was only twenty-two years old when the work took s present form, and we have none of the compositions he may have roduced after that date. This view, however, is in conflict with 1e opinion that those of Sanetomo's poems, which are based on *Man'yôshû*, date only from about the eleventh month of 1213, when 'eika presented him with a copy of that ancient anthology. Never- 1eless we cannot escape the conclusion that the appearance of the ext in the possession of Teika dated 1213 shows that Sanetomo must lready have made acquaintance with the style of *Man'yôshû* some time efore that date.

Although the actual bulk of *Kinkai Wakashû* is not very great, it 1ust be accepted as a collection of poems notable not only for the uthor's own style but also for its merit as representing the then xceptional Man'yôshû style of the Middle Ages.

HEIKÉ MONOGATARI

(Tales of the Heiké)

The Middle Ages are marked by much notable "battle literature," known as *senki-bungaku* or *gunkimono*, among which the most outstanding is undoubtedly *Heiké Monogatari*. This famous Japanese epic narrative, which now consists of twelve books, was for long handed down by oral tradition. It used to be recited to the accompaniment of the *biwa* (lute), played by blind bonzes, and, inevitably, in the course of its oral transmission underwent many changes before it arrived at its present form. The work deals with the fate of that powerful oligarchy, the Taira or He ké clan, presenting them in all their glory and ending with their tragic defeat by the Minamoto or Ge ji clar, who wrested power from them.

The note of the tragic story is struck by the opening description of the bell of the monastery of Gion (Jeta-vana) tolling the knel of all earthly things, while the beautiful flowers of the majestic Indian sal-tree bloom to reveal the eternal truth that "pride goeth before a fall." The prosperous never live long, but their glory i destined to be as brief as a dream on a night in spring. The valian also are subject to the same doom, passing like grains of dust in the wind.

Now, the power and glory of Taira-no Kiyomori, the Presiden of the Council (Dajôdaijin), surpassed all belief. At one time simpl a military commander, he had risen rapidly to the highest rank an the greatest prosperity possible to a subject. He, and all the mer bers of the Heiké family, boastful of their high honours and might power, had risen like the mounting sun.

There were many who bitterly resented the Heiké's high-hande ness, among them Narichika,, the new Chûnagon (Counsellor c Middle Rank). He mustered an army under his banner at Shishigata in Kyoto in order to attempt the overthrow of the Heiké famil Knowledge of this attempt, however, leaked out prematurely, an

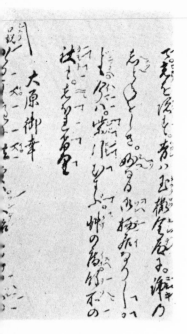

HEIKÉ MONOGATARI.
...xt-book with musical note. print.
... in the 19th century. Owner : To-
...o University.

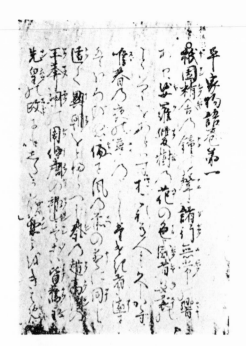

HEIKE MONOGATARI
(TALES OF THE HEIKÉ).
Manuscript copy in the 15th
century. formerly owned by the
Ômura family.

NIFON NO
COTOBA TO
Historia uo narai xiran to
FOSSVRV FITO NO TAME-
NI XEVA NI YAVA RAGVETA-
RV FEIQENO MONOGATARI.

...VS NO COMPANHIA NO
...llegio Amacusa ni voite Superiores no go men-
...jio co aru coto no fan ni qixamu mono nari.
Go xxxxx yori M.D.L.XXXXII.

WANDERING BLIND MU-
SICIAN. A CHANTER OF THE
HEIKE MONOGATARI.
(From a scroll made in the 15th
century.)

HEIKÉ MONOGATARI. Writ-
ten in spoken Japanese and
Romanized by Fabian, a Japanese Jesuit. Printed in 1592 at
Amakusa, Kyûshû.

Narichika, the leader, was exiled with Priest Shunkan, while Priest Saikô was beheaded. Kiyomori was even inclined to suspect the ex-Emperor Go-Shirakawa, who had entered the religious life, of complicity in the plot; he was only prevented from laying irreverent hands on him by the tear-laden petition of his eldest son, Shigemori, who hastened to him to urge on him the duty of loyalty. So troubled indeed was Shigemori at his father's growing arbitrariness, which he felt presaged a quick doom for the Heiké,, that he made continual prayer to die, and as if in answer to his prayer, he was soon afterwards carried off by a brief illness.

After his son's death, Kiyomori's tyranny became still harsher, and all the highest positions and offices passed into the hands of his family. The Heiké confined the ex-Emperor to the Palace of Toba-den, and, installing a three-year-old prince as the Emperor Antoku, governed the country subject to no other control but their own desires. By such despotism the number of their enemies was greatly increased. In the fifth month of 1180, Minamoto-no Yorimasa took up arms under the banner of Prince Mochihito, the second son of the ex-Emperor. But the time was not yet ripe and the plot was revealed. The prince had to flee, disguised as a woman, to the temple of Mii-dera. The priests of that temple had long been awaiting an opportunity of avenging themselves on the hated Kiyomori. They gladly welcomed the prince and took up arms in his defence, but they were outnumbered, and after a severe fight were driven in defeat across the river Uji, where Yorimasa killed himself with his own sword, while the unfortunate prince was shot to death. To consolidate his position further Kiyomori next transferred the capital from Kyoto to Fukuhara in Settsu province, causing the Emperor to be removed there. By this time the whole country was filled with dissatisfaction owing to the extreme arbitrariness and violence of the Heiké which had caused widespread suffering among the people.

It was on the advice of a fierce militant priest, Mongaku Shônin, and with the secret support of the ex-Emperor Go-Shirakawa that Minamoto-no Yoritomo took up arms in Izu province where he gained the victory in his first battle. After this victory, Yoritomo marched on the capital, and to meet this dangerous threat to their power the Heiké sent an army eastwards under Koremori and Tadanori which encountered the Genji army at the river Fuji.

Meanwhile the whole of the eastern district had fallen into the hands of Yoritomo, who was now in possession of a force that greatly outnumbered his enemy. The Heiké samurai were dismayed when confronted with the might of the Genji. They were defeated before a battle was fought, for, trembling at the fires kindled by the m untain farmers, and terrified by the noise of the flapping w'ngs of waterfowl at dead of night, they took to an ignominious flight, so that there was not a single enemy soldier to thwart the advance of the Genji forces next morning.

While this was happening, Kiyomori found himself forced to yield to the growing public anger and dissatisfaction over the transfer of the capital to Fukuhara, and decided to return to Kyoto.. Once this decision was known, everyone hastened back thither. Kiyomori himself led an expedition against the troops of the Kôfuku-ji temple at Nara, which had taken the side of the unfortunate Prince Mochihito, and utterly crushed them. In the course of this expedition, numerous famous temples, shrines and Buddhist images at Nara were destroyed by fire. Among them was the celebrated Daibutsu, the great image of Buddha standing in the Daibutsu-den of the Tôdai-ji temple. It suffered serious damage, but was later restored to its present appearance.

About that time the ex-Emperor Go-Shirakawa's son, the Emperor Takakura, who had recently abdicated, passed away, his life shortened with anxiety and despair over the state of the times. He was the wisest leader of the time, and the people who had thus lost him grieved as though the light of the sun and moon had been taken from them. From his boyhood, the Emperor Takakura had been distinguished by a rare refinement and a merciful spirit, and *Heiké Monogatari* relates mar.y stories about him. One of the most pathetic of these deals with his sad love affair with a beautiful young Court lady, Kogô-no Tsuboné. This lady stood high in the favour of the Emperor, and Kiyomori therefore plotted to kill her. So in order to escape him she fled in secret one night from the Imperial Palace, not a soul knowing where she had gone. The Emperor was heart-broken at losing her and bade Nakakuni, his attendant, find her at all costs. The moon was shining brightly when he set out, and he remembered that Kogô was an accomplished *koto* player and would love to play to herself on such a moonlight night. Whipping up his horse he went on to search all over Saga plain, and at last was rewarded by hearing the music of Kogô's *koto* from a humble cottage. The tune she was playing was the ancient *Sôburen*, telling of conjugal happiness; as she played she was no doubt thinking of the Emperor. In obedience to the Emperor's fervent desire, she suffered Nakakuni to bring her back to Court, but when Kiyomori heard of her return he had her arrested and banished to the seclusion of a convent.

The news was brought post-haste to Kiyomori that the Genji adherent, Kiso Yoshinaka, had roused the northern districts to revolt, in concert with Yoritomo in the east, and was about to march on the capital. He mustered the army of the Heiké, but, just as he was about to lead it to the front, he was taken suddenly ill. In great anguish of body and spirit, Kiyomori died at the age of sixty-four. He had brought the Heiké clan to its zenith; but now, deprived of their central figure, the Heiké immediately felt their feet were set on the road to ruin.

Caught as they were between the two forces of the Genji, Kiso Yoshinaka in the north and Minamoto-no Yoritomo in the east, the fate of the Heiké now hung in the balance. Not even then, however, were they able to rouse themselves from their long dream of peace, success and luxury. They continued to pass their time in the aesthetic pursuits of poetry and music, and in viewing the cherry blossoms and the moon, while Kiso Yoshinaka daily approached nearer to the capital with his irresistible army. One by one, the provinces broke away to join the Genji, until there was scarcely an inch of ground on which the Heiké could live in peace. They had to tear themselves away from the capital, and, after tearful partings from wives and children, fled with the Emperor Antoku to the west. On that autumn night the dewy hedges wetted the sleeves of the fugitives as if with still more tears, while the very brightness of the moon seemed to be dimmed with the weeping of the Heiké clan, uprooted from the capital where they had once so proudly vaunted themselves.

They found a temporary resting place in the seat of Dazaifu Government in Kyushu, only to be soon ejected thence. Endless was their journeying, as they struggled along unfamiliar mountain paths with their long sleeves tucked up or were tossed about on the sea in small boats. It was a tragic ending for them.

Yoshinaka meanwhile had occupied the capital and established himself in the place of the Heiké, but becoming flushed with his victory gave offence to the ex-Emperor Go-Shirakawa.. His outrageous oppression of the people also aroused general hatred, and eventually, Yoritomo, by Imperial command, despatched a force to subjugate him under Minamoto-no Ysohitsuné, his younger brother. The two armies met at the ferry of the river Uji, where Yoshinaka's forces were utterly defeated and he killed himself.

Meanwhile the Heiké had gradually rallied their forces in the central part of the country, taking up their positions at Ichinotani in Settsu province. But Yoshitsuné's troops attacked them from the rear by surging down the steep precipice of Hiyodorigoé behind Ichinotani, and the Heiké army, thus taken unawares, was quickly routed. They rushed down to the sea in front of them, where most of them were slain or drowned.

Most pathetic of all was the death of the youthful Atsumori. This young Heké samurai was spurring his horse into the sea towards the boats lying just off the shore, when he was challenged from behind by one of the Genji samurai named Kumagai-no Jiô Naozaré. Older, stronger and more skilful, Naozané forced the Heiké warrior to dismount on the beach and removed his helmet in order to cut off his head. But as he looked in his face and saw a handsome youth, his face lightly powdered and of about the same age as his own son fighting in the same battle, in pity Naozané would have spared the boy, but, unfortunately, he was surrounded by men of his own side and could find no way to let him escape. Since the youth was destined to be killed, he preferred to slay him with his own hands and afterwards say masses for the repose of his soul. So he cut off his head, weeping when he saw the youthful form of the samurai with a flute at his side and bearing every evidence of elegance and taste, lying dead at his feet. This rugged samurai from the east was so deeply touched that, realizing the pity and uncertainty of human life, he afterwards entered the priesthood.

The defeated Heiké who had managed to escape in boats were carried along at the mercy of the winds and tides. They found temporary shelter in the Island of Yashima, but there Yoshitsuné, again in obedience to the command of the ex-Emperor, pursued and attacked them. The Heiké fought a long and desperate battle from their boats. At the height of the battle, the Genji army on shore saw a beautiful lady beckoning to them from a richly ornamented boat, and pointing up to a fan, decorated with a crimson disk on a white ground, which had been placed at the top of a long pole. Yoshitsuné ordered Nasu-no Yoichi, an expert archer, to accept the challenge. He rode some distance into the sea after the boat as it receded into the distance and loosed his bolt. The crimson fan, shining in the evening sun, fell fluttering down on the white waves, while friend and foe joined in an outburst of admiration at his skill.

Worsted once again, the Heiké resumed their endless journey until they were finally overcome in the decisive sea-fight off Danno'-ura in Nagato province. All the members of the once prosperous Heiké clan were annihilated on this sea-shore in the distant west.

As an aftermath of this victory of Yoshitsuné, his elder brother, Yoritomo, afraid of his brilliant deeds and mounting power, proved a ready listener to the slanders of Kajiwara Kagetoki and interrupted the triumphal return of Yoshitsuné, even sending a large force against him. In face of this, Yoshitsuné decided to turn back to the west and there take refuge until his elder brother relented. He sailed out of Daimotsuno'ura, but was shipwrecked in a gale and beaten back to shore. On landing he made his way to Yoshino-yama in Yamato province, where Yoritomo's men again attacked him. So he fled to Nara and then returned to the capital, eventually to escape north to Ôu.

Such is the outline of *Heiké Monogatari*, a mixture of history, tradition and fiction. It gives a sympathetic picture of the rise and fall of the Heiké, and, although the work as a whole is concerned with the struggles between the Heiké and Genji clans, it has the character of a national epic. Or one may describe it as a romance, wrought out of historical facts with lyrical and tragical power. A plaintive note is struck in numerous episodes subsidiary to the main plot, but yet a strain of gaiety often relieves the predominant pathos. We see how the aesthetic nobles of the Heian period, devoted to a dreamy, emotional and refined idea of life, never, even in the theatre of battle, unmindful of graceful accomplishment, were confronted and quickly crushed by the military genius and native vigour of the newly-risen Genji clan, as tender blossoms are scattered by the wind. The sad melody of the life of the Heiké still lingers in this prose elegy.

The chief contemporary idea running through *Heiké Monogatari* is the Buddhist view of the mutability of life, tinged with the theory of nemesis. The work opens with an exposition of the Buddhist view of the transience of all earthly things which permeates the whole, forming the directive idea behind the various phases of life presented. One battle follows another, the glories of this world pass quickly away, and all life is vain and precarious. It is no wonder that those who witnessed the process of the rise and fall of the Heiké clan should have been brought to dwell on life's mutability taught by Buddhism. Yet, offering a sort of contrast to this, great emphasis is also laid upon loyalty to the samurai's code of Bushido.

The literary value of the work is enhanced by its style which is a blend of the virility of the Chinese Han writing and the delicate lyricism of the Heian tale, making it a popular favourite as well as a masterpiece of battle literature. We can mark the beautiful rhythm and modulation and gauge its effect when it was originally recited; notable also is the impressive power of its plain and concise style— a general characteristic of most battle literature—its skilful and suggestive, albeit sometimes bombastic, expressions and the vivid, heroic quality of its battle scenes. In addition to this, the plaintive charm of its accounts of various wanderings and the episodical love stories, with a style varying according to the need of the subject, are enough to win for it a high place among the finest Japanese literary compositions. Finally, as a national epic, offering abundant material to later writers, it holds an important and permanent place in the history of our literature.

In the nature of the case there can be no definite opinion as to authorship. In the course of oral transmission and popularization, the work inevitably underwent a long and gradual process of revision, and may fairly be styled a product of the collaboration of the whole nation. The result is that there are more variations in the text of this than of any other outstanding literary work. The best of these from a literary point of view is the current text, the most widely read and therefore the most beautifully polished. Yet, as an example of the variety of the texts, we may mention *Genpei Seisuiki*, which, with its forty books, is much more voluminous and almost gives the impression of being a different work. The date of *Heiké Monogatari* also is unknown, but it may be roughly ascribed to 1250.

HÔJÔKI

(Notes of a Recluse)

Hôjôki belongs to the category of diaries, fugitive essays and records of journeys figuring so largely in Japanese literature. Although such works have not so high a place in literature as poetry, fiction and the drama, nevertheless there are among them some of considerable literary merit. One quality, indeed, they possess that one cannot expect to find in such works of imagination as poetry and fiction: they are usually written without any self-consciousness or literary ambition on the part of their authors, and so present their thoughts and deeds with greater frankness. Like *Makura-no-Sôshi* and *Tsurezuregusa*, *Hôjôki* is usually classified as a *zuihitsu* (fugitive essay), but it is much more systematic than these.

The work deals with the life of Kamo-no Chômei who lived the life of a hermit on Mount Hino-yama during the Kamakura period. It gives the motive for his retirement from the world and his views on life, and, although brief, is an impressive and touching account of the ideas and general attitude towards life held by Kamo-no Chômei and his generation.

In the opening lines the author expresses his view of life's mutability by comparing the life of a man to an everflowing stream. He develops this theme by describing the vicissitudes he himself has experienced. As illustrations of the chances and changes that mortals have to undergo, he gives vivid descriptions of the fire that ravaged the capital on the twenty-eighth of the fourth month, 1177, the great storm of the fourth month of 1180, and the transfer of the capital in the same year, together with various famines and earthquakes and other calamities. This picture of the evanescence of the material world provides the fundamental motive of Chômei's retirement. From this he proceeds to describe his life as a hermit. At the age of thirty or so, he had removed to a small cottage only one tenth the size of his former dwelling, but as he grew older, being then be-

tween fifty and sixty, he ardently desired a still greater seclusion. So
he built himself a small retreat, only one *jô* (ten feet) square on Mou.
Hino-yama. He describes his tiny abode in detail and his life within
it. Hence the title of the book, *Hôjôki*, which means "Life in a
dwelling one *jô* square (*hôjô*)."

Although the main purpose of his days was to devote himself to
prayer and the chanting of sutras, he had other interests, playing
musical instruments such as the *koto* (harp) and the *biwa* (lute). Also
he beguiled the long hours by making friends with the children who
lived at the foot of the mountain or by gazing in the direction of the
capital from the summit. He would also meditate on life and quietly
observe the various phases of existence, insisting that, if one is in
quest of a self-centred life as opposed to one of self-effacement in the
service of others, the tranquil existence of a hermit affords the best
conditions. Chômei had definitely adopted the negative attitude of
an anchorite, affirming that a man had a perfect right to live for his
own sake alone, so long as this involved no harm to others.

Hôjôki is only one of a number of literary works produced by
hermits at that time, all of them taking an egocentric view of life
based on the same acute feeling of life's uncertainty as shown by the
vicissitudes of human fortune. Not indeed that such a negative attitude was universal. On the contrary, even in those days, the production of the *gunkimono* or *gunki monogatari*, the battle literature,
shows that many samurai preferred to throw themselves boldly into
the midst of life's struggles. Nor again is the attitude of Chômei,
and those who follow the same trend as he, entirely negative. In
his hermit seclusion he was also pursuing the changeless, constant
values amid the ever shifting scenes around.

The style of *Hôjôki* is eminently suitable for the spirit and attitude
it expresses. The work rings true in that it is not only systematically
composed, but also expresses an attitude based on the author's own
concrete experience. There is a harmonious blending of Japanese
and Chinese Han styles of writing which gives an effect of vigour
touched with tenderness. Throughout, the profound learning of the
author is revealed, and the work appears as the crystallization of his
own life-long experience. We feel that within Chômei there is a
genuine passion which he has succeeded in harmonizing with his
reason to produce a deeply reflective nature.

He was the first man of letters to lead a solitary hermit's life, remote from the haunts of men, and this not as the outcome of mere caprice or a momentary impulse but of deliberate reflection. In a sense, this is to accept the mutual antagonism between natural impulse and reason, which is the keynote of Chômei's character and of his work. The same attitude was also found among his contemporaries in the early middle ages ; it is also the main reason for the continued popularity of this work.

Although the work is usually ascribed to Kamo-no Chômei, the late Dr Sakutarô Fujioka would not admit his authorship. He has won a certain amount of support for his view on the ground that the work is an imitation of the *Chiteiki* of the Heian period, a composition in the Chinese Han style. One can, however, readily admit the influence of the earlier work upon *Hôjôki* without it being necessary to deny Chômei's authorship. Indeed, it is hard to see who else could have written it. For, although the form is influenced by the earlier work, it is Chômei who describes his own life and expresses his views on life.

From the author's note we learn that the work was finished at the end of the third month, 1212, while internal evidence shows that it was written when the author had reached the age of sixty. Of the various different texts, that in the possession of the Daifukukô-ji temple, which has been reproduced by the Koten Hozonkai (the Society for Preserving National Classics), is more naive and concise than the current one. One may take it that this text in the Daifukukô-ji, which was copied during the Kamakura period not long after Chômei's death, is nearest to the original, and that it has been revised and enlarged until it has taken the form of the current text.

The author, Chômei, was also called Kikudayû, his name in religion being Ren'in. He was sixty-three or sixty-four years of age when he died in 1216. He was born of a family of Shinto priests in the hereditary service of the Kamo-jinja shrine in Kyoto, his father dying while Chômei was still a youth. In response to a summons from the ex-Emperor Go-Toba, who admired his poetic genius, he entered the service of the Imperial Poetry Bureau. As a poet, he was a disciple of the priest Shun'é, the son of Minamoto-no Toshiyori, and, like Shunzei, he followed the *yûgen*, the " lonesome," school of poetry. According to *Iyenaga Nikki*, failure to become a Shinto priest drove him into the Buddhist priesthood. His tonsure and his awakening to the mutability of the world are due to some such similar cause.

His reputation as a poet is witnessed to by the gracious words of the ex-Emperor who entreated Chômei to remain in the service of the Bureau even after his renunciation of the world. *Azumakagami* shows that he made occasional visits to Kamakura to see the Shogun Sanetomo, and, despite his seclusion, he never lost his interest in Buddhism and in art. Together with Saigyô and Kenkô, he holds a brilliant position in the history of Japanese literature as one of the mediaeval hermit-authors.

Besides *Hôjôki*, Chômei wrote *Mumyôshô*, *Hosshinshû* and many other works, while others are wrongly attributed to him. His poems are, for the most part, included in *Kamo-no-Chômei-shû* (Works of Kamo-no Chômei), while twenty-five of his lyrics are also to be found in *Shin-Kokinshû*.

TANNISHÔ

(Sorrow for Misbelief)

Tannishô is included in the Analects of the great religious leader Shinran (1173–1262) whose life is obscured by innumerable traditions. Still the following facts about him can be accepted with considerable confidence.

Shinran entered the priestly life while still a youth and lived austerely on Mount Hiyei. Later he became a devout disciple of Hônen, accepting, like his master, with complete conviction the efficacy of *Nenbutsu*, the Invocation of Buddha Amitâbha. With his master also he suffered banishment and betook himself to the province of Echigo, where he married and had one child. On the termination of his period of exile, he built a hermitage at Inada in the province of Hitachi, where he preached to the rustic inhabitants during a space of more than twenty years. Later he returned to Kyoto where he lived nearly thirty years, dying at the ripe age of ninety.

His master Hônen had accomplished a great revolution in Japanese Buddhism. Prior to him Buddhism had been employed, at least in his view, for the advancement of earthly interests, whether by means of magical incantations or prayers or by the teaching of a strict and profound philosophy. He transformed it into an other-worldly religion of pure faith with implicit belief in the saving grace of Buddha Amitâbha. By a single stroke, he made what had been up till then rather a religion for the aristocracy into a faith for the masses, and translated the aim of Buddhism from the earth to the skies. With the rise of Zen Buddhism as a new Buddhist sect appealing to the samurai class, the appearance of Hônen was the greatest event in the early Kamakura period, marking an epoch in the history of Japanese Buddhism.

The form of Buddhism known in the Nara period had already undergone a great change during the Heian period, when Dengyô and Kôbô between them had brought about its Japanization. Hônen went a long way further. Yet his work had been largely among the samurai and the aristocracy, among whom he had many powerful devotees, for though he had many enemies who brought about his banishment, he certainly enjoyed a great popularity during his life-time. Shinran, on the other hand, was an obscure figure, whose activities brought him little prominence among his contemporaries. Yet, for that very reason, he served as the necessary complement to the distinguished Hônen, having a much more suitable character for building up a religion for the masses, such as the teaching of Hônen, by its very nature, was destined to become.

Shinran lacked the originality of Hônen. Although tradition has associated the Buddhist toleration of meat diet and marriage of the clergy with his name, there is little historical justification for this. As is clear from the present work, his chief characteristic was his implicit obedience to the teachings of Hônen. The purity of his faith turned his commonplace character into an extraordinary one, making him a man of originality high above the common capacity for such attain-ment.

Tannishô is not from the pen of Shinran himself. Indeed, the authorship is uncertain, although it is usually ascribed to the priest Yuiyen who is mentioned in the text; still even if not from his pen, it truly represents both the views and the spirit of Shinran.

We are told in the Preface that the expression "tani" is intend-ed to represent the grief felt by Shinran "over the widespread mis-understanding of the faith that is contained in the oral teaching of our late Master, Hônen." The aim of the work is then to combat the false views that had already begun to arise by putting on record the sayings of the dead Master which were still ringing in the ears of the compiler. The work is held in high esteem today as showing a purer aspect of Shinran's personality than has been conveyed in his own works. This personality comes out clearly in the extracts that follow below.

"Belief in the most merciful Amitâbha is everything, for he swore that he would never hope for Buddhahood for himself unless his desire for the salvation of all people was realized.

"My sole way of life lies in my unquestioning belief in the sayings of my predecessor, Saint Hônen (Hônen Shônin). I cannot tell whether I shall be born again in Paradise or fall into hell. Yet will I never repent even if my whole-hearted faith in my master, Saint Hônen, should lead me away from the path to Buddhahood. It would be pitiable indeed, if I were to be tricked into falling into hell by virtue of the Buddhist invocation (*Nenbutsu*), when I could have sought Buddhahood by the other method of self-reliance! I, however, who could never become a Buddha by any other means but was destined from the first to go to hell, would have nothing to repent of. Amitâbha proposes to save me, regardless of my great sins and worldly lusts. Because his Original Vow is true, Sakya's teachings cannot be false. And if his teachings are true, then Saint Zendô Daishi's interpretation of Buddhism and the sayings of Saint Hônen, which are definitely based on it, must also be true.

"There is no distinction of good and evil in the way of the *Nenbutsu*. There is no virtue higher than the *Nenbutsu*. No other virtues are necessary, nor are any vices to be dreaded, for there is no vice strong enough to resist the almighty power of the Amitâbha's Original Vow.

"People say that Paradise admits even the wicked, but still more the virtuous. But this is a mistaken way of putting it. Those who seek to attain Buddhahood by self-reliance have no particular need for the Lord Amitâbha's Original Vow. This is intended to aid those people who are not destined to be saved by their own self-reliance; that is to say, it is the wicked who are the main objects of Amitâbha's Vow. Therefore it is more correct to say that Paradise admits even the virtuous, but still more the wicked."

On being asked why the repetition of the *Nenbutsu* does not give rise immediately to the feeling of joy, nor to an impatient longing for Paradise, the Master Shinran confessed that he himself had harboured the same doubt as that which afflicted me. He admitted that it appeared strange indeed that we did not rejoice in those things which had originally made us dance for happiness. But we ought to console ourselves in the knowledge that it is this very fact that proves we are destined for Paradise. For it is the lusts of the flesh that keep joy far away from our hearts. It was his knowledge of this that caused Amitâbha to call men poor creatures possessed by earthly lusts, yet these very creatures are the main objects of the Original Vow. Therefore the lack of joy on our part only serves to show more convincingly our salvation by the Lord Buddha. Further, it is only these earthly lusts that overwhelm us with the fear of death whenever we are taken slightly ill, instead of causing us to long impatiently for Paradise. In other words, it is the very excess of our earthly lusts that makes us actually long after this world of suffering instead of leading us to yearn after Paradise. Amitâbha takes pity on such a state of mind, which is the object of his salvation. People would suspect that we had no earthly lusts at all, if we danced for joy and at the same time yearned for the attainment of Paradise.

"I have no disciple. If, according to my own discretion, I were to persuade others to pray to Amitâbha, then I might call such men my disciples. But everyone who has entered on a life of invocation by the recital of the *Nenbutsu* has done so through the invitation of Amitâbha himsefl, and so he must not be called a disciple of mine."

TSUCHI-NO-RÔ GOSHO

(An Epistle to One in a Dungeon)

Nichiren (1226–1282) affords a most striking contrast to Shinran. Owing to the intensity of his faith, he was filled with an impetuosity like that of a thunderbolt or a whirlwind. He was the fiercest man even in that fierce age which witnessed a great event unprecedented in Japanese history, the Mongolian invasion of these shores.

He was the founder of a powerful Buddhist sect, now known as the Nichiren-shû, or the Sect of Nichiren, and spent his whole life in one incessant conflict by pen and tongue for the propagation of that particular sutra of the Buddhist Scriptures in which he so fanatically believed. This was the *Hoké-kyô* (the Saddharma Pundarika Sutra) which he held to be the very quintessence of Buddhism; to him it was no mere constituent of the Buddhist Scriptures, but superseded them all, being the perfect synopsis of all that they contained. It was one with the Lord Buddha himself.

An age in which this sutra was despised, and in his opinion "openly violated," was too much for Nichiren to suffer without rebuke. He excluded nothing and nobody from his condemnation; he censured the central administration, the Kamakura Shogunate, and proclaimed that all the sects of Buddhism were blasphemous contradictions of the genuine teachings of Buddha. His unceasing denunciations declared, "The devotees of the Nenbutsu sect will fall into an everlasting hell; those of the Zen sect are possessed by evil spirits; the Shingon sect will destroy the State and the members of the Ritsu sect show themselves traitors to their country." The sect that he detested above all was the first of these, the Nenbutsu His fanatical ardour inevitably provoked retaliation. He was assaulted, exiled, and once was on the point of being beheaded by the officials of the Shogunate; but, undaunted, he regarded all these persecutions as proof of all that is taught in the *Hoké-kyô*. No man has ever been so perfectly convinced from first to last of the absolute rightness of what he taught and did as Nichiren; no man has ever been so persevering in the face of foes. Yet, on the other hand, it is doubtful if ever man was tenderer towards his friends than he.

The epistles he sent to his pupils, whether priests or laymen, are eloquent of his tender heart. Yet their tenderness is not of the kind ordinarily met with in daily life. It is much more than a vague sentimentalism. Just as much as his denunciations of his enemies, so these letters to his friends are a most convincing expression of genuine emotion. They are shot through and through with passionate expressions that penetrate the reader's mind. They are the throbbings of a living heart. And they are literary gems of a very high order.

It is noteworthy that in spite of the popularization of teachings by the founder himself, the Nichiren sect has exercised practically no influence on literature, whereas from the Nenbutsu sect which he hated so much has flowed a great literary influence. Besides his epistles, his other works, like *Kaimokushô* (First Glimpse) in which he expounds his beliefs and *Shuju Onfurumai Gosho* (Apology for Various Actions) where he gives us something of his life, are also to be regarded as masterpieces of belles-lettres.

Of his epistles, the work under consideration, *Tsuchi-no-Rô Gosho*, is an excellent example. It was written by Nichiren when on the point of setting out on his journey to exile in Sado, a punishment that he had brought upon himself by his unsparing arraignment of other Buddhist sects and the political administration of the Kamakura Shogunate. It was addressed to one of his friends and disciples, Nichirô, confined in a dungeon-cave near Kamakura.

"Nichiren is starting out for the province of Sado tomorrow," it begins. "Tonight's cold makes me wonder with all the more concern how you are faring in your prison. Nevertheless, since you have devoted yourself, body and soul, to the reading and practice of the whole *Hoké-kyô*, you are thereby endowed with the power of alleviating the lot of parents, of relations to the sixth degree of affinity, and of all men. Others read the *Hoké-kyô* only with their mouths, not with their hearts. And even if there be such as read it with their hearts, they fail to practice its precepts. How much the more then are you to be honoured, who both read the sutra with your heart and express it in your deed! Says the Sutra, 'Guarded by all those akin to Buddha, the devotees of this Sutra of the Wonderful Law

shall never be harmed either by swords and staves or by poisons.'
This promise assures me that nothing mortal can ever harm you. So
soon as you obtain your freedom, come to me at once; I assure you
of a warm welcome."

The last words should be translated literally, "I shall see you
and be seen by you," typical of the vivid way in which Nichiren
expresses himself. Nichirô to whom these kindly words were
addressed was a favourite disciple of Nichiren. He had attached
himself to Nichiren at the age of twelve, and the beautiful relationship between these two as teacher and disciple is even today a
favourite theme for dramas and novels. But it is noteworthy that the
great religious leader does not reserve his tenderness for any favourite,
not even such a one as Nichirô. We find the same deep tenderness
expressed in many letters sent to followers such, for example, as the
epistle to Shijô Kingo, a layman and one of the saint's earliest pupils,
that to Sennichini, wife of Abutsubô and afterwards a nun, whose
husband began by seeking to kill Nichiren while he was in exile in
Sado but afterwards was converted by hearing the saint's sermons,
and the last epistle he ever wrote, which was sent to Hagii, a devoted
follower and, in his master's later years, his protector, facilitating his
retirement to Minobu by giving him land there, building him a hermitage and generally looking after his well-being.

"Respectfully I beg to state," begins his last letter to Hagii, "that
I have safely arrived at Ikegami. The hills and valleys on the way
were rather difficult for me to cross, but I am glad to say that I have
come so far without mishap, thanks to the guidance of your sons.
Though I purpose to travel back again by the same road before long,
I cannot help fearing that I may die at any moment on account of
the poor state of my health. Your great kindness is always in my
thoughts. For nine long years you have taken good care of Nichiren who is regarded as a problem by all the people of Japan. I
cannot possibly express my thanks in words. Wherever I may chance
to die, I want you without fail to make my grave at Minobu. That
chestnut horse of yours pleases me very much, and I should like to
have him with me always, even to ride him as far as the hot-spring
of Hitachi. But then I feel what a pity it would be if the horse
should be stolen, so I have decided to leave him in charge of our
friend Mobara at his house in Kazusa until my return from the hot-

ring. In any case it would worry me if the horse were in the nds of a groom I did not know, so I do not want him to go out the hands of the man who looks after him at present."

This letter was written from the house of Ikegami Sôchû at egami in Musashi province, just after Nichiren's arrival there, to exess his thanks to Hagii for all his kindness and also to reassure him out his own health, especially since Hagii's regard for Nichiren's mfort had led him to furnish the saint with a horse and groom d to arrange for his sons to accompany him.

The circumstances in which the journey was undertaken were as llows. Nichiren, as is clear from the letter, fully realized that he as not far from death and wished, while he still had strength, to pay e more filial visit to his parents' graves. He was a very devoted n, and whenever he received an unexpected grant of alms or was ved from some impending danger, he attributed all this to the uardianship of his departed parents, who, he thought, never ceased om their merciful vigilance on him. He also intended to make se of the opportunity to go round to Hitachi in the hope that the ot-spring would be of some benefit to his health.

At the time of writing this letter, we can see that Nichiren was illy expecting to be able to continue his journey. But almost immediately after writing it, his illness took a critical turn and he died t the house in Ikegami.

———————

YÔKYOKU

(Noh Texts)

Yôkyoku (literally "chants") is the name given to the texts of the Noh plays, of which there are two hundred and forty-one in the combined repertoire of the various Noh schools.

The *yôkyoku* may be classified under the following five heads :

1. *Wakinômono,* "God pieces."
2. *Shuramono,* "Warrior pieces."
3. *Kazuramono,* "Woman pieces."
4. *Yobanmemono,* "Fourth pieces,"—better described as "Miscellaneous pieces."
5. *Kirinômono,* "Final pieces."

1. The God pieces usually open with the appearance of a God in the guise of an old man, who addresses himself to a visitor to the scene, giving him an account either of the history of the shrine dedicated to himself, or of some locally famous tree. Afterwards he assumes his divine appearance and entertains the visitor with the *kamimai* (god-dance) or some similar dance. In a few of the pieces in this group the leading characters are Goddesses.

2. The Warrior pieces have as their heroes the warriors of the Taira (Heiké) or Minamoto (Genji) clans. *Shuram no* might be literally rendered as the "Asura pieces," for the name derives from the inferno of fighting and bloodshed ruled over by Asura. According to Buddhist doctrine, all those who participate in battle, whether among the killers or the killed, are destined to eternal torment in this hell. These plays often describe how the spirit of one of these warriors seeking to escape such a destiny, may take advantage of an unguarded moment to fly back to this world where he may accost a bonze to entreat a mass on his behalf, through which he may obtain translation to paradise. In all the pieces in this group battles are presented rather as descriptions and do not necessarily form the principal theme.

3. Following the strictest principles of the Noh drama, the Woman pieces form the most important group, for beauty and elegance, their principal characteristics, are the essential features of a Noh play. The regular *kazuramono* contains a *jonomai*, a dance consisting of five movements and a prelude, but those with only a *chûnomai*, a dance of five movements without a prelude, are much more popular among the moderns who find the full *jonomai* rather tedious.

4. The Fourth pieces contain miscellaneous types, such as the *kuruimono* Mad pieces, the *onryômono* Revenge pieces, the *genzaimono* Earthly pieces. All are distinguished by their more human, and consequently more dramatic plots. Most interesting are the *kuruimono* with the theme of a mother crazed by grief over the loss of her child, the majority of such pieces ending in the happy reunion of the mother and the child. The Revenge pieces are chiefly ba ed upon jealousy and the action taken in retaliation for disappointed love. The term Earthly pieces is a curious one. In most of the Noh plays historical persons appear as spirits, whereas in the Earthly pieces they are represented as if they are still living in this world. As can be well understood, these are the most dramatic of all the Noh plays.

. The Final pieces, one of which should form the finale of a Noh programme, consist of the lively, even violent, performances of monters or other supernatural beings.

The regular Noh programme should consist of five plays, one from each of the five groups; but the programme may be reduced to three or expanded to seven pieces. Moreover, the order of the pieces may sometimes be changed; one of the Fourth pieces may come second, while sometimes a Finale may even be given first.

A count of the number of pieces extant in the different groups of the *yôkyoku* reveals the tendency taken by this form of drama over a period of five hundred years; there are forty God pieces, sixteen Warrior pieces, forty-one Woman pieces, ninety-two Fourth pieces, and fifty-two Final pieces. Needless to say, more than that number were composed—we have a list of over a thousand—but, in the course of time, these two hundred and forty-one plays have come to comprise the traditional repertoire. The enumeration given above shows that the Fourth pieces are by far the most numerous and this can be taken as evidence that they are the most popular.

It has been pointed out by Zeami that in the Muromachi period which saw the full development of the Noh, the quality of *yûgen* (gracefulness) was regarded as the chief essential of the plays. Since this was most fully expressed in the Woman pieces these came to be valued most highly. Even to this day, this high appraisal of the Woman plays is accepted as being logically correct, although the audiences clearly prefer the Fourth pieces. If we ask why the Fourth pieces have attained the first place in popularity, the answer will lie in finding out why the quality of *yûgen* has lost its fascination.

What is *yûgen*? "The essence of *yûgen* is beauty and elegance"— such, as we find from *Gakushû Jôjô*, is the answer given by Zeami himself. It finds its most perfect manifestation in pieces with a lyrical inspiration, and thus is best expressed in the Woman pieces. But while Zeami stressed the significance of this quality, his father Kan'ami, had placed *monomané*, the quality of realism, first, although he still regarded *yûgen* as necessary. Thus, although under Zeami' influence the quality of *yûgen* came to be given precedence, the quality of realism was present from the start and eventually has again taken precedence.

In the space available, it is difficult to do more than barely outline the history of the Noh drama. Briefly, the Noh, as we have it today, was brought to perfection by Kan'ami Kiyotsugu (1333–1384) and his son, Zeami Motokiyo (1363–1443). We must go much further back, however, for its origins, as far back as the Kamakura period. In those days the Noh, then called *Nôgei* (Noh performance) was staged by the actors of the mediaeval farces (*Sarugaku* and *Dengaku*). Gradually these performances took on a professional character, and in the provinces near the capital many groups of players were organized in guilds (*za*). Thus, in the early Muromachi period, we have in Yamato province four *za* of *Sarugaku* actors, and three *za* in Ômi province ; while there were also two *za* of *Dengaku* actors, one in each of these provinces. For a time these different *za* were in competition, but in the end the *Yamato Sarugaku* emerged the victor. The four *za* of the *Yamato Sarugaku* were the Yûsaki, Tobi, Takeda and Sakato, which later became respectively the Kanzé, Hôshô, Konparu and Kongô schools. Among these the dominant position was

eld by the Yûsaki, under Kan'ami, the victory of the Yûsaki mean-
g a triumph for his realism. This tendency was superseded by the
gen of his son Zeami, who raised his father's art to a higher degree
f perfection.

The art of Kan'ami won the patronage of the Shogun Ashikaga
oshimitsu, and thenceforth the Noh drama was regarded as an aristo-
atic pursuit. After Kan'ami's death, Zeami received even stronger
ıpport from the Shogun, and using his abilities to the utmost devel-
ped the Noh into an extremely elegant theatrical art. One may
escribe these two artists in the drama as the Japanese Aeschylus and
ophocles. But in the Noh drama there was no Euripides to bring
to perfection. It was the influence of Euripides' genius on Greek
agedy that laid down the lines which the modern drama in the West
ollowed; but since, in Japan, no greater artist followed Zeami, later
ges have rather devoted themselves to preserving the traditions of
ie Noh drama as it was left by him and Kan'ami.

It was in the Edo period especially that the feudal government
ave the Noh official recognition, so that it became increasingly for-
ıalized and polished in its technique. The extant pieces afford ample
vidence of how the style became encrusted with artificial ornamen-
ation. At the present day some of the freer spirits among the Noh
ctors are attempting to modernize and adapt the Noh to the require-
nents of the present age by reviving the free and experimental spirit
vhich the art enjoyed in its prime, rather than allow it to linger
ın as a relic preserved from the middle ages, but, so far, with little
ıerceptible effect.

In such an atmosphere as this, only the ancient playwrights are
steemed. Among them Zeami has left the greatest number of pro-
luctions, more than half the current repertoire being from his hand.
Other representative playwrights are his father, Kan'ami, his eldest
ıon (Kanzé) Jûrô Motomasa, (Kanzé) Kojirô Nobumitsu, Nobu-
nitsu's son (Kanzé) Yajirô Nagatoshi, Zeami's son-in-law Konparu
Zenchiku, Zenchiku's grandson Konparu Zenpô, Hiyoshi Saami
ınd Mimashi.

The general principles on which the *yôkyoku* were composed were
aid down at an early date. In actual practice, however, the construction varies greatly, and, strictly speaking, conforms in only a few
cases to the fundamental principles, for the Noh dramatists, even

Zeami himself, constantly sought variety in structure and aimed at originality in creative art.

Since the Noh play is a kind of operatic performance, the chief parts of the *yôkyoku* are those chanted by the chorus. The actors are mainly occupied in singing or chanting, and, except in the Fourth pieces, dialogue plays only a minor part both in bulk and importance. But the interest of the performance centres in the *mai* or dance. Although this cannot be discerned merely by reading the *yôkyoku*, the character of the play is actually determined by the kind of *mai* danced by the *shité* (First Actor); while the very words of the *yôkyoku* are also based on the *mai*.

The chief rôles are those of the *shité* (the Protagonist or First Actor) and the *waki* (the Deuteragonist or Second Actor). On occasion a Boy Actor as well as Third and Fourth Actors may be employed. In most of the plays the Second Actor appears on the stage as the representative of the audience, and during the performance of the principal part of the play sits down by a pillar merely as a spectator of the *mai* performed by the First Actor. This suggests that the dramatic intention of the Noh is to present the performance of one actor only. Yet although this may hold good with regard to many of the pieces, it is not so with others. Indeed, in the *genzaimono* which are included in the Fourth pieces, the Second Actor generally meets the First Actor on equal terms, giving rise to marked dramatic action.

TAKASAGO

Takasago, one of the most typical of the *wakinô* (God pieces), is performed chiefly on occasions of congratulation, being chanted notably at marriage ceremonies. It was written by the leading Noh dramatist, Zeami (Yûsaki Motokiyo : 1363–1443), and was originally titled *Aioi no Matsu* (The Pair of Pine-Trees Grown Together), which was abbreviated to *Aioi* (Grown Together).

One of the two old pine-trees stood on the sea-shore at Takasago in Banshû (Harima province), and the other on the beach at Sumiyoshi in Tsu no Kuni (Settsu province). Why then should they be called " aioi "—grown together—when thus separated by a stretch of the Inland Sea ? The mystery is explained by the fact that these two pine-trees were lovers, the pine-tree of Sumiyoshi being the husband and that of Takasago the wife, who, in spite of the estranging sea, were happy in the union of their hearts. Two may live together under the same roof and yet be unhappy, if their hearts are not in accord, but this pair of pine-trees were happy in their oneness of heart, although living far apart.

In the Noh play, the pine-trees appear on the stage as an Old Man and an Old Woman. The Old Man of Sumiyoshi used to visit the Old Woman of Takasago every night, and together they swept clean the ground beneath the pine-tree there and enjoyed the beautiful view. On one occasion a Shinto priest from Higo province in Kyushu, accompanied by his attendants, stopped at the shore of Takasago on his journey to Kyoto, the capital, in order to see the famous pine-tree. On landing, he met the old couple.

The stage presentation begins with the entrance of the Priest, the *waki* (Second Actor) taking this rôle. He wears a garment called *itsuita*, with a kind of white skirt called *ôkuchi*, a *kariginu* robe and a special head-dress, his attendants being similarly attired. His entrance is marked by the introductory music known as *shidai*. The first chant reveals the purpose of his journey, while in the second he tells how far he has come and of his arrival on the shore of Takasago.

〔145〕

Then to the introductory music called *shin no issei* enter the *shite* (First Actor) in the guise of an Old Man and his *tsuré* (Companion) dressed as an Old Woman. In accordance with Noh convention, both wear masks, the First Actor, the *koujijô* (or *kojô*), a noble mask for an old man, and his companion, a gentle-looking mask for an old woman called *uba*. Each also wears an appropriate wig and a pale robe called *mizugoromo*, the Old Man having a white *ôkuchi*, while both of them carry brooms. It is a spring evening and the evening-bell is rolling from a mountain temple. Then the two together chant in unison a passage that recalls the length of their peaceful existence and their expectation of a long life in the future.

Thereupon the Priest greets the old couple, who tell him the story of the pine-tree in the manner of a dialogue. As it develops, however, the place of the old couple is taken by the chanting of the Chorus, the most important passage which recounts the theme of the story being known technically as *sashi* and *kusé*.

The pine-tree is venerated among trees because as an evergreen it is the symbol of the eternal, never-failing prosperity both of the State and of the families that compose it. The pine-tree of Takasago owes its peculiar importance to its being one of the Aioi, the Pair of Pine-Trees Grown Together, which implies, first, the union of husband and wife, and so the harmonious union of all things, the family and the State. Further the word is taken in a philosophic and mystical sense to suggest the complementary nature of the positive and negative. It may, of course, be questioned whether the author himself really intended the meaning to be pressed so far as this, but it remains true that *Takasago* has always been taken as implying such a meaning.

When the old couple's story is finished, the Priest, already suspecting that they are no ordinary old couple, asks them to reveal their identity. After confessing that they are in fact the spirits of the sacred Aioi, they tell him they will wait for him in distant Sumiyoshi and then disappear into the sea. This means that the First Actor, with his Companion, makes his exit by way of the *hashigakari* (the bridge) to the greenroom beyond the raised curtain.

This ends the First Scene of the play.

The Priest, however, remains on the stage with his Attendants. As the strange couple have invited him to make the voyage to Sumiyoshi, he seeks a Boatman. The Boatman, who plays a comic rôle, comes into his presence, and the Priest tells him of the mysterious couple and their invitation. The Boatman advises him to set sail at once, since, without doubt, he has been addressed by the sacred spirits of the Aioi, and he undertakes to take him over in the newly-built boat of which he is the happy possessor. During the course of this inter-scene dialogue the First Actor changes his dress.

The Second Scene begins. The Priest and his Attendants, standing up together, chant in unison the *machi'utai* (the waiting song). This is to suggest that the Priest and his party have now arrived at Sumiyoshi across the sea, where they await those who have invited them.

Then to a brisk kind of entrance music called *deha*, the First Actor reappears, but now as the God of Sumiyoshi; he is seen as the Spirit of the sacred pine-tree of Sumiyoshi. His costume consists of a *kariginu* robe with a white skirt (*ôkuchi*), a wig of long black hair, surmounted with a head-dress or crown called *sukiganmuri*, and he wears a *kantan'otoko*, the mask of a pale young man. In the past, instead of this kind of mask, the *mikazuki*, a dignified brown mask, was customarily used.

He declaims an old song :—

> " *Waré mitemo hisashiku narinu*
> *Sumiyoshi no kishi no himematsu*
> *Ikuyo henu ran !* "
>> O time-honoured pine,
>> Ancient slender-leafed pine-tree,
>>> For ages growing
>> On the Sumiyoshi shore—
>> To what age hast thou attained?

After this, in order to entertain his visitors he begins, to the accompaniment of music, to perform a swift and blood-stirring dance called the *kamimai* (god-dance). Then, through the mouth of the Chorus, the Priest, who is deeply moved, expresses his gratitude. The God responds by praising the upright, divine and sovereign reign and informs him that the peace of the country rests on this harmony between heaven and earth.

This marks the end of the play, but one may add a few remarks by way of illumination. According to the opening lines, the Priest is merely visiting a noted pine-tree. It is on his arrival there that he finds it is one of Aioi, and this gives rise to various topics, the everlasting, the harmony of man and woman, the unity of the ruler and the ruled, the complementary nature of the positive and negative, and the nature of eternal peace.

The phrases "the ruler" or "the sovereign reign" are interesting. They do not refer to the Shogun, who at that time wielded supreme administrative power in Japan, but to the secluded Emperor. In the Noh plays not a single word in praise of the Shogunate is ever to be found, and this despite the fact that the Noh writers (who were also Noh actors) were under the constant protection of the Shogun, who granted them fiefs. This bears eloquent testimony to the reverence which was felt for the Emperor as a special being belonging to Japan from the days of its creation. Not only do we find this in the *Takasago*, but in many other *wakinô* (God pieces), more notably in *Yumi-Yawata*, which Zeami specifically wrote to express his reverence for the Emperor of his day, as is clear from the extant record of his talk on this matter to his son.

Next, one ought to note how classical Japanese poetry is touched on in *Takasago*. The simple beauty of the lyrical odes of *Man'yôshû*, our oldest anthology, is brought into contrast with that of *Kokinshû*, a later collection of the most refined lyrical songs, since *Man'yôshû* is symbolized by the pine-tree of Takasago, and the *Kokinshû* by that of Sumiyoshi, and these collections are contrasted in such a way as to emphasize the equal respect in which the two should be held. A distinctive feature of the days of the author, Zeami, was the tremendous influence of the poetical tradition of *Kokinshû*. Yet he felt that this should not lead to the neglect of the more ancient poetry. Even here he is stressing the necessity for harmony, in this case that between things old and new.

Lastly, one must remember the fact that, in the traditional taste of the Japanese, the *matsu* (the pine-tree) is the most highly esteemed of all trees—more than the *umé* (the plum-tree) with its fragrant flowers, the *sakura* (the cherry) with its cloud of beautiful blossom, the *momiji* (the maple) in autumn all brocaded with crimson leaves, or any other tree. This reflects how typical of the Japanese character is a simple, unaffected taste as well as a moral predisposition towards endurance and chastity.

KIYOTSUNÉ

(Kiyotsuné's Ghost)

Kiyotsuné is one of the *shuramono* (Warrior pieces). Most Noh plays of this group begin with the entrance of a travelling Bonze, who is entreated by the ghost of a dead Warrior to recite a prayer for his translation to heaven. But in this piece, instead of a Bonze, the dead Warrior's Retainer appears. His master Kiyotsuné has drowned himself off the shores of Kyushu in despair after his defeat, and he has returned in secret to the capital, Kyoto, in order to inform his mistress of her husband's death.

The Mistress (played by the *tsuré*, the Third Actor) is the first to appear, the scene being her dwelling. She sits down by the *wakibashira* (the third pillar), and, to the entrance music known as *shidai*, the Retainer (the Second Actor) takes the stage. He recounts his reason for his journey from the battle-field to the capital and, with the end of his *michiyuki* (travelling song), is supposed to have arrived at his destination, his Master's house. The Mistress rises to her feet and demands of him why he has come back alone. After much hesitation from fear lest she be overwhelmed with grief at her bereavement, he informs her of his master's tragic end.

Amid her tears, the Mistress shows bitter resentment against her husband. She could have accepted his fate with resignation, had he fallen in battle or died of sickness, but she finds it hard to forgive him for taking his own life. For thus he had broken his promise to live united in love with her forever.

Towards the end of this lament the chanting of the Chorus takes up the theme in her place. Up to this time she had wept in silence, for as a member of the fallen Taira (Heiké) clan she had to live in secret. But, since things had now come to this hopeless pass, she now expresses her grief aloud, like the cuckoo crying to the wan moon at dawn.

The Retainer tries to comfort her in her sorrow by producing an amulet bag containing a lock of her husband's hair, discovered in his boat. He hands this to her, suggesting that she look on it as a relic of her beloved and seek comfort from it. She, however, is so full of reproaches of him for his suicide and broken promise, that her inclination is to send it back to her dead husband, yet her deep love causes her to yearn for one more sight of him, even if it be only in a dream.

The dream scene follows.

Kiyotsuné (the First Actor) quietly appears. He wears *chûjô*, a mask representing a noble, a fine head-dress, a beautifully embroidered robe with a white skirt, a long sword, and a thin overrobe bright with gold adornments, one sleeve of which is hanging loose. As in a dream he moves slowly towards her and takes up the song by Ono-no Komachi in *Kokinshû*.

> " *Utatané ni koishiki hito o miteshi yori,*
> *Yumé chô mono wa tanomi someteki.*"
>> She who once did see
>> A vision of her lover
>>> As she lay in sleep,
>> Ever since has come to trust
>> In what she sees in a dream.

Then he cries, " O my love, I, Kiyotsuné, have come to you." But the Mistress cannot be sure whether it might not be a reality after all, and not a dream. Yet she rejoices to see him, although she cannot forget the resentment she feels against him.

Kiyotsuné is displeased that she has thrust back at him the lock of his hair, which he had sent as a keepsake, while she defends herself by saying that the sight of it disturbs and tortures her. The mutual reproaches of this lovers' quarrel are chanted emotionally by the Chorus. Finally, Kiyotsuné entreats her never more to utter bitter reproaches against him, since he has come back in order to tell her why he took his own life. This explanation forms the principal part of the play.

Kiyotsuné begins by telling her how the forces of the Taira (Heiké) clan, to which he belonged, were so hard pressed by the enemy clan of the Minamoto (Genji) that they could scarcely reach the shore of Yanagiga'ura in Buzen province, how they offered up prayers at the ancient shrine of Hachiman (the God of War) at Usa nearby, seeking an oracle, and how the oracle prophesied their failure, so that all were dismayed, especially Kiyotsuné himself, who was led thereby to desire death.

The rest of the pathetic story is then chanted by the Chorus in a passage that is technically termed *kusé*. It tells how the despairing nobles of the Taira clan set out on a voyage to which there was no end, since the neighbouring regions, wherever they turned, were crowded with hostile troops. The very sight of the white egrets, perching in flocks on the rows of pine-trees by the sea-shore, curdled their blood with fear, for they mistook them for the banners of the enemy, which were white, in contrast to the red ensigns of the Taira clan. " Woe is me ! " Kiyotsuné cried to himself, " Sooner or later death comes to every man. Forever drifting miserably at the mercy of the waves will not save us. The glory of the past can never return, while the cares of this world are unending. Life is nothing but a long, weary pilgrimage. I have lost all hope for this world."

Having thus reached his decision, he stood on the deck at dawn. There he gazed upon the pale moon as it sank in the west and prayed it to take him to that far western bourne where is Sukhâvatî, the blessed Paradise of Buddha. So, for the last time on earth, he played an *imayô* song on his flute, and then, crying, " Hail Amidha Buddha, receive my soul, I pray ! " he plunged into the waves.

To the accompaniment of the chanting of the Chorus and the strains of the Musicians, the First Actor performs a dance suggestive of Kiyotsuné's actions at this fatal time.

After Kiyotsuné had thus drowned himself he descended into *naraku* (hell), for, according to the Buddhist tradition already mentioned, everyone who engages in battle in this world is destined after death to be confined in that infernal region ruled over by Asura, to suffer the eternal torment for fighting and bloodshed.

This scene of torture Kiyotsuné finally describes in gestures. Chaos rules over all and there is an endless rain of arrows ; swords lie scattered everywhere, and the mountains are crowned with strong castles touching the clouds ; and amidst these scenes the damned do unending battle. Wave after wave of troops surge forward and recede ; endless war-cries mingle confusedly with the ceaseless clash of resounding arms. When he found himself involved in this terrible scene, he was at his wits' end; but by virtue of the final prayer he had offered from the boat, he was ultimately released from his torment.

This present piece, like the majority of the Warrior pieces, is of Zeami's composition. Also, like so many of these plays, the material is derived from *Genpei Seisuiki* (The Rise and Fall of the Genji and Heiké Clans) and *Heiké Monogatari* (Tales of the Heiké) It is distinguished from other similar pieces mainly by its more dramatic construction, due to the fact that the dramatis personae consist entirely of contemporaneous characters. Further, it lacks a travelling Bonze as the representative of the audience. Therefore the actions performed before the Mistress are developed along different lines from most Warrior pieces which usually deal with the actions as seen by the Bonze; while the presence of the Mistress on the stage throughout heightens both the aesthetic and emotional effect. For this reason, this play of Kiyotsuné of all the Warrior pieces may be regarded as approaching nearest to the lyrical quality of the Woman pieces.

It is noteworthy that none of our Noh writers sought to extol the glories of battle: what they sought rather was its elegiac beauty Hence the choice of the nobles of the defeated Taira clan, since they met the artistic demands of the Noh dramatists better than the brave generals of the victorious Minamoto clan. The same tendency is also found in the tradition of the writers of the *senki monogatari* (war chronicles) of the preceding age, from which the Noh dramatists derive much material; but, nevertheless, the insistence of the Noh drama on gracefulness and elegance enhanced that tendency to a much higher degree. On this account, *Kiyotsuné*, although differing so much from other Warrior pieces, deserves to be regarded as outstanding among them. In this connection also it should not be overlooked that Zeami went further still in the development of this tendency in his *Atsumori*, the pathetic story of the aristocratic youth Atsumori of the Taira clan, who was killed in battle at the early age of sixteen. The end of one so young was too tragic to be handled in the manner common to the heroes of the Warrior pieces Zeami overcame the difficulty by having the pitiful hero perform a *mai*; as a rule, the Warrior pieces never contain that sort of dance out only a short fragment of a *mai* called *kakeri*. The great Noh dramatist found so much beauty and religious faith united in the hero Atsumori, with his budding life so tragically cut short, that he completed the piece with the young hero enjoying eternal bliss. What enhances the dramatic as well as the pathetic quality of the play is that the brave samurai, whose fate it was to kill Atsumori in battle, was struck with grief and repentance and became a bonze, and in that character visited the grave of his victim to entreat Buddha to lead the wandering soul of the miserable boy to Sukhâvatî, the abode of the blessed.

The Noh audiences of the Edo period, however, singled out as their favourites among the Warrior pieces the plays of *Tamura*, *Yashima* and *Ebira*, which they called " The Three Victors," all the heroes being men who had triumphed in battle. This suggests that, under the influence of the militaristic ideals of the feudal government, their standard of appreciation was lowered. The Noh writers of the highest rank, however, always set themselves to lead the audience up to a world of grace (*yûgen*) and never praised those who were victorious. It is significant, indeed, that the Hôgan Yoshitsuné, the victor in *Yashima*, as well as Genda Kagesué, the hero of *Ebira*, find themselves unable to bear the eternal torture of the inferno into which they have fallen, and must turn to a traveling bonze for help. Sakanoué-no Tamuramaro in *Tamura* is the only warrior who did not suffer torture in the nether world because his victory was due to his religious faith, through which he had erected a temple to his tutelary deity, Avalokitêsvara. *Tamura* is one of the few plays dealing with the miraculous intervention of a goddess.

HAGOROMO

(The Heavenly Robe of Feathers)

An angel descended to the sea-shore in Suruga province, where she hung her robe of feathers on a pine-tree before bathing in a secluded spot. But some fishermen found the robe and, struck by its marvellous beauty, were about to take it back with them to their village, when the distressed maiden called to them, entreating them to return her robe, since without it she could never ascend to heaven again. The fishermen at first refused but, moved by her piteous plight, they agreed to return it if she would perform for them the famous " Heavenly Maiden's Dance." On this understanding, the maiden donned her robe and performed the dance.

Such is the story of *Hagoromo*. It recalls the myth of the Swan-maiden current in many parts of the world which may be derived from " The Tale of Hassan of Bazrah " in *The Thousand and One Nights*. The same myth, however, appears in coun less other forms, with the heroine as a swan, a dove, a fish or a serpent, the basic idea of these various transformations being that of a man wedding a supernatural maiden whom he is unable to keep on earth. Mythologists tend to hold that this group of stories have their origin in the taboos of the totemism of primitive peoples ; and Andrew Lang suggests that the story of the fairy maiden who only remains with her captor-spouse so long as he preserves her supernatural robe is representative of the Stone Age.

In *Hagoromo*, however, the fishermen faithfully return the robe of feathers, not one of them thinking of seeking her in marriage or even of falling in love with her. They are quite willing to return the robe to her, wishing only a dance in compensation. Here we have a refinement on the Swan-maiden myth. The fishermen had no intention of keeping the maiden on earth ; they sympathized with her in her plight, making no attempt to restrain her from ascending to her home and kin in the heavenly regions. For them the heavenly

A SCENE FROM THE NOH PLAY HAGOROMO (THE HEAVENLY ROBE OF FEATHERS).

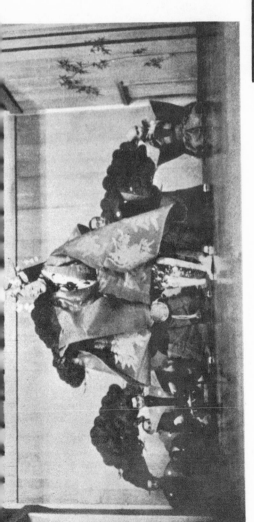

A SCENE FROM THE KYÔGEN TSURI-GITSUNÉ (THE FOX-TRAPPING)

maiden was a symbol of grace, beauty and purity, admitting of no ea:thly affection.

Yet one would not deny the existence of other stories much closer to those of the Swan-maiden myth type current in ancient Japan. In *Ômi Fudoki* (Topographical Survey of Ômi Province) we find the story of the eight heavenly maidens who descended from heaven in the guise of swans. These were surprised while bathing by a man, who caused his dog to take the feathered robe of one of them and then, since she could not escape to heaven without it, wedded her. A variant of this story is in *Tango Fudoki* (Topographical Survey of Tango Province), where it is a childless old couple who surprise the eight maidens bathing and hide the feathered robe of the youngest of them to keep her on earth as their daughter. Further, even in connection with Suruga province, with which *Hagoromo* is associated, there is a similar very ancient story regarding a heavenly maiden who descended to the beach of Udonohama there.

Such old stories have been revised and consummated in the much more refined story of *Hagoromo*, which bears evidence of the fastidiousness or purity of mind of the author of this piece. Some may indeed accept the refinement of the story but regard it as too simple and unsophisticated, as being too childish even. Yet it accords fully with the spirit of the Noh drama, whose ideas of beauty, grace and purity are in no way marred by the simplicity and innocence of the theme. Noh plays, and this kind of play in particular, are devoted to the pursuit of the highest beauty, excluding the lower desires.

In the hands of its author, Zeami, the dances of the Heavenly Maiden are made the centre of the piece with the object of unfolding before the eyes of the audience the supreme beauty of the Noh. So two dances are introduced, the first the quiet, formal dance with a prelude, the *jonomai*, and the second, the slightly quicker *hanomai*. Unlike most of the Woman pieces, *Hagoromo* is accompanied by the *taiko* or flat drum, which gives forth bright, elegant notes, suggestive of the eternal felicity of heaven.

The play begins with the entrance of the Second Actor in the part of Hakuryô, a fisherman, with two other fishermen as his attendants. The entrance music is not, as is usual in Noh, the *shidai*, but the *issei*, which is customarily reserved for the First Actor's entrance. Their costumes are not those of fishermen, being what are called *noshimé*, a dress suggestive of the humbler classes generally, and consisting of a white skirt and a thin garment called a *mizugoromo*; but each one carries a fishing-rod on his shoulder. The three fishermen, grouped face to face, chant a *sagé'uta* (an ode of low tone), and an *agé'uta* (an ode of high tone), and this is supposed to mark their arrival at the shore of Miono'ura, where a picturesque avenue of pines stretches along a sandy beach.

There they land, and there Hakuryô finds a beautiful robe hung on a pine branch. He is about to take it home when he is hailed from behind the curtain by the First Actor in the rôle of the Heavenly Maiden. The First Actor wears a *surihaku*, a tinselled garment, over which is an embroidered dress (*nuihaku*) wound round the lower part of his body in the *koshimaki* style, the purpose of which is to suggest delicately and artistically that he is really naked. He also wears the mask of a lovely and graceful woman, with a heavenly crown on his head.

The Maiden demands the return of the robe of feathers which has been reft from her, explaining its true nature and importance. Her request, however, is not immediately granted, for when the fisherman learns that it belongs to a heavenly maiden, his determination to keep it only becomes the stronger, for he regards it as a treasure to preserve and hand down to posterity. Eventually the sight of the maiden tearfully protesting that without her robe she cannot go back to heaven moves his compassion, and he consents to give it back in return for a heavenly dance. She readily agrees, but stipulates for the robe in advance. The fisherman, however, is suspicious, fearing that once she has the robe she will return to heaven without dancing as she has promised. At this the Maiden indignantly exclaims, "Oh, no. Doubt is for mortals. There is no deceit in heaven." Struck with shame, the fisherman gives the robe of feathers back to her.

There follows the *monoki*, the dressing interval, during which the First Actor puts on the feathered robe. Then, thus attired, the Maiden begins to tell the story of the heavenly dance about to be performed, a dance transmitted in this country under the name of *azuma-asobi*. The story tells how in the palace of the Moon there are thirty maidens, half dressed in white robes and the other half in black, fifteen maidens dancing every night. On the last night of the month the dance is performed by the fifteen maidens in black robes, but on the next night one white-robed maiden joins the company and one black-robed one withdraws. So they continue every night until, on the night of the full moon, fifteen white-robed maidens are dancing. The Heavenly Maiden is one of this company, and if her dance could be learnt, the tradition of the heavenly dance would be handed down in this country.

The above story is chanted by the Chorus in the *kusé* form, the Maiden meanwhile maintaining a slow rhythmical movement. Then she dances the *jonomai*, followed by the *hanomai*, ending in the Maiden ascending into the sky, far above Mount Ashitaka and Mount Fuji, until she vanishes in the spring mists.

There is no need to treat this play as a moral allegory, pointing to any such a lesson as that righteousness exists only in heaven and not on earth, for it is clear that the author had no intention of writing a moral play. His purpose was to exhibit the performance of a divinely beautiful and graceful dance. Prior to this revelation of her beauty and grace the Maiden had been weighed down with profound melancholy and grief. Then with the revival of hope, she displays her divine perfection in the joyous performance of her two dances, culminating in her impressive disappearance behind the curtain.

The Noh playwrights aim at bringing before us something of the divine. Here we have the Heavenly Maiden personified, while in other plays they show us the spirits of flowers and trees, whose dancing is more noble and charming than anything seen in the accepted beauties of earth.

YUYA

Yuya is, with *Matsukaẓé*, one of the most popular of the *kaẓura-mono* (Woman pieces). There is a proverb which says, *Yuya, Matsukaẓé ni komé no meshi*, the meaning being that we no more tire of seeing those two Noh plays than we do of eating *komé no meshi* (boiled rice); they never pall on the appetite.

Yuya and *Matsukaẓé* are differentiated from all the other *kaẓura-mono* by the simple, rather rapid dance, called *chûnomai*, performed by the heroine, in place of the usual quiet and more formal dance, *jonomai*, and also by the fact that the Second Actor appears in the guise of a historical person instead of the usual travelling Bonze. These differences contribute to a more dramatic effect than in most of the Woman pieces.

Yuya was a beautiful courtesan from Tôtômi province, high in the favour of Munemori, the chief of the Taira (Heiké) clan, and living in his palace at Kyoto. She was most anxious to return to the country to visit her old mother who was seriously ill and yearning for a glimpse of her daughter, but her master would not grant her the required permission. It was the time for going on picnics to view the spring flowers, and Munemori was looking forward to taking her with him on a cherry-viewing excursion to Higashi-yama.

The play opens with the entrance of the Second Actor in the rôle of Munemori, who relates the story up to this point in a form technically termed *nanori* (the self-announcement). He wears a *kaẓaori-eboshi* (courtier's head-dress) and an elegant robe called *kariginu*, with a white skirt, and is accompanied by an Attendant (the Fourth Actor), his sword-bearer.

Then, to the accompaniment of *shidai*, entrance music, Asagao (the Third Actor) appears. She is a young woman sent to the capital by Yuya's mother with a letter for her, and wears a woman's mask and a beautiful dress, *kara-ori*. Asagao chants the *michiyuki*, the travelling song, the termination of which is supposed to indicate hat she has reached the capital and is visiting Yuya. From under the raised curtain appears the First Actor in the rôle of Yuya, wearing an exceedingly gay *kara-ori* and a beautiful woman's mask. Her appearance on the stage is called *Sômoku no dé* or entrance beginning with *sômoku* (plants and trees). This name is derived from the entrance song which she begins to chant on the bridge, standing just in front of a pine-tree. Even those who regularly attend Noh plays always listen with rapt attention to this song with its charming words : —

> " *Sômoku wa uro no megumi,*
> *Yashinai eté wa hana no fubo tari;*
> *Iwan'ya ningen ni oité oya !* "

> " Plants and trees grow through the beneficence of rain
> and dew, and to them the blossoms feel grateful as to
> their parents. How much more should mankind feel
> grateful to theirs ! "

So Yuya expresses her anxiety about her aged mother lying ill far away in the country.

Asagao greets her and hands her the letter she has brought. On opening it, Yuya learns the seriousness of her mother's illness. So, thinking that she must return home at once, she comes down on to the stage, accompanied by Asagao, in order to ask her master's permission. On being told of her wish, the Attendant brings her into the presence of Munemori, to whom she shows the letter and explains how dangerously ill her aged mother is. This is known as the Letter Scene and is of absorbing interest to the audience. The usual custom is for the letter to be read by the First Actor only, but sometimes it is chanted in unison by the First and Second Actors, while yet another variation is for the first half to be read by the Second Actor and the second half by the First.

The letter, written in extremely poetical language, is charged with an old mother's tender affection for her daughter. The sufferer likens herself to an old decaying cherry tree which will probably never blossom again in this world, and she yearns for her daughter to return quickly that she may see those scanty flowers before they fall. In deep grief she writes, " Should I fail to see my daughter again in this life, then I fail for ever, for the Buddhist proverb says *Oyako wa issé*," referring here to the belief that, though the bond between husband and wife extends beyond death, and the relations of master and servant can be traced back to a past life, the affinity between parent and child is limited to the present life alone. The letter ends by quoting the famous old poem from *Kokinshû* by the mother of Ariwara-no Narihira :—

> "*Oinuré ba*
> *Saranu wakaré no*
> *Arito iyeba,*
> *Iyoiyo mimaku*
> *Hoshiki kimi kana !* "

expressive of the old mother's desire to see her son, lest she might meet with some unforeseen accident.

The letter, however, fails to move Munemori, for his mind is wholly bent on revelling with Yuya under the beautiful cherry blossoms. So he orders his ox-carriage to be made ready, determined to start at once for Kiyomizu at Higashi-yama.

A simple model of a carriage is now brought on the stage, which the First Actor enters, while the Second Actor takes up a position close by. This is to suggest that actually both have entered the carriage, that Asagao and the Attendant have followed them, and that Munemori's procession has set out for Higashi-yama, although the movement is indicated by chanting, not by action.

On arrival at Kiyomizu, the first thing Yuya does is to fall on her knees at the temple of Kannon (Avalokitêsvara), to pray for the recovery of her mother. Meanwhile, the carousal has begun under the cherry trees in the precincts of the neighbouring Jishu-Gorgen shrine. Summoned there, she hastens to the place, where the beauty of the cherry blossom in all its glory moves her deeply. Recollecting an ancient poem on the beauty of spring, she chants :—

> "*Kazen ni chô mô, funpun taru yuki ;*
> *Ryûshô ni uguisu tobu, henpen taru kin.*"
> Around the cherry blossom the butterflies flutter,
> Like falling snow-flakes ;
> And over the willows, warblers are flying,
> Like glittering leaves of gold.

She then urges the whole company to compose impromptu

poems on the charming scene, although she herself has little mind to take pleasure in it. She cannot free herself even for a moment from the thought of her sick mother.

Her mood is suggested by the chanting of the Chorus according to the *kusé* form. The tolling of the temple bells reminds her, as it did Buddha, of the transience of all earthly things, and the sight of the passing beauty of the cherry blossoms in the grounds of the shrine tells how all creatures must soon perish. At this juncture she finds peculiar comfort in remembering the merciful words of the goddess Kannon, " Trust only in me and you shall be saved." Subduing her anguish, she serves her lord with saké. He bids her dance, and she obeys by dancing the *chûnomai* with her fan spread open. A shower begins to fall, and the blossoms are scattered. "Oh, the heartless rain!" cries Yuya, and then, ever mindful of her dying mother, likens the rain-drops to the tears of a woman lamenting the scattering of the flowers. With her fan spread out, she tries to catch the falling petals, as if she might thus ward off death from her dear mother.

Sitting down among the fallen blossoms, she takes from her sleeve a strip of poem-paper, on which she writes a verse improvised on the spur of the moment. This she places on her fan and tenders to Munemori, who takes it and reads it. The poem runs :—

> *Ikani sen,*
> *Miyako no haru mo*
> *Oshikeredo,*
> *Nareshi Azuma no*
> *Hana ya chiru ran !*
>
> Fair indeed is Spring
> Here in the capital—
> But what if meanwhile
> In my distant East-land home
> That dear blossom is passing!

The poem does not fail to move Munemori, and he grants her leave to go. Delighted, she attributes it all to the divine favour of the merciful Kannon in whom she trusts, and pauses for worship at the temple. Then, accompanied by Asagao, she immediately leaves the capital for the east.

The leading motif of this drama is the contrast between her uneasy melancholy and the gaiety and mirth of spring. Were the heroine free, she would obviously speed at once to her sick mother's side. Instead, because she is bound to a self-centred lord, she has to take part in the cherry-viewing festival with an outward air of pleasure which veils the sadness of her heart. We see the cherry blossom as a symbol of human life, and underlying all is Buddhist fatalism.

This work well deserves to be ranked among Zeami's master-pieces. For, although the contrast between the gaiety of the world and the loneliness of sorrow is a favourite theme among the Noh playwrights, in this play it is treated with peculiar harmony. As we have seen, the Second Actor is not, as usual in the Woman pieces, a travelling Bonze, but a person directly concerned with the heroine, and this improves the dramatic construction and quality of the play considerably.

The presentation of the play given here is that most commonly adopted, but there are no less than six other recognized versions.

––––––––––

SUMIDA-GAWA

(The River Sumida)

In the early days of the Tokugawa period, the river Sumida, which flows through the city of Tokyo, formed the boundary between the provinces of Musashi and Shimôsa. Tokyo was then known by the name of Edo, and had been founded on the plains west of the river in the closing years of the sixteenth century. To appreciate the play under discussion we must picture Edo as it was at that time, with the wide and unbridged Sumida-gawa flowing through broad, desolate plains. The only means of crossing available for the public was a ferry understood to have been near the present Kototoi Bridge.

The play opens with the entrance of the Ferryman (the Second Actor), who introduces himself to the audience, explaining that the river is running high (probably because of the melting of the snow upstream), making his task very difficult, so that he wishes to take over as many passengers as possible on one trip.

Then, to the type of entrance music known as *snidai*, enters a Pedlar (the Third Actor), who is returning from a business trip to the capital, Kyoto, to the eastern part of the country and asks the ferryman to take him across the river. He is told to wait until more passengers have assembled, and then the Ferryman's attention is attracted by some disturbance which can be heard without. This leads the Pedlar to tell him about a mad woman whom he has encountered at various times on his journey. The Ferryman says he will wait until she comes and then cross over. One has to imagine that other passengers have gathered at the ferry before the arrival of the mad woman, but, in accordance with the Noh convention of omitting all non-essentials, no passengers other than the Pedlar actually appear on the stage.

Here it may not be amiss to pause for a brief explanation of the frequent appearance of mad women in the Noh. The use of the term mad women does not imply that they are actually insane, but rather that they are temporarily deranged by intense emotion. They are invariably seeking some dear one lost, usually a child, and once they have found the object of their quest they are freed from their derangement and become normal again; nor are their outbursts of madness entirely beyond their control. One meets with about a score of such stories of mad women in the Fourth Group of the Noh pieces, and among them the story of the mad heroine of *Sumida-gawa*, who ultimately fails to find her long-sought child alive, is one of the most pathetic.

To the music known as *issei* the Mad Woman (the First Actor) appears on the stage. She wears the mask of a middle-aged woman called *fukai* or *shakumi*, a woman's hat, a robe of one colour (*mizugoromo*), and carries a twig of bamboo grass in her hand, this costume signifying a mad woman in Noh. Already she has been wandering over a year in search of her missing boy. She begins to chant :—

" *Hito no oya no kokoro wa yami ni aranedomo......*"— a pathetic confession that though her mind is not utterly dark, yet a mother's heart is apt to lead her astray through affection for her child. She then sings another *uta* (song) :—

> *Kikuya ikani,*
> *Uwa-no-sora naru*
> *Kazé danimo*
> *Matsu ni oto suru*
> *Narai ari-towa?*
>
> Do you hear the winds?
> Even fickle winds that blow
> Across the heavens high
> Are mindful enough to greet
> As they pass between the pines.

Thus she expresses her longing to hear her lost boy calling out her name.

In her frenzy she performs *kakeri*, a short dance, which might well be described as an aimless movement to and fro, and then proceeds to relate the story of her life. She lived in the suburbs of the capital, the widow of a man named Yoshida, and devoted herself entirely to the care of the only child. But the child was kidnapped, and probably brought to the eastern part of the country. In her distraction she has followed in vain search of him. Seeing that the

Ferryman is about to put off, she hails him, but he refuses to take her on board until she has first danced for him. She upbraids him for his harsh attitude towards a distressed woman traveller, an attitude quite unworthy of the ferryman of the famous Sumida.

To her overwrought mind come the words of a song by Ariwara-no Narihira, the ancient poet, on his banishment to this district:—

> *Na ni shi owaba*
> *Iza koto towan,*
> * Miyako-dori,**
> *Waga omô hito wa*
> *Ariya nashiya to.*

> If unto your name,
> O Bird of the Capital,
>   You are true, tell me—
> Is the one whom I love so
> Alive—or is she no more?

And of the birds which are wheeling in confusion over the river she asks where her lost boy is, but receives no answer. They cannot help her, she reflects, for they are *hina no tori*, country birds, not *miyako-dori*, birds of the capital.

Out of pity the Ferryman takes her on board and puts off. When the boat is midway across the stream, the Pedlar asks about the chanting of prayers faintly audible from the opposite bank. The Ferryman replies that the people are saying a mass for the dead, explaining that on the 15th of March, exactly a year ago that day, a young boy who had been kidnapped arrived at the village from the capital on his way up to the north-eastern district. A sudden illness had prevented him from going further and the heartless kidnapper had left him there. The kindly villagers had taken him in and nursed him, but he had died without seeing his mother again who had been left behind in the capital. So, since that day was the first anniversary of his death, a memorial service was being held.

The boat touches the shore, and all the passengers depart, urged by the Ferryman to say a prayer for the repose of the dead boy's soul, but the Woman is unwilling to leave the boat and asks the Ferryman to tell her the dead boy's name. When she hears that his

---

* *Oyster-catchers*, literally *birds of the capital*.

name is Yoshida Umewakamaru, twelve years old, she knows that this dead boy is her long-sought child. Her grief breaks out anew, and the sympathetic Ferryman helps her to land and takes her to the grave, shaded by an overhanging willow and carpeted with young spring grass just putting forth its shoots.

In the Noh performance we see only the Ferryman and the Pedlar standing with her there, but we are expected to imagine many friendly villagers standing around the grave. The grief-stricken mother throws herself prostrate before it and bursts into tears of uncontrollable grief. Up to now she had been living in hopes of seeing her child again, and all the while he has been lying here, buried in this far distant place. She turns to the people and passionately urges them to open the grave to give her just one glimpse more of him.

The moon appears over the distant horizon, the wind blows from the river, the villagers chant prayer after prayer, but she still lies motionless in her grief. At last, the Ferryman helps her to her feet and ties a small prayer-bell round her neck. He advises her to ring this as a memorial for him, telling her that the dead child will be much more pleased with the prayers said by his mother than with those of anyone else.

So she lifts up her voice and repeats, "Namu Amida Butsu," and the others say it after her, until as dawn comes near a high-pitched voice is heard, mingling with the prayers of the people. It is the voice of the dead boy, and the Mother, like one crazed and desiring only to hear that voice again, continues to chant, "Hail, O Amita Buddha," to encourage a reply. It comes; the same words, in his clear, high-pitched voice, are twice repeated by the dead boy.

At the same moment the boy himself appears in front of the grave. The Mother rushes to embrace him, but the phantom disappears. It reappears on the other side; the distracted mother rushes there, only to see it vanish again—not to reappear. Morning has broken, and there is nothing but the grass-grown mound, to which she clings without ceasing to wail.

The Boy Actor, who performs the part of the apparition, wears a white robe with long sleeves (*mizugoromo*) and a wig of long black hanging hair. The Boy Actor has been concealed since the beginning of the performance in a grave-mound at the back of the stage in front of the musicians, out of which he steps at the proper time.

This introduction of the Boy Actor was the subject of some discussion between Jûrô Motomasa, the author, and his father Zeami. Motomasa held that the actual appearance of the dead boy in the person of the Boy Actor would make the performance more effective, while his father maintained, in the orthodox manner, that the appearance should be left to the imagination. Motomasa's opinion is more popular today and, as a rule, the Boy Actor is employed.

It is not clear whether the piece was based on some event that happened or was talked of in the author's day, or was purely a product of the imagination. We find similar themes in other Lunatic pieces such as *Sakura-gawa*, *Mii-dera* and *Hyakuman*, and also in *Kagetsu* which belongs to a different Noh group; while in *Jinen-Koji* the Second and Third Actors appear on the stage in the parts of kidnappers. So it is highly probable that kidnapping and slave-dealing were frequent and greatly feared in those days.

One thing to be noted is that, even when they adopted ordinary domestic materials of this kind, the Noh playwrights did not treat them in a direct, realistic way, but always transformed them into charming and pathetic lyrical dramas. The atmosphere they aimed at creating is greatly enhanced in the present play by means of the numerous quotations from *Isé Monogatari*.

AOI-NO UÉ

(The Lady Aoi)

This play is the dramatized version of a famous episode in *Genji Monogatari* concerning the Lady Aoi, one of the consorts of Hikaru Genji, the Radiant Prince Genji. She had incurred the jealousy of Rokujô-no Miyasudokoro, Princess Rokujô, widow of the Sovereign's brother and a rival for Genji's affections. The jealous princess caused her spirit, her wraith, to haunt Aoi-no Ué and so tormented her that she fell seriously ill. It is at this point that the play begins.

Despite the title, Aoi-no Ué does not appear in person on the stage, but is represented by a beautifully embroidered silk garment called a *kosodé*, spread in the foreground to indicate the young lady lying on her bed. This suggests a comparison with the *Prometheus Bound* of Aeschylus, in whose opening three characters (beside a mute) participate, but in which Prometheus himself does not utter a word, his part presumably being taken by a lay-figure.

The action of the play hinges upon Princess Rokujô, whose jealousy of the Lady Aoi furnishes the motive. The Princess Rokujô pronounced a curse upon the Lady Aoi, praying the gods to remove her from the land of the living, and as a result of this curse the unfortunate lady became critically ill. The Courtier (the Fourth Actor), taking his place on the stage, tells how the Lady Aoi's illness refuses to yield either to medicine or prayers, and explains how he has had to send for Teruhi, a female diviner, in order to discover the author of it. Through her supernatural powers and by making use of the bow-strings, she will find out whether the illness is the work of some wraith or spirit.

The Diviner (the Third Actor), wearing the mask of a young woman and a white robe, is already seated by the *daijinbashira*, the third pillar, and thereupon begins her necromantic incantation :—

Ten shôjô, ji shôjô, naigé shôjô, rokkon shôjô,
Yoribito wa imazo yorikuru, Nagahama no

Ashigé no koma ni tazuna yuri-kaké.
Heaven pure, earth pure, the inside and outside pure,
the six organs of sense pure, may the one I invoke now
appear, as if holding the reins of her grey horse.

ιen, through this incantation, a wraith, in the guise of a woman,
·pears on the bridge. It is the living spirit of Princess Rokujô
ιe First Actor).

Her mask, called *deigan* (gilded eyes), represents the face of a
·autiful woman with an expression of hatred and wrath, while her
·ir, which is a wig dishevelled and disordered, shows that she has
st the dignity of her station. Also the skirt of her splendid dress
 tucked and girded up in the *tsubo-ori* style. To the music of *issei*
·e reaches the stage and begins her entrance song :—

> *Mitsu no kuruma ni nori no michi,*
> *Kataku no kado oya idenu-ran.*

The opening words are a Buddhist parable and imply that the
·raith, the living spirit, of the Princess Rokujô has left her body.
·he phrase *mitsu no kuruma* (the three carriages) and many phrases
ι the passages that follow contain word-plays on the word "car-
·age." Thus there are *Yûgao no yado no yareguruma*, the broken car-
·age standing at Lady Yûgao's gate ; *ushi no oguruma*, the little
·x-carriage ; *kuruma no wa*, the carriage wheels ; all of which refer
·o a recent incident at the summer festival of the Kamo shrine
·hen the ox-carriage of Princess Rokujô had collided with that of
·ιe Lady Aoi, with the result that Princess Rokujô had suffered the
·ιdignity of having her carriage forced into a side-street, this making
·er bitterly angry. And, at the same time, by means of the word-
·lay human life is likened to the turning wheels of a carriage.

When the female Diviner has enticed the spirit on to the stage
·y the twanging of her bow-string, she declares that, to her clair-
·oyant eyes, Princess Rokujô appears as a noble female figure sitting
ι a broken ox-cart, to whose shafts a young lady in tears is clinging.
·he Courtier understands the significance of this vision. The Spirit
·f Princess Rokujô then confesses her relentless hatred, sayiι g that
·er persecution of the Lady Aoi is in retribution for the indignities
·hrust upon her by her successful rival.

In her fury she is about to strike the Lady, but the Diviner restrains
·er, reproving her for her mean and vulgar conduct, nothing better

than the sort of attack made by a divorced woman of the lower classes upon her supplanter. The Spirit of the Princess pays no heed to her, and crying, "I will have my revenge," strikes the invalid. The vindictive princess fears that, if the Lady Aoi recovers, she will continue to live happily with the Radiant Prince, and so she resolves to carry her off in her broken carriage. While the Chorus is chanting this, she pulls her *kara-ori* or embroidered robe over her head, and then with gestures indicating that she is carrying off the stricken lady takes her place in front of the Prompters' seats.

All is confusion in the Palace, and the Courtier summons a servant whom he bids haste to Yokawa on Mount Hiyei to bring the Exorcist. The servant (the Comic Actor), standing on the bridge facing the curtain, calls at the Priest's dwelling. The Priest (the Second Actor) is engaged in religious devotions in his cell, but he cannot refuse to receive this urgent messenger from so important a quarter as the palace of the Minister of the Left, Lady Aoi's father. So he consents to come down the mountain to the capital at dead of night.

His appearance on the stage marks his arrival at the palace, where the Courtier ushers him into the sick-room. He is in the dress of an itinerant priest, wearing the small head-dress called *tokin*, and a *suzukaké*, a kind of stole, over a *mizugoromo* and a white skirt. He is confounded at the evil atmosphere of the room and, losing no time, begins to tell the beads of his rosary in prayer.

While he is praying the Spirit of Princess Rokujô, her robe still pulled over her head, draws near to him. She has exchanged her *deigan* mask for one called *hannya*, which, with its two protruding horns, gives her a terrible, fiendish appearance. She is in fact a female monster, the personification of jealousy.

She now girds her robe about her waist and attacks the Priest with a T-shaped staff, a struggle ensuing between the forces of good and evil. At first the issue is uncertain, the Priest begins by pressing the Spirit back close to the curtain, but she rallies and drives him back again to the stage. But the Priest refuses to relax his efforts and continues his exorcism by invoking the Five Conquering Kings :—

Namaku Samanda Basarada,
Senda Makaroshana,
Sowataya Untara Takanman.

ese are corrupt Sanskrit words used for incantation, appealing to
most potent forces to arise and subdue the raging evil spirit.

Under the spell of the incantation the Spirit of Princess Rokujô
inally overcome, and she swears she will never attack the Lady Aoi
iin. Praising the power of Buddha, she proclaims her repentance
l her intention to reform.

This play belongs to the *onryômono* (Revenge pieces) of the Fourth
oup, and is certainly the work of Zeami. It has been wrongly
ributed to Konparu Zenchiku, but the strongest and most con-
isive piece of evidence against this attribution is the existence of
:ords showing that it used to be performed by Dôami (Inuô), a
ingaku actor, who was an older contemporary of Zeami. But since
Sami died when Zenchiku was only nine years old, it is impossible
at Zenchiku could have written this piece. *Aoi-no Ué* has always
en regarded as one of the finest plays in the Noh repertoire.

HACHI NO KI

(The Dwarf Trees)

The traditional samurai valued his honour so highly that, no matter how low he had been brought by poverty, he would never lower his standard of conduct. Among the virtues of ancient knighthood that of hospitality was not the least esteemed. Hence, Genzaemon Tsuneyo, the hero of *Hachi no Ki*, is regarded as a model samurai, for he retained even in the midst of ruin his integrity and his observance of the duty of hospitality.

One winter evening, so the story goes, when the snow lay deep an itinerant priest arrived at the door of Tsuneyo's thatched cottage to beg for a night's lodging. Here he was given shelter and food, coarse though it was, while, lacking any other fuel, the samurai made a fire for him of his treasured dwarf trees. Not only was the bonze deeply grateful for such hospitality, but he appreciated his host's scrupulous ideas of honour which he had preserved in spite of his adverse circumstances. His devoted observance of the duty of hospitality had indeed passed the severest test, and eventually it received an ample reward. For the bonze was none other than the Shogun Hôjô Tokiyori, called the Lay Brother (*Nyûdô*) of Saimyôji, who in the disguise of an itinerant priest was then inspecting for himself the conditions of the people in the provinces.

The play proceeds thus. The Bonze (the Second Actor) appears on the stage in a priest's robe and a hat of rushes, explaining that, because of the heavy snowfall in Shinano province he intends to return to Kamakura to stay there until the following spring. He chants a *michiyuki* (travelling song), during the course of which he must be supposed to cross the skirts of Mt Asama, to descend the bed of the river Usui, and to arrive in the Sano district near the present city of Takasaki. The thickening snowstorm prevents his going further and so he knocks at the door of a solitary hut to ask for lodging.

The Wife of the samurai (the Third Actor), who actually entered

[172]

he stage before the Bonze, has meanwhile remained seated. But
ow she rises to answer the knock. She explains that the absence of
er husband prevents her from welcoming him in at once, whereupon
he Bonze says that he will await her husband's return and takes shelter
nder the eaves.

Genzaemon Tsuneyo (the First Actor) then returns, bemoaning
he sight of the heavy snow. Such a scene, he declares, is as distres-
ing to poverty-stricken people like himself as it is pleasing in the
yes of the well-to-do in their comfortable homes. Surprised to find
is wife standing outside the hut in the bitter cold awaiting his return
e inquires the reason and learns that a pilgrim priest, overtaken by
he snow, is seeking shelter.

The Bonze comes forward and repeats his entreaty, but Tsuneyo
egrets that it is impossible to give him shelter as his wretched hovel
s barely large enough for two. So he advises the wanderer to hasten
o a decent inn in the village less than a mile away. The Bonze com-
plains that he should have been kept waiting all in vain, and leaves the
ut.

When he has gone, the Wife, touched with pity, suggests that such
misfortunes as theirs may be due to their failure to observe the com-
mandments of Buddha in their previous lives, and asks whether they
may not be assured of some happiness in the next world if not in
his, if they welcomed such a poor pilgrim. Tsuneyo is greatly
moved by her compassion and, declaring that she ought to have given
im this advice sooner, hastens from the hut.

The Bonze is still standing in the snow shaking the snow from
is sleeves. Tsuneyo runs up to him, catches him by the arm and
nvites him to stay at least that night at his cottage, shabby though it
s. So the Bonze retraces his steps to the hut, while the Chorus
hants the following song :—

> Geni koremo tabi no yado,
> Geni koremo tabi no yado,
> Karisomé nagara chigu no en,
> Ichiju no kagé no yadori mo
> Kono yo naranu chigiri nari.
> Soré wa amé no kokagé, koré wa yuki no noki furité,
> Uki-né nagara no kusa-makura,
> Yumé yori shimo ya musubu ran,

This meditative chant gives expression to the Buddhist teaching that to shelter from the rain under the same tree, to cross a river together in the same ferry-boat, to stay for one night under the same roof, or to be husband and wife even though only for one day, reflects close relations in a former existence. Life itself is but a journey, and as much a temporary abode as the poor hut in which the Bonze was given a lodging. But although life is thus transient and ephemeral, the karmic relations are unbreakable and everlasting.

The scene changes to the interior of the hut, where the host and hostess have nothing but boiled millet to set before their guest, who, however, receives it gratefully. The cold increased as the night wore on, but the host, eager though he was to make a fire that his guest might be warm, had no fuel at all. Then he remembered the dwarf trees growing in their pots, his prized possessions, sole relics of the abundance of the days of his affluence. Now, in his low estate he had but three of them, a plum, a cherry and a pine, which, covered with snow, stood outside the window, waiting for the return of spring. Precious though they were in his eyes, he resolved to use them as fuel for the comfort of his guest.

Despite the priest's protestations the host and hostess persisted in their intention; they remembered how, of old, the great Sakya himself had gone out and sought fuel from the Snow Mountain to serve a poor hermit's need, and they regarded their own service as an act of ascetic devotion. Yet the host himself, as he stood in front of the dwarf trees, brushing the snow-flakes from their branches and gazing earnestly at them, was loth to part with them. This tender mood is delicately brought out in the *kusé* and the section preceding it.

The guest was eager to know the name of his host, who had touched his heart with his gracious courtesy; but the samurai, ashamed of his humble circumstances, at first refused to give it. At last the Bonze's importunity compelled him to speak, and he told him that he had formerly been lord of the Manor of Sano, but that his field had been usurped by other members of his clan. On the guest asking why he had not gone up to Kamakura to bring an action against the usurpers, the samurai replied that, although he had great respect for

Lord Saimyôji, the Shogun, he had given up the idea of appealing to him, because he was then absent on religious pilgrimage. He went on to declare his loyalty as a samurai, that should any emergency arise at Kamakura he would be ready to take up arms on behalf of the Shogunate. The sole ornament of his poor rooms was his arms, and a lean horse was housed in a wretched stable close by. Yet strong though he was in knightly honour, he could only regret that death from starvation in his great poverty might prevent him from sacrificing his life in the way that his loyalty prompted.

When the Bonze left at dawn, the host and hostess saw him off with regret. But he invited the samurai to come and see him at Kamakura, promising him his aid in any suit he instituted against those who had wronged him.

The second scene is laid in Kamakura a few months later. In order to test the sincerity of Genzaemon Tsuneyo, the Shogun has instituted an extraordinary levy in mass of the Eastern provinces.

The Second Actor enters, now in the dignified dress of the Nyûdô Shogun, and takes his seat by the third pillar. Near by stands the Chief Retainer (the Fourth Actor) together with an Attendant (the Comic Actor). They represent the headquarters of the central government, where, of course, many other daimyo are supposed to be present, although they do not actually appear.

To the music of *haya-fué* Genzaemon Tsuneyo enters. His dress suggests the man-at-arms; he wears a dress called *sobatsugi* over the *dan-noshimé*, white skirt and a head-band. He has a halberd on his shoulder and, to suggest the mounted retainer, he carries a whip in his hand. Though he had been eager to reach Kamakura from Sano in Kôzuké province, he had been compelled in the end to dismount from his horse and lead it, because it was too feeble to travel at any speed. The assembled company look with sneering contempt on his shabby appearance.

The Shogun then bade the Chief Retainer bring forward the most shabbily attired of all the samurai who had responded to his call. This order was passed on to the Attendant who summoned Genzaemon into the Shogun's presence. The astonished Genzaemon could only think that he had been thus singled out because of some accusation of treachery by his traducers, and feared he would be put

[175]

to death.   So he fell on his knees before the Shogun only to be greeted by the kindly words, "Welcome, Genzaemon-no Jô Tsuneyo of Sano! Do you not recognize the man to whom you once gave shelter from the snow?"

Thus accosted, Tsuneyo lifted up his eyes and saw before him the man to whom he had a short time before given a lodging for the night.   Deeply moved, he could only prostrate himself once more. Then the Shogun told him that his object in summoning the present military levy was to test his honesty.   First of all he praised him for his great loyalty in thus coming forward, and declared that the next business was to deliver judgement regarding any of those present who had any complaint.   He then pronounced that Tsuneyo's fief should be restored to him, and, further, that he should receive a reward for his unselfish fidelity to the duty of hospitality.   In place of the three dwarf trees he had sacrificed three fiefs should be added to him —for the *umé* (the plum), the fief of Umeda in Kaga, for the *sakura* (the cherry), of Sakurai in Etchû, and for the *matsu* (the pine), that of Matsuida in Kôzuké province.

After receiving this signal honour, Tsuneyo remounted his lean horse and started back for Sano in high spirits, while those who had just been sneering at his shabby appearance now gazed after him in envious amazement.

This brief synopsis should be enough to show why this particular play has long remained the favourite of the samurai class, and indeed one of the most generally popular pieces in the Noh repertoire. Although it falls into the *genzaimono* group of pieces, it has certain exceptional features; it lacks the *otokomai* (the knightly dance) on the part of the First Actor, and also the *kirikumi*, which one may render as the grapple-scene, both of which are characteristic of the *genzaimono*.   Some scholars ascribe its authorship to Zeami, but the probabilities are that it is a work of Kan'ami.

KYÔGEN

(Comic Interludes)

The *kyôgen* developed from the same origins as the Noh drama, the difference being that whereas the Noh has developed along lines of classical severity, and the Noh plays are usually, though not necessarily, of a tragic character, the *kyôgen* plays are comedies, or rather, farces. It is not known with any certainty when the *kyôgen* drama assumed the form in which it has come down to us, but the probabilities are that, with the Noh, it took its present form about the beginning of the Muromachi period, or about the years 1330-1340.

Tradition attributes the origin of the *kyôgen* to the priest Gen'é; but it is probable that the many texts attributed to him (of which there are fifty-nine, according to one count) served rather as prototypes of the actual *kyôgen*. After him came Hiyoshi Yahei, Hiyoshi Yatarô and their successors, who carried on the hereditary art of *kyôgen* from generation to generation. The sixth of this line, Hiyoshi Yaemon, imparted this artistic tradition to Konparu Shirôjirô, son of Konparu Zenchiku and an actor of great talent. He composed numerous texts, greatly improving *kyôgen* from what it had been in the days of the priest Gen'é, and winning recognition as the founder of the Ôkura school of the *kyôgen* drama.

At a later date, in the early Edo period, another school, the Sagi, came to rival the Ôkura school. The third and last school to arise was that of Izumi, which still survives today with the Ôkura school, the Sagi school having disappeared during the Meiji era.

There are about two hundred and fifty *kyôgen* plays extant, which can be roughly classified as *wakikyôgen* (Celebration pieces) corresponding to the *wakinô*; *hyakushômono* (Farmer pieces); *daimyomono* (Daimyo pieces); *mukomono* (Bridegroom pieces); *bôzumono* (Priest pieces); *onnamono* (Husband and Wife pieces); *otomono* (Wooing pieces); *yamadachimono* (Highwayman pieces); *zatômono* (Blind Minstrel pieces); *yamabushimono* (Itinerant Priest pieces); *kajamono* (Apprentice

[177]

pieces); *onimono* (Devil pieces); *tachishûmono* (Retainer pieces); and *shimaimono* (Dance pieces) in which Noh plays are parodied.

Whereas the sister drama, Noh, centres on singing and dancing, the *kyôgen* concentrates on dialogue and action, and belongs, moreover, to the genre of the comedietta or farce, in contrast to the Noh which can be defined as musical drama or opera. With very few exceptions, the *kyôgen* lacks entirely the chorus and musical accompaniment. It differs also in that it is secular and critical, whereas the Noh is meditative and declamatory. The *kyôgen* writers sought their material almost entirely in the happenings of the world around them which they treated in a spirit of satire or irony. Accordingly the language employed is that of everyday usage, and is never in the grand style like that of the Noh. Finally, the characters of the plays are by no means so distinguished and heroic as those of the Noh but are taken usually from the middle and lower classes, a fact that strengthened its appeal to its audience in the past.

Also the *kyôgen* actors were of a different school from those of the Noh, for they needed to be specially trained for humorous and witty dialogue. Yet the fact that the *kyôgen* were acted in the intervals between the Noh prevented the actors from going too far in over-waggish remarks and vulgar gestures, which would be disagreeable to a Noh audience.

The First Actor in the *kyôgen* is called *omo*, the Chief Person, but sometimes *shité*, the Doer, as in Noh. The Second Actor is known as *ado*, the Person addressed, while the Third Actor is *ko-ado*, the vice-*ado*. The number of actors can be increased indefinitely according to requirements.

It has long been customary to stage the *kyôgen* as part of the Noh programme, the usual arrangement being three or four *kyôgen* pieces given alternately with five Noh plays.

The purpose of this insertion of the *kyôgen* in the Noh programme is to enable the audience to relax; they serve the same purpose as the satyric plays with the Greek tragedies. The more serious and tense the Noh play, the more need is felt for the diversion offered by the farcical *kyôgen*. The *kyôgen* actors, moreover, play in the rôle of clowns in the Noh drama itself. Hence in olden times a *kyôgen* actor was called *okashi*, the Joker, and his buffoonery was welcomed and even admired. Recently, a sober joker is sometimes substituted, reflecting the aversion of the modern Noh audience to playfulness and facetiousness. It is doubtful, however, if he is necessarily an improvement on the former buffoon.

KANI-YAMABUSHI

(The Crab and the Ascetic)

The word *yamabushi* literally means a mountain-dweller, and is used to denote an itinerant bonze who by the assiduous performance of religious austerities and asceticism aspires to eminent virtue through complete self-control. Even in the past, few of the *yama bushi* ever succeeded in attaining this difficult goal, despite their large numbers. Since the Middle Ages their numbers have gradually diminished, and very few can be found today. These *yamabushi* were often caricatured by *kyôgen* writers as ineffective, pretentious and cowardly blunderers, *Kani-Yamabushi* affording an excellent illustration of this type of play.

A *yamabushi* from Dewa province (the First Actor) takes the stage attended by a mountain-coolie (the Second Actor). For the practice of austerities he has been tramping over Mt Ôminé and Mt Kazuraki in Yamato province, and is now on his way back to Mt Haguro, his native place.

With his confidence in his supernatural powers greatly increased as a result of his recent ascetic discipline, the *yamabushi* boasts to the Coolie about what he can do. Why, he declares, he could even bring a flying bird to the ground by prayer. The Coolie supports him with flattery, saying that his calm and imperturbable demeanour would make people believe that Fudô Myôô, the God of Fire (Arya Acalanâtha), had returned again to this world. Greatly elated with this, the *yamabushi* replies in like manner, comparing the Coolie to Kimkara or Cetaka, who is represented as standing on each side of Fudô Myôô. Naturally, the Coolie in his turn is highly gratified.

Indulging in this mutual flattery, they travel on until they have penetrated deep into the heart of the mountain. As they are following a path in a ravine a strange roaring is heard, which at first they take to be the soughing of the wind among the pine-trees or the gurgling of a shallow stream. But the sound grows louder and louder until it swells out like a peal of thunder. The place suddenly becomes dark and a mysterious form appears.

"Oh, what has appeared?" cries the *yamabushi*. "Oh, how dreadful!" shrieks the Coolie. The *yamabushi* bids the Coolie go forward and find out what it is, but he refuses, saying, "I am too frightened. You go yourself!" The *yamabushi*, very angry at this, says, "It is just to have your services in such a case that I have brought you at all." But the Coolie only pushes his master forward, asking, "Aren't you a brave leader among the *yamabushi*? Haven't you supernatural powers?"

The *yamabushi* sees the force of these words. He puts his hand on the hilt of his sword and accosts the monster, "Who dares to stand in the way of the divine *yamabushi*?" In answer, the Monster declaims in a terrifying voice, "My eyes soar to the sky; my carapace never touches the earth; and with two great limbs and eight small ones I walk sideways to the right and to the left."

"Why, Coolie, it is the spirit of the Crab," says the *yamabushi* in a more confident tone to the Coolie who also feels bolde and, determined to chastise the saucy fellow, raises his staff to str ke. But the Crab nips his ear with his great claws and holds on tightly, and the Coolie screams out with pain. The *yamabushi* thereupon thinks that this is just the occasion for employing his hard-earned super-natural powers, and sets to work to cast a spell over the creature. His incantations and prayers, however, only increase the Monster's strength and consequently the Coolie's pain. "O, leader, leader," shrieks the Coolie, "pray stop your incantations!" But the *yama-bushi* continues, saying, "Don't worry, Coolie, the pinch always gets stronger just before he has to let go." The Crab then moves forward to catch the *yamabushi* also. Although he tries hard to escape, the Crab catches his ear with his other claw and pinches and shakes his two victims to his heart's content, finally flinging them aside and making off.

The rôle of the Crab is played by the Third Actor, who wears a *kentoku* mask with goggle eyes and clenched teeth, and this, with his head covered with long black hair, is enough to suggest the

Monster. In this play, even more than in the *Uri-Nusubito*, one ca[n]
see how largely the *kyôgen* pieces consist in sheer slapstick comedy.

———————

URI-NUSUBITO

(The Melon Thief)

A Melon-grower (the Second Actor) had set up a scarecrow to keep the birds and animals away from his melon-patch. The Villager (the First Actor), in straitened circumstances owing to a succession of misfortunes, had come under cover of darkness to steal some of the ripe melons. He was at first somewhat hesitant to steal the fruit of another man's labour, but, in the end, deciding that it had to be done, he broke through the fence and entered the melon-patch. For a while only dead leaves met his groping fingers, but then he began to find melons which he plucked as he wandered about here and there.

Suddenly he caught sight of the scarecrow silhouetted against the sky. Believing it to be the watchman, he prostrated himself before it and began to beg forgiveness. Crying out, " Forgive me ! Forgive me ! " he was just about to return the stolen fruit, when he realized that it was only a scarecrow. Annoyed at having been so easily fooled, he kicked it down and then ran off with the melons.

When the Melon-grower came to his patch next day he could see from the broken fence and the prostrate scarecrow that a thief had broken in. So he decided to lie in wait for him that evening, pretending to be a scarecrow. As still as a statue he sat waiting, with a whip and a rope in his hands. After sunset the Villager came again. " Ah," he said admiringly, " they've set the scarecrow up again. How lifelike it is ! "

It so happened that the people of that village had decided to stage as part of their coming festival the old folk-play in which the devil tortures dead sinners. Recalling this the thief thought that this would be a fine opportunity to rehearse the play, with the realistic scarecrow in the rôle of a dead sinner, and himself in the rôle of the devil. So he took the whip from the scarecrow and, accosting it, began to mimic the gestures of putting it to torture.

"Ho, ho, you dead sinner," he cried, laying it on with the whip. With the greatest patience, the Melon-grower remained as still as a statue and let the thief have his way.

Then it struck the thief that, since the parts in the drama were assigned by lot, it might fall to him to play the part of a dead sinner. So, reversing the rôles, he placed the whip again in the hand of the scarecrow, and kept hold of one end of the rope as if he were going to be whipped. He bagan to chant the words of a dead sinner, "Ah, woe is me! Please don't torture me so cruelly! Oh, what a place is hell! When I try to get away the rope pulls me back, and when I stop I get a thrashing!"

Suddenly he felt a stinging blow on his back. Wondering where it came from, he spun round to find nothing there but the scarecrow. But each time he pulled the rope, up went the whip in the scarecrow's hand; when he slackened his pull, down came the whip on his back. "Truly, this scarecrow is most skilfully made!" he exclaimed, and, full of admiration, went on with the rehearsal. Finally the Melon-grower rose to his feet, shouting out, "You thief!" and began to rain blows upon his back. With cries of "Mercy, mercy!" the thief ran off, with the Melon-grower pursuing him and roaring out, "You shall not escape, you shall not escape."

TSURIGITSUNE

(The Fox-Trapping)

In the Middle Ages, and even much later, the country-people believed that the cunning of the fox was due to its possession of supernatural powers. It was even thought that the fox frequently assumed the form of a human being or even of a god.

Once upon a time there lived a good huntsman who was so skilful in trapping foxes that he spread consternation amongst that cunning community, and the old head of the family began to fear that all his kin would soon be extirpated if the huntsman's activities were allowed to continue. So he decided to assume the form of the old priest Hakuzôsu, the uncle of the huntsman, and in that guise advise him to give up fox-trapping.

The First Actor enters as the Bonze, in a hood and a long robe, carrying a cane. He also wears a mask called *hakuzôsu*, which, although it has the features of an old priest, gives us a hint of the fox in the cast of the eyes and the protruding lips. Also the howling of a dog causes him to show signs of great perturbation.

He calls at the house of the Huntsman (the Second Actor), who rises to receive his venerable visitor. "Is it true, as people say, that you go in for trapping foxes?" asks the Bonze. At first the Huntsman denies the rumour, but in the end he is forced to admit its truth. After having trapped his first fox, he had become interested in the game and altogether might have trapped five foxes. Asked how he disposed of his catch, he explained that he used their skins for rugs, their flesh for food, while the bones he would char and sell to the apothecaries.

The Bonze shuddered as he heard of the fate of the foxes and admonished the Huntsman to give up such a dangerous sport, as the foxes are so vindictive that they harbour deadly resentment after death. The Huntsman showed signs of listening to his advice, and the Bonze went on to give examples of the formidable nature of the fox family, telling the story of one fox which took on the guise of Tamamo-no Maé, a court-lady, in order to do harm to its captor, and, even after its death, brought him harm through assuming the shape of a stone.

Finally the Huntsman pledged himself to hunt no more foxes and, at the Bonze's advice, went off to dispose of his snare. Greatly relieved at his success, the disguised fox said good-bye and went away to his lair humming a tune. But on the way he encountered a snare baited with a young fried mouse. He could hardly resist the temptation to devour the succulent morsel, but he knew that if he touched it carelessly he would be trapped. As he remembered how his young fox kin had been unable to resist such a temptation, he felt bitter against the little decoy mouse and struck it vindictively with his cane.

Yet he cannot help turning round repeatedly and gazing at the tempting morsel. He actually makes an attempt to pick it from the snare, but realizes the danger just in time. So he determines to go back home for a while and return later without his disguise.

Meanwhile the Huntsman, who had not been quite convinced by his Bonze uncle, looked back on the recent interview and recalled several strange points in it. For one thing the language used by the Bonze had sometimes been incomprehensible, and, quite unlike his real uncle, he had used a roundabout way of talking. Further, it was very strange that the visitor had suddenly vanished almost as soon as he had seen him off at the gate. So he visited the snare he had laid and saw signs of its having been tampered with. This gave him the idea that the old fox, whom he had been daily trying to snare, had actually visited him in human guise. Knowing that a fox will always return to a bait he has once sampled, he lay in wait for him by the side of the snare.

The First Actor now enters on all fours in the form of the old fox. He runs across the bridge to the stage, howling, " Kwa-a-a-ai, kwa-a-a-ai," and performs many antics around the snare until at last he tries to snatch away the fried mouse. " Splendid, I've got him ! " shouts the Huntsman and pulls the rope, bringing the fox down into the snare. Then he goes up to beat him to death with his stick, but the fox puts up a violent resistance and, in the end, succeeds in getting away.

The theme of this farce is not so much the cunning of the fox as that of man. The fox is fighting for its own life and for that of its kin, whereas man's craftiness and insincerity are represented as contemptible and beyond all forgiveness ; it is a satire on man rather than on the foxes.

———————————————

OTOGI-ZÔSHI

(Fairy Stories)

Otogi-zôshi (the book of fairy-tales) is the generic name of collections of popular short stories which were in circulation around the Muromachi period, the later Middle Ages from about 1300 to 1600. These stories, as their name *otogibanashi* shows, were fairy stories written with the general intention of delighting young and old of both sexes. With their artlessness of thought and expression, they were addressed primarily to children, but it would be a mistake to think that they were intended exclusively for the young.

The origin of these stories can be sought in the lyric narratives of the Heian period. Like other works of their day they show a yearning for the aristocratic life and atmosphere of the monarchical age, and the influence of Buddhist philosophy and Confucian morality, reflecting the current of social ideas in the early part of the modern age. To the literary taste of those days are due their similarity of plot, their conventional style, their simplicity and their quaint choice of subjects. And, because of their wide appeal, we can see in them the growing influence of the middle classes.

If we are to attribute to them any special value it must be as works of a period of transition. It is vain to search in *otogi-zôshi* high literary qualities, their sole claim to literary importance being that they form a repository of material derived from a period extending over several hundred years up to their own day. It serves no useful purpose to treat these stories as the compositions of authors whose identity has ceased to be known either through the passage of time or their own unimportance; their significance consists rather in their being productions of the native genius, bringing with them the unsophisticated heart and voice of the people.

Let it suffice that from them we can learn something of the social conditions and of the life, habits and customs of those days; that they provide valuable material for the study and exposition of the literature of a period of transition; and that in them can be found the germs of the new literature which was to come to maturity in the following period. If they have a quality which deserves special emphasis it is that the curious blend of attitudes we find in them, one looking backwards to the romance of the monarchical age, the other suggesting rather the self-consciousness of the newly-risen commoners, gives them a certain "popular" elegance, and a touch of fantasy. The charm of the *otogi-zôshi* is in its being a link between aristocratic and popular literature.

It is possible to make a rough classification of the themes of the stories, but this must not be pressed too closely, since each tale contains a diversity of elements which cuts across any classification. Again, as may be gathered from what has already been said, these tales by their very nature go beyond any specific grouping, to bear witness to this or that social aspect and to reflect this or that current of contemporary thought. Below then is what seems the most satisfactory classification:

1. Nursery tales.
2. Tales dealing with non-humans, such as birds and insects.
3. Religious tales, such as deal with Buddhistic preaching and seclusion from the world.
4. Tales of stepchildren and their ill-treatment.
5. Tales of love.
6. Tales of heroes, great warriors or monster-killers.
7. Tales of filial piety.

As a sample of the tales we will outline four of the stories: *Issun Bôshi, Hachi Kazuki, Shuten Dôji*, and the very popular *Urashima Tarô*.

1. *Issun Bôshi* (The Dwarf)

A certain old couple, regretting their childless state, besought the aid of the god Sumiyoshi Myôjin, who blessed them with a son. The child, however, was exceedingly small, only one *sun* (about one inch) in height, and so he was given the name of Issun Bôshi, One-inch Dwarf.

Having reached the age of twelve without showing any signs of growth he came to be neglected by his disappointed parents, who even went so far as to enter upon arrangements for giving him to another family. When he heard about this, little Issun Bôshi took the initiative and asked for permission to depart. With his old mother's help he equipped himself for his entrance into the great world. For a sword he took a needle with a single straw for its scabbard, and then embarking in a bowl for a boat he punted it along with a chopstick and set off from Naniwano'ura for the capital. Having safely arrived there he went to the mansion of the State Councillor of Sanjô, where he knocked at the door. The Councillor himself opened it, but could see no signs of anyone. He looked around in bewilderment and then heard a tiny voice, apparently from beneath his feet, exclaiming, " Please don't step on me ! " He was still more amazed when he saw that the speaker was a tiny dwarf, peeping out from between the supports of a *geta* (wooden clog).

The Councillor found Issun Bôshi such an amusing little fellow that he took him into his service. There he continued until his sixteenth year, when he fell in love with his master's daughter. Realizing that it would be impossible to win her by ordinary means, he thought out a cunning plan. He smeared her mouth with honey and stuck a sacred rice-offering over it. Then he slandered her to the Councillor, who in his anger turned her out of the house. But the dwarf went with her and set sail for his native place.

On the way the ship was wrecked and they were cast ashore on the Island of the Ogres. One of the ogres desired the Princess for himself and so, to get rid of the dwarf, attempted to swallow him. But every time the orge swallowed him, Issun Bôshi tormented him by rushing out of his eye, until in the end the ogre dashed away howling with pain. In his flight the ogre dropped his mallet of good fortune which the dwarf picked up. Shaking the mallet as well as he was able, the dwarf prayed that he might grow taller. This was granted and he became a young man of normal size. Shaking the mallet again he obtained a sumptuous repast for himself and the Princess, and then a great supply of gold and silver treasure. Thereupon he returned to the capital with his Princess and entered the service of the Emperor, where he attained great distinction. Nor in his good fortune did he forget to discharge his obligations to his old parents.

From this synopsis it is clear that this tale belongs to what Baring-Gould calls the world-wide " Tom Thumb " type. In addition to the description of the success of the god-given child and the divine mercy which brought him into being and watched over him, other matters of interest are the drifting to the Island of the Ogres and the vision of Nyoi-Hô, the "Soul-satisfying Treasure."

2. *Hachi Kazuki* (The Pot-Wearer)

Once upon a time a man named Sanetaka had a beautiful daughter. When the girl was thirteen years old her mother fell ill. Just before she died she called her daughter to her, and set a large pot upon the girl's head, at the same time praying to Kannon (Avalokitêsvara) to watch over and protect her. After the funeral, the father essayed to remove the pot from the girl's head, but all his efforts to do so failed; the pot remained firmly fixed.

It was not long before her father married a second wife, who hated her "deformed" stepdaughter and did all she could to get rid of her. At last, by means of wicked lies and insinuations she succeeded in getting the father to turn his unfortunate daughter out. Poor, helpless girl, she wandered about for some time until, overcome by despair, she flung herself into the river. But the pot kept her from sinking and she was rescued. Then she was taken into the service of Yamakagé-no Chûjô, where she toiled as a kitchen drudge, a sad life for the delicately brought-up maiden.

But the youngest of Chûjô's four sons, a noble-minded and handsome youth, had sympathy for the forlorn maiden. Attracted by her elegant and gentle speech and demeanour, and also by the comeliness of her appearance despite the fantastic disfigurement caused by the pot on her head, he told her of his love in secret.

Rumours of this came to the ears of his mother who was greatly concerned and sought by every means to separate them. At last she devised a scheme she believed would certainly succeed, which was to call together the wives of her other sons and force the girl into a competition with them. Both the lovers were so overwhelmed when they heard of the plan that in their desperation they determined to run away. They had just set out when, wonderful to relate, the pot which had stuck so long on the maiden's head suddenly came off of its own accord and fell with a thud at their feet. Then, in place of a poor, forlorn girl, there was revealed a beautiful princess, and from the fallen pot there rolled out rich stores of gold and silver and jewels, as well as a dazzling ceremonial dress.

Full of joy, she immediately put on the dress, and together with her lover set forth to take part in the wife-competition. The mother, meanwhile, with her other sons and their wives, had been impatiently awaiting the arrival of the girl, prepared to heap every humiliation upon her. Conceive of their astonishment when, in place of the humble maiden they had expected, they saw approaching a maiden as charming and fair as a heavenly being, accompanied by her lover. They stood in blank dismay not knowing what to do.

But the mother, jubilant at the unexpected splendour of the appearance of the one-time pot-wearer, invited her to the chief place nearest herself, doing everything in her power to entertain her. The princess soon showed that she was the superior of the wives of the other sons not only in beauty but also in her accomplishments in music and poetry. So completely did she win the admiration of the parents that they decided to make the fourth son their heir, passing over his three brothers.

Some time afterwards the princess encountered her father, Sanetaka, at the Kannon shrine at Hasé, who told her that, soon after her flight, he had been convinced of his error and had wandered all over the country in search of her. He had offered up prayers to Kannon to aid him in finding her, and now, thanks to the goddess, they were once more united. And so the story ends that, through the divine favour of Kannon, they all lived happily ever after.

This singular story centres on the mysterious pot which adheres to the heroine's head. Because of this she was despised and turned out of her home as " deformed " by her stepmother, and yet by its means great fortune and happiness came her way. For the rest, it is a stepmother story, although the miracle worked on the heroine's behalf by Kannon also shows the strong religious colour which marks mediaeval Japanese literature.

3. Shuten Dôji

There once lived on Mount Ôé-yama in Tanba province a demon called Shuten Dôji, who spread terror far and wide by carrying off people from the provinces around, but especially young girls from the capital, among them the beloved daughter of Ikeda Chûnagon

Kunitaka. When the father had learnt through a diviner that the monster was the cause of his daughter's disappearance, he hastened to submit the matter to the Throne.

Minamoto-no Yorimitsu, the hero of his day, receiving the imperial order to slay the demon, accepted the commission with pride and decided to take with him to aid him in the great task five companions, Yasumasa, Sadamitsu, Suetaké, Tsuna and Kintoki.

When the hero and his companions had offered up prayers for success, they started for Mount Ôé-yama in the guise of itinerant priests. On their way up the steep mountain path they came to a cavern in which they saw three dignified old men seated, who spoke thus to them: " Our wives have been torn from us by the demon of Mount Ôé-yama and we have come thus far seeking revenge. Since you also, it appears, in obedience to the Imperial order, are determined to destroy this demon, we offer ourselves as your guides. But, first, please rest yourselves here awhile."

Then one of the old men produced a bottle of saké, explaining, " This is a miraculous saké; it will redouble your courage, but from demons it takes away their supernatural power and renders them unconscious." Giving them the saké, the three old men led them along the rugged and precipitous path, until they reached a mountain stream where the old men stopped and said, " Further upstream you will see a beautiful young girl. She will show you the way. We are Gods incarnate who have made this brief appearance in order to help you." No sooner had they spoken than they vanished. Yorimitsu and his followers at once fell on their knees and offered thanks for this divine protection. Then, with courage renewed, they went on until, as they had been told, they saw a young girl of seventeen or so washing by the stream.

When they asked her where lay the cavern of the demon, she burst into tears and replied, " I belong to the capital, but I was kidnapped by the demon and am forced each day to suffer terrible torments. There are more than ten other maidens, bewailing a like fate, who are waiting only for death. The demon tortures them daily and sucks their blood." The tears of Yorimitsu and his companions flowed in sympathy, and they consoled her, declaring that they would deliver her and the other maidens. So they struggled

[193]

along until the girl at last brought them to the front of the demon's abode.

An iron gate rose high between steep cliffs, and on the path before it dreadful demon-sentries blocked the way, looking as if they would fall on them and crush them with one blow. So in order to allay suspicion, Yorimitsu and his companions put on a modest demeanour and humbly said, "Please give us shelter for the night. We are itinerant priests who have lost our way. Fortunately we have with us some excellent saké which we would like to offer to Shuten Dôji." So soon as the demon heard them mention the saké of which he was inordinately fond, he bade them be admitted at once.

Soon a banquet began, at which the drink served by the demon and his attendants consisted of blood squeezed from kidnapped women with some of the flesh still accompanying it. Nevertheless the brave men put up a bold front and talked fearlessly with the ogres. Then they urged Shuten Dôji to partake of the charmed saké they had brought, and it soon took effect, for Dôji fell fast asleep.

During the night Yorimitsu and the others donned their armour and stole into the demon's bed-chamber. They had seen the demon earlier in the human form that he assumed during the day, but now in sleep he had resumed his true and terrible form of a demon. They hacked the horrible creature to pieces, slew all the vassal demons, delivered the captive maidens and returned in triumph to the capital. The Emperor was highly pleased with their great exploit and the whole world resounded with the fame of Yorimitsu's prowess.

As the outline shows, we have here a feat of traditional demon hunting ascribed to that historical hero Minamoto-no Yorimitsu also known as Raikô. So while it embodies the belief in demons which was general in those days, it also suggests the prevalence of outlaws and robbers at that time and Yorimitsu's activity in suppressing them. This work also is characterized by the contemporary faith in divine protection.

4. Urashima Tarô

Once upon a time, in the province of Tango, lived a fisherman named Urashima Tarô. One day he caught a tortoise, but taking pity on it, he put it back unharmed into the sea. The following day he was out fishing again when, some distance out at sea, he espied a small boat in which a fair lady was sitting, which was soon carried ashore by the waves.

Wondering, he approached her and asked whence she had come. The lady replied that she had been shipwrecked and had drifted to this place, and begged Urashima to take her back home. Moved with pity he boarded the boat and pulled out to sea, but did not reach her home until he had been rowing for over ten days. Then they came to the glittering Palace of the Dragon King, enclosed with silver fences and roofed with gold! Urashima was received with great courtesy and soon afterwards married the lady who was the mistress of the Dragon's Castle. But after three years of dreamlike happiness had passed, Urashima became homesick and said he would like to return to pay a brief visit to his parents' home.

On parting, his wife for the first time disclosed her identity. "I am in truth the tortoise-queen of this Dragon's Palace, whom you once spared from death, and I married you out of gratitude for your kind-heartedness. But I fear that we shall not meet again." She then produced a beautiful casket, which she presented to him, saying, "Take this as a souvenir, but I warn you never on any account to open it."

With his heart full of sorrow at parting, Urashima retraced his way across the sea to his native place. There he found only a desolate wilderness; nothing remained of the once familiar village. Amazed and unable to believe his own eyes, he found an old man in a lonely hut and hesitatingly asked him if he happened to know the whereabouts of a man named Urashima Tarô. To his astonishment, the old man replied, "Well, well, that's a strange question to ask. For there is a tradition that Urashima lived here as far back as seven hundred years ago."

"What can this mean?" Urashima asked himself. Then he told the old man in a few simple words just what had happened, but the old man shook his head sceptically. "Look!" he said, pointing to a stone monument. "That is said to be Urashima's grave."

Standing before his own grave, Urashima was overcome with

tears, and in the excess of his grief scarcely knew what he was doing. Without thinking he lifted the lid of the casket that he had been forbidden to open!

Immediately three columns of smoke arose from within, and Urashima, from being a young man of twe.ty-four or so, was at or.ce transformed into an aged, white-haired man and was wafted up into the sky in the form of a crane. The seven hundred years of his life had been stored in the casket.

This Urashima afterwards reappeared in the province of Tango in the form of the god Urashima-no Myôjin, with the tortoise as the Myôjin goddess. These twain afterwards married and saved the world.

The famous legend of Urashima is recorded in *Tango Fudoki* (Topographical Survey of Tango Province), and is also the subject of a poem in *Man'yôshû*. The story deals with the marriage of a human and a non-human, and a sojourn in a fairyland, a theme found all over the world. The fairy-tale of Urashima is based on this ancient tradition, transformed under the influence of the times, and the later addition of the tortoise's gratitude is due to the moralistic note common in stories for the young.

TSUREZUREGUSA

(Gleanings of Leisure Moments)

Tsurezuregusa composed about 1330 by the priest Kenkô Hôshi is one of the finest collections of occasional essays in Japanese literature, ranking with that famous collection of the Heian period, *Makura-no-Sôshi*.

This work was produced at a time when a succession of wars had plunged people into the depths of pessimism and hatred of this world, turning their thoughts to Buddhism with its quiet rejection of the present and peaceful contemplation of a future life of happiness. *Tsurezuregusa* was naturally dominated by this Buddhist influence and the Chinese philosophy of Lao-tse and Chuang-tse. It was further inspired by the Japanese classics and the attractive emotionalism fostered by the literary ideals of the time—reverence for tradition and a wistful looking back on the flowery culture of the monarchic age of the Heian era.

For the author the beauty of the monarchic age derives itself from the philosophic depths of Buddhism and Taoism—the calm resignation that succeeds emancipation from worldly troubles, profound observation of life and nature, and the ideal of an intellectual life which is a harmony of literature with religion and ethics. In giving expression to such views *Tsurezuregusa* is unique in Japanese literature.

It is a collection of stray notes devoid of any attempt at consistency and unity in substance and form, jotted down from time to time as fancy dictated by a philosopher who sought and loved the solitary life. In them he gives expression to philosophical reflections, views on religion, statements and arguments reflecting his attitude on life, rules for conduct, moral ideas, views on love, observation of nature, items of information and the results of various investigations, all of which bring many aspects of his age into sharp but unstudied relief.

The work opens with the passage, "Overcome with ennui, I jot down whatever random thoughts occur to me." The word here rendered "ennui" is *tsurezuré*, and although it could well be translated "leisure," since it suggests a tranquil freedom from the pressure of secular affairs, there is in it as used here by the author more than a hint of forlorn loneliness. Lover though he was of solitude, the author sometimes found the loneliness irksome, and this contradiction pervades his thinking. But the word "leisure" may be preferable when we translate the title of the whole collection : hence the rendering of *Tsurezuregusa* as "Gleanings of Leisure Moments."

There are 244 chapters in all, out of which we will select the most characteristic and interesting in order to discover something of the mind of Kenkô. In Chapter 3 he reveals the temper of the monarchic age with its quest for emotionalism thus : "No matter how talented a man may be in every way, unless he has been a lover, he is just as unsatisfactory as a beautifully jewelled saké cup that lacks a bottom." Chapter 5 presents the author as so yearning for solitude that he is in complete agreement with an ancient who expressed a wish to live in exile without being guilty of any crime. The point of Chapter 10 is that although this world offers us but a brief stay, yet it is delightful to live in a tasteful dwelling. Houses in an unostentatiously harmonious style suggest the personalities of their masters. In Chapter 22, the author yearns for the charms of the monarchic age.

The author narrates in Chapter 43 how he happened to pass a wretched cottage in the mountains, where, through the torn bamboo-blinds, he was attracted by the sight of a handsome young man serenely reading a book on a calm spring evening. On another occasion he saw another young man pass out from his humble bamboo gate on a beautiful evening in autumn playing on a flute and following a narrow moonlit path, until he entered a mountain temple fragrant with incense.

Chapter 137 develops as its theme how, in all things, it is their beginning and end that hold the greatest charm and interest. It is more pleasing to watch for the coming of the moon when the sky is obscured by clouds than to view it when it is bright and full, and this suggests to him why it is more delightful to remain at home ather than seek abroad to witness all the scenes of passing spring. n the matter of the cherry blossom also, the author finds his chief pleasure in the twigs on which delicately blushing buds are just bursting into flower or in a tastefully laid-out garden where the fallen blossoms lie scattered on the ground. Yet an unimaginative man, on regarding the passing of the bloom, would only say, " The cherry blossoms are over. They are all dead ! " The same is true of love. Love stirs the depths of our hearts, not only in the bliss of longed-for meetings, but also in the mutual yearning that does not end in meeting, in the grief over a short-lived love throughout a lonely, wakeful night, in the sweet yearning for a lover far away, in the sight of a house now desolate that recalls the memory of a bygone love. Again, what can be more desirable than to talk quietly with bosom friends when, near dawn, the long-awaited moon, all slender and pale, silvers the tops of the trees among the mountains ; when the moon is screened by drifting clouds ; or when the glittering moonlight hangs on the glossy leaves of trees ! None but a lout needs to break off and carry away a branch of cherry blossom to give expression to his admiration for the beauty of the flowers, or must thrust hands and feet into pellucid springs or tramp ruthlessly about in a beautiful garden on a snowy day—unable to appreciate the beauties of nature unless he can take them in his grasp.

In Chapter 191 we find Kenkô praising the beauty of lamp-light, stressing the peculiar charm lent by it to commonplace utensils and clothes. He takes pity on anyone who is so absorbed in the struggle for fame and riches that he is content with the realist's insensitivity to beauty.

If we would see his attitude to Buddhism, we may turn to Chapter 7. His conception is based on his realization of life's uncertainty, in which he is strongly influenced by contemporary thought. How monotonous life would be if, instead of being as evanescent as morning dew or the smoke of a funeral pyre, it should continue everlastingly ! Life owes its fascination to the very fact that it is so mutable and uncertain. To seek to cling to life, to be greedy even for the welfare of one's posterity, to wish for a long life—all these are unworthy aims. To live long is merely to outlive much. Since one is destined to die, then much better is it to die at forty, when one is in the fulness of one's manhood. In this world, ever-drifting, precarious as the pools and shallows of a river, both pleasure and grief alike come to an end. To the thinker, life is but vanity, and vain are all the glories of the past. What folly also to plan and labour for the welfare of one's posterity !

The author's profound ideas on life are characteristically expressed, for example, in Chapter 92. There he tells how a man, beginning to learn archery, took his place before the target with two arrows in his hand, when his teacher thus admonished him : " A novice must never face the target with two arrows, for he will be careless with his first shot, depending on the second. He must learn how to concentrate on the one arrow available." This is an immortal saying of universal application. When a student, in the morning, begins to rely on the morrow or even the evening, he is falling into a habit of procrastination against which he must always be on guard, for although the call of indolence may only be momentary, it can have lasting effects. How is it that a man is so apt to lack the determination to carry out his resolutions as soon as he makes them ? Accordingly, in Chapter 98, he quotes the following three lessons of a great and holy man :—

1. One should leave undone anything one hesitates about doing.
2. In order to fix one's thoughts on a future life one should possess nothing in this life.
3. Holders of rank must abandon it ; the wise must become simple, and the rich poor.

In a similar vein he teaches, in Chapter 108, that it is of the first importance to know the value of every moment. " Time flies like an arrow." Death is approaching with every second. Yet the short moments, piled up, make a long life. Any man who idles away even the least fraction of time is foolish enough ultimately to waste a day, a month, or even a whole life. In Chapter 150 he says that a resolute will and unfaltering efforts are essential to accomplish anything. Possessing these even a fool will succeed where a man of talent fails. Chapter 233 deals with sincerity, the best and surest policy with which to entertain one's friends.

He has many observations to make on nature. Chapter 19, for instance, deals with the changes of the seasons, each of which has its own special attractions. Thus, while autumn is characterized

a tranquil beauty, spring is exhilarating. In spring there is the
ng of the birds, the young grass pushing its way out to the mild
nlight, a warm haze trailing over the earth and flowers budding.
'hile we are still grieving to see the flowers scattered by the heartless
ind and rain, we are surprised by the sudden arrival of the season
green foliage. Then come the sweet odour of orange blossoms
ousing old associations, the delicate charm of the yellow roses,
d then the fragile grace of the wistaria. All these things please
, each in its own way, and early summer stirs our hearts. In late
immer moon-flowers bloom white by humble cottages that we have
arcely deigned to notice, whose eaves are caressed by the curling
noke of smudge fires—a beautiful and pathetic scene to gaze upon!
'ith autumn comes the chilly wind that daily blows with increasing
rength. The wild geese cry overhead, the leaves of the bush-clover
dden, and in the golden rice-fields the work of harvest goes on.
desolate winter scene also has its fascination. How lovely indeed
a winter's morning when tinted leaves drift at the water's edge, the
ost glittering white and a soft mist rising from the little streams!
much does the author admire the beauties of nature in every
ason that, in Chapter 20, he expresses agreement with the man who
id that, in spite of his complete detachment from the world, he
uld not help regretting that nature was so everchanging—he
uld never tire of a spring evening, never tire of gazing at the ex-
uisite autumn moon, feeling at one with nature.

Further, *Tsurezuregusa* contains a number of pointed anecdotes
d curious stories having a philosophical bearing on life. Chapter
gives us the strange story of " The Priest and the Three-legged
ot." During a noisy revel, a young bonze jumped up and began
dance. He took hold of a three-legged pot and pulled it over his
ead, and his droll appearance evoked general applause and roars
f laughter. But when, after a while, he tried to remove the pot
e found it impossible, for he had forced the small pot too far over
is head. This sobered the whole party and, raising a clamour, they
l joined in trying to remove the pot. But all their efforts proved
ain. The iron was too strong for them to break and, indeed, each
me they struck it, they only caused a clangour that almost burst
is ear-drums. So, leading the priest by the hand, they trooped off

to find a doctor, but he too proved helpless. They were at their wit's end with anxiety and, feeling that they must save his life at any cost, tugged so hard at the pot that they nearly pulled his head from his shoulders. In the end they could only remove the pot at the sacrifice of his nose and ears, which were torn off in the process of extrication.

In Chapter 109 is the story of a skilful tree-climber. He had ordered one of his men to climb a tall tree, and, while the man was perched on a high and dangerous branch, watched him without saying a word. When the man had almost completed the descent to the ground, however, the master uttered a warning cry, "Take care!" The author demanded in amazement, "Why do you warn him when he has reached a safe place? Why didn't you do it when he was up there in danger?" The master answered, "That's just the point. Everybody takes care of himself in a dangerous place. He makes blunders when he feels quite safe and so gets careless."

There are many such brief anecdotes pregnant with point and meaning, while the whole work possesses a high literary value because of the beauty of its style and language. It blends perfectly two distinct styles; one, the flowing elegance characteristic of the classical literature of that Heian period for which the author yearned in particular, *Makura-no-Sôshi*; the other, the concise and vigorous style typical of the new age. The author's simple, unworldly, yet resourceful, touches create a medium flexible enough to vary according to the subject-matter of each chapter. When he is delineating scenes in the Heian style he employs the elegant manner of classical narrative; but when he is recounting anecdotes and strange events his style is impressively concise, pointed with epigrams and satire. It is the employment of this lucid, unrestrained and polished style to reveal the secrets of humanity that makes the work a masterpiece in the field of the occasional essay, fully deserving of the high place it holds in Japanese literature.

The author's real name was Yoshida-no Kaneyoshi, Kenkô being his name in religion. He was born of a Shinto priestly family in the hereditary service of the Yoshida shrine in Kyoto, and as a youthful samurai he entered the service of the Imperial court. There he enjoyed the special favour of the Emperor Go-Uda, and be-

ne highly respected as a poet. On the death of the Emperor, he
s overwhelmed with sorrow at life's uncertainty, and so secluded
nself from the world to lead the life of a Buddhist recluse.

Later, when Kyoto had become the scene of civil strife, he travel-
. as a solitary among distant mountains to escape the turmoil.
ter a while he came back to Kyoto and built himself a hermitage
Narabigaoka, where, it is said, while leading a leisurely life in the
oyment of nature, he composed his great work *Tsurezuregusa*.

Born a Shintoist, becoming well versed in poetry and in close
ich with Confucianism and Taoism, and later entering the religious
e as a devout believer in Buddhism, Kenkô Hôshi was fortunate
being blessed with wide culture and with scholarship and talent
well as a profound knowledge of Japanese literature. The result
is, as this work clearly shows, to produce in Kenkô a philosopher
whose mind such contrasts as pessimism and optimism, feeling
d reason, fantasy and realism, could find a harmonious meeting
ace.

———————

JINNÔ SHÔTÔKI

(The True Genealogy of the Sacred Emperors)

The author of *Jinnô Shôtôki* was Kitabataké Chikafusa, who wro
it in the autumn of 1339 in the castle of Oda at the foot of N
Tsukuba in Hitachi province (Ibaraki prefecture). Except for
concise chronological table which he kept by him for referenc
Chikafusa wrote the whole book from memory.

The strangest feature about this compilation is that Chikafus;
a prominent court-noble, should have undertaken it, not only i
the midst of war, but in a small castle remote from the capital. T
understand it one must go with some detail into the circumstanc
that led him to undertake the task. Chikafusa, who enjoyed th
full confidence of the Emperor Go-Daigo, had come to the conclusio
that the disorganization of the administration and the feebleness o
the Court had resulted from the appointment of the Shogun as militar
dictators. Originally, the Shogun had been but an official in th
service of the Court, but by this time he had come to exercise a
authority greater than that of the Throne itself. Or rather, it was nc
the Shogun, but one of his vassals, Hôjô Takatoki, who now hel
the supreme power. Accordingly, the Emperor felt that he must a
all costs regain control of the reins of government and retrieve th
administrative power. Then only, with the Emperor actually rulin
as well as reigning, could peace and order be restored to the country

The Emperor Go-Daigo therefore surrounded himself with me
of outstanding ability, Kitabataké Chikafusa, Madenokôji Fujifus
and Hino Suketomo among them. Chikafusa rose steadily from on
high position to another until, at the age of thirty-one, he was ap
pointed to the important position of Dainagon (Chief Councillor o
State), ranking next to the President of the Council. This positio:
he filled for six years, at the end of which period he entered a lif
of religion.

The reason for this unexpected action was this. Of all the youn;

rinces the one who had shown the greatest promise and had enjoyed he special favour of the Emperor was the youthful Yonaga Shinnô. Chikafusa had been appointed his guardian ; he had loved his charge nd served him devotedly, but unfortunately the young prince had een suddenly taken ill and had died at the early age of eighteen. n his grief, Chikafusa resigned his responsible office and took the onsure on the day Yonaga Shinnô died. As a monk he was now lebarred from any direct concern in politics, but he continued to how his devotion to the Emperor by aiding his own son Akiié to upport the Emperor in his high ideal of regaining control of the dministrative power.

This restoration could be achieved only by the destruction of Hôjô Takatoki, an exceedingly difficult task, since he controlled both he police and military forces. But this was eventually accomplished n 1333. Then, only two years after the Hôjô had been overthrown, Ashikaga Takauji raised the standard of rebellion. Chikafusa's son Akiié did manful service in the attempt to subjugate Takauji and, l h)ugh only eighteen years old at the time, he actually succeeded n recapturing Kyoto from the rebel who had been in occupation f it for a while. But disasters followed for the Imperial Army. Such great commanders as Kusunoki Masashigé and Nawa Nagatoshi vere slain in battle, and then, in a battle fought in the fifth month, 338, Akiié himself fell, to be followed very little later by Nitta Yoshisada. The dire straits of the Imperial Army with so many llustrious leaders falling in quick succession aroused Chikafusa, vho now determined to offer his services in the suppression of the Ashikaga.

Chikafusa decided to use the province of Mutsu (including Aomori nd other prefectures) as his base of operations. Thanks to the nfluence of Akiié, who had formerly been governor of that province, oyalty to the Imperial cause there ran high. His purpose was, after is army had thoroughly recouped its energy in this province, to march on Kyoto and destroy the Ashikaga clan. The Emperor Go-Daigo approved his decision, and then, since the land was overrun by the enemy forces, he embarked his own men and set sail from the coast of Isé province (Mié prefecture) to accompany Prince Norinaga o Mutsu. But a heavy storm overtook Chikafusa and his party,

and the boats were separated. The Prince's boat was driven bac
to the shores of Isé and he was obliged to return to Yoshino, whil
Chikafusa's boat was cast away on the coast of Kasumiga'ura i
Hitachi (Ibaraki prefecture).

There the Ashikaga forces swarmed down on Chikafusa, but h
succeeded in routing them and eventually was able to establis
himself in the castle of Oda at the foot of Mt Tsukuba. Using thi
as his base he put up a good fight desperately for four years. I
was in the ninth month of 1338 that he entered the castle of Oda
and in the eighth month of the following year, the Emperor Go
Daigo having died at Yoshino, the young Prince Norinaga suc
ceeded his father on the throne, with the posthumous title of Go
Murakami Tennô. Full of anxiety about the future of the nation
the Emperor Go-Daigo from his death-bed had urged his son to
have complete trust in Chikafusa's management of affairs.

The news of the Emperor's death reached Chikafusa just whei
he was engaged in a severe conflict with the besiegers of Oda Castle
Not long before when he had been bereaved of his ward, the youny
Prince Yonaga, his grief had driven him to resign office and ente
the priesthood. But now there was no time to indulge in lamenta
tion. His duty now was to assist the still youthful Emperor Go
Murakami in the administration of the country to the utmost of hi
powers. Beleaguered as he was by a powerful enemy, he was unabl
to hasten to Yoshino to offer his services. This explains how i
was that Chikafusa came to write *Jinnô Shôtôki*, and why he, one o
the chief court-nobles, composed this work in a besieged castle fa
away from the capital.

The main aim of this history is to elucidate the principle on whick
the Japanese nation is established. It sets itself to recount how the
country of Japan was brought into being, by whom the country has
been governed and the character of its administration. The thesis
put forward by Chikafusa is that, as a matter of historical fact, Japan
was founded by the gods, that the emperors are the descendants
of the gods, and that they have always ruled, do still rule and will
always continue to rule the country.

Composed as it was in the midst of war, with no other written
authority available except one small chronological table, this work

lacking in historical detail. Nevertheless, with *Nihonshoki* (History Book of Ancient Japan) and *Dai Nihon Shi* (History of Great Japan), is one of the most important of Japanese histories.

The account it gives of the country's past shows keen insight and is entirely free from the false conceptions of history current at the time, the "Prophetic theory" introduced from China, and the "Decadence theory" of Indian Buddhism.

The Prophetic theory, long held in China and most widely in the age of the Later Han Dynasty, may be briefly outlined as follows. Human history proceeds according to natural law and necessity and owes nothing to contingency or the arbitrary will of man. Consequently, by studying the law and elucidating the principle of historical evolution, we shall be able to foresee and prophesy the future course of events. Since all man's life is held to be in accordance with the law of necessity this theory of history does not admit the freedom of human will and reduces all human effort to insignificance. It follows that the prevalence of such a theory involves the acceptance without question of the various evils that beset men. In Chikafusa's day it was very generally accepted, but he resolutely rejected this mistaken view of history.

The Decadence theory is a Buddhist conception of history originating in India. It divides history after the death of Sakya, the founder of Buddhism, into three ages—(1) The age of "True Buddhism" covering the first one thousand years after Sakya's death, when his teachings prevailed and people could be sure of salvation by practising the austerities enjoined by those teachings, (2) the age of "Nominal Buddhism," the succeeding period of one thousand years, during which, no matter how desirous people were of following the law of Buddha, they could never attain enlightenment, and (3) the age of "Decadent Buddhism," covering the next ten thousand years, a period of continual deterioration of mankind. Men cease to practise the discipline of asceticism and, guided by their natural appetites, engage in continual strife, bringing the world into an absolutely hopeless condition. This theory, according to which mankind entered upon an age of darkness two thousand years after Sakya's death, was widely favoured in the Middle Ages of Japan, and a number of historical works were written from this standpoint.

Chikafusa rejected both these theories and understood and ex
pounded history much more in accordance with actual facts. H
opposed the current pessimism by maintaining that "Japan is
Divine Land." He was by no means the first to assert this; indeec
the divine character of Japan had been widely accepted from antiquity
His merit was that, at a time when it especially needed saying, h
reasserted this principle and began his history with the emphati
declaration of the divineness of his country. He laid it down tha
Japan was founded by the gods and that its rule was entrusted to th
Emperors as the descendants of the gods, hence its name, Kami n
Kuni, the Land of the Gods. He made this the basis of his con
ception of Japanese history and the standard of his moral, cultura
and political principles.

He bases the moral obligations of the Japanese people on the fac
that they owe everything to the favour of the gods and their des
ce·dants, the Emperors. The rice eaten and the water drunk eacl
day should not be looked on as private possessions but as blessing
received from the divine Emperor. By His grace we live, and i
return we owe Him absolute allegiance. Ethically regarded, this al
legiance follows as a simple matter of course without any expectatior
of remuneration, even if it involves the sacrifice of life. In the spher
of politics too the same principle holds good. No matter how power
ful a subject may be, he can never measure himself against the Em
peror who ascends the throne in virtue of His divine origin. Indeed
ultimately, no subject can be said to possess any power, since it al
lies in the hands of the Emperor alone. This is the basic ide
of his history.

The work dates from a time when morality had deteriorated and ε
rebel such as Ashikaga Takauji had used his power to capture Kyoto
and it was at this very juncture that Chikafusa presented the young
Emperor Go-Murakami with his *Jinnô Shôtôki*, with the idea of in
forming him correctly in Japanese history and in the basic principle:
of Japanese morals and politics.

Jinnô Shôtôki has, however, exercised an influence far wider than
that of a mere hand-book on politics for the Emperor's use. Not
only did it inspire the loyalty of those who read it at the time, but
this book, with *Taiheiki* (Chronicles of the Peaceful Reign), may be

egarded as one of the main inspirations of the Meiji Restoration, aving, so to speak, waited for three centuries to be appreciated completely and to find its fullest expression.

———————

TAIHEIKI

(Chronicles of the Peaceful Reign)

Taiheiki is the record of nearly fifty years of the chequered history of the Kamakura Shogunate, beginning with the Emperor Go-Daigo's ill-fated effort to subjugate it. At the time when the Emperor Go-Daigo ascended the throne in 1318, the Shogun had acquired such power that in actual fact Kamakura, the seat of their feudal system of administration, had become the centre of government to the exclusion of Kyoto, where the Emperor lived and reigned. One of the worst features of this deplorable state of things was the enormous power that Hôjô Takatoki had come to wield; originally only a vassal of the Shogun, he was now more powerful than his master, ruling arbitrarily without the least regard for the sufferings of the people or their needs. In such circumstances, the Emperor Go-Daigo decided that he must restore the course of Japanese politics to its proper channel; the supreme power must be brought back into the hands of the Emperor who, loving his subjects as his children, would rule in conformity with the moral law.

But the Hôjô family was so powerful that they were able to impose some of their members on the Imperial Court, where they exercised such close surveillance that it was almost impossible for the Emperor to make any progress with his projects for reform. Finally, in 1324, the plan was ferreted out by the Hôjô, the samurai involved were all put to death, and the court-noble, Hino Suketomo, regarded as the moving spirit in the plot, was arrested and exiled to the distant island of Sado. The Emperor refused to be turned from his purpose, and had made some progress with a further attempt, when that too was discovered, and the Hôjô dispatched a large army from Kamakura to Kyoto to arrest and disperse the conspirators. Thereupon the Emperor hastily fled from Kyoto to Mount Kasagi, where, at the head of the Imperial forces, he sought to defend himself, but the castle being ill-equipped for defence and his men outnumbered by the enemy,

e castle fell and he himself was exiled by the successful rebels to
e remote island of Oki. The triumphant Hôjô Takatoki sent
inces and courtiers into exile in all parts of the country and estab-
hed Kôgon'in on the throne at Kyoto. He was bound to set up
a Emperor, since Japan can never be without one, and moreover,
ily members of the Imperial family, as Kôgon'in was, can ascend
ie throne.

The Hôjô were now challenged from a new quarter, by Kusunoki
Iasashigé, a loyalist general who had raised an army in Kawachi.
'he Hôjô mobilized an enormous army of a million men and laid
ege to his castle, but even after six months of strenuous fighting
iey were unable to capture it. The resistance of Masashigé in-
)ired the loyal samurai all over the country who rallied round Prince
Iorinaga, known as Daitô-no Miya, a son of the Emperor Go-
)aigo, and, under his leadership, made a surprise attack on the
Iôjô.

Meanwhile, the Emperor Go-Daigo had effected his escape from
he island of Oki and, making his way with Nawa Nagatoshi to Mt
enjô-sen, he sent out Imperial orders summoning volunteer samurai
rom all quarters. So large and powerful an Imperial Army was
ssembled that it was able to capture not only Kyoto but also
Kamakura, where, in May 1333, Hôjô Takatoki was completely de-
eated and committed suicide. From the moment of his enthrone-
nent fifteen years before, the Emperor Go-Daigo had striven to
uppress the Shogunate, and it now seemed as if the great work of
estoring the Imperial authority had been achieved.

Greeted by Kusunoki Masashigé and other loyal samurai, the
Emperor returned in triumph to Kyoto, and forthwith set himself
) the task of effecting the great reforms necessary to the Restoration.
But the work had not advanced very far when another serious prob-
em arose, the rebellion of Ashikaga Takauji.

Originally, Ashikaga had sided with Hôjô Takatoki and had led
an army against the Emperor, but seeing the growing strength of
the Imperial forces, he had suddenly deserted the Hôjô and regained
Kyoto for the Emperor by attacking the Hôjô army there. His action
in attaching himself to the side of the Emperor had been inspired
by considerations of self-interest ; he was merely waiting for a suitable

opportunity to seize political power. Prince Morinaga, seeing through his evil designs, attempted to suppress him, but fell a victim to his cunning and was imprisoned at Kamakura. While he lay there the remnants of the Hôjô raised the standard of revolt and delivered an attack on Kamakura, and Tadayoshi, younger brother of Takauji, took advantage of the confusion to slay the Prince. Then the two Ashikaga rose in open rebellion at Kamakura. The Emperor sent an expedition against them under the command of Nitta Yoshisada, the same general who not long before had captured Kamakura and annihilated the forces of Hôjô Takatoki. But Yoshisada was defeated and had to return to Kyoto, pursued by Ashikaga Takauji with an irresistible force. Thus only two years after the fall of the Hôjô, Kyoto was again captured and the country was once more thrown into confusion.

But after a while, Nitta Yoshisada and Kusunoki Masashigé succeeded in defeating Takauji, and, with the help of Kitabataké Akiié, they regained Kyoto, while Takauji had to flee to remote Kyushu. Takauji, however, was a man of infinite resources and rallying the local samurai to his side was soon able to lead another powerful army against the capital. Yoshisada and Masashigé advanced as far as Hyôgo (now Kobe) where they prepared a defensive stand against him. But for some reason or other Masashigé's strategic plans were not properly carried out; anticipating failure and defeat Masashigé, on his way to battle, left a final testament for his eldest son Masatsura, then a boy of eleven, at Sakurai no Eki. "The coming battle," he said, "will be a very severe test and I am afraid this will be our last meeting on earth. When you hear of my death, you will know that the Ashikaga have gained the upper hand. No matter what happens, you must never surrender to the disloyal and unjust Ashikaga. So long as a single relative or vassal survives, you must lead him against that rebellious family." After giving his son this command he sent him back to his native place.

With a small force of only seven hundred men he then set out for Hyôgo, where he gallantly engaged the powerful enemy force of five hundred thousand, inflicting heavy losses on them before he was defeated. Then he disembowelled himself. Takauji went on to recapture Kyoto and set Kômyôin upon the Imperial throne. Thus like Hôjô Takatoki before him, he deluded the people with the pretence that he was assuming the direction of state administration under the command of this Emperor.

With the death of Kusunoki Masashigé and Nawa Nagatoshi, all serious opposition melted away. The Emperor Go-Daigo was compelled to retire to Mount Yoshino, where, putting himself in command of the loyalists throughout the country, he continued to plan the overthrow of the Ashikaga, hoping to stir up the loyalists in different parts of the country to simultaneous action, so that the Ashikaga forces in Kyoto could be attacked from all sides. But when the time came for the carrying out of his plan, his two chief leaders, Kitabataké Akiié and Nitta Yoshisada were killed in action. Roused by the news of the miscarriage of this plan and of the death of one Imperial general after another, Kitabataké Chikafusa, father of Akiié, came out of retirement to lead the Imperial forces. Under the leadership of Prince Norinaga he and his men set forth by sea for northeastern Japan (the provinces of Mutsu and Dewa), when they were overtaken by a storm and scattered to various coasts. Chikafusa's boat was cast away on the coast of Hitachi (Ibaraki prefecture), where he landed and carried on a desperate resistance for six years.

In the meantime, the Emperor Go-Daigo passed away in August 1339 on Mount Yoshino, after a troubled life of conflict against the two rebellious families of the Hôjô and the Ashikaga. He remained to the end undaunted by his many distresses, still keeping firm to his resolve to suppress these rebels and bring back Japan to her proper state, and so replace an administration based on crude self-interest by one ruled by the moral law.

Prince Norinaga succeeded him as the Emperor Go-Murakami, but could do nothing to halt the growing power of the Ashikaga. In 1348 Kusunoki Masatsura, son of Kusunoki Masashigé, fell in battle, and six years later the aged champion Kitabataké Chikafusa also died. The Imperial army was all the while growing weaker in strength and resources, but never relaxed its efforts, upheld as it was by the determination to destroy the insurgents. *Taiheiki* ends with the year 1376, describing the confused and desperate efforts of that year.

The author of *Taiheiki* is unknown. In the Diary of Tôin Kinsada under an entry dated May 3rd, 1374, the Priest Kojima, who had died a few days earlier, is referred to as the author, and Kojima was for long assumed to be the author. But both tradition and internal evidence show that *Taiheiki* cannot have been the work of a single writer, but that it is rather a joint production that has undergone gradual enlargement and revision. One thing is obvious, that *Taiheiki* is not a record prepared later, but is based on personal experience, the authors themselves being witnesses of the social upheavals and disturbances they describe. Its character as a joint production is well shown by a story in *Nan-Taiheiki* (Taiheiki Denounced) written in 1402 by Imagawa Ryôshun, a vassal of the Ashikaga and Governor-General of Kyushu, to the effect that when Ashikaga Tadayoshi, younger brother of Takauji, who died in 1352, had read *Taiheiki*, he had pointed out some statements at variance with the truth. This early reference, before 1352, to a work, which was not completed until 1367, shows how it had grown up from one hand to another.

Taiheiki, although it begins coherently enough, becomes more and more disconnected and inconsistent as it proceeds. This is partly owing to its joint authorship, but also, to a much larger extent, to the increasingly chaotic state of the country in the course of the struggle. It is indeed to be marvelled at that a history dealing with fifty years of such grave disorders should be as concise and coherent as it is. The style is magnificent, lucid and vigorous, admirably suited to the matter. That the style is of a flowing character, sometimes with a touch of poetic rhythm, bears witness to the fact that the work was recited in public.

It gives a vivid picture of the greatest disturbance in thought and morality in the whole of Japan's long history. Though living through such a time of disorder the authors are faithful to the Japanese tradition and to the lofty ideals of the Emperor Go-Daigo. They give us an imperishable record, wrought in sympathetic detail, of the deeds of those who remained loyal to the Emperor. Their own greatness is thus revealed.

Unfortunately the Ashikaga gained the victory and all the loyalists perished in battle. With their fall all the records of their families were obliterated. *Taiheiki* alone keeps the knowledge of what these loyal heroes wrought from being utterly lost. To this work posterity owes the transmission of the exploits of such men as Prince Morinaga (Daitô-no Miya), Hino Suketomo, Kusunoki Masashigé, Nawa Nagatoshi and Nitta Yoshisada. In the course of years the great impression made by these loyalists upon the nation has but deepened and, undoubtedly, the national consciousness has its prime source in the influence exercised by *Taiheiki*. Kusunoki Masashigé in particular has been praised and loved with a religious fervour as a great national hero, and his parting from his young son Masatsura at Sakurai no Eki treasured as one of the most pathetic incidents in our history.

Eventually the noble example of these heroic loyalists bore fruit, after the lapse of five and a half centuries, in the Meiji Restoration, of which, therefore, *Taiheiki* can truly be said to have been the motivating force.

NOTE. Although the literal rendering of the title *Taiheiki* is " The Chronicles of the Peaceful Reign," the work is not concerned with what the title suggests but deals exclusively with the wars and internal troubles of the preceding period, now recollected in tranquillity in a peaceful reign.

GIKEIKI

(A Life of Yoshitsuné)

Gikeiki is one of those battle stories (*gunkimono*), so typical of the age (the latter half of the fourteenth century) in which it was written, which depict scenes of fighting and striking historical events. To this class of work *Soga Monogatari* (Tale of the Soga Brothers) also belongs, but these two differ from the general run of such battle stories in that they are limited in the main to the exploits of one individual hero, the principal figure in *Gikeiki* being the great national hero, Minamoto-no Yoshitsuné.

Undoubtedly, a great deal of the popular sympathy for the ill-starred Yoshitsuné sprang from the fact that he was a great general known for his ability and valour, a samurai commanding general admiration and respect, whose life was nevertheless a succession of misfortunes and vicissitudes. *Gikeiki* is the expression of this sympathy ; it is the popular voice raised in homage to him. Also, in order to appreciate fully the character of *Gikeiki*, regard must be paid to the fact that the very weakness and failure of Yoshitsuné, a victim of the cruel jealousy of his elder brother Yoritomo, evoked that compassion for the righteous when weak and oppressed, which is one of the characteristics of the Japanese people. Under the influence of such compassion, the Japanese go to the extreme in embellishing the actual sufferings of such unfortunates so as to bring them nearer to the ideal victim demanded by their tender emotions. In this way *Gikeiki* is meant to give what must be regarded as a romantic rather than a severely historical picture of Yoshitsuné, with a very free use of legends and fantasy.

To give expression to the intense sympathy felt by the people to this unfortunate hero, the phrase *Hôgan-biiki* (Devotion to the Hôgan) was coined from his title as a high police official.

The following is an outline of the contents of the work. Yoshitsuné, known in his childhood as Ushiwakamaru, was sent to study

ILLUSTRATIONS TO GIKEIKI (A LIFE OF YOSHITSUNÉ). Printed in 1672.

ILLUSTRATIONS TO SOGA MONO-GATARI (THE TALE OF THE SOGA BROTHERS). Printed in the 17th century.

on Mount Kurama, near Kyoto, after his father Yoshitomo had fallen in the Battle of Heiji. There, from about the age of fifteen, he devoted himself in secret to the study of military arts, with the firm determination of destroying his father's foes, the Heiké clan, and of regaining control of the administrative power for his own clan, the Genji. At the age of sixteen he fled from Kurama with the aid of Kaneuri Kichiji, a merchant, who took him to Ôu (the provinces of Mutsu and Dewa in north-eastern Japan) where he found asylum with Hidehira of the Fujiwara family, hereditary friends of the Genji. He stayed there for over a year and then returned to the capital, Kyoto, in order to watch for an opportunity of raising an army.

There was living at that time in the capital a tactician, named Kiichi Hôgen, then at the height of his fame. To gain access to his treasured books on tactics, Yoshitsuné made love to his daughter, and with her help succeeded in seeing the books. When Hôgen discovered what had happened, he was greatly enraged and planned to kill Yoshitsuné, who, however, turned the tables on him and killed him.

Meanwhile, he had gained the services of Musashibô Benkei, a loyal and trustworthy retainer of unparalleled daring. The story tells that Benkei was carried eighteen months in his mother's womb and that he was of uncommon size at his birth, precocious of speech with the looks of a demon. His father had sent him to Mount Hiyei, to be trained as a priest, but his reckless daring and iron nerve led to his being very quickly expelled for unruliness. Then he went to Mount Shosa, where his wilfulness and spirit of mischief displayed themselves by his starting a forest-fire which consumed the whole mountain-side.

Benkei's ambition was to collect one thousand swords to be treasured as an heirloom, and at night he used to fall on passers-by and rob them of their swords. He was only one short of the thousand when, one night, he caught sight of a handsome young man wearing a gold-decorated sword. It was no other than Yoshitsuné himself, who, apparently nothing more than a young man of fashion, was strolling along, playing on a flute. But when Benkei attacked him, he soon found that his brute strength was no match for the skill of the young man, and in the end he had to yield to him. Thus

Yoshitsuné won a retainer of peerless loyalty and valour, whom he took with him when he went once more to Hiraizumi in Ôu, there to await an opportunity to rise in arms.

As soon as he heard that his elder brother Yoritomo, who had been exiled to Izu, had raised an army, Yoshitsuné hastened to join him. The two brothers had been parted since childhood, and they threw themselves into each other's arms, weeping tears of joy. The elder brother appointed young Yoshitsuné commander-in-chief of an expeditionary force against the Heiké, and so well did he execute his task that, after pursuing the enemy from one hard-fought battle to another, now in the valley of Ichinotani, now on the fatal seashore of Danno'ura in Yashima, he succeeded in annihilating the whole clan.

Flushed with victory, he set forth eastward to bring his brother the good news of his spectacular success, and reached Koshigoé near Yoritomo's base of operations at Kamakura. There he was amazed to receive orders from his brother forbidding him to advance further, and, indeed, Yoritomo had even sent a punitive force against his army. This was due to the machinations of Kajiwara Kagetoki, whose pusillanimous conduct had aroused Yoshitsuné's resentment in earlier battles, and who now took his revenge by reporting that the younger brother was harbouring rebellious designs. Yoshitsuné at once sent his brother a passionate defence, which forms the well-known *Koshigoé Jô*, the Epistle from Koshigoé, in which he protested that he had a perfectly clear conscience and that, so far from being guided by self-interest, he had only achieved the subjugation of the Heiké at grave risk of his own life. But nothing was able to dispel the elder brother's deep-rooted suspicion, and therefore, overcome with depression and despair, Yoshitsuné turned back to Kyoto, there to wait until his brother's wrath had died down. But Yoritomo's bitter anger did not permit him to find any peace even there, for he dispatched a force against him under the command of Tosabô.

Yoshitsuné and his men gave themselves up for lost, and, indeed, they only just managed to succeed in beating off the forces of Tosabô. They were forced to leave Kyoto and seek refuge in some less accessible district, and accordingly Yoshitsuné and his men set sail for Shikoku, accompanied by a number of Yoshitsuné's ladies, including his favourite concubine Shizuka. But, en route, a violent storm arose which drove them ashore at Daimotsuno'ura, where the buffeted and bewildered fugitives succeeded in making a landing, only to find a new peril awaiting them. For orders had been sent all over the country for the apprehension of Yoshitsuné, and he had the greatest difficulty in effecting his escape to Mount Yoshino in Yamato province (Nara prefecture). He had hoped to have his beloved Shizuka's company in all his exile, but he now felt it necessary to send her back to the capital.

His hiding-place was a room in a small chapel still thickly covered with snow, but here he was sought out and attacked by the monk-soldiers. He offered a long but hopeless resistance, and then, guarded by Benkei and other stout, faithful retainers, he escaped from the mountain to find shelter for a while in the house of Kanjubô at Nara.

Meanwhile, after parting from Yoshitsuné, the weeping Shizuka descended Mount Yoshino quite alone and at Kyoto was given shelter by her mother, Iso-no Zenji, who was a Zen priestess there. But Yoritomo had both Shizuka and Iso-no Zenji arrested and hailed before him at Kamakura. There he sought to extort from her information regarding Yoshitsuné's whereabouts, but she resolutely refused to give it.

Yoritomo, therefore, gave orders that if Yoshitsuné's child which Shizuka was carrying proved to be a girl, it should be allowed to live but that if it were a boy it should be killed. The child was a boy and, in accordance with this merciless decree, was at once torn from her and thrown into the sea. So far was Yoritomo from showing the least regard for Shizuka's sorrowing heart that he ordered her to dance before the shrine of Tsurugaoka Hachiman, so that he could enjoy the wonderful art of this famous dancer. This broke her heart; but it was the spectators who were moved to tears, when the beautiful dancer, her eyes haggard with grief, danced before the detestable Yoritomo, fluttering her sleeves gaily and bravely as she sang a song of love for her absent lover.

The ill-fated Yoshitsuné, driven from one place of concealment to another, at last made up his mind to flee from the capital and to turn to Hidehira in the Ôu region for help. He brought together his few remaining men, ten in number, including the loyal Benkei, and they set out on their dangerous journey, disguised as mendicant priests so as to elude the severe interrogations they were bound to encounter.

On their way northward, they only just escaped arrest at the barrier of Sannokuchi-zeki, where Benkei's quick wit enabled them to elude the vigilance of the samurai in charge who had received special orders from Yoritomo to keep a very strict watch at that point. They succeeded in passing the next dangerous barrier of Togashi no Tachi, but when they came to the ferry of Nyoi no Watashi they were viewed with great suspicion. This was only dispelled when the watch saw Benkei strike Yoshitsuné as one would strike only a coolie. Thus they managed to cross the river safely, but the thought of the pitiable plight to which they and their lord had been reduced made them choke with tears. Eventually, after further narrow escapes, they succeeded in reaching their destination at Hiraizumi in Ôu, where Hidehira greeted them and gave them the use of his castle at Takadachi.

In this province, far beyond the reach of Yoritomo's influence Yoshitsuné found himself for the first time in a place of safety. But he was fated to misery! Not for long could he know rest. Hidehira, his faithful friend, fell ill and died, and his son Yasuhira, blinded by the desire for gain, went over to the opposite side and under Yoritomo's orders attacked the castle where Yoshitsuné and his ten men had taken refuge. Beset by a large hostile force, they put up a desperate but vain defence against hopeless odds. All his men were killed and then Yoshitsuné, after setting fire to the castle, committed suicide and thus brought his hapless life to an end.

Such is the story of Yoshitsuné as recounted in the eight books of *Gikeiki*. We see Yoshitsuné presented, not as a triumphant hero, but as one dogged by misfortune and misery who, unable to stem the opposing tide, was carried along to his miserable doom. To heighten the effect, the first half of the book shows us the youthful Yoshitsuné as popular imagination loved to picture him, outstanding in intelligence, valour and personal beauty. Then, in the second half, his misfortunes awaken our pity, for, despite the favourable circumstances of his birth and character, we see him suddenly brought low by the slanderous tongue of a villain. It was these contrasting aspects of Yoshitsuné—his heroic character, evoking admiration and worship, and the unjust misfortunes that pursued him, calling forth pity—that combine to produce the "Devotion to the Hôgan," which is the inspiration of the whole book.

Yoshitsuné, so strong and brave and wise in the first half of the story, suddenly shows himself passive and non-resistant, incapable of giving events any turn for the better, even with the aid of the sagacious and valiant loyalists who remained true to him. This almost feminine temperament ascribed to the Hôgan has no historical foundation, and it certainly does not show Yoshitsuné as a great hero, except in his youth. It is due to the desire of the author and the mood of the people to draw what tears could be drawn from the misfortunes of their hero. This sentimental presentation accords well with the general yearning for the aristocratic and classical refinements of the Heian period which was just as truly a characteristic of the thought of the later Middle Ages, during which the book took shape, as was the very different taste for bold and warlike heroes.

The work takes on colour from the two figures who stand nearest to Yoshitsué in love and misfortune, Shizuka, the sorrow-laden mistress, and Benkei, peerlessly loyal, outstanding alike for wisdom and valour. Like Yoshitsuné himself, they have both been idealized in the work, ennobled and magnified in various ways to increase our sympathy with their tragic destiny and move us the more to tears. Posterity has always taken Shizuka as an ideal of true womanhood and Benkei as the type of what a courageous warrior should be. This is one aspect which the "Devotion to the Hôgan" has assumed.

Few other historical characters are surrounded with such a wealth of romantic traditions as Yoshitsuné, and *Gikeiki*, wrought of romantic adoration, is the fount from which they have flowed. The "Devotion to the Hôgan" expressed in this book rose to such a height that it was believed that he did not die in the castle of Takadachi but managed to escape to Ezo (Hokkaido), there to become governor, and later to be even deified and worshipped as Gikyô Daimyôjin. Stories are also told of how he went to Manchuria and Mongolia to appear there as Genghis Khan. In this way did the people give form to their belief in the immortality of their hero.

The events of his boyhood, in particular, owe much to tradition; indeed, one is tempted to ask whether tradition is not the sole source of all his youthful activities. Of those narrated in the first half of the work, the most famous youthful exploit is the incident at the Bridge of Gojô, which tells of the first meeting and fight between Yoshitsuné and Benkei. The most famous story in the second part is the incident at Ataka, on which the famous *kabuki* play *Kanjinchô* (The Subscription Book) is based. In this play the famous incident in which Benkei strikes his lord is treated as having happened at Ataka, whereas in *Gikeiki* it is placed at the river ferry of Nyoi. The Noh play *Ataka*, which is based on *Gikeiki*, first made the change to the Barrier of Ataka, and the *kabuki* play follows it.

The traditions that have sprung up from *Gikeiki* are numberless, not only about Yoshitsuné but also about Shizuka and Benkei. In addition to the story of Shizuka's descent from Mount Yoshino and her dancing in front of the shrine of Tsurugaoka Hachiman, other stories enhance her as the representative type of Japanese womanhood, with her gracious charm, her undying fidelity and her will of iron. And so also with Benkei and his comrades as models of faithful retainers. These traditions maintained a remarkable hold upon later literature, especially the drama; they were employed so frequently in the Noh and *kabuki* plays as to create an important cycle called *hôganmono* or *yoshitsunemono* (the Hôgan, or Yoshitsuné, plays).

In literary quality, *Gikeiki* is far inferior to such other *gunkimono* (battle stories) as *Heiké Monogatari* and *Taiheiki*, the construction and the narrative being often marred by commonplaces, crudities and clumsiness. Yet it has the lyricism of the later mediaeval tales and that touch of rough classicism which marks the *gunkimono*, as it tells of tender love and stirring scenes of battle, and depicts with some little skill in characterization the leading personages concerned.

There is no certainty as to the author or the date of composition. It was composed between 1340 and 1400, and one may presume it was the work of some admirer of Yoshitsuné who, in accordance with popular feeling, presented the sad fate of his hero with this blending of historical fact and oral tradition.

SOGA MONOGATARI

(The Tale of the Soga Brothers)

Like *Gikeiki*, this tale is a product of the heroic tradition and so is usually reckoned among the *gunkimono* (battle stories), although both differ from the main body of *gunkimono* in being concerned rather with individual heroes contemporary with the time of their production than with wars and battles of long ago.

Soga Monogatari is the story of two brothers who after eighteen years of varied hardships at last succeeded in taking their revenge on their father's irreconcilable enemy; it covers the whole period from their childhood until their glorious self-sacrifice on the altar of filial piety. Throughout the greater part of the work the marked contrast between the powerful position of their proud enemy, Kudô Suketsuné, and the youth and weakness of the two brothers, as they patiently endured and surmounted the poverty of their circumstances, inevitably evokes feelings of tender sympathy towards such brave and dutiful sons. Just as in regard to the unfortunate hero of *Gikeiki* there sprang up the "Devotion to the Hôgan," so we get here "Devotion to the Soga" (*Soga-biiki*).

Interwoven into the romantic story of the chequered careers of the two brothers is the tale of the lives of those who aided them in the adversities they had to endure in the cause of honour, their mother, torn between her love for them and her sense of duty, and a courtezan of intrepid spirit and faithful heart. Though quite in the tradition of such *gunkimono*, yet these are idealized to give an added lustre to the young Soga brothers, representing them as veritable national heroes.

In his method of approach, the author follows the author of *Gikeiki*. The characters of the two heroes in their virtues and weaknesses aptly balance each other: Jûrô, the elder, had cool courage and discretion, while Gorô, the younger, was rash and hot-tempered. The author emphasizes and idealizes the sincerity and purity of the martyrs, as he presents them sharing hardships and devoting their lives to the cause of filial duty.

These two brothers, Soga-no Jûrô Sukenari and Soga-no Gorô Tokimuné, were the sons of Kawazu-no Saburô Sukeshigé and grandsons of Sukechika. Sukeshigé's cousin Kudô Suketsuné, bearing malice against his uncle Sukechika, plotted the assasination of the son, Sukeshigé. Accordingly, while Sukeshigé was returning from hunting in Okuno in Izu province (Shizuoka prefecture), he was waylaid and killed on Mt Akazawa by two of Suketsuné's vassals, Ômi and Yawata. At the time of this sad event, the boys were still young, being yet known by their childhood names of Ichiman and Hakoô. The grief of these two little ones was great. But still more moving was the heroic resolution of little five-year-old Ichiman, who clung to his dead father's body vowing to avenge his father when he grew up.

In order to bring up the two fatherless children, their mother married Soga-no Tarô Sukenobu. Ever cherished by the two boys as they grew up was the memory of their father, intensifying their whole-hearted determination to console their mother's sorrow by avenging him as quickly as they could. When they saw a pair of wild geese happily winging their way side by side across the sky, the two boys could not help thinking of their father torn from them by death ; and then they would secretly practise with small bows and arrows or swords.

The boys were only eleven and nine, when their enemy Suketsuné used his venomous tongue to such effect that they were summoned before the Shogun Yoritomo and condemned to be beheaded. Together young Ichiman and Hakoô stood on the scaffold erected on the seashore of Yui at Kamakura calmly awaiting death, when fortunately Hatakeyama Shigetada intervened, his eloquent plea on their behalf securing their release.

Two years later Ichiman, then thirteen, took the adult name of Soga-no Jûrô Sukenari, and applied himself diligently to military arts. Hakoô, however, in accordance with his mother's wish that prayers should not be wanting for the repose of her husband's soul, entered the priesthood at a temple at Hakoné. When he was fourteen years of age, Kudô Suketsuné happened to come there on pilgrimage in the train of his lord Yoritomo. Hakoô's heart almost burst with rage at being thus brought face to face with his father's murderer and yet forced to remain an idle spectator.

Finally, the thought of his father's foe being still alive becoming unbearable, at the age of seventeen he renounced his orders and fled from the temple to join his elder brother, changing his name to Soga-no Gorô Tokimuné. When his mother heard what he had done she was so angry that she disowned him. But his burning desire for revenge never faltered, and the two brothers went on secretly plotting and hoped to achieve their object very soon. Encouraging them in their hopes and consoling them in their disappointments was Tora Gozen, the beautiful mistress of Jûrô, a courtesan, but a woman of refinement, sympathy and understanding.

Their chance for revenge seemed to have arrived when Yoritomo, confident that nothing could now disturb the peace of the country, began to indulge in revelry all day long and, on one occasion, decided to summon the warriors from the neighbouring provinces for a great hunting party on the plain of Asamano in Shinano province (Nagano prefecture). Kudô Suketsuné would naturally be one of the party, and the brothers were full of joy, for they believed that it would be quite easy to slip among the assembled crowds and take their enemy unawares. They had managed to obtain entrance to Suketsuné's hunting-lodge, when the guards became suspicious and questioned them. It was only the intervention of Hatakeyama Shigetada, who had already saved their lives when they were boys, that enabled them to escape. They made a further attempt, this time with the assistance of Wada Yoshimori, but were again unsuccessful.

It was not long, however, before another chance occurred. The brothers learned that Yoritomo was so pleased with the success of the hunt at Asamano that he had arranged for another to be held at the foot of Mount Fuji. The young men decided that this time, even at the cost of their lives, they would see justice done, and so Jûrô set off to pay a farewell visit to his mistress, Tora Gozen. But at her house he encountered the veteran Wada Yoshimori, who had conceived a great affection for her. Tora Gozen thrust herself between the two men to screen Jûrô from danger, but he was so hurt in his manly pride and honour at such an intervention, that a desperate quarrel threatened between him and Wada Yoshimori.

[225]

Gorô, who had remained at home, suddenly had a feeling that his brother was in danger, and he sprang at once on his horse, without even troubling to saddle it, and rode at full speed to her home. There, from outside the paper sliding-doors, he saw the situation and drew himself up to his full height ready to stab Jûrô's opponent. But Yoshihidé, Yoshimori's son, was there and chanced to see his shadow on the paper door. He swung it open and dashed at Gorô, trying to drag him into the room by the tassels of his armour; but Gorô stood as firm as a rock. Both the young men were notable for their strength, and, shouting defiance at each other, they now exerted it to the full. All Yoshihidé's efforts were in vain. He could not move Gorô. But he tugged so hard that at last the tassels gave way and he fell backwards into the room in a heap. This proof of Gorô's strength was conclusive. None ventured to lift a finger against him, and, after Yoshimori had offered him a cup of reconciliation, the two brothers quietly left the house.

The two brothers then went to pay a farewell visit to their mother. They assumed a casual air, but their hope was to receive some present from her that would make more dear the world they were so soon to leave. They began to talk in an easy manner about the hunting party that was to be held at the foot of Mount Fuji, saying that it would be quite a fine show and they would have to go and see it. In this way they persuaded her to make them a present of silk garments, but she gave them reluctantly because of her gloomy forebodings about their real purpose. She even tried to dissuade them from going, but, failing, she listened to Jûrô's intercession and forgave Gorô with whom she had hitherto remained unreconciled since he had left the priesthood. She gave him also a silk garment, and then, restraining their tears, the two brothers bade her a last farewell and set out on their fateful journey.

They found the skirts of Mount Fuji thronged with warriors from all over the land, clad in gorgeous attire. All were engaged in hunting, striving to outdo one another in order to catch Yoritomo's eye. In such a confusion the brothers found it difficult to keep a watch on their enemy, Kudô Suketsuné; it seemed to them that once again they would be thwarted in carrying out their act of filial piety. They were greatly encouraged, however, by the sympathy of

Hatakeyama Shigetada, who urged that, since this was the last night of the hunt, they must act at once, for so good an opportunity would never occur again. They therefore sent their attendants back to their mother's house with their keepsakes, and waited for nightfall.

It was the 28th day of the 5th month of the 4th year of the Kenkyû era (1193), on a pitch dark night with the rain falling in torrents, that the brothers dressed themselves and bravely set forth on their enterprise. They gazed for the last time into each other's faces in the light of their torches. Taking heart, they wiped the tears from their eyes. They succeeded in passing the barriers at the corners of the roads and eventually reached their destination, the hunting-lodge of Suketsuné. The friendly Honda-no Jirô Chikatsuné happened to be on guard that night, and so they were able to steal with ease into Suketsuné's sleeping quarters.

They shook their enemy out of his sleep, told him their names, and then plunged into his breast their swords burning with the enmity of eighteen years. Finally they cut off his head with the fierce, unfaltering strokes of sons fulfilling a filial duty. Now that they had attained their life's ambition they had nothing to regret, and stepping out into the garden they shouted forth their names and in triumphant voices offered combat to all who would.

Many dashed upon them only to be beaten back by the vigorous blows of the brothers, who appeared irresistible. At length, however, Jûrô, exhausted, fell a victim to the sword of Nitta-no Shirô. He was then twenty-two years of age. Seeing his brother fall, Gorô fought his way through a crowd of opponents and reached the place where his brother's body lay, and there he abandoned himself to his grief. He escaped, and when at last he was caught, it was by an enemy disguised as a woman. He was haled before the Shogun Yoritomo, who was greatly moved by the intrepidity and filial piety of the young man, as well as the bold and dignified replies he made to his questions. Then the head of Jûrô was brought in and when Gorô, his hands bound behind his back, beheld it, the tears flowed down, while the whole company wiped their tears with their sleeves.

Gorô was handed over to the Suketsuné family and condemned to death to the deep grief of his mother and Tora Gozen. Even

Yoritomo deplored the death of the brave young men and later erected a temple where prayers could be offered to Amita Budaha for the repose of their souls.

Such is the brief outline of the Soga vendetta. Based upon historical facts, the story is characterized by the consistency of its conception and execution, and has been an inspiration to many authors, both of that period and later. It has always appealed strongly to Japanese feeling, and indeed, both *Soga Monogatari* itself and the Soga traditions that sprang up later are the fruit of the deep sympathy and admiration for the sad fate of the brothers. Just as national compassion for the sad fate of just but oppressed men expressed itself in the case of the " Devotion to the Hôgan," it has given rise to the " Devotion to the Soga Brothers."

Like *Gikeiki*, *Soga Monogatari* has no great significance as a work of literature. Its great and continued popularity is due to the fact that the tragic and heroic tale of how two young men sustained their resolve to have revenge through eighteen years of hardships, and accomplished it in the end at the cost of their own lives, appeals to a burning human instinct, and that the motives which actuated them are in such close accord with the Japanese moral teaching regarding filial piety (*kôkô*). It also makes a good biographical novel, with its single ethical concept permeating a rich whole of sad, heroic and beautiful deeds. It has the virtue of presenting dramatically scenes of brotherly love and maternal affection. Among its defects must be counted the frequent use of Chinese fables to point a moral and the tedious discussions on Buddhism carried on between the brothers and Tora Gozen. Yet in this respect it reflects the current thought of the Middle Ages (the Kamakura and Muromachi periods) and is characteristic of the literature of that time.

The story is sufficiently coherent, yet is more ornate and Buddhistic than *Gikeiki*, probably because it is the work of a priest. We do not know his name, but presumably he belonged to the Kamakura period. Since then several different texts have appeared, and the current text emerged in the Muromachi period, at about the same time as that of *Gikeiki* (the fourteenth century).

This work also has had such great influence upon later literature that there have come into being various cycles of Soga pieces (*Soga-mono*) in the Noh plays, the *jôruri* and the *kabuki* drama. In *kabuki* especially a great number of Soga pieces have been produced, and it has become a time-honoured tradition to stage a Soga piece in the month of January every year. In addition, among *Kabuki Jûhachiban* (the Eighteen Classical *Kabuki* Pieces), *Sukeroku* and *Yanoné* are connected with the Soga tradition.

Further, the tale of the Soga brothers is popularly associated with the story of the Forty-Seven Rônin of Akô in the Edo period (the story dramatized as *Chûshingura* or The Loyal League), *Soga Monogatari* presenting the virtue of filial piety, *Chûshingura* that of loyalty, which virtues forever inspire and guide the souls of the Japanese people.

───────

BASHÔ SHICHIBUSHÛ

(The Seven Haikai Anthologies of Basho's School)

The original meaning of the word *haikai* (poetic epigram) w
" humour," the humour of that type of poetry known as *hai*
renga (humorous linked-poems). The *haikai* poem began as an a
breviated form of the *renga*, Yamazaki Sôkan and Arakida Morita
having established this humorous type of poetry as an independe
form by the later Muromachi period (middle of the sixteenth centur
The *haikai* was revived at the beginning of the Edo period (ea
seventeenth century) by Matsunaga Teitoku, whose *haikai* were o
sportive character, full of humorous punning and partaking of som
thing of the elegance of the earlier *renga*. This type of *haikai*
known as *kofû* (Ancient Style) or as *Teimon no haikai* (*haikai* of t
Teitoku school).

The next type of *haikai* to develop was that of the *Danrin*
(Danrin style) originated by Nishiyama Sôin. This style also h
a humorous basis, but its was a fresher and wilder kind of humo
which won wide popularity. Next Matsuo Bashô effected a gre
reform of the Danrin type of *haikai*, by stripping it altogether of i
humorous punning and its jocularity and uniting the *haikai* for
to a gravity and loftiness of thought. Indeed, Bashô may l
said to have recast and completely changed the character of tl
haikai.

Moreover, the sphere of the *waka* had been limited to what we
termed " things graceful." But Bashô refused to be encumbere
by such narrow considerations as the refinement or vulgarity of them
and gave a much wider scope to the subject, vocabulary and conten
of the *haikai* until, in this freedom, a new world of beauty was create
a beauty which, in his view, as may be seen more clearly in the ess:
Oku no Hosomichi, was both derived from and symbolized in Natur

The title *Bashô Shichibushû* is applied to the collection which i
cludes the seven representative selections of *haikai* of the school (

猿蓑集巻之一

冬

初しぐれ猿も小蓑をほしげ也　芭蕉

あし引の山鳥の尾のしだり尾の　其角

ながき夜を一人かも寝む　千那

　　　　　　　　　　　　文州

　　　　　　　　　　　　正秀

(MONKEY'S RAINCOAT).
...k of haikai (poetic epigram), pub...
...in 1691.

MATSUO BASHÔ
(1644—1694)

...YASHI ISSA
1763—1827)

YOSA BUSON
(1716—1783)

asl:ô (*Shômon*):

The earliest of these, *Fuyu no Hi*, was published in 1684, and the latest, *Zoku Sarumino*, in 1698. They were not published together until 1774, when they were given the title of *Haikai Shichibushû*. At a later date the collection came to be known as *Bashô Shichibushû*, to distinguish it from the *Buson Shichibushû* (Seven Haikai Antholoies of Buson's School) and numerous other similar collections of haikai which were compiled in imitation of the first *Shichibushû* that had won wide favour and esteem.

The process by which the genius of Bashô recast the *haikai* form an be clearly traced. He began by imitating the old style *haikai* of he Teitoku school and then fell under the fascination of the Danrin tyle before he gave expression to his originality in what is now nown as *Shôfû* or the Bashô style. *Fuyu no Hi* represents the first tage of his characteristic style, and this and the remaining six selec- ons show the successive stages of his development, in which his ollowers see five, or more usually three, main steps. Although some ter scholars have questioned the appropriateness of some of the elections as representative of the steps, they are generally approved f by the great mass of critical opinion.

Before commenting on each of these collections in turn, it would e well to note the two varieties of *haikai*: *haiku* and *renku*. A *haiku* onsists of one stanza, generally of seventeen syllables, divided into hree lines of five, seven and five syllables, making a complete and ndependent whole both in form and content. A *renku* consists of a ong series of *haiku*, and is of various lengths, the number in the series arying between wide limits, the two commonest types of *renku* eing the *kasen*, a series of thirty-six *haiku*, and the *hyakuin*, which onsists of one hundred.

In all types of *renku* the first poem, which is complete in itself and sually contains seventeen (5, 7, 5) syllables, is known as the *hokku*

(the opening verse). Taken by itself apart from the series whic
follows it, the *hokku* may be regarded as an independent *haiku*; it
from the *hokku* that the current, independent *haiku* are derived.

The opening poem is followed by one consisting of fourtee
(7, 7) syllables, which is called *wakiku* (the supporting verse), or *wak*
for short. Thereafter the succession consists of alternate poems i
seventeen (5, 7, 5) and fourteen (7, 7) syllables, differing from th
first, the *hokku*, in that they are not completely independent but at
linked to the others of the series by association of feeling. The
is no distinctive name for each of these, except for the third, which
called *daisan* (the third), and the last, the *ageku* (the closing verse
the rest being called *hiraku* (common verses). The first of any tw
consecutive poems in the *renku* is styled *maeku* (the fore verse) an
the second *tsukeku* (the supplementary verse). With the sole excep
tion of the *hokku*, then, every poem in a *renku* may be regarded a
a *tsukeku* to the preceding poem. In the anthologies of *haikai* we at
now considering, the *haiku* (including both independent pieces an
hokku) number 2,030; while the *tsukeku* (using the word in its broades
sense to mean any poem of a *renku* except the first) total 1,452. Bash
himself is the largest contributor, with 130 *haiku* and 157 *tsukeks*
He is followed in the order of number of contributions by Kake
Kikaku, Etsujin, Kyorai, Yasui, Bonchô, Jôsô, Shikô, Yah:
Shôhaku and Ransetsu. Though the mere number of contributior
is scarcely reliable as a standard of poetic achievement, still thes
seven anthologies include practically all the chief works of th
leading poets of Bashô's school.

1. *Fuyu no Hi* (Winter Days)

Fuyu no Hi was published in the winter of 1684. This and th
remaining anthologies, with the exception of *Haru no Hi*, its im
mediate successor, were printed by Izutsuya Shôbeé, publisher c
Kyoto. It was compiled by Yamamoto Kakei, Bashô's discipl
at Nagoya, probably under the eye of the poet himself, who calle
public attention to it as an epoch-making selection, definitely establish
ing his style (*Shôfû*).

In the autumn of the year in which this selection was publishe
Bashô set out on that journey to his home which inspired h
Nozarashi Kikô (Weather-beaten Trip) and arrived at Nagoya in th

rovince of Owari with the winter. There he foregathered with
is disciples to compose *renku* (*haiku* sequences). The subtitle to
ıe anthology, *Owari Go Kasen* (Five *Kasen* from Owari), makes it
lear that it contains five *kasen* harvested from this *renku* meeting at
Jagoya, to which are added six *haiku* poems as an *omoté-awasé* (poems
1 the style of opening verses of a *kasen*). The title *Fuyu no Hi*
Winter Days) was obviously suggested by the season of its composi-
on.

The first *kasen* in the anthology begins with the following *kyôku*
comic *haikai* poem) by Bashô, which is preceded by a brief explanatory
ote in prose : —

"Having been exposed to bitter wind and rain on my long journey, I
struggled into this province of Owari a most forlorn and utterly exhausted
traveller, as did an ancient master of *kyôka* (comic *waka* poem), whose
memory inspired the following piece ":—

KYÔKU
Like Chikusai
Buffeted by wintry blasts
To this place I come.

This Chikusai was a quack doctor, hero of *Chikusai Monogatari*
Tales of Chikusai), a work belonging to the type known as *kana-*
ôshi (popular tales current in the early Edo period), probably written
y Karasumaru Mitsuhiro in either the Genna era (1615–1623) or
1e Kan'ei era (1624–1643) telling how this itinerant *kyôka* poet,
·hile on his way from Kyoto to Edo, spent three years in Nagoya.
s Chikusai had also come there struggling against the wintry blasts,
 point the resemblance between them Bashô called the short *hokku*
ppening poem) given above a *kyôku* as a contrast to Chikusai's *kyôka*.
he use of the word *kogarashi* (wintry blasts) here suggests the season
f its composition, for all *hokku* and *haiku* generally contain, either
 word or allusion, some suggestion of the season in which they were
·ritten ; this symbolism of the changing phases of Nature forms the
ɔre of the whole anthology.

Through the use of this convention Bashô was able to express a
ew world of beauty. Moreover, in *Fuyu no Hi* one glimpses the
awning of *yûgen* (abstract beauty) as the aim to which Bashô's art
ointed in his renovation of the *haikai*, as well as the coming of that

[233]

quietism which developed from the circumstances of his life. He ha
not, however, rid himself yet of passionate emotion and had yet muc
of life's mystery to plumb.

2. *Haru no Hi* (Spring Days)

Haru no Hi was compiled by Kakei and published by Nishimu
Ichĭroemon of Kyoto in the autumn or winter of 1686, two yea
after the appearance of *Fuyu no Hi*.

In April of the previous year, Bashô had returned to his hermitag
in Edo after his "weather-beaten journey," which had contribute
so much to the development of his style. His visit had proved
great inspiration to Kakei, Etsujin, Yasui and other *haiku* poets i
the Owari district, and the present anthology was the fruit of the
enthusiasm. During its compilation it was, presumably, revise
by Bashô himself.

The choice of the title *Haru no Hi* (Spring Days) was partly due t
the fact that it followed on *Fuyu no Hi* (Winter Days) and partly t
the fact that all the *renku* in it were written in spring. It contains thr
kasen with six supplementary *omoté-awasé haikai* and some *haiku* poen
classified according to the season. Among these latter is the follow
ing famous, practically untranslatable, composition by Bashô :—

> An old tranquil pond
> Into which a frog plunges
> With a lonesome splash !

The *renku* are modest and unaffected in style, but represent a noticeab
advance in refinement and repose, while the *haiku* bear evidence
deeper meditation.

3. *Arano* (Waste Land)

This is also a compilation by Kakei and was published three yea
after *Haru no Hi*, probably in the summer of 1689. This, the large
of the anthologies, has an important preface by Bashô, in which
draws a distinction between this and the two preceding works, *Fu*
no Hi and *Haru no Hi*. These two works, he points out, still have
tendency towards "floweriness," whereas by contrast the thi
anthology seeks after substantiality and opens up an unlimited sphe
of abstruseness. Hence its title of *Arano* (Waste Land), which syr
bolizes the ideal aimed at.

It consists of eight books of *haiku*, totalling 735 poems, with ten supplementary *kasen* at the end. The *haiku* are classified under more than a dozen heads, including "noted places," "travels," "love" and others in addition to the usual division into the "four seasons," the bulkiness of the work being apparently mainly responsible for this more minute classification. In addition to the works by Bashô's school, this compilation also contains some by earlier poets that are judged to conform to the standard established by Bashô. It is clear then that the purpose of this anthology is to demonstrate to the *haikai* schools in general the standard already established by Bashô's school. The critical standard, however, is not uniformly high. The majority of the thirty-five *haiku* contributed by Bashô are travel pieces, of which the following is widely renowned :—

> Karasaki Pine !
> More dream-like than cherry flowers
> In misty moonlight !

And, apart from his travel poems, we find such a distinguished piece as this, an elaborate variation of his earlier effort :—

> On a leafless branch
> A lonely crow is perching
> On an autumn eve !

4. *Hisago* (The Gourd)

Compiled in August, 1690, by Hamada Chinseki, a disciple of Bashô at Zezé in Ômi province, this volume is, like *Fuyu no Hi*, a *renku* collection containing five *kasen* with a preface by Ochi Etsujin, of Bashô's school in Owari, in which he appeals for the approval of the public. These *kasen* were composed in the spring and summer of that year, mostly by Bashô's disciples in Zezé, which the master had frequently visited. Here then we have a new centre, the province of Ômi (Shiga prefecture), all the three previous anthologies having been compiled in Owari.

The rhythm and spirit of the work are so similar to what is found in its immediate successor, *Sarumino*, that this is usually regarded as a sequel to *Hisago*. Both these anthologies represent Bashô's school in its maturity and mark a turning-point in its development, but since *Hisago*, consisting exclusively of *renku*, contains some weak as well as fine examples, one would suggest that *Sarumino* better reveals the quality of Bashô's art at this stage.

5. *Sarumino* (Monkey's Raincoat)

Sarumino, published in 1691, was compiled by Mukai Kyorai and Bonchô (surname unknown), two of Bashô's disciples in Kyoto with a preface by Kikaku and a postscript in Chinese by Jôsô. Bashô dwelt in the Genjû-an hermitage in Ômi from April to August, 1690 and spent much time in Ômi and Kyoto until the year following. It was in this year, as is now known, that, thanks to the strenuous efforts of the compilers, this anthology was completed under the close supervision of the master himself. It is a most careful selection of *haiku* and *renku* by poets from all over the country, with those around Kyoto predominating, and includes the finest and most typical examples of Bashô's mature style. That is why the anthology has ever since been known as *Haikai Kokinshû* (Anthology of Haiku, Ancient and Modern), thus suggesting a comparison with the *Kokinshû* of the Heian period, one of the three great anthologies of Japanese poetry. The contents are *haiku* on the four seasons, followed by four *renku*, each representing a season, to which are added *Genjû-an no Ki* (Records from the Genjû-an Hermitage) by Bashô, and *Kiyû Nikki*, a collection of the works of those who visited the hermitage. The arrangement as a whole is systematic. The opening poem is a winter song by Bashô, from which the title of *Sarumino* was derived:—

> First wintry drizzle!
> The monkey seems yearning for
> A small raincoat too!

The first poem is a poem on winter, for the seasons are suggestively rearranged in the order of winter, summer, autumn, spring.

Bashô and Bonchô contributed the greatest number of *haiku*, Bonchô being, next to the master, one of the most highly esteemed poets, followed by Kyorai and Jôsô. Like the winter poem already given, most of Bashô's poems were naturally composed on his journeys, another fine travel piece being:—

> Throw my sorry self
> Into greater loneliness,
> Birds of Solitude*!

---

* These birds are the *kankodori*, Himalayan cuckoos.

The six *omoté-awasé* poems of the first *kasen* are here quoted, the name of the composer of each being appended. It should be noted how each two consecutive *haikai* are linked together by associations of the same emotion.

> Smoothing out again
> The kite's disordered plumage,
>   First wintry drizzle !   (Kyorai)

> Those sharp gusts of wind rustling
> Among the leaves now die down.   (Bashô)

> With my skirts drenchéd,
> From morning have I waded
>   Across these rivers.   (Bonchô)

> The scarecrow stands, bow in hand,
> To frighten badgers away.   (Fumikuni)

> On the lattice-door
> Clad in dun ivy, shines pale
>   The evening moon.   (Bashô)

> Denied to others the trees
> Laden with pears of renown.   (Kyorai)

6. *Sumidawara* (Charcoal Sack)

Appearing three years later, probably in the autumn of 1694, this anthology was compiled by Shida Yaha, Koizumi Ko'oku and Ikeda Rigyû, Bashô's disciples in Edo. In the preface by Soryû we are told how the compilers planned the selection under the title *Sumidawara* after calling on the master in his hermitage (Bashô-an) in the winter of 1693, when he gave his view that the word *sumidawara* should be admitted into the *haikai* vocabulary. The *haiku* and *renku* it contains are classified according to the seasons, the *renku* consisting of seven *kasen* and one *hyakuin*.

This anthology has been regarded as a harbinger of its successor, *Zoku Sarumino* (Sequel to *Sarumino*), in giving expression to that *karumi* (the lighter touch), characteristic of Bashô's later style. Still, it is somewhat erroneous to regard it as an exemplification of that lighter touch at its most perfect. True, in his last years Bashô made frequent reference to the *karumi* to which at the same time he was giving definite expression in his work, but what he meant by the term was by no means a merely elaborate playing with words and design,

but rather something more in the nature of *kotan* (chaste refinement)
His "lighter touch" was the spontaneous flowering of the depth
of a poet's mind impregnated with the atmosphere of *haikai*, a state
which could not possibly be attained without that maturity of style
which Bashô himself displays in *Sarumino*. Even those who strove
to lead the life of a true poet under Bashô's guidance, lacking such
maturity, sometimes could rise no higher than the merest imitation
of his lighter touch.

One would not like to regard Yaha, who is noted for his "lighter
touch," as nothing more than an imitator of Bashô. Yet he certainly
fails to express the "chaste refinement" of his great exemplar in
his "lighter touch," which is in his case due rather to the high spirit
resulting from his shrewd worldly wisdom. With Bashô it flows
spontaneously from the soul of a perfect poet, while with Yaha it is
rather an expression of his life as head clerk of the Echigoya Exchange
the forerunner of the present Mitsui Bank. It is probably enough
to compare the two following examples of the lighter touch, one by
each poet on the occasion of the New Year :—

> O please, Hôrai,*
> Sure you can tell me the first
> Tidings from Isé ?   (Bashô)

> Even Chômatsu**
> In the name of his father,
> Brings us best wishes.   (Yaha)

Thus the *renku* in *Sumidawara* reveal two different types of lighter
touch, Bashô being responsible for the more chaste type, and Yaha
for the more worldly one. Indeed, the great decadence of *haikai*
in the Tenpô era (1830–1844) has been largely attributed to the bad
influence of *Sumidawara*, as it encouraged the imitation of Yaha's
somewhat superficial gusto through failure to see the subtle distinction between it and what Bashô understood by the term *karumi*.

7. *Zoku Sarumino* (Sequel to *Sarumino*)

This volume was published in the summer or autumn of 1698
four years after the appearance of *Sumidawara* and the death of Bashô

---

* The *hôrai*, a New Year decoration, is associated with the Great Shrine at Isé, the centre
of worship at New Year.
** A common name for a merchant's son.

An epilogue by Izutsuya Shôbeé, the printer, recounts the circumstances of its publication and states that the book is an exact replica of the drafts made by Bashô himself, a statement which has given rise to great discussion.

The anthology begins with five *kasen* on the seasons, followed by *haiku* on the subjects of " seasons," " Buddhism " and " travels." On the whole the compilation is lacking in unity and cohesion and appears to have been retouched after Bashô's death. Some scholars, accepting the verdict of Etsujin on the collection, deem the collection a forgery by Kagami Shikô. But this seems far too sweeping, and there is a good deal of evidence throwing light on the very complicated and delicate circumstances in which it was compiled. It would seem that, from 1693 o. , Bashô had been assisting Hattori Senpo, his Edo disciple, in the compilation of an anthology. Death intervened to prevent its completion, and then it passed into the hands of Shikô who published it with his own corrections.

Quite rightly, this anthology is regarded as expressing the same quality of *karumi*, the lighter touch, as *Sumidawara*, but much nearer to Bashô's ideal. Its contents are less tainted with the worldliness that perverts the outlook of so many of the poems in *Sumidawara*, and, although there may be still room for polish, they are in many ways finer than the latter. Shikô and Senpo, who contribute more poems than anyone else except Bashô, here reveal their powers at their height, Shikô being the more able poet of the two. Some of the poems of Bashô found here may be accounted a little too rigid, but he has several delicate masterpieces, as, for instance :—

> The lightning flashes
> In a dark corner of sky,
> A winging hern cries.   (Bashô)

Although Bashô s style underwent many changes as his mind grew more mature, yet throughout he held clearly to a definite course. The great poet who attained his ideal of *kotan* (chaste refinement) may well be said to have developed his style to its ultimate point of achievement.

After the death of Bashô, his disciples lost their unity and fell away. And since Bashô's school was the very centre of the composition of *haikai*, its decadence meant degeneration everywhere. Still, the more marked this falling away, the more was this notable legacy of Bashô's school, *Bashô Shichibushû*, held in reverence. When eventually, the *haikai* renaissance dawned as a movement with the cry "Back to Bashô," similar collections began to appear on the model, such as *Buson Shichibushû* (The Seven Haikai Anthologies of Buson's School), while around the original itself there grew up a vast literature of studies and annotations.

———————

OKU NO HOSOMICHI

(Journey to Ôu)

Oku no Hosomichi is a book of travel written by the famous poet Matsuo Bashô, who founded a new school of *haiku* (poetic epigram), and whose name is also associated with several *haikai* books of travel like the present one. It well exemplifies the *haibun*, that prose literature popularized by Bashô and his followers which is illustrated and enriched with *haiku* poems. The title *Oku no Hosomichi*, which means the Ôu Road, is taken from the name of that portion of the road which he traversed between Sendai and Shiogama on his way to Ôu, the two northern provinces of Mutsu and Dewa.

The book opens with some reflections by Bashô on certain ancients, Li Po and Tu Fu of T'ang China and Saigyô and Sôgi of Japan, for whom he had a great reverence and who all died while on a journey. For himself, he says, whenever he set out on a journey, it was always with the feeling that he might not return alive, and that he had that presentiment especially on setting out on the present journey because it was much more hazardous than any he had yet undertaken. So, as he set out he disposed of his dearly loved hermitage, Bashô-an, after taking a tender farewell of it

Accompanied by his disciple, Kawai Sora, he left Edo on the 27th, 3rd month, 1689, to make his long journey of over five months to the provinces of Ôu and through the districts facing the Japan Sea, Hokurikudô, a distance of 600 *ri* (about 2,400 kilometres). He first made a pilgrimage to the shrine dedicated to the Princess Konohana Sakuya Himé at Muro no Yashima, and then on the 30th put up at an inn at Imaichi-machi at the foot of Mt Nikkô-san, whose proprietor Gozaemon was nicknamed " Hotoké " (Buddha) on account of his strict honesty. On the 1st, 4th month, he set out towards Kurobané, but had great difficulty in crossing the plain of Nasu on the poor horse he had hired. Then he visited Jôbôji, the caretaker of the castle at Kurobané, and also the site of the hermitage of the priest Butchô Oshô, behind the temple of Ungan-ji, where he had once studied and practised the Zen discipline. He stopped to see the Sesshôseki, the Stone of Death, and then passed the barrier of Shirakawa no Seki, after which he felt in the best of moods for travelling. At Sukagawa he spent several days at the house of Sagara Tôkyû, on which occasion he wrote the following piece :—

> Ôu rice planting song !
> Of all elegant pursuits
> This the earliest !

He went on to view the Shinobu Mojizuri no Ishi, a famous stone, and the site of the castle of Satô Shôji, the henchman of the hero Minamoto-no Yoshitsuné. Then he fell sick with a recurrence of a chronic complaint, but, saying to himself, "What if I do die on my journey ! Providence has ordained it," he took heart and went on to see the Pine of Takekuma, which reminded him of the priest-poet Nôin Hôshi. It was on the 5th of the 5th month, the day of the Boys' Festival, that he arrived at Sendai. He stayed there several days and made the acquaintance of Kaemon, a *haiku* poet and painter, who showed him over the neighbouring beauty-spots and also gave him pictures of Matsushima and Shiogama.

This led him to travel along the "Oku no Hosomichi" where he saw, among other things, the Tsubo no Ishibumi, the stone monument at Tsubo, and the Myôjin shrine of Shiogama. Then he went over to visit Matsushima, regarded as one of the Three Great Scenes of Japan, where he worshipped at the Zuigan-ji temple. He writes copiously about the natural beauties of Matsushima, declaring it "the most charming view in Japan." "Far beyond all description and words is this masterpiece of creation," he says, too much moved to be able to compose a poem about it.

On the 12th he started for Hiraizumi, but missing the way, found himself at the little port of Ishinomaki. Still, this enabled him to see the mountain-island of Kinkazan. Fetching a long detour, he came at last to Hiraizumi, where traces remained of the bygone glory of the three generations of the Fujiwara family, who, after their protection of Yoshitsuné, had sunk into ruin in the early Kamakura period (end of the twelfth century). At Takadachi in Hiraizumi, where Yoshitsuné and others had fallen in battle, Bashô composed the following poem :—

> How the wilderness
> Of summer grass hides what remains
> Of the warriors' fame !

The impression made on him by the Konjiki-dô, the Golden Hall, of the Chûson-ji temple, is shown in this poem :—

> As if beyond reach
> Of the early summer rain,
> Stands the Golden Hall !

He now turned west and entered the province of Dewa, where, at Obanazawa, he lodged at the house of Suzuki Seifû, a wealthy disciple, and found repose after the hardships of his journey. Then he went south to visit the Risshaku-ji temple, founded by Jigaku Daishi, then under the control of the lord of Yamataga castle. It was a veritable haunt of peace, situated in the very heart of rocky mountains, and inspired him to a poem that is regarded as his masterpiece :—

> How deep the silence !
> The shrill chirp of cicadas
> Pierces the very rocks.

No less impressive is the poem he composed as one fine day he went down the Mogami-gawa river :—

> Swollen by showers,
> The waters of Mogami
> Rush on swiftly past.

From the 3rd to the 8th, 6th month, he made a pilgrimage to the well-known Haguro-Sanzan, the Three Great Mountains of Haguro, as the three neighbouring peaks of Haguro-san, Gassan and Yudono-san are called, over which itinerant priests climb as part of their ascetic pilgrimages. From there, he sailed down to the port of Sakata at the mouth of the Mogami-gawa, on the Japan Sea, where he turned northward to Kisagata, a beauty-spot which ranks with Matsushima on the opposite, the Pacific side. He writes thus of the scenery there :—

" Although in general appearance it resembles Matsushima, it makes quite a different impression. If one compares Matsushima to a smiling woman, then Kisagata is a mournful beauty, whose desolate and sorrowful features induce a feeling of sadness."

Taking a southwesternly course, he set out for the Hokurikudô
district. At Izumozaki in Echigo, he composed the famous piece :—

> Beyond raging waves
> Past where lies the Sado isle
> Hangs the Milky Way !

After passing Oyashirazu, one of the most perilous points on
his trip, he stopped for the night at the Barrier of Ichiburi. Here he
and his disciple had as fellow lodgers two courtesans making a
pilgrimage to the Shrine of Isé, who mistook the two men in their
clerical-looking robes for two priests. Terrified at the loneliness of
the place in which they found themselves, the two women begged
the protection of their company. Before he left the inn, however,
Bashô was able to calm their fears by assuring them that the
protection of Heaven would see them safely to their journey's end.

Entering Kaga from Etchû province, he sings of their journey
through air laden with the fragrance of early rice-plants, with the sea
of Ariso on their right. So he came to Kanazawa in Kaga on the
15th of the 7th month and found there the burial mound of the young
haiku poet, Kosugi Isshô, who had died the previous year while impatiently awaiting the arrival of Bashô. In front of the mound
Bashô composed an elegy of unusual force and passion :—

> Shake, shake, O grave,
> In response to my lament
> In the autumn wind !

Visiting the Tada shrine he was also deeply moved by the sight
of the armour and *hitataré* robe, once worn by that aged warrior,
Saitô Sanemori, who had never faltered, fighting desperately to the
end. Then he bathed in the hot-springs of Yamanaka and praised
their efficacy.

It was here that he lost the companionship of his disciple Sora,
who decided to leave before Bashô in order to get some relief in
his sickness from an acquaintance in Isé. Sora left the following sad
poem :—

> What though I may die
> On my wanderings, in this
> Paradise of *hagi* flowers !

So Bashô was left alone. But Tachibana Hokushi, a disciple

who lived in Kanazawa, accompanied him as far as Echizen, where he worshipped at the Eihei-ji, a temple founded by the priest Dôgen Zenji. Thence he went on to his old friend Tôsai in Fukui, who took him to the port of Tsuruga on the 14th of the 8th month, where he worshipped at the Myôjin shrine of Kei by moonlight. The following night it rained and the full moon was obscured, but the day after, the 16th, turned out fine, and he went boating. Another follower, Yasomura Rotsû, welcomed him to Tsuruga and accompanied him as far as Mino, where he stayed in the house of another disciple, Kondô Jokô of Ôgaki. There Sora rejoined him from Isé, and several other disciples gathered together to welcome Bashô, with as much joy as if he had been a dead man restored to life. But he only stayed a brief while with them before sailing to Isé, on the 6th of the 9th month, in order to view the removal ceremony of the Isé shrine.

And here the work ends.

This is not only one of the best of the travel books in that body of occasional writings which is such a feature of Japanese classical literature, but also the finest of Bashô's works in this genre. Bashô had a peculiar genius for expressing the delicate quality of the *haikai* poetry in his prose, so that both are vehicles of the same spirit. The great improvement which he wrought in the *haikai* poetry is equally visible in the *haibun*, of which the present work is so finely representative. His style combines the traditional floweriness with the essential conciseness of the *haikai*, the *haiku* poems being so ble:ded wi h the prose description as to form a lyrical whole such as belongs to the *uta monogatari*.

His passion for travel had a great effect on the development of his poetical ability, this long journey to Ôu marking a turning-point in his life and his poetry, since it was followed by the publication of *Sarumino*, the highest achievement in Bashô's style of *haikai* poetry.

His attitude towards life is based on the ever-changing aspect of Nature. Impermanency, he holds, is of the eternal nature of things, and the changing seasons express this essential mutability. Nature is the symbol of the fleeting character of all life. Accordingly, the *haikai* whose inspiration derives from the ever-changing phase of nature becomes a poetical symbol of life itself. Man, like a traveller, wends his way through life, and life, in turn, is constantly moving and flowing. By travel one comes into closer touch with Nature and its meaning, and one's poetic outlook is deepened. That was the significance of travel for Bashô.

He refused to regard Nature and Life as mutually antagonistic, since Nature includes Life. So his interest in Nature involved an interest also in human life and history : the frequent mention of his visits to local shrines and ruins shows this. One may say that the blending of Nature, History and Man is the characteristic of this work.

Bashô polished and retouched the work until it assumed final perfection about 1694, some five years after the actual journey. Soryû, a friend of the author who made a fair copy of the text, calls attention, in his epilogue, to the many varied strands out of which this noted composition is woven. It is " quiet and gay, heroic and transient," and even the most critical reader, he avers, will be forced to admire it and read it with delight. It first appeared in print in 1702, and its immediate success gave rise to a fashion among poets of rehearsing his wanderings in the Ôu district.

Matsuo Bashô, who gave new life to *haiku* poetry, came of a samurai family descended from the Heiké clan, and was born in 1644 at Ueno in Iga, near the Great Shrine of Isé. He had four sisters and an elder brother Hanzaemon. While still a boy Bashô attended the *haiku* poet Yoshitada, son of General Tôdô of Ueno. Yoshitada, a disciple of Kitamura Kigin and a writer of *haiku* under the penname of Zengin, died at the early age of twenty-five, when Bashô himself was twenty-three. For some unknown reason he left his feudal service soon after this, and spent some years in wandering.

Bashô is believed to have lived chiefly in Kyoto afterwards, occupied with the study of Japanese classics and the *haiku* poetry of the Teitoku school under Kitamura Kigin himself and others. In 1672, when he was twenty-nine years of age, he went to Edo, where he published his *Kai-Ôi*. This volume contains the choicest fruit of the period of his imitation of the Teitoku school, and also his criticisms of poems presented on the occasion of the *ku-awasé* (*haiku*-contests).

Then for many years he suffered the hardships of a wandering life, while his growing mastery of *haikai* attracted growing attention. In 1675, with Nishiyama Sôin, the founder of the Danrin school, who had just come to Edo, he composed a *haikai*-sequence. Hitherto he had written under his real name of Munefusa, but during the period in which he was under the spell of the Danrin school he adopted the pen-name of Tôsei. Ihara Saikaku, later the celebrated *ukiyo-zôshi* novelist, who was two years senior to Bashô, was also studying at the same time under Sôin and had established a reputation as a poet of the Danrin school.

In the following year (1676), Bashô returned for the first time to his native place, but this journey produced no travel book. It was between 1677 and 1680, probably, under the necessity of gaining a livelihood, that he occupied himself with the construction of water-works at Sekiguchi in Edo. But in the winter of 1680, when he had reached the age of thirty-seven, he was able to establish himself in a tiny hermitage at Fukagawa, thanks to the kindness of Sugiyama Sa pû, one of his admirers. Thus his period of wandering ended and he entered upon the life of a hermit.

In the following year his disciple Rika presented him with a banana-tree, which was planted in the poet's garden. From that time people began to speak of his hermitage as Banana Hermitage (Bashô-an) and eventually the poet began to call himself Bashô, although to the last Tôsei remained his chief pen-name.

Unfortunately in December, 1682, the year that saw the publication of Saikaku's first *ukiyo-zôshi*, the Bashô-an was burnt down, and Bashô for a time retired to Kai province. Somewhere about that time, probably just before or after the fire, Bashô began to study and practise the Zen discipline under Butchô Zenji of the Chôkei-ji temple at Fukagawa in Edo. With his hermitage rebuilt in the following year, he returned from Kai to Edo, and in that same year was achieved the compilation by his disciple Takarai Kikaku of *Minashiguri*, the first memorable anthology of the works of Bashô and other *haiku* poets. In August, 1684, at the age of forty-one, he made a second journey home, which lasted into the following year, and of which an account is given in *Nozarashi Kikô*. Further, as the fruit of his work in Nagoya during the winter of that year (1685), he published a *haiku*-sequence under the title of *Fuyu no Hi*. In this volume his

〔 247 〕

new and revolutionary style of *haiku* is now revealed as firmly established. This new style is called the *Shôfû Haikai* (*haikai* in Bashô's style).

Although the Bashô-an still remained his headquarters, he continued to make frequent expeditions, which are closely connected with the unceasing growth of the poet's mind. The relation of his journeys to his travel books and the *haiku* anthologies of his school may be listed as follows :

Date of journey	Companion	Chief destination	Record	Anthology
Summer, 1676		His native place		
August, 1684 to April, 1685	Chiri	His native place, with Yoshino, Nagoya, Kyoto, etc.	*Nozarashi Kikô* (*Kasshi Ginkô*)	*Fuyu no Hi*, 1684 *Haru no Hi*, 1686
August, 1687	Sora and Sôha	Kashima (moon-viewing)	*Kashima Kikô*	
October, 1687 to 1688	1. Etsujin 2. Tokoku	His native place and Yoshino	*Utatsu Kikô* (*Yosh no Kikô, Oi no Obumi*)	
August, 1688	Etsujin	Sarashina (moon-viewing)	*Sarashina Kikô*	
March to September, 1689	Sora	Ôu, Dewa and Hokurikudô	*Oku no Hosomichi*	*Arano*, 1689
September, 1689 to November, 1691		His native place, Ômi, Kyoto and neighbourhood		*Hisago*, 1689 *Sarumino*, 1691
May to October, 1694	Jirobeé	His native place, with Kyoto, Osaka, etc.		*Sumidawara*, 1694

Oku no Hosomichi (Journey to Ôu) stands out significantly because it marks a cardinal stage in the continuous development of his poetic art. Between this long journey and his return to Edo in the 11th month, 1691, he made several journeys to his native place as well as to Ômi and Kyoto. From the 4th to the 8th month, 1690, he lived quietly in the Genjû-an (Hermitage of Vision) on Mt Kokubu-yama behind Ishiyama near Lake Biwa-ko, where he wrote an account of his life in *Genjû-an no Ki* (Records from the Genjû-an). During the 4th and 5th months, 1691, he stayed at the abode of his disciple Mukai Kyorai in Saga, which was called the Rakushi-sha

(Hermitage of Fallen Persimmons), and there composed *Saga Nikki* (Saga Diary).

In the 5th month of the same year the epoch-making *haiku* anthology of Bashô's school, *Sarumino*, was published after two years of compilation. In the 11th month the master returned to Edo where Sanpû and other followers had built a new Bashô-an near the site of the old. Another banana-tree had been planted, and this was the occasion of his prose work *Bashô o Utsusu Kotoba* (On Transplanting the Banana-Tree).

For the next three years he did not leave the hermitage, for during that time he had two invalids with him at the Bashô-an, his nephew Tôin, and Jutei, an old sweetheart, probably of his Kyoto days; and besides, he had had a difference of opinion with some of his disciples. This accounts for his work *Heikan no Setsu* (On Seclusion), written in the autumn of 1692. Tôin died in the following spring. Yet, even during these days of retirement, he could neither avoid company completely nor lay aside his art, for that would have been contrary to his true nature. So he was only too glad to give a lodging to his disciple, Hamada Shadô, when he came from Zezé to Edo in the 9th month, 1692.

In the year following he aided Shida Yaha and other followers in compiling the anthology, *Sumidawara*, and in similar tasks. *Sumidawara*, which represents Bashô's later style, was published in the 6th month, 1694. Just a month or so before that, invalid Jutei seems to have rallied and so, after a confinement of three years in his hermitage, Bashô set out on another visit home, accompanied by Jirobeé, the son of Jutei. This proved to be his last expedition. Only a month later Jutei was dead, and at the *bon* (lantern festival) in his native place Bashô sadly held a requiem for her.

Leaving his native place he came to Osaka by way of Nara, and there he developed dysentery, and in spite of all the devoted care of his disciples, he passed away on the 12th, 10th month, 1694, in his fifty-first year, closing his life with the following famous *haiku*:—

> Ta'en ill whi'e travelling
> My dreams wander round and round
> O'er withered moorlands.

In obedience to his wishes, his remains were carried to the Gichûji temple in Awazu and were buried by the side of Kisozuka, the grave of Yoshinaka.

The vicissitudes of life played their part in bringing Bashô's rich poetical gift and noble personality to their full development; the death of his lord, his wandering life, his study and practice of the Zen discipline, his frequent excursions into the heart of nature and his habit of seclusion from the world, all these things were transmuted by him into poetic expression, so that he brought *haiku* poetry to such perfection that all new movements, originating in later periods when the *haikai* art had declined, have always meant in effect a return to Bashô.

The Genroku period, extending from the later seventeenth to the early eighteenth century, is well called the Japanese Renaissance. For, in addition to Matsuo Bashô, the great *haiku* poet, there were such other representative figures as the Priest Keichû who did so much in the study of the classics, Ihara Saikaku, famed for his *ukiyo-zôshi* (genre novels), and Chikamatsu Monzaemon whose work in *jôruri* (dramatic ballads) has earned him the name of the Japanese Shakespeare. All these were almost contemporaries. Saikaku died a year before Bashô, Keichû seven years la.er, while Chikamatsu outlived him for thirty years.

BUSON SHICHIBUSHÛ

(The Seven Haikai Anthologies of Buson' School)

Yosa Buson stands out as the leader of the *Haikai* Renaissance, the "Back to Bashô" movement. In his age *Bashô Shichibushû* (Seven Haikai Anthologies of Bashô's School), more properly called *Haikai Shichibushû* (Seven Haikai Anthologies), was enjoying an ever-increasing popularity; and when, towards the end of his life, in 1774, these anthologies were put together and published in one small volume, this more convenient form caused them to find a still wider public.

It was the popularity of these Bashô anthologies that began the fashion, which was to last for several decades since 1787, of compiling seven-volume editions of other *haiku* poets both ancient and modern. Of all these one of the most valuable is that named after the leading figure of the *haikai* renaissance, Buson himself, *Buson Shichibushû* (Seven Haikai Anthologies of Buson's School), issued in July, 1808, twenty-five years after the death of the poet. It was produced by a publisher who, seeing the probable demand for such a collection, had busied himself in collecting the *haikai* written by Buson and his school. It is a matter for some regret, perhaps, that it should have been a shrewd publisher rather than some thoughtful disciple of Buson who was responsible for these anthologies, since he seems to have based his selection rather on the fame of the poets and the desire to be as inclusive as possible than on a careful consideration of the value of the poems themselves. Certainly, the result is exceedingly uneven.

If we compare the present collection with the original editions of these anthologies, published as separate volumes, we shall find both abridgements and additions, as well as abbreviations and inversions. Further, owing to the fact that two anthologies were included in one of the original volumes, these were mistaken for a single collection, and the original titles were misrepresented, with the result that *Buson Shichibushû* contains not seven but eight anthologies.

The following table affords a comparison between the contents of the original separate editions and *Buson Shichibushû* :—

Buson Shichibushû	Original Editions
1. *Sono Yuki-kagé*	1. *Sono Yuki-kagé* (two volumes compiled by Kitô)
2. *Aké-garasu*	2. *Aké-garasu* (one volume by Kitô)
3. *Ichiya Shi-kasen*	⎧ 3. *Kono Hotori : Ichiya Shi-kasen* (one volume by Buson) ⎩ 4. *Kachô Hen* (one volume by Buson)
4. *Momo Sumomo*	5. *Momo Sumomo* (one volume by Buson)
5. *Zoku Aké-garasu*	6. *Zoku Aké-garasu* (two volumes by Kitô)
6. *Gosha Hôgo*	7. *Gosha Hôgo* (two volumes by Korekoma)
7. *Kachô Hen*	8. *Zoku Ichiya Shi-kasen* (one volume by Kitô)

Of the original anthologies in this list only the last named, *Zoku Ichiya Shi-kasen*, was compiled after Buson's death, the remainder being either compiled by Buson himself or under his supervision, so rightfully claiming a place in *Buson Shichibushû*. The imperfections of these anthologies as included in the later collection can be corrected by comparison with the original separate editions, and today, therefore, there exist more perfect editions of *Buson Shichibushû*.

Contrasted with *Bashô Shichibushû*, which contains anthologies so arranged as to represent the stages of the development in Bashô's style (*Shôfû*), the collections in *Buson Shichibushû* lack any such clear purpose. In any case, there is a great difference between the two poets in the matter of stylistic development ; Buson's style remained practically unchanged after he had reached maturity, whereas, as has been shown, we can discern three stages in Bashô's development, the final one being the definite establishment of his own distinctive style. Accordingly, it is not so important to distinguish the transitions in the growth of Buson's art.

Buson Shichibushû has a preface by Matsumura Gekkei, one of

Buson's chief disciples, followed by a portrait of Buson by Matsumura Keibun, Gekkei's younger brother, and a biographical sketch of Buson.

After the death of Bashô, not only his school but *haikai* poetry generally showed signs of deterioration, which became more and more pronounced until at last reaction set in towards the renaissance of *haikai* in various parts of the country, with the cry of " Return to Bashô." In this the leading figure was Buson, who was also a painter seeking to establish a new style of painting. As a poet he was always interested in the revival of *haikai* as it had been established by Bashô and this characteristic became most marked around the year 1770. By 1772 he had reached the pitch of his artistic development, anything after that being in the nature of a deepening. Buson never attained the same degree of refined simplicity as Bashô. Still, the work of his maturity covered by the seven collections compiled in his lifetime shows great polish and ease.

Survey of the eight parts of *Buson Shichibushû* will be made in the order of their publication.

1. *Sono Yuki-kagé* (The Snow-Shade)

Compiled by Takai Kitô, one of Buson's chief disciples, this anthology appeared in the winter of 1772, the title being derived from a supplementary verse (*tsukeku*) in one of the *renku* by Kitô himself. He made the compilation to commemorate the thirteenth anniversary of the death of his father Kikei, a disciple of Hajin, an epilogue being added by Miyaké Shôzan, another of Hajin's disciples, while Buson contributed the preface. The first of the two volumes in which the collection appeared consists almost entirely of *renku*, the second of *haiku*. In the first volume is a commemorative *hyakuin*, with a short introduction by Kitô, and three other *kasen*, with three *haiku* also appended as commemorative pieces. The second volume has memorial portraits of Hajin, Kikei, Bashô, Kikaku and Ransetsu by Buson, then Kitô's explanatory introduction, followed by a collection of *haiku* on the seasons.

Although this is a memorial collection and contains some commemorative poems, for the greater part it is an ordinary collection of *haiku*. Buson's " Back to Bashô " style had reached a degree of development that entitled his school to publish an anthology, and the thirteenth anniversary of Kikei's death furnished them with a good opportunity. Actually, this anniversary is of quite secondary importance, the prime intention being to introduce Buson's school to *haikai* circles. Some of the poems were well worthy of that purpose, such as Buson's distinguished poem :—

> The peaceful spring sea
> Now swells, now sinks languidly
> All the long day through.

The current edition of *Buson Shichibushû* lacks the commemorative *hyakuin* with its introduction, as well as one *kasen*, in the first volume. It also contains some inversions in the order of the poems.

2. *Aké-garasu* (Morning Crow)

Also compiled by Kitô and published in the autumn or winter of 1773, this anthology has a preface by Kitô himself, then four *kasen*, followed by *haiku* "without distinction of the seasons." Unlike *Sono Yuki-kagé* it has no commemorative purpose and was specifically intended to bring the reformist tenets of Buson's school to the notice of the public.

Kitô's preface clearly states the motive. He tells how, inspired by the widespread interest in the revival of Bashô's style and feeling that the time was ripe for a renaissance of *haikai*, he had consulted with a fellow student, Yoshiwaké Banan, who was in complete agreement with him. Then he took to Buson the *kasen* that he and Banan had produced on that occasion, and consulted him about compiling an anthology based upon it. Buson gave the title of *Aké-garasu* to the anthology, to which the poet also contributed, among others, the following famous *haiku* :—

> Beneath the young leaves
> Does the whole world lie buried—
> Save for Mount Fuji.

3. *Kono Hotori*: *Ichiya Shi-kasen* (All around this Place: Four *Kasen* Composed on One Night)

Compiled by Buson, this collection probably appeared in the winter of the same year as *Aké-garasu*. Buson tells in the preface how he came to compile it. In September that year, Buson, Kitô and Miura Chora from Isé, another leading figure in the Bashô renaissance, happened to be together in Kyoto and one evening went to call on Ranzan, a fellow poet although of a different school, and their host suggested that all four of them should each set to work to compose a *kasen* before they separated for the night. These four *kasen* were brought together in the collection *Kono Hotori*, which derives its name from the opening poem (*hokku*) of the first *kasen* by Buson :—

> All around this place
> Does the pampas grass grow thick.
> Why not *hagi* flowers ?

Since it is a joint production by poets of different schools it holds a comparatively unimportant place in *Buson Shichibushû*. The current edition is based upon a reprint of *Kono Hotori* (also called *Ichiya Shi-Kasen*) together with *Kachô Hen* (Book of Birds and Flowers) in one volume, and that is why we find it combined with *Kachô Hen* and bearing the title of *Ichiya Shi-kasen*.

4. *Zoku Aké-garasu* (Sequel to Aké-garasu)

This was compiled by Kitô and published in the winter of 1776 with a preface by Higuchi Dôryû, one of his fellow-students. Consisting as it does of two volumes, it is the largest of all the anthologies included in *Buson Shichibushû*. As the title clearly indicates, it was intended to be a sequel to *Aké-garasu* published three years earlier, and it is similar to it alike in structure and contributors. But it differs in being divided into four parts representing the four seasons, each part containing *haiku* and three *renku*, so that the whole work is more skilfully arranged than the earlier work.

It happened that the year of its publication corresponded with the seventeenth anniversary of Kikei's death, and so a commemorative *renku* is inserted at the end of both the " summer " and " winter " sections. These, however, were apparently added only for form's sake, and the anthology cannot be regarded as commemorative in essence. The *renku* at the end of the " winter " section has a foreword by Muchô, the pen-name of Ueda Akinari, the famous author of *Ugetsu Monogatari*, who was a disciple of Kikei's.

This anthology has special value as being a representative selection of the best work of Buson's disciples and other poets who conformed to his standards. Here we see clearly how Buson had refined his style to that perfect freedom which caused him to play a leading part in the *haikai* renaissance of his time.

This puts the selection on much the same plane as *Sarumino* in *Bashô Shichibushû*, standing out as the finest achievement of *Buson Shichibushû*. Below are quoted a few notable pieces by Buson himself :—

> O, rape-flowers, o'er you
> Does the moon hang in the east,
> The sun in the west.

> Such a sharp shower—
> A flock of little sparrows
> Cling to the grasses!

> The wrestler, at night,
> Recounts to his wife the match
> He should not have lost.

5. *Momo Sumomo* (Peaches and Damsons)

Compiled by Buson, *Momo Sumomo* appeared towards the end of 1780, with a preface by the poet. During that year, Buson and Kitô by the interchange of letters elaborated two *kasen*, one opening with a poem (*hokku*) by Buson, the other with one by Kitô.

> Of scattered peonies
> Two or three petals lie piled
> In a little heap.
>   (Buson)

> Through a wintry grove
> Does the chill moonlight descend
> To pierce the bones tonight!
>   (Kitô)

These two *kasen*, most typical of the *renku* in Buson's style, were included in this anthology. The preface describes it as nothing more than a collection of older works now published for the first time, and justifies this by appealing to the rotary movement of fashion as symbolized by the title, for the words *Momo Sumomo* (*mo-mo-su-mo-mo*) are the same whether read from the beginning or from the end.

6. *Kachô Hen* (Book of Birds and Flowers)

This compilation by Buson was published in the summer or autumn of 1782, with a preface by Buson himself and illustrations both from his own hand and also Keishi's. In the preface Buson tells how he invited *haiku* on the cherryblossom from his disciples and friends, intending to publish them together under the title of *Hana Sakura Jô* (The Book of Cherry Blossom), but that little progress was made in carrying out the task. Fortunately, just at that time, he had completed a *kasen* which began with a poem (*hokku*) on the cuckoo composed by Nishiyama Sôin, founder of the Danrin school of *haikai*. Combining this *kasen* with the projected *Hana Sakura Jô*, Buson rather hastily published the collection with the somewhat apologetic title of *Kachô Hen*. In addition, the anthology includes a *renku* beginning with a poem by a poetess named Umé as well as other works. In excuse for the haphazard character of the work, it must be remembered that it was compiled by Buson in the last years of his life and simply for the sake of the pleasure and interest it gave him to do it.

7. *Gosha Hôgo* (Big Library)

This anthology consists of two volumes and is the second largest of the Seven Anthologies. It was compiled by Kuroyanagi Korekoma, with Kitô's help, to commemorate the thirteenth anniversary of the death of Shôha, Korekoma's father, both father and son being disciples of Buson's. Buson himself contributed a preface and Kitô an epilogue. It is a collection of *haiku* and *renku* classified according to the seasons, only the *renku*, of which there are five, being commemorative. Each of these five *renku* begins with a poem (*hokku*) by Shôha, and the title is derived from one of these pieces :—

> Irksome confinement
> Of winter do I enjoy, with
> My big library.

While it is apparently a collection of the works of Buson and kindred poets brought together in imitation of *Sono Yuki-kagé* as a commemorative publication, it is also intended to serve as a sequel to *Zoku Aké-garasu*, the latest collection of the works of Buson's school to appear. Its fine poems representative of Buson's later years cause it to rank second only to *Zoku Aké-garasu* in importance, these two anthologies being the cream of *Buson Shichibushû*.

Gosha Hôgo was published towards the end of 1783. Buson wrote his preface for it in November of that year while he was sick in bed.

As he died a month later, this collection proved to be the crowning glory of the great poet. Three *haiku* among those he contributed are concerned with the approach of old age, of which we quote the following :—

> More lonely feel I
> Than in the year that has gone,
> Oh, this autumn eve !

The seven anthologies we have dealt with above were all compiled during Buson's lifetime, and may properly be held to constitute *Buson Shichibushû*. But, as has been already mentioned, the current edition includes one more, *Zoku Ichiya Shi-kasen*.

8. *Zoku Ichiya Shi-kasen* (Sequel to Ichiya Shi-kasen)

This was compiled by Kitô and seems to have been published in the summer of 1787. The preface by Kitô makes the motive clear. It was in imitation of *Ichiya Shi-kasen* (or *Kono Hotori*), compiled in Buson's lifetime, that Kitô and three other poets, Gekkei, Seira from Harima and Gyôdai from Owari, while asembled together one night in Gekkei's inn at Kyoto, composed the four *kasen* that give the title to the work. The inclusion of this anthology in the current edition of *Buson Shichibushû* was due to its being mistaken for *Kachô Hen*.

Yosa Buson, leading figure in the *haikai* renaissance of the An'ei (1772–1780) and Tenmei (1781–1788) eras, was born in 1716, twenty-two years after the death of Bashô. He was renowned not only as a poet, but also as a painter ; indeed, he had already established his reputation as a painter before he became known as a *haiku* poet. Thus occupied with two arts, he adopted a number of names, and of his real name we know only the surname Taniguchi.

His birthplace was the village of Kema-mura in Settsu province, not far from the river Yodo-gawa, where he spent his boyhood. From early days he had been fond of painting and at the age of twenty he set out to pursue his studies in that art by making a roving journey to Edo. There he also studied *haikai* under Uchida Senzan, a disciple of Sentoku's, and later under Hayano Hajin on the latter's return from Kyoto. Buson was twenty-seven when Hajin, who had sat at the feet of Kikaku and Ransetsu, passed away, and he then attached himself to Isaoka Gantô of the same school at Yûki in Shimôsa.

With Gantô's home as his headquarters, he used to travel about the neighbourhood to observe Nature, mainly, however, for the furtherance of his art of painting. Yet he found time to write a good deal of verse and, in 1744, at the age of twenty-nine, he published at Utsunomiya in Shimotsuké a *Saitan-jô* (A Collection of Poems on the Year-end and the New Year), under the pseudonym of Buson instead of Saichô which he had been using.

After leaving Edo he spent about ten years in wandering. The winter of 1751, when he was thirty-six, found him at Kyoto. Three years later, he left to spend four years in Tango province, facing the Japan Sea. Rumour has it that his mother had been born at Yosa in Tango, famous for Ama no Hashidaté, one of the three most beautiful places in Japan. During his stay in Tango he communed with Nature, striving earnestly to improve his technique both as poet and painter. It was at this time that he changed his family name from Taniguchi to Yosa.

After 1766, when he was fifty-one years old, he also spent three more years in making frequent tours to the Sanuki province in Shikoku to seek greater perfection in both his arts. The result was that he achieved not only the recognition of his own style of painting, known as *Yosa-fû* (Yosa's style), but also of *haiku* marked by the reactionary note of the "Return to Bashô."

After the Meiwa era (1764–1771), he grew increasingly fond of *haikai* composition. A circle of *haikai* poets, with Buson as leader, had already been formed in 1766, but, when in 1768 he returned from Sanuki province, this was expanded into a much larger group. In March, 1770, he succeeded to the name of Yahantei, one of Hajin's pen-names, and under the name of Yahantei Nisei (Yahantei II), he came to be revered as a great *haikai* poet.

But he had not reached perfection yet. With redoubled zeal he devoted himself to *haikai* until he attained the full development revealed in *Aké-garasu*, and went on to advance his impressive, sensuous and gorgeous style (so eminently the blending of the two arts of poetry and painting) to the further refinement and freedom of *Zoku Aké-garasu*. He had now reached his zenith—there is no further development of style seen in *Gosha Hôgo*—and he was unquestionably the most prominent figure in the *haikai* renaissance.

He was stricken by illness in October, 1783, and, in spite of the devoted attention of his family and disciples, he ended his brilliant career on December 25th of that year, at the age of sixty-eight. His last moments are described in *Kara Hiba* (Withered Cypress) by his leading disciple Kitô, who after his master's death was called Yahantei Sansei (Yahantei III). His grave is in the precincts of the Kinpuku-ji temple near Kyoto.

The inspiration behind this great leader of the *haikai* renaissance was to revive the spirit of the incomparable Bashô. He shows that clearly in his work *Bashô-an Saikôki* (The Bashô Hermitage Refounded), which he wrote when the famous hermitage was rebuilt in the compound of the Kinpuku-ji in 1776. But Buson always had his own original genius. It was this that inspired him from youth, led him to break away from the style of his master Hajin, and in the end brought him to base the *haikai* revival on the " Return to Bashô."

He was not indeed so human as Bashô, whose mind was deepened by his many travels and who also kept Nature blended with Life. Buson's genius was more purely artistic, with little regard for the world that Bashô loved so much. He built up his character rather through travelling and reading and evolved a sensuous and picturesque style that had touches both of romanticism and classicism. Great though he was, Buson never quite attained the humanistic depths of Bashô.

ORA-GA HARU

(My New Year)

This notable work from the pen of Kobayashi Issa, a village poet of Kashiwabara in Shinano, purports to be a diary for the year 1819, when the author was fifty-seven years old. As a matter of fact it was not all written in that year, and the entries as a rule are not regularly dated after the fashion of a diary. The contents are a well-balanced mixture of prose and *haiku*, most of the prose taking the form of explanatory introductions to the verses. Here and there are inserted a few *haikai uta* or *haikaika* (comic *haikai*) and, as occasion demands, *haiku* written by the author's friends and disciples, as well as *renku* fragments, and *haiku* and *waka* by earlier poets, with seven illustrations by the author's own hand, adapted from earlier examples. The work certainly commences as a diary under the date of January 1st, but the entry takes the form of an old tale, followed by two *haiku*, testifying to the comfort which the author had found in Buddhism. Long ago, one New Year's Eve, he writes, a bonze of the Fukô-ji temple in Tango province wrote a letter to himself as if from Amitâbha Tathagâta announcing his visit with an invitation to the bonze to return with him to Paradise. This letter he handed to an acolyte, who was bidden to bring the letter to him on the following morning. The acolyte duly presented the pretended invitation, which the priest read with tears of joy streaming down his cheeks. After the story comes a poem by Issa to show that he too greeted the New Year in poverty but in the grace of Buddha :—

> Now do I welcome
> With but only half my heart
> The coming New Year.

The second poem describes how with joy he prepared a first New Year's feast for his little daughter Sato, then entering on the second year of her life. Then come a number of *haiku* on spring, and another story. The head priest of the Myôsen-ji, Issa's family temple in the village, had a little son of eleven years named Takamaru. On March 7th the little fellow went out gathering herbs and accidentally fell into a river and was drowned. This was a great shock to his father, accustomed though he was to preaching and practising resignation to life's uncertainty. Issa, who attended the funeral, composed an elegy, the conclusion of which likened little Takamaru's plucking of the spring herbs, destroying them in the first flush of their blooming, to the child's untimely death.

After several more *haiku* Issa inserts another delightful bit of prose. The rumour having spread through Issa's village that every eighth day from January 1st music had been heard flowing from heaven, a number of friends gathered in Issa's house on the evening of March 19th to listen to this heavenly music. They waited in vain, but just at the first glimmer of dawn the song of the nightingale (*uguisu*) reached their ears.

This story leads up to a *haiku*, which is followed by forty-two more, including one which is the work of his disciple, some of them on spring, but the most part on summer. Here are a few of them :—

> O baby sparrows,
> Quick, quick, get out of the way,
> A horse is coming !

> 'Neath the summer moon
> Isn't it pleasant to beat straw
> Just for diversion ?

> Flies swarming on the rice ;
> One more fly could share the diet,
> If the world were better !

He then tells how he planned a journey to the northeast and set out on April 16th, but after walking eight or ten kilometres, he began to wonder whether, since he was nearly sixty years old, he would ever return alive. So he sat down under a tree and turned his homesick eyes in the direction of his native village of Kashiwabara, and a *haiku* was the result : —

> Though firmly resolved
> Not to think of turning back,
> Yet how dear my home !

We are not surprised to learn that after all he does turn back.

Next come two humorous *waka* poems, or *haikai uta*, and a number of *haiku*, including one by a disciple. We are told how Nabuchi, his disciple, had in the village of Naganuma in Shinano a famous peony garden that attracted visitors even from considerable distances. One day when Issa was there, he was much impressed to see among the variegated blooms some black and yellow specimens which, although highly commended by the visitors, seemed to him to be lacking both in charm and vigour. They proved to be artificial, the owner of the garden having made them out of paper for a joke. This inspired Issa to write the following *haiku* :—

> In guise of petals,
> Does waste paper resemble
> Genuine peonies.

A prose piece follows entitled *Kawazu no No-okuri* (The Frog's Funeral). The heartless boys in the author's neighbourhood used to bury frogs alive, covering them with earth and leaves, and chanting as they did so :—

> Mr Frog is dead, he's no more;
> With leaves of grass let's bury him.

The author expresses his feelings in a *haiku* :—

> Even the flowers and leaves
> To sorrowful tears are moved
> At the frog's grave-side !

He then goes on to tell about the toad—not troubling to distinguish between toads and frogs—which once taught a Chinese hermit (referring to Gama Sennin, the Toad-hermit) how to fly, and recounts also how in ancient Japan the frogs won much fame for their military prowess in the great battle of frogs fought at Tennô-ji in Osaka, but that in the present peaceful reign, the frogs have taken on milder qualities. As we sit at the back door in the cool of the summer evening, if we call out, " *Fuku yo, fuku yo* (Frog dear) ! " a toad will come lumbering up to us out of a nearby thicket to share with us the cool air. Issa then gives us the following *haiku* :—

> Oh so peacefully,
> A frog is sitting, looking
> At the far mountains,

followed by two *haiku* on toads by ancient poets, and a number by

Issa himself on toads and summer-time.

The succeeding lines in prose give an illustration of the Buddhist doctrine of retribution in the story of how the father of Nakamura Santetsu, a doctor in the village of Sumisaka in Shinano, died the very night he killed a snake, and how the retribution even overtook his son. This piece of prose is followed by a number of *haiku*, one being by a friend of Issa's, and by two *waka* by ancient poets.

Issa tells of three chestnuts brought from the sacred mountain forest of Mukawa in his own province and planted in a corner of his garden. They budded most promisingly, but the house newly built to the east kept the sunlight from them, and the tender saplings were never able to grow to a height of more than one foot, for, when the winter snow piled up on the roof was swept off, as is the custom in that snowy province, its weight snapped the stems off at the root. This went on year after year, and at the end of seven years the trees were still only a *shaku* (about one foot) in height and barely alive. Issa compares the fate of these unfortunate little trees with his own bitter experiences as a stepchild, with *haiku* and *renku* by ancient poets on children and stepmothers, and an old *waka* by one who was a stepson.

Issa recalls his own unhappy childhood, how, motherless and left to play alone by the other children, he chanted :—

> Come and play with me,
> You little baby sparrow,
> Poor orphan sparrow !

This poem is signed " Yatarô (aged 6)," using his boyhood name, though this piece was not composed by the poet at that tender age, but is known to express what he felt about his childhood when he looked back on it in later years.

He goes on to tell an old tale of a stepchild in the village of Tatsuta in Yamato province starved by a cruel stepmother. Once, after giving him scarcely any food for ten days, she set a bowl of rice in front of him and mockingly said, " If that stone image of Jizô were to come and eat this, I would give you another bowlful." In response to the child's prayers the guardian deity of little children did come and eat the rice, when the mother repented of her cruelty and heartless-ness and treated her stepson with the same love as her own child

he image of Jizô, the poet adds, that rendered such notable service
ɔ stepchildren is still carefully preserved, while Issa himself rounds
ff his narration with a *haiku*.

As a contrast to these stories of unhappy childhood Issa proceeds
ɔ write about his own baby daughter Sato, born the summer before,
rhom he and his wife adored. In the following *haiku* we see his
rife Kiku fondling her little one :—

> While I count over
> The long tale of her flea-bites,
> I suckle my child!

hen there are a number of *haiku* by Issa and other poets on the in-
ocence of children. Among them are such famous pieces as :—

> Wanting me to get
> For her the moon from the sky
> My child still cries on.
>> (Issa)

> Women planting rice—
> They plant the rice towards the place
> Where their children cry.
>> (Kisha)

Issa next tells the tale of a divorced woman who, anxious to see
he carp streamer hoisted for the first time on the Boys' Festival for
he little son she had had to leave behind, came stealthily back to her
ɔrmer home under cover of night. There is a *haiku* attached to the
tory followed by others by Issa and certain ancient poets on parental
ɔve as revealed in man and animals.

The poet's infant daughter Sato died of smallpox on June 21st,
nd Issa describes the sufferings of the little patient as well as the
rief felt by his wife and himself :—

> Though I know 'tis true
> That all things must change and go,
> My loss o'erwhelms me!

n the next section there are several *haiku* elegies by earlier poets on
he death of their children, and other poems on various aspects of
e relationships of children and parents.

A few lines of prose precede a *haiku* on the stunted growth, owing
ɔ the cold climate, of the trees and shrubs of Issa's neighbourhood.

Most of the next thirty *haiku* treat of summer, although the later ones are on autumn.

> A mountain temple !
> From its verandahs one hears
> The belling of deer.

> The baby tried to pick
> Dew-drops in hand—so like pearls
> Did they look indeed.

In the next passage Issa quotes a proverb that utters the soun
opinion that " it is good to shelter under a large tree.* " Th
can be applied to the towering chestnut tree in the precincts of th
Suwa shrine in Kashiwabara. At first sight, one cannot see ar
fruit under the great mass of leafage, yet no one can pass under
without finding some chestnuts.

The themes of the following fifty-six *haiku* (two of which wei
composed by disciples of Issa) vary from autumn to winter.

> Under the lantern
> Hanging from a pine-branch, a girl
> Is beating washings.

> On cold nights my heart
> Is filled with thanks to my sons—
> So old have I grown.

> " The rice-cake maker
> Is working at the next door ! "
> Cries my child with joy.

> Plump falls the urchin
> Rooting up with all his main
> A radish too large.

On the subject of rice-cakes, Issa tells how on December 27th h
was staying in a temple, which some other evidence suggests wa
sittuaed in the village of Furuma near his home. Early in the morr
ing when the lady of the home was boiling the rice, she said to hin
" They are making rice-cakes next door and they usually bring u
some. Be sure and eat yours while they are hot, as they are not goo
for you when cold." But though Issa waited and waited the hc

---

* Cf. *Don Quixote*: "It is good sheltering under an old hedge. He who leane
against a good tree, a good shelter findeth he." The interest of the coincidence may perhaj
excuse the irrelevance here.

rice-cakes never came. And meanwhile his boiled rice got cold.

> O those rice-cakes
> That every passing minute
> We were expecting.

The work concludes with a brief essay dated December 29th, which strikes the same note as that with which the diary opened on January 1st, the comfort that the author had derived from Buddhism. His life beyond the grave he submits entirely to the disposition of Amitâbha Tathagâta, praying that he lead him wheresoever he will, be it to Hell or Paradise. With a mind so composed he is confident of Buddha's protection, whether or not he says his prayers, an attitude he holds to be in accordance with the teachings of the Buddhist sect to which he belonged.

> Whatever befalls
> All comes from the divine will,
> So I end the year!

Ora-ga Haru, as we have seen, is a collection of fugitive essays (*zuihitsu*) in diary form, with prose and verse skilfully blended. But the prose style is quite ordinary and matter-of-fact, in this differing from that *haibun* prose of Bashô, in whose hands it was distinguished by an atmosphere of *haikai*, conveying the same emotion as that of his *haiku*. This atmosphere is altogether missing from Issa's prose, as it is from his verse.

Yet, though in another vein, *Ora-ga Haru* is a fine piece of writing. There is a lyrical quality about the stories that capture the attention, interest and sympathy. Unlike the symbolistic *haiku* perfected by Bashô and derived from a peculiar intimacy with Nature, Issa's *haiku* express his own subjective reaction to Life in a very familiar way with a skilful mastery of colloquial language.

Such a technique was not novel, yet Issa's achievement is unique because of the way he harmonizes the form and content. The *haiku* that Issa has included in this work, whether composed at the time or previously, may be regarded as a selection of his favourite pieces, and all have the quality of distinction.

Issa's manuscript, still extant, contains three blank spaces, two among the prose essays and one among the *haiku*, from which we may infer that he intended to insert two more illustrations and another *haiku* before publication, but this is the only sense in which th work can be regarded as incomplete.

The manuscript remained in the hands of one of Issa's disciples Yamagishi Baijin, of the same province, until his dea h, when i passed into the hands of Shirai Isshi, a friend and neighbour of Baijin who published it in 1852, twenty-five years after the death of Issa Isshi's edition is a wood-block replica of the original manuscript wit! a preface by Kodama Itsuen of Edo, a friend of Issa's, an epilogue b Matsudaira Shisanjin, the daimyo of Mori, Izumo province, whe was also a *haiku* poet, commemorative *renku* and various *haiku* an *renku* by other poets, and a final epilogue by Fusho Saiba, a discipl of Itsuen's. There have been various editions at inteivals sinc Isshi's, Issa's own handwriting being reproduced in a collotyp edition by the Kokonshoin of Tokyo in 1926.

Issa was born on May 5th, 1763, the eldest son of Kobayash Yagoheé, a farmer in the village of Kashiwabara in Shinano province Bereft of his mother at the age of three, he was brought up by stepmother from the time he was eight. The lack of sympath between his stepmother and himself developed into a prolonge feud that vitally affected his life and career.

Issa was ten years old when his stepbrother, Senroku, was born and the affection which his stepmother lavished upon her own chil only increased the ill-feeling between her and Issa. His grandmothe used to intercede for him, but unfortunately she died when he wa fourteen, and his father then sent him to Edo as an apprentice as th only way of bringing peace to the family.

In Edo he studied *haikai* under Chikua of the Katsushika schoc which had been founded by Yamaguchi Sodô, a friend of Bashô* and wrote under the pen-name of Ikyô. Chikua died when Iss was twenty-eight and the next year he returned to his home for th first time. In the following January he changed his pen-name t Issa, thus signifying his determination to cultivate his own style o *haikai*, independent of the Katsushika school.

In the same year he made a pilgrimage to the Hongan-ji templ in Kyoto as proxy for his father, and so began a period of extensiv travel through the Kansai district lasting four years, both for diversio and for the development of his art. He then published a collectio of his own and others' works gathered on his journeys under the title of *Tabi Shûi* (Harvest of Travel), an anthology which still shows traces of the old tradition and marks a transitional period in his life.

He then went back to Edo, only, however, to return to the Kansai district the following year where he travelled about for another three years. The fruit of this was his second anthology, *Sarabagasa* (Hat of Farewell).

His father died when Issa was thirty-nine. The poet was present at his death-bed, and afterwards wrote *Chichi no Shûen Nikki* (Diary on the Death of My Father), a fine piece of work, meriting comparison with his *Ora-ga Haru*. His stepmother still persisted with her feud, preventing his father's wish that the inheritance should be divided between the two sons, Issa and Senroku, from being carried out.

He returned to Edo and spent the next few years in wandering about eastern Japan. Meanwhile, the note of originality in his poetry became more marked.

At the age of forty-six he again returned to his home to keep the thirty-third anniversary of his grandmother's death, and this was made the occasion for bringing about a settlement of the inheritance dispute through the good offices of a mediator. He had scarcely returned to Edo, however, when his stepmother and Senroku broke the agreement arrived at, and it was not until he was fifty-one that a mediator was able to bring the long and bitter dispute to a close and ensure that the terms of his father's will were properly carried out. After that Issa settled down in his native place.

The following year he married and had four sons and one daughter. Unfortunately all died young, and his wife Kiku also died when Issa was sixty-one. And still misfortune pursued him. He married a second wife, Yuki, a year after the death of his first wife, but their conjugal life was not a happy one, and soon she was divorced. A year later he married Yao, who survived him. But two years after this marriage, in 1827, the village was swept by a fire that burnt down his house ; and he lived afterwards in a godown saved from the flames. Then in August his old complaint of paralysis returned and proved fatal, carrying him off on November 19th, when he was sixty-five years of age. By an ironical chance he never saw the one child who was to reach maturity, a daughter, Yata, who was born posthumously and through whom his line has been continued.

Yet with these misfortunes we cannot call him wholly unfortunate. Undoubtedly the originality that marks his work was largely due both to his peasant origin and the difficulties and disappointments he suffered. Even during his lifetime he had the satisfaction of being hailed as a great *haiku* poet, and later generations have more than confirmed the verdict of his contemporaries.

HAIFÛ YANAGIDARU

(A Collection of Light Verse)

Haifû Yanagidaru is the title of a series of selections, in 167 books, which appeared between 1765 and 1833. It was compiled from many anothologies of that form of light verse which is known as *senryû*, compiled by the poet Senryû I and his successors.

The word *senryû* is now used to denote a modern form of verse consisting of seventeen syllables, arranged as 5-7-5. Although this is exactly the verse form of the *haiku*, it did not derive directly from it, having its origin in a special form of the *renku* (*haiku* sequence) called *maeku-ʒuké*.

The history of this form of light versification is briefly as follows. Karai Hachiyemon, living in Edo in the Meiwa era (1764–1771), attained fame, under the pen-name of Senryû, in the writing of *maeku-ʒuké*, a verse form with a long history. Senryû compiled an anthology of some of the best examples, known as *Senryû-ten no maeku-ʒuké* (Senryû's Selection of *maeku-ʒuké*), or *Senryû-ten* (Senryû's Selection), or, still more briefly, as *Senryû*, from which another selection was compiled later and published under the title *Haifû Yanagidaru*, or simply *Yanagidaru*, in the year 1766. This consisted of those particular *tsukeku* or second lines that the compiler believed were intelligible by themselves.

This proved to be the first of the long series of *Haifû Yanagidaru* that appeared at frequent intervals, twenty-four books being published during the lifetime of Senryû himself. After his death, his name was carried on by Senryû II, Senryû III and Senryû IV, but without doubt the collections made by the original Senryû I contain the largest number of masterpieces.

Despite the modernity of the name *senryû*, this verse form dates from the remote Muromachi period when there appeared Yamazaki Sôkan's *Inu Tsukuba-shû*. This is a collection of two-line *renku*, composed on the following principle. The first line, or *maeku*.

is composed in what Matsunaga Teitoku termed the *mushôtai* style; that is, having in itself no fixed meaning or character. The first and second halves of this line usually contradict, or modify, each other, so that the next line, *tsukeku*, derives its interest as an answer to a riddle or the solution of a difficult problem. Below are some pieces from *Inu Tsukubashû* :—

> "In one way lonely, in another not, I feel . . .
> Having money with me in a brushwood cabin and weary of the world."
> "Something exalted, something otherwise, the bonze . . .
> Having the flying bird brought to the ground by prayers, only to devour it."

Obviously, the second line, or *tsukeku*, may vary considerably as in the following three efforts in supplementing the *maeku* :—

> "To cut, or not to cut, that is the question."
> A. "Catching a burglar and finding him your own son."
> B. "The flowery branches hiding the bright moon."
> C. "An arrow a little too long but agreeable to hit the mark with."

It will be seen that the greater variety of associations the first line possesses, the better it is for this form of composition. Examples of first lines with a great elasticity are the following :—

> 1. "Pushing and being pushed."
> 2. "Dreadful and dreadful."
> 3. "Little by little."
> 4. "Slowly and slowly."
> 5. "Often and often."
> 6. "Funny and funny."
> 7. "Lonely and lonely."

First lines of this kind were given to a number of competitors to be completed or capped, and the best of the results were selected and their superiority discussed. This sort of capping, or *maeku zuké*, became a very popular poetical pursuit. For instance :—

> "Little by little,
> The hair fading into baby's down on a bald head."
> "Funny and funny,
> My lantern blown out, to be shown the way by a blind man."
> "Slowly and slowly,
> Carrying a paper lantern, shielding it from the wind with my hand."

These supplementary or capping lines can be full of wit or waggery, satire or irony. Since, by comparison, the first lines seem to be merely explanatory, the second or capping lines came to have a separate existence and to be known as *senryû*.

Morphologically, the *senryû* is commonly characterized by the imperfect endings of the verbs and their auxiliaries. For example, in the original Japanese of such a line as, " The hanger-on, how bashfully he holds out his bowl for a third helping, " the last word is *dashi*, the imperfect ending of the verb *dasu* (to hold out). This characteristic is in a sense due to the development of the *senryû* from these capping competitions, since the second line is to be explained by the first line, and the complete meaning understood by continuing from the second to the first line. Thus some pieces, on being read from their second to their first line, form perfect *kyôka*, or comic poems. For instance :—

> " Looking around from side to side,
> The bill-collector forestalls, ' Ahem, is the man out again ? ' "

This can be read conversely, and so makes a perfect *kyôka*. But in order that one may pass back from the second line to the first, the imperfect ending is necessary. This type of ending has become a convention, and even characterizes the perfectly independent *senryû*.

But there is a further reason, apart from the historical one, for the use of imperfect endings after the *senryû* had been established as a separate form, and that is the very nature of the verse itself. It is light and gay, or, even if ironical, it is never serious. Nothing is so suggestive of what is light and casual as these abrupt imperfect endings. For instance, in the piece quoted about the hanger-on, the piece would have a much more serious air if *dasu* were substituted for *dashi*.

There are various ways in which *senryû* may be classified, but here let it suffice to give examples of a few different types. There are some whose peculiar quality is due to their very realism, to the light and easy fashion in which they bring a complete picture before our minds, rather than to anything particularly witty or ironical. Take the following piece :—

> " O withered flowers in a vase in a country inn ! "

Nothing could better objectify what is in the poet's mind. A wretched room, a shabby alcove with its cheap vase and neglected flowers, all this we see, and remember, perhaps for the first time, those humble tea-houses in out-of-the-way villages that we usually pass heedlessly by. Or take another piece like this :—

"An embroidered crest, the sucking child is scratching it!"

This raises up the picture of a baby unconsciously digging his tiny nails into the embroidered crest on the mother's dress, and we smile with pleasure at the expression of the child's serene contentment.

Sometimes the chief interest of a verse is in the subtlety of some ironical comment, especially on human foibles and weaknesses, a subtlety that at times trembles into real beauty. Thus :—

"The long sleeve with which girls cover their mouths after a slip of the tongue,"

or, even better, this trait of girlishness :—

"The girl ran to her mother out of breath—on no urgent business at all."

In such a piece as the following we have a bitterly ironic comment on the egotism that may be found lurking in any one of us :—

"Sons, with weeping eyes, watching the dividing up of their parent's mementoes,"

or this :—

"Saying, 'I dare not presume to ask you to make me another loan,' the debtor comes to prove the falsity of his own words."

Irony often gives a humorous twist to historical facts and traditions, even in speaking of the deities or Buddha.

"Stripping himself, the doctor approached Kiyomori to feel his pulse."*
"The elephant sneezing, Samantabhadra** was shaken off its back."

Occasionally non-human creatures are the subject of the jest, as in these two :—

"A dragon-fly on a stone image of Jizô (the guardian deity of children), resembling the god's hair."
"A lobster decked out on an orange looking as if it were feasting on the fruit."***

This form of verse is also often employed to show the mental workings of maid-servants and hangers-on, particularly the latter.

---

* Taira-no Kiyomori was suffering from a terrible fever. His body grew so hot that even those around him all felt the heat.
** A Buddhist deity mounted on a white elephant.
*** A rice-cake with lobster, orange, etc. forms a New Year decoration.

" A maid lost in thought, hardly able to bring herself even to use the floor-cloth."

" A hanger-on, too talkative, but much too slow."

" The hanger-on, using his master's ink-slab from the opposite side."

" Whether to dare to eat or, out of deference, to refrain, either is hard for a hanger-on."

It was in Edo more than anywhere else that the *senryû* type of verse delighted the citizen, and so we see the life of Edo fully dealt with by it. Many subjects are taken from the popular *kabuki* and the gay quarters. Further, since *senryû*, unlike *waka* poetry which is more conservative and traditional, has not to stand on its dignity, it can take its themes freely where it will, from everyday life and personal affairs. It is also quite distinct from the *kyôka* (comic verse) which is full of puns and jokes. *Senryû* in fact, although following quite different rules owing to the difference of language, seeks to achieve almost exactly the same result as the light verse of the Western world.

SHINJÛ TEN NO AMIJIMA

(The Lovers' Suicide at Amijima)

During the long period of peace from 1603 following the end
of the Age of Civil Wars, with a wider diffusion of the benefits
of culture, a variety of arts arose designed to appeal to popular
tastes. Among these the puppet theatre (*ayatsuri*) and the *kabuki*
drama were the most prominent, offering a marked contrast to the
earlier forms of Japanese drama, the Noh and the Noh Comedy
or Farce (*kyôgen*), whose appeal was limited to the upper classes.
Thus in the realm of the popular drama were produced many works
of great literary value. Indeed, the greatest of all Japanese dramatists,
Chikamatsu Monzaemon (1653-1724), revealed his genius in his
writings for both the puppet theatre and *kabuki*. His *kabuki* plays,
however, survive only in the form of short synopses of the plots,
while the plays he wrote for the puppet theatre have come down
to us, most of them, exactly as they had issued from the author's
pen. Owing to some degree of resemblance in the structure of
their plays, to the wealth of their vocabulary and to their continued
popularity with succeeding generations, Chikamatsu has, with good
reason, been called "The Japanese Shakespeare." A further
similarity between these two great playwrights is that, despite
much speculation and research, the details of their lives outside
their work for the stage are hidden in obscurity. By some Chikamatsu is said to have been a Buddhist priest, by others a samurai in
the service of a court-noble. Nor is opinion agreed as to his birthplace. It is clear, however, from various evidences that he was
of good family and well-educated, a thing which was then rare
among playwrights.

Puppet plays as well as *kabuki* plays are generally classified
under the two headings of *jidaimono* ("historical pieces") and
sewamono ("social pieces"), in both of which Chikamatsu has left
masterpieces of dramatic art. It is in his social pieces that he shows

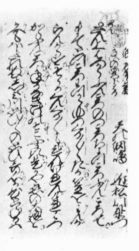

CHIKAMATSU MONZAEMON
(1653—1724)

ILLUSTRATION TO THE
JÔRURI TEXT-BOOK OF
KOKUSEN'YA KASSEN
(THE FIGHTS OF KOKU-
SEN'YA). Printed in 1715.

greater originality, for, being based chiefly on contemporary events, these give the author a wider scope for the exercise of his personal observation and expression, whereas the historical plays, derived mostly from ancient literature and popular ballads based on it, are often marred by lapses into a triteness that is almost entirely absent from the social pieces.

One of the principal themes of these social pieces was that of *shinjū*, the double suicide of lovers who, despairing of happiness in this life, die together in the hope of finding it in the next. Double suicide was exceedingly frequent at the time, and since the public enjoyed seeing them dramatized both in the puppet and the *kabuki* theatres, Chikamatsu raised the dramatic representation of this theme to its highest pitch of perfection. We may therefore take *Shinjū Ten no Amijima* as typical of his social pieces.

This is a puppet play that tells the story of an actual event, the double suicide of a young merchant and a courtesan at Amijima in Osaka in 1720. According to tradition, Chikamatsu was carousing in a restaurant in a suburb of the city, when he received word from his theatre of this suicide which had taken place the previous night, with the request that he should prepare a dramatic representation of it immediately. As he hurried home in his palanquin the plot came to him which he wrote down as soon as he arrived home, and so we have our present play.

Jiheé, the hero of this tragedy, was the young master of a paper-shop who, in his infatuation for the courtesan Koharu, had run heavily into debt. This liaison was not to the wishes of Koharu's mistress who had her own reasons for wishing to keep them apart ; she favoured the suit of another of the girl's patrons, Taheé, a base type of fellow, but very wealthy, who was on the point of ransoming her and making her his wife—for in those days a courtesan had no choice but to marry any man who paid her ransom, no matter how much she disliked the prospect.

Accordingly, since Jiheé and Koharu saw that their love was hopeless, they decided to run away together and commit suicide, if they could escape the watchful eye of the girl's mistress.

The issue was complicated by the fact that Jiheé had a wife, Osan, and two children. Osan, a devoted wife and a judicious woman, heard rumours of the death pact that her husband and

Koharu had made, and so she wrote secretly to the girl, asking her to give up Jiheé and save him from ruin. The tender earnestness of Osan's appeal distracted Koharu, but, rising to the occasion, she made up her mind to save Jiheé at the cost of her own happiness. It is against such a background that the play begins.

Act I. The scene opens with Koharu entertaining a country samurai at a tea-house to which she has been summoned. Although she does not know him, he knows about her, and her sadness and depression convince him that the rumours he has heard are true. He ventures to remonstrate with her on the grave folly of such an act, and she confesses everything, except the one vital fact that is now disturbing her, the pathetic request in Osan's letter and her own resolve regarding it.

"Yes," she says, " it is true we have promised to die together. But life once lost is lost forever, and I am not now so eager to die."

So she suggests that the samurai should visit her often, thinking that thus the bond between Jiheé and herself might be weakened, and Jiheé discouraged from his plan.

But Jiheé had heard about this rendezvous at the tea-house, and was waiting outside, in the hope that he and Koharu would afterwards be able to take this opportunity to carry out the project of dying together. When, however, he overheard her talking in that strain, he angrily drove his sword through the paper of the *shōji* door to kill her for her inconstancy. The thrust fell short, however, and the samurai seized his hand and tied it to the doorpost.

Then Taheé, Jiheé's rival, happened to come along and, mistaking the bound man for a robber, began to cuff and kick him. This caused the samurai to come out of the room and fling Taheé to the ground. Then, taking off his hood, he showed himself to be Jiheé's elder brother, Magoemon, who had come in the guise of a samurai in order to learn Koharu's real feelings.

He could not help feeling deeply chagrined at what he took to be the coldness of Koharu's attitude towards his brother. And Jiheé, in his turn, confessed to Magoemon his folly in being so long deceived by Koharu. As evidence of the severance of all connection with her, he now requests his brother to give back to her the written vow she had given him in return for the one he had given her. While engaged in this, however, Magoemon discovers the letter that Osan had sent to Koharu. He now understands clearly the reason for the girl's apparent heartlessness, but decides not to show the letter to Jiheé, who continues to reproach her for her faithlessness and goes off with his brother.

Act 2. The scene is laid in Jiheé's house, where Magoemon enters with Osan's mother. He speaks of the rumour that Koharu is being ransomed and accuses Jiheé. Jiheé meanwhile is pretending to be asleep over the charcoal brazier, but he hears every word and, knowing that the hateful Taheé must be the man, weeps tears of mortification. Osan believes that her husband's tears show that he still loves Koharu, but when she charges him with this he protests that that is not so.

" Should tears of sorrow flow from my eyes, and tears of bitterness even from my ears, then no words would be needed to show my heart." He is not weeping because of his old love, he protests, but rather that he has been put to shame by the rumours which his successful rival, Taheé, has circulated about his having dissipated his whole fortune.

Then Osan, understanding what is in his heart, cries out, in her compassion for Koharu in being forced by pressure of circumstances into the power of Taheé for whom she feels no affection, " Oh, the pity of it that Koharu should have to die."

Thereupon she confesses that Koharu's apparent heartlessness is due to her own entreaty, and begs her husband to do justice to Koharu and spare her life. The dialogue at this point is wonderfully written and vividly reveals an ideal Japanese woman sacrificing herself on the altar of justice and charity. She concludes by offering all she has to ransom Koharu, even if she has to pawn her own and her children's clothes to obtain the money.

By chance her father enters at this moment and, hastily jumping to the conclusion that Jiheé will never cease philandering, forces him to agree to a divorce and takes his daughter away with him.

Act 3. Here we arrive at the culmination of the tragedy. Jiheé, now reduced to utter despair, entices Koharu to come out to him. He stabs her and hangs himself with her sash.

The characteristic feature of this play is that it reveals the ideal of Japanese womanhood through the two strongly contrasting characters of Osan and Koharu, the respected mistress of a better-class household, and a courtesan. Osan's nobility is shown in her clear and generous recognition of the other's noble qualities, so that, at the cost of her own interests, she is eager to ransom her. Koharu, for her part, is willing to give up her love for the sake of Osan, and finally prefers death to marriage with a rich man she detests. The main action centres round these two, with Jiheé, the hero, playing a somewhat hesitating and passive rôle.

From its first presentation this play has retained its popularity on both the puppet and *kabuki* stages. One of the most famous actors associated with the rôle of Jiheé was the late Ganjirô Nakamura (d. 1935), whose performances never failed to attract crowded houses. In the course of its long history on the *kabuki* stage, however, the play has been so much modified and adapted to meet the demands of popular taste that an almost new version has resulted, a version no doubt more effective for dramatic representation, but lacking in the literary quality of the original.

HAKATA KOJORÔ NAMIMAKURA

(Kojorô and the Pirates)

Like *Shinjû Ten no Amijima* (The Lovers' Suicide at Amijima), *Hakata Kojorô Namimakura* (Kojorô and the Pirates) is one of Chikamatsu's social dramas based on contemporary events, although differing greatly from the former in its incidents and characters. It was produced in the puppet theatre, two years before the appearance of *Shinjû Ten no Amijima*. Both are three-act plays.

In Chikamatsu's time, foreign trade was still strictly forbidden except with Holland and China, but the ban was frequently violated by adventurers who sought big profits by trading with foreign ships offshore out of range of the authorities. Occasionally they were detected and brought to book, and in the year 1718 over sixty people, including women, were arrested for this sort of smuggling.

Their leader was an outlaw in Nagasaki named Hachiyemon, and the women associated with him, mostly of courtesan origin, seem to have been responsible for disposing of the smuggled goods. The two ring-leaders were sentenced to death the following year. Chikamatsu, however, wrote this play in the year in which the arrests were made and before sentence had been passed and carried out. It should be noted that it was illegal to portray contemporary events either in books or on the stage, and consequently the names of the persons in the play are different from those of the actual criminals, who, moreover, are referred to not as smugglers but as pirates.

Act 1. The opening scene is laid off the Straits of Shimonoseki, where a big ship is lying at anchor. Kezori Kuemon, the captain, who is really a pirate, is waiting with four subordinates for some merchandise that is to be brought, and finding time hang heavy on their hands, is chatting with a passenger, a young merchant named Komatsuya Sôshichi.

The master, Kuemon, brags of how in his younger days he had a quarrel with a Satsuma man on the occasion of the festival of the tutelary deity of Nagasaki, and half killed him, thus revealing his own wild, lawless nature and his pride in his brute strength. He then calls on the young merchant, Sôshichi, to tell his story. The young man says that he is the son of a merchant of Kyoto, travelling to Hakata on business, and confesses that he has long been passionately in love with Kojorô, a courtesan of that town, whom he has promised to ransom and marry. Disgusted with such a milk-and-water story, Kuemon loses all interest in Sôshichi and returns to his cabin.

Just then two of Kuemon's gang arrive with the smuggled goods in a small boat, and Sôshichi happens to peep out of his cabin window as they are being taken on board. Kuemon spots him doing so and, fearing he will betray the secret of his contraband trade, orders his men to throw him into the sea. Fortunately the young man falls into the boat and succeeds in making his way to the shore.

The next scene is a tea-house at Hakata. Sôshichi enters in the rags of a beggar, and finally succeeds in seeing his beloved Kojorô. He tells her what has happened to him and they embrace each other in tears.

Into the next room enters a noisy crowd of swaggering pleasure-seekers. It is Kuemon and his gang all decked out in foreign-made materials of great value, silks, woollens, brocades and velvets, crying out to the reception clerk to bring forth the choicest beauties of the house for them, and spreading out in front of the mistress and her family generous gifts of ginseng, coral ornaments, damask silk and satin apparel. It is a scene of riotous gaiety.

Kojorô, roused from her weeping with the unfortunate Sôshichi and envious of the revelling throng, peeps into the next room and recognizes Kuemon, whom she knows quite well. She goes in and entreats him to lend her money for her ransom, in order to leave the house and marry her lover. Kezori generously agrees to do this and so she brings in Sôshichi to express his thanks also. The unfortunate man finds himself in the midst of the gang of pirates who had thrown him into the sea. The recognition is mutual; scarcely has he opened his mouth than the gang jump to their feet in a way that makes clear their intention of effectually silencing him this time. But the leader remains seated and perfectly calm ; facing Sôshichi he tells him that he will have to join the gang.

"You see, Master Sôshichi, much as we may regret the past we can never recall it. It's no use worrying over what has been done. The best thing you can do is to throw in your lot with us. Kojorô's ransom shall be paid and you shall marry her. It's true that the more there are of us, the less each one gets. But our profession, after all, depends on luck, and a lucky fellow like you ought to be very useful. I go down on my knees, my dear sir, and beg you, entreat you, to join us."

But these polite words were spoken in such a threatening tone that Sôshichi knew he would be killed if he refused the offer. He did not want to join these men, but if he did not, then that would mean death as well as giving up Kojo ô. Even as he hesitated, Kojorô cried out : "I refuse to live if you don't marry me. Marry me or kill me ! Is it yes or no ? Your answer decides my fate."

Yielding to her persuasions Sôshichi at last decides to join the gang. Kuemon feels quite satisfied that he will keep his word, so he calls in the others, pays down 1,500 *ryô* for seven courtesans including Kojorô, and they all leave the house together.

Act 2. The pirate Sôshichi now has a fine house in Kyoto and is living in luxury with Kojorô. Hearing of this, his father Sôzaemon comes up to visit the house. It happens that the young couple are away on a journey at the time, and the father finds that all his suspicions are justified. Indignant that a son of his should be living on ill-gotten gains, he takes charge of all their household goods and sells them, intending that Sôshichi and Kojorô shall have a chance to make a clean start.

When the young couple return they feel that it must be the police who have seized their property and make plans to flee. Just then Kuemon happens to call on them and notices their restless behaviours. He becomes suspicious and demands the return of the Tally for Voyaging among the Islands, the much-valued licence to trade in the South Seas, which had been placed in Sôshichi's charge. Unfortunately the young man could not return it, since it had been sold off with everything else. Naturally, this only makes Kuemon more suspicious still. Believing that Sôshichi intends to part company with the gang and to keep the tally to set up in business on his own and so monopolize all the profits, he draws his sword and attacks Sôshichi.

From outside the house Sôzaemon hears the desperate fray and is eager to hand over the cause of it at once, for the tally is the one thing he has not disposed of. But he cannot get in, since the front door is firmly locked and nobody can hear his shouts. At last, he manages to make a hole in the wall of the garden and throws in the tally, which Sôshichi picks up and returns to Kuemon, who thereupon leaves.

The young couple cannot see the father's face, but he stretches his hand through the hole for them to take and so bid him a sad farewell. He then throws in the proceeds of the sale so that they can use it to pay the expenses of their flight from Kyoto. Gratefully they receive it and set forth on their escape.

Act 3. While the two fugitives are urging the bearers of their palanquins to make all the speed they can, a posse overtakes them. Feeling that the end has come, Sôshichi commits suicide with his short sword, while the weeping Kojorô is taken and bound. Then Sôshichi's fellow pirates and the women they had ransomed from the tea-house at Hakata pass by, escorted by the police. Soon sentence is passed on the criminals. The men are all liable to the death penalty, but on the auspicious occasion of an Imperial enthronement, the death sentence is commuted, while the women are acquitted. To the bereaved Kojorô the chief official addresses the following words :—

" Although your husband, Sôshichi, was associated with these men, his criminal acts sprang from his youthful indiscretion in permitting himself to be infatuated by a woman's charms. Yet his crime was a grave one. You must now take your husband's place and render filial duty to your father Sôzaemon, and make your prayers for the repose of your husband's soul."

With this the play ends. Like *Shinjû Ten no Amijima* it is written as a love tragedy, with Sôshichi and Kojorô as the leading characters, yet, both in the puppet play and the adaptation of it made later for the *kabuki*, it is the scenes in the pirate ship and in the tea-house from Act 1 that have held the stage ; and in both these scenes, it is Kuemon, not Sôshichi and Kojorô, who takes the lead.

The popularity of these two scenes is due both to their dramatic quality and to the interest aroused by Kuemon's character. After all, Sôshichi and Kojorô are types frequently met with in the works of Chikamatsu, and also in the puppet theatre and the *kabuki* generally. But Kuemon is an unusual creation, vividly drawn, blending in himself the brutality of an outlaw and the cheerful and generous innocence that gives him the charm of a hero. Further, the exotic meal served in the pirate ship scene and the still more exotic dresses donned by Kuemon and his band were bound to strike the imagination of the Japanese, who at that time were isolated from all contact with foreign things. This fact served greatly to make the play popular both in the puppet theatre and the *kabuki*, and to give these two scenes a place in the hearts of the public that has outlived all changes of taste.

KOKUSEN'YA KASSEN

(The Fights of Kokusen'ya*)

Kokusen'ya Kassen is a very different type of drama from the two plays of Chikamatsu already described. They were social pieces in three acts, whereas this is a historical drama, and, in accordance with the convention of the time, is built up on a more massive scale in five acts.

The subject is derived from historical events in China in which a partly Japanese hero played an important rôle. When the Ming Dynasty yielded to the Ch'ing Dynasty in 1644, a certain Tei Seikô, a surviving retainer of the Ming Dynasty, carried on the conflict against the new order. Seikô's father, Shiryû, had lived in Japan and there taken a Japanese wife, and Seikô was the offspring of this marriage. Because of his Japanese associations Seikô turned to the Japanese Government with a plea for military assistance in his revolt against the Ch'ing Dynasty. This plea could not well be granted, but Seikô continued to make frequent raids on Chinese territory, finally establishing himself in Formosa. He did not live long after that, but his son who succeeded him ruled Formosa for almost thirty years and maintained the conflict with the Chinese Government. Although Japan had not rendered any aid to Seikô, the fact that this rebel who was continually harrassing the Chinese Government had Japanese blood in his veins riveted the interest of the Japanese people upon him and inspired Chikamatsu to write the present play.

Chikamatsu was not born until seven years after Seikô had made his unsuccessful appeal to the Japanese Government, and he was only ten years old when the hero died in Formosa. But that widespread interest in Seikô was long sustained is shown by the fact that it was not until 1718, when Chikamatsu was

---

* Or Koxinga, as usually spelt by Europeans.

sixty-six years old, that the drama was first staged as a puppet play.

The name *Kokusen'ya* which Chikamatsu uses in his title refers to Seikô. The Ming court had honoured him with the family name of *Shu* which was the family name of the Ming emperors, and accordingly he changed his name to Shu Seikô. Thus he became popularly known as the "Old Man with the Emperor's Family Name," that is, Kokusen'ya.

Act I. The play opens with the arrival of an ambassador from Tartary with the news that his King was anxious for the hand of the Empress Kasei, favourite consort of the Emperor Shisô, in return for which he would conclude a treaty of peace with China. Ri Tôten, the General of the Right, urged upon the Emperor the necessity for acceding to the proposal, which, however, was vigorously opposed by Go Sankei, the War Minister, who did not mince his words in voicing his opinion of the impertinence of the Tartar King. The Tartar ambassador was about to depart in a rage when Ri Tôten checked him and, as evidence of the sincerity with which he had urged the Emperor to accept the proposal, gouged out his left eye. Such a display of self-sacrifice placated the Tartar and also deeply touched the Emperor himself.

This Ri Tôten wished to marry the beautiful younger sister of the Emperor, named Princess Sendan, and the Emperor approved of the match. But the Princess refused. Thereupon the Emperor proposed that the matter should be decided by a game between the ladies of the court, one hundred on either side, those on the one side bearing a plum-flower and those on the other a cherry-flower. If the plum-flower team were defeated, then the Princess must marry General Ri Tôten. The Emperor had indeed ordered the plum-flower team to lose, and as a result the Princess was pressed to accept the marriage.

At this point Go Sankei entered hurriedly on the scene to remonstrate with the Emperor, saying that Ri Tôten was a traitor. He declared that even his gouging out his left eye was no proof of loyalty, but was rather evidence of the extent to which he had gone in his secret and treacherous negotiations with Tartary.

He was immediately justified by the arrival of a Tartar army under the command of the ambassador. Their sudden attack was successful, the Emperor was captured and beheaded, and his consort made prisoner. Go Sankei, however, put up a strong resistance. He sent off his wife with the Princess, and then, having set free the Empress, he made his escape with her, also taking along with him, tied to the handle of his halberd, his own child whom his wife had been forced to abandon.

In crossing a ferry the Empress, who was then pregnant, was killed by a bullet, and Sankei cut the infant prince from her womb. But in order that the enemy should not know that the child had been saved, he destroyed his own beloved infant son as a substitute for the prince. Then, overwhelmed with grief at his own loss, he carried the imperial prince away in his arms and continued his escape.

His own wife also had fallen a victim to the enemy on reaching this ferry, and the Princess Sendan, all alone, drifted away in a small boat at the mercy of wind and waves.

Act 2. The scene is laid in Japan, where dwells Tei Shiryû, who had been exiled from China years before because he had incurred the displeasure of the Emperor whom he had admonished· Under the name of Rô Ikkan he had married a Japanese wife who had borne him a son, Watônai.

This Watônai had grown up and married, and one day he went down to the seashore with his wife to gather shells. They found there a curiously shaped boat that had drifted ashore, in which was a beautiful foreign lady, who proved to be the Princess Sendan. Watônai had learnt Chinese from his father and so was able to learn from her of the great rebellion in China. He proposed to his father that they should cross over to their country to help suppress the rebels, and his father agreed, sending Watônai on ahead in one of his ships.

Ikkan and his wife soon followed, but, on their arrival, Ikkan went on alone in order to seek out his daughter, the wife of General Kanki. Watônai joined his mother and, in the course of their journey, they had to pass through a great thicket, known as the *Senri-ga-také*, the Wide Bamboo Plain, haunted by tigers. The soldiers of Ri Tôten happened to be on a tiger hunt, and a fierce tiger, maddened with fear, attacked the two travellers, but Watônai boldly grappled with it and overcame it, just as the soldiers in hot pursuit appeared on the scene. They surrendered, however, to the power of Watônai and the tiger.

Act 3. According to the convention of the time the third of the five acts formed the climax, on which playwrights concentrated all their art. It is so in this play.

We see the *Shishi-ga-jô*, the Lion Castle, under the command of Ikkan's son-in-law, General Kanki. Watônai and his mother, having joined Ikkan, had managed to reach it and found it closely guarded. They knocked at the gate, with Watônai calling out, " We wish to see the lord of the castle ! " while Ikkan added, " If the master is absent, I would like to see the mistress. She will be sure to remember a man from Japan."

The guards, however, took him for an enemy and were about to shoot him down, when the daughter Kinshôjo, wife of General Kanki, appeared on the upper story of the gate. She had heard the word " Japan," and demanded to know who Ikkan was, whereupon he briefly explained to her their relationship.

Could he really be her father ?—wondered Kinshôjo, and she demanded proof of his identity.

" When I had to leave this country," replied Ikkan, " I left my portrait as a keepsake."

" Ah, your words prove who you are," she cried, and produced the portrait which she wore next her heart. With a mirror she reflected her father's face in the moonlight and looked from one to another. She could have no doubt, and weeping she threw herself in his arms.

But when Rô Ikkan asked to be admitted to the castle on the ground that he had a most important request to make of his son-in-law Kanki, the guards firmly refused, because the Tartar King had definitely forbidden them to admit any foreigners. The utmost they would concede after much argument was that his wife might enter if she agreed to have her hands bound.

" What can your request be ? " asked Kinshôjo. " Still I will do my best to persuade my husband to meet you and, if I succeed, I will pour white face-powder into the castle moat. But if I fail, then I will use rouge instead."

General Kanki was absent at the time in conference with the King of Tartary who had conferred high rank on him. But Kinshôjo entertained her stepmother kindly, and then, on Kanki's return, brought her before him so that he might learn of Watônai's desire for an interview.

"So this Watônai is my wife's younger brother!" ejaculated Kanki. "Certainly I shall take your side." Thereupon, to the horrified surprise of the mother, he drew his sword and made as if to stab his wife Kinshôjo. To her protest Kanki replied thus: "The Tartar king has appointed me commander-in-chief of an expeditionary force against this Japanese hero Watônai, who plans to re-establish the Ming Dynasty. Not knowing that Watônai was my wife's brother, I vowed to the king that I would not fail to return victorious. Therefore, should I now throw in my lot with Watônai, I should certainly be accused of having failed in my duty as a samurai merely because my wife is his relation. The only thing I can do in the circumstances is to kill my wife, before I can honestly take your part."

Kinshôjo professed herself quite willing to be sacrificed for the sake of her parents, but her stepmother refused to let her. "For," said she, "if I allow you to be killed before my eyes, it will be said, both to my shame and to the shame of Japan, that a Japanese stepmother left you to your fate in remote China because she hated you."

In face of this Kanki decided he could not kill his wife, although this meant that he must refuse to aid Watônai.

Watônai, meanwhile, was watching the colour of the water coming from the castle, anxious to know the result of his stepsister's petition. After a time the water flowed out tinged with red. Thinking therefore that Kanki had refused to see him, Watônai tried to enter the Castle by climbing the wall in order to find his mother. There he confronted Kanki, and the two were about to cross swords when Kinshôjo intervened, crying out, "Look at the source of the red water!" She flung open her dress. The red stain was from her blood; she had stabbed herself with a dagger.

"Since I have killed myself," she pleaded, "please take the side of my parents and younger brother!"

Her husband promised her he would, and then the mother, rejoicing at these words, tore the dagger from Kinshôjo's body and plunged it in her own throat to vindicate herself before her heroic stepdaughter.

With this the Act ends. This remarkably dramatic presentation of Oriental morality by means of these four characters—two heroes, one Japanese and the other Chinese, and two heroines, one from either country—has a quality that never fails to move the audience.

Act 4. The scenes in this Act change almost as rapidly as in a film, and in fact were devised for the sake of employing elaborate stage machinery.

In the first scene Princess Sendan appears, seeking to return to her native country accompanied by the wife of Watônai. On the way, they encounter a youthful prodigy asleep in a fishing-boat, and by means of this boat they reach their destination.

Then we turn to Go Sankei who, fleeing from mountain to mountain, has devoted himself to bringing up the infant prince. On the summit of M Kyûsen-zan he found two very ancient men with white hair playing a game of *go*. They told him that Watônai was actively engaged in fighting and offered to bring him just as he was before their eyes.

So the scene changes to the Castle of Shokuto in the spring-time, which is captured by Watônai. Then to the Barrier of Unmon Kan in the summer, defended by Tartar soldiers, where Watônai breaks down the gate and kills the enemy general. Another change shows a mountain castle in autumn, and Watônai making a night attack and destroying it with cannon. Finally, we are shown the Castle of Chôraku covered with the snow of winter and occupied by Watônai.

Each time that he saw Watônai, Go Sankei could scarcely help rushing to him with the prince in his arms, but the two old men kept him back, saying, " Though he appears for a moment before your eyes, he is in reality hundreds of miles away. Again, though you think you have spent but a few minutes on this mountain, actually five years have passed." Then, after informing him that they were the Emperor Kô, the founder of the Ming Dynasty, and his faithful retainer, Ryû Hakuun, they vanished from his sight.

When the astonished Sankei came to himself again, he found that his beard had grown long and that the prince was quite a tall boy. To that place came Rô Ikkan accompanied by the princess and Watônai's wife, and the prince and princess talked together.

Suddenly the party were attacked by a large enemy force led by the general who was seeking the princess. In this grave peril Sankei and the prince uttered prayers to the two old men, while the princess and Watônai's wife prayed to Sumiyoshi Daimyôjin of Japan. Marvellous to relate, a bridge was thrown across the sky and they passed over it to a distant mountain. The enemy troops dashed after them across the bridge, but before they could get across it was snapped in the middle by a strong blast of wind. All of them fell down headlong, except the leader who managed to scramble up, only, however, to be killed by Sankei who struck him with the checker-board the old men had been using.

Act 5. The scene is the Castle of Nanking where the Tartar King and Ri Tôten are holding Rô Ikkan prisoner, bound to a shield. Watônai, following up a succession of victories, had opened an attack on the castle, but they warned him that if he did not call off the attack they would kill Rô Ikkan. This threat caused Watônai to hesitate, but the difficulty was solved by Sankei and Kanki. These two generals pretended that they were surrendering to the enemy, and then turned suddenly upon them. They managed to capture the King, whom they sent back to his own country, while Ri Tôten they killed. Thereupon the young prince ascended the imperial throne and the Ming Dynasty was restored. This ends the play.

When the play was first performed in 1718 as a puppet play, it is said to have held the stage for seventeen months. This lengthy run, almost unprecedented, shows how it was welcomed by the public. Regarding the composition of the play, there is a tradition that it was composed while Chikamatsu lay in prison. This was on a charge of blasphemy because of his adaptation of *Nippon Furisodé Hajimé* from the history of the Age of the Gods. When the officials read *Kokusen'ya Kassen* they realized that it was not at all surprising that Chikamatsu should have been able to write about the remote Age of the Gods, since even in prison he could produce out of his imagination such a remarkable work dealing with foreign countries, and so they released him at once.

Ill-supported as this tradition is, it is but a further testimony to the play's popularity. As already suggested, a good deal of its success was due to its fanning of national pride with its description of the adventures of a semi-Japanese hero, but undoubtedly its stage value was also greatly enhanced by its spectacular qualities, particularly in its presentation of foreign manners and customs, so strange to the almost hermit nation of that day. Then one cannot overlook the popular appeal of the cinema-like changes of scene and action, as in the scenes on Mt Kyûsen-zan, to say nothing of the wealth of underplots and the brilliant skill with which myths and legends are blended with historical facts, all of which would greatly appeal to the mind and eye of the audience.

After its great success as a puppet play, it was, and still is, frequently staged as a *kabuki* play in various theatres. At the present time, however, Act 3 is usually performed alone for its high dramatic interest.

SUGAWARA DENJU TENARAI-KAGAMI

(Sugawara's School of Penmanship)

The dramatists who followed Chikamatsu Monzaemon employed a very different method of writing; Chikamatsu had conceived and written the whole of his plays, but the custom among his successors was to collaborate, one dramatist making himself responsible for the plot of a play, while the different acts were each written by different men. The two main reasons for this collaboration were first, the growing complication of the plots to suit the public taste which made it difficult for any one writer to prepare a play within a reasonable time, and secondly, the great increase in the number of playwrights, who could only be kept in adequate employment by some such division of labour.

Three dramatists who frequently collaborated were Takeda Izumo, Miyoshi Shôraku and Namiki Senryû, and the five-act play *Sugawara Denju Tenarai-kagami* (often referred to shortly as *Sugawara* which was staged for the first time as a puppet-play in the year 1746 was one of the fruits of their partnership. It is a popular presentation of the tragic life of Tenjin-sama, worshipped in Japan as the god of literature and calligraphy.

Tenjin-sama is the name of the deified Sugawara Michizané a historical personage who died in 903 and was at one time Minister of the Right. He rendered great political and cultural services to the state, but the intrigues of his political enemy, Fujiwara Tokihira brought about his downfall and he ended his life in despondency. Legends gathered around his name very soon after his death, and it is told how his revengeful ghost, transforming itself into a thunder-bolt, struck the Imperial Court with such effect as to kill his enemy Tokihira and all his party. It was for the purpose of placating his vindictive spirit that he was deified as Tenjin-sama and a chief shrine to him set up in Kyoto with subsidiary shrines throughout the country, where even to this day festivals in his honour are held

n the 25th of every month. There also grew up a widespread tradi-
on that this god is particularly responsive to prayers for scholarship
ld calligraphy, and on this account he was worshipped by school
ildren as their patron deity up to the Meiji era.

With Tenjin-sama as the chief figure, topical events were also
oven into the play. Thus, just before its appearance, a woman
1 Osaka had given birth to triplets, on which rare achievement
le had received nation-wide congratulations and an award from
le government. These triplets, under the names of Umeômaru,
Latsuômaru and Sakuramaru, are brought into the play as retainers
f Sugawara Michizané.

Act 1. The opening scene is the Imperial Court to which the
Chinese priest Ten Rankei had come with instructions from the
Emperor of China to draw and bring back to him a portrait of the
apanese Emperor, because of his reverence for the latter's noble
irtues. Unfortunately the Japanese Emperor was ill, and so it
ras decided that the priest should draw the portrait of a substitute,
ttired in the Imperial robes. Tokihira, Minister of the Left, tried
o get himself appointed as the Imperial substitute, treacherously
lanning to use the opportunity to usurp the throne. Suspecting
hat this was his intention, Michizané, Minister of the Right, opposed
lim and recommended that the substitute should be Prince Tokiyo,
he Emperor's younger brother. The Emperor agreed, and so it
ras Prince Tokiyo who sat for the Emperor's portrait to the Chinese
riest.

The scene changes to a river bank near the Kamo shrine, where
he Prince is going in an ox-carriage to pray for the Emperor's
ecovery. A faithful attendant, Sakuramaru, accompanies him
s driver, and later his wife appears on the scene, accompanying
Princess Kariya Himé, adopted daughter of Michizané. Prince
Tokiyo and Kariya Himé are deeply in love with each other, and
he faithful couple, Sakuramaru and his wife, have arranged for
hem to meet in the ox-carriage. Then Miyoshi Kiyotsura, one
f Tokihira's followers, comes on the scene and wishes to look into
he carriage, but, fortunately, the lovers have time to flee without
lis discovering their presence there.

The next scene is laid in the mansion of Michizané, who has
Deen ordered by the Emperor to instruct his ablest pupil in the secret

of calligraphy in which he had made himself illustrious. The able
of all his pupils was undoubtedly Takebé Genzô, but it so happen
that he had once been expelled from Michizané's household f
having formed an illicit union with one of the ladies-in-waitir
This unfortunate incident did not, however, prevent Michiza
from choosing him, although, much to Genzô's grief, the c
intimate relationship was not at the same time revived.

In the meantime Prince Tokiyo and Princess Kariya Hir
had eloped together, and this afforded Tokihira a suitable prete
for bringing about Michizané's downfall. He accused Michiza
of planning to make the Prince Emperor, ambitious to see l
daughter Empress, and as evidence of his treacherous intentions
adduced Michizané's strong recommendation of the Prince as t
Emperor's substitute for the portrait. The result was that Micl
zané was cast into prison. His wife and young son were also
grave danger, but Genzô and his wife helped them to escape.

Act 2. After spending some time in prison, Michizané w
sentenced to banishment, and, guarded by officers, was carri
in the prison palarquin to the quay at Osaka whence to set s
for his place of exile. The Prince and Princess overtook him, f
of profound regret at having been the cause of the false char
made against him, and in the hope that it might help in provii
Michizané's innocence, the Prince gave up Kariya Himé and
himself be taken back to the capital by Sakuramaru.

Not far away lived Michizané's aunt Kakuju, the mother
Michizané's adopted daughter, Kariya Himé, with her elder daught
Tatsuta who had married a man named Sukuné Tarô. Kaku
now an ailing old woman, sent for Michizané, desirous of seei
him once again before she died. The chief of the guards in char
of Michizané was a kind-hearted man and consented to Micl
zané's paying the visit.

Accordingly, Michizané spent some time at his aunt's hou
but the time came when he had to set out again at two o'clock
the night with the second cock-crow. But Tatsuta's husband, Suku
Tarô, and her father, Haji-no Hyôé, who were both rogues
secret communication with Tokihira, plotted together to ma
the cock crow earlier than the hour appointed for the real escort
arrive for Michizané, so that he should go off with a false esc

who had orders to assassinate him on the way.

The unfortunate Tatsuta overheard the two rascals, but before she could do anything she was discovered and put to the sword and her body hidden in a pond. Having heard that if a cock is put on the water near a drowned person it will always crow, the two murderers did this, and the crowing woke up Michizané who was hurried away by the false escort.

After Kakuju had bidden him farewell she found Tatsuta's body in the pond with a fragment of Sukuné Tarô's dress in her mouth. Having thus identified the criminal, the old woman slew him with the same sword. Then the cock crew at the right hour and the real escort came to fetch Michizané. Kakuju told him that the escort had already arrived and that Michizané had gone off with them. The leader of the escort refused to believe her, and, while they were disputing, Michizané himself came out of an inner room.

Then the false escort returned, reporting that they had not found Michizané inside the palanquin but only a wooden image of him. Doubting her senses, Kakuju lifted up a blind of the palanquin, and, to the astonishment of them all, exposed, not a wooden image, but Michizané himself. While this was going on, Haji-no Hyôé had joined the false escort, only to be arrested by the genuine escort whose arrival had exposed their imposture, the other criminals seeking safety in flight.

Once again Kakuju examined the interior of the palanquin and found this time only a wooden image, not the real man. Then the real Michizané appeared, to explain that he had carved this wooden image with his own hands, intending to leave it behind with his aunt as a keepsake. But while he was asleep his soul had entered into it and brought it to life. So deep a mystery moved the whole company with awe.

Kakuju determined to end her days in a convent and for that purpose cut short her hair with the very sword that had killed her daughter and that she had used to kill her wicked son-in-law. The rascal Hyôé was beheaded, and Michizané started on his long journey into exile in the official palanquin. Although the divorced Princess Kariya Himé had not been permitted to see her foster-father when she had overtaken him with her husband, she was now able, through the good offices of Kakuju, to bid him farewell.

Act 3. Umeômaru, one of the triplets, had been in the service of Michizané, his master's banishment leaving him a lordless man (*rônin*). Joining his brother, Sakuramaru, who had taken Prince Tokiyo back to the capital, they were deploring the heavy misfortune that had overtaken Michizané, when Tokihira passed by in an ox-carriage. The two brothers tried to attack him, but they found themselves opposed by their third brother, Matsuômaru, who was then in the service of Tokihira. Both sides parted, breathing defiance at each other.

The scene changes to the house of Shirodayû, the father of the triplets, who was a farmer in charge of Michizané's villa and was now celebrating his seventieth birthday. His three daughters-in-law had the congratulatory dishes already prepared, but, as their husbands had not yet appeared, the dishes were served instead before the three trees that Michizané prized most in the garden, a plum (*umê*), a pine (*matsu*) and a cherry (*sakura*), from which the triplets had received their names of Umeômaru, Matsuômaru and Sakuramaru.

Shirodayû had gone to visit the shrine of the tutelary deity in company with Sakuramaru's wife, when Matsuômaru arrived, followed shortly afterwards by Umeômaru. Remembering their quarrel of the preceding day, the two brothers began to fight and in their struggles struck the cherry-tree, breaking off a branch. This is suggestive of Sakuramaru's suicide later.

On their father's return, they both proffered requests to him; Umeômaru wished to go to attend on Michizané in his place of exile, but his father would not agree to this and, instead, bade him search out the missing wife and young son of Michizané and make himself their protector; Matsuômaru, out of his loyalty to Tokihira, proposed to dissociate himself from the family; Shirodayû agreed to this and turned him out.

When Matsuômaru and Umeômaru had departed with their wives, Sakuramaru's wife was left filled with anxiety regarding her husband's delayed return, but when he did appear, to her surprise, from the inner room, it was only to kill himself as a proof of his sincere regret for the troubles he had brought upon Michizané by acting as go-between in the love affair of Michizané's daughter and Prince Tokiyo. Knowing all this, the father had visited the tutelary shrine to ask for the oracle as to how Sakuramaru should dispose of himself, and the oracle had turned out unfavourable. Act 4. Michizané in exile composed the following ode :—

> Upon the east wind,
> Send forth your fragrant perfume,
> O ye plum blossoms,
> And though left now masterless
> Forget not the Spring's coming!

And his plum tree, left in the care of Shirodayû, was miraculously transported to the place of his exile in a single night, already in bloom.

Then a vassal of Tokihira's, who had been sent from the capital to assassinate Michizané, crept on the scene. But Umeômaru, who had come by the same ship as he, appeared in the nick of time to capture him. From this would-be assassin Michizané heard for the first time that Tokihira was definitely plotting to sacrifice the Emperor and usurp the throne himself. So Michizané at once turned into thunder and winged his way to the capital to destroy the traitor.

All this was seen in a dream by Michizané's wife. She was now living secretly in a suburb of Kyoto, carefully tended by the wives of Umeômaru and Sakuramaru. But Tokihira's soldiers discovered the hiding-place and descended upon them. In the struggle Sakuramaru's wife was killed, but, just when the wife of Michizané was on the point of being captured, a masked itinerant bonze appeared on the scene and rescued her.

Meanwhile, Takebé Genzô, Michizané's ablest pupil, was established with his wife in a private school in a mountain village some distance from the capital, where, under cover of teaching the village boys the art of penmanship, he was able to bring up the young son of Michizané in secret, but it reached the ears of Tokihira, who sent his retainer Shundô Genba to summon Genzô before the village headman and demand the death of the boy.

Genzô had to consent, but his intention was to put another boy in the prince's place. So, when he returned home, he accounted it fortunate to find a handsome young boy there, who had entered the school in his absence. It was this boy he beheaded.

Then Genba came, bringing with him Matsuômaru, who because

[299]

of his old association with Michizané, would be able to identify the head of the decapitated boy. This Matsuô did without hesitation, and the party left, carrying their grim trophy.

Just as Genzô was congratulating himself on having saved Michizané's son, the mother of the boy he had substituted arrived to take her son home. Fearing that his secret might be revealed, Genzô was about to kill her, when Matsuômaru burst into the room. It was Matsuômaru's own son who had been sacrificed, his loyalty to Tokihira had been only a pretence and he had entered the traitor's service temporarily only in order to render what help he could to Michizané, to whom he had always been faithful. It was he who, in the guise of an itinerant bonze, had rescued Michizané's wife, and, still greater proof of loyalty, it was he who had deliberately sent his own son to Genzô's school in order to offer a substitute for the son of Michizané.

Act 5. A tremendous clap of thunder broke over the Imperial Court, terrifying all, and striking dead all the rascals on the side of Tokihira, and gravely endangering the life of Tokihira himself. The chief villain, however, after being tormented by the ghosts of Sakuramaru and his wife, finally perished at the hands of the young Prince Tokiyo and Princess Kariya Himé, and the drama ends in the enrolment of Michizané among the gods on account of his loyalty.

As is obvious from this synopsis, the play is a very long one with an extremely complicated plot and many underplots. Performance of the whole play tends to be very wearisome, and, indeed, at the present day would be impossible owing to the shorter time now allowed. Accordingly, portions of it only are staged, by far the most popular being the fighting scene in front of the ox-carriage in Act 3 and the school scene in Act 4, which are both staged repeatedly at the present day. The appeal of the fighting scene lies mainly in the appearance, dress and conventional gestures of the triplets and Tokihira, affording a wonderful blend of colour, form and movement.

In this scene, but more especially in the second one from Act 4, it is the character of Matsuômaru that makes the chief impression on the audience. Until the culminating moment, Matsuômaru appears as an ungrateful rogue. Then, through changing situations of deep emotional appeal, the audience, after watching the grave dilemma of Genzô and his wife when reluctantly they decide on the sacrifice of another's son because of their loyalty to Michizané, is led on to the pathetic lamentations of Matsuômaru and his wife for the dead son whom Matsuô had deliberately brought to serve as substitue for the son of their honoured lord. And, in addition to the tragic quality of this scene, there is here als the local colour of a private school in the Edo period to add to the inte est of the audience, with its portrayal of the manners and customs of the time, another reason for the continued popularity which this scene from Act 4 has enjoyed ever since its first performance on the stage.

———————

KANADEHON CHÛSHINGURA

(The Loyal League of the Forty-Seven Rônin)

Chûshingura is another of the joint productions of the three authors of *Sugawara Denju Tenarai-kagami*, produced on the puppet stage two years later (1748). *Sugawara* deals with remote events of 800 years before, while *Kokusen'ya* by Chikamatsu, although the events on which it is based go back no more than 60 years, still has its scene in a distant foreign country, so that these plays lent themselves readily to the introduction of many fantastic elements, myths and fairy-tales. The present play, however, not only deals with events no more remote than fifty years before, but also has its scene in Japan itself, and there is then little room for any fantastic elements, the play keeping close to reality. It has in this respect something in common with such social dramas as *Ten no Amijima* and *Hakata Kojorô*, but contains elements of greater historical and social interest.

The historical event on which the plot is based had achieved great fame among the Japanese : it was the action of forty-seven samurai who, after successfully avenging the death of their lord, committed *seppuku* (*harakiri*), and whose tombs in Tokyo are even to this day continually visited by large numbers of worshippers.

The story is, briefly, as follows. In the year 1701 an Imperial messenger was despatched from Kyoto to the Shogun's court in Edo, and a daimyo named Asano Takumi-no Kami was appointed to receive him officially. He appealed for guidance in the proper discharge of his duties to Kira Kôzuké-no Suké, an official who was responsible for the ceremonial etiquette on such occasions. On the pretext of being inadequately rewarded, Kira did not instruct Asano properly in every detail, with the result that the unfortunate daimyo blundered in carrying out his functions. Derided moreover in foul terms by Kira, he ended by drawing his sword on Kira, who had a narrow escape, receiving only a mere scratch. But Asano had been guilty of the grave offence of disturbing the peace of the Shogun's

OPENING SCENE OF THE KABUKI PLAY KANADEHON
CHÛSHINGURA (THE LOYAL LEAGUE OF THE FORTY-
SEVEN ROSHI).

LAST ACT OF THE PUP-
PLAY SUGAWARA
U TENARAI-KAGAMI
AWARA'S SCHOOL OF
ANSHIP), AT BUNRA-
HEATRE, OSAKA

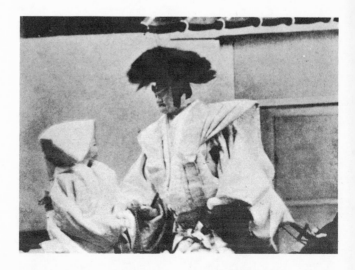

court and was condemned to commit *seppuku* with the confiscation of his fief.

The ruin of the Asano family left all his vassals "lordless men" (*rônin*). Among them were forty-seven loyal samurai who, under the leadership of Ôishi Kuranosuké, vowed to avenge their lord's death. After many hardships, they finally realized their purpose in a night attack on Kira's mansion, and then, in obedience to the law, all committed *seppuku*.

In the dramatic presentation of this tragedy, the names of persons and places were deliberately changed so as to give the impression that it had taken place 350 years earlier, in the Ashikaga period. Such an alteration was for the purpose of evading the law prohibiting the dramatization of any contemporary event. For us, as well as for the contemporary audience, these Ashikaga personages in the drama are easily identified with the characters of the real tragedy of the Edo period, and any anachronisms found in it do nothing to disturb the pleasure of the performance.

The play is divided into eleven acts :—

Act 1. Tadayoshi, younger brother of the Ashikaga Shogun, was proposing to visit the shrine of Hachiman, the War God, at Kamakura in order to offer there the helmet of Nitta Yoshisada, an enemy general killed in a recent battle. But it so happened that forty-seven helmets were lying around the spot where Yoshisada had been killed, making it difficult to know which one was actually his. So Kaoyo, wife of En'ya Hangan, who knew the dead general's helmet, was summoned before Tadayoshi to identify it.

But Kô-no Moronao, the secretary of the Shogun, made adulterous advances to the beautiful Kaoyo, and when he was thwarted by Momonoi, the equal in rank of the absent Hangan, denounced him. Moronao corresponds to the historical Kira, and Hangan to Asano, while the forty-seven helmets suggest the forty-seven *rônin*.

Act 2. Smarting under the insults and denunciation of Moronao, Momonoi determined to kill the secretary next morning in the Shogun's court. He confided in Honzô, his principal retainer, and entrusted his affairs to him. Honzô apparently approved of his purpose, even encouraging him by snapping off a twig from a pine-tree in the garden as a figure of the cutting off of Moronao's life. Yet immediately afterwards he galloped off to visit Moronao with the intention of trying to avert the threatening clash by means of a bribe, since Moronao was very avaricious.

Act 3. The bribe proved effective, so that when, later, at the Shogun's court, Momonoi was about to carry out his threat, Moronao offered no resistance but bowing humbly apologized for his insolence. Just then Hangan entered and gave Moronao a letter from his wife, Kaoyo. Moronao jumped to the conclusion that this meant that Kaoyo had resolved to surrender to his desire and eagerly opened it, only to find an ancient *waka* poem, reproaching him for his unlawful desires.

Finding himself thus spurned, he turned in hate on Hangan and addressed him in the most insulting terms. Hangan, unable to restrain himself, whipped out his sword against Moronao. But Honzô was able to seize Hangan from behind and hold him until Moronao had effected his escape.

Act 4. Hangan, confined to his quarters for having drawn his sword at the court, was ordered to commit *seppuku*. He was quite prepared for this and meantime had been impatiently awaiting the arrival of Yuranosuké, his most faithful retainer, to whom he wished to entrust the management of his affairs. Yuranosuké, however, was away at his master's fief, and was unable to arrive in time. However, just as Hangan was about to close his dying eyes, Yuranosuké rushed on the scene. All Hangan could do was to hand him his blood-stained sword, hinting revenge.

All Hangan's loyal samurai were eager to take up arms forthwith against Moronao, all except Kudayû, superior in rank to Yuranosuké. He was too egotistic and poor-spirited to favour a course involving so much self-sacrifice, but nevertheless even he pretended to approve. Yuranosuké, most loyal of all, yet also most discreet, used his influence to control his companions and led them quietly from the palace. This Yuranosuké, of course, represents the historical Kuranosuké.

Act 5. This act and the next are concerned with the fortunes of Kanpei, a young samurai and vassal of Hangan. He had been absent when his lord attacked Moronao, on account of a clandestine meeting with Okaru, one of Hangan's ladies-in-waiting. Full of remorse, he would have committed suicide but for Okaru, with whom he was fleeing to her native place to lead the life of a hunter.

On his way he chanced to meet an old friend, Senzaki, and learned that vengeance was being planned against Moronao and that funds were being collected to assist Yuranosuké in carrying it out. He entreated Senzaki to intercede for him with Yuranosuké so as to be allowed to take part in the plot.

Okaru, meanwhile, was much troubled, blaming herself for her husband's reduced circumstances and most anxious to see him restored to his old rank of samurai. She thought it would help him if she could raise money for the cause. She consulted her parents, and her father, Yoichibeé, a most worthy old man, agreed with her that the only way in which she could raise the money was to sell herself to a house of ill fame in Kyoto, he himself going there to arrange the contract.

The contract completed, the brothel keeper loaned him the money he desired, and the old man set out to return and hand it over to Kanpei. But a bandit, waylaying him, killed him and took the money. This bandit was Sadakurô, the depraved son of Kudayû. Kanpei, after leaving Senzaki, chanced to come that way and saw the bandit, but in the dark he mistook Sadakurô's stealthy movements for those of a wild boar. So he shot at him, and was surprised to learn he had killed a man. He found the purse in the dead man's pocket and determined to use it as a contribution to the fund, of which Senzaki had told him.

Act 6. While Okaru was waiting with her mother for Yoichibeé's return, the master of the brothel came to fetch her away. Just then Kanpei returned to learn for the first time what his wife was doing on his behalf. He insisted that such a sacrifice was now quite unnecessary, since he had already got the requisite sum of money on him; and in any case, he refused to let her go until Yoichibeé returned with the money the brotherl keeper said he had paid him.

As a proof that he had indeed paid the money, the man produced the contract signed by Yoichibeé, adding that he had lent him a purse to carry the money in, made out of the same cloth as the clothes he was wearing.

On hearing this, Kanpei looked from the man's dress to the purse he had taken from the dead body. They were made of exactly the same cloth, and then came the dreadful thought that in the darkness he had shot his own father-in-law. In agony, he urged that Okaru need not wait for Yoichibeé's return but should go off at once with the brothel keeper.

She had scarcely gone before Yoichibeé's body was brought in by his hunting companions. Kanpei's guilty manner was observed by the widow, who accused him of having brought about her husband's death. To complete the young man's anguish, Senzaki and another comrade entered to say that their leader, Yuranosuké, had refused to allow Kanpei to participate in the plot and would not accept his contribution. And when Okaru's mother turned and told them that Kanpei had murdered her husband in order to get that money, they covered him with reproaches for such a horrible crime.

In the belief that he had indeed killed his father-in-law, Kanpei committed suicide. But before he died, it became clear that it was the bandit Sadakurô, not Yoichibeé, whom he had killed, and he was permitted to join the cause of revenge and sealed the covenant with his blood just before breathing his last.

Act 7. In order to keep the existence of any plot quite secret, Yuranosuké pretended to give himself up to dissipation, leading a riotous life in a house of ill fame in Kyoto. Even when Senzaki or any other conspirators called on him to ask about the time of the attack, he refused to answer, and paid no heed to the eager petition of Heiyemon, Okaru's elder brother and a loyal *ashigaru* (soldier-servant), who begged to be enrolled in the conspiracy. And when Kudayû, who had become a spy on behalf of Moronao, came to visit Yuranosuké, hoping to learn his intentions, Yuranosuké did nothing but play the drunken fool and mock at the idea of having a plan at all.

When Yuranosuké thought that he was safely alone he opened a letter from Kaoyo, wife of his late lord, giving some information regarding the plot, and read it by the light of a lantern hanging from the eaves. But Kudayû had remained behind, hidden under the verandah, and was able to obtain a glance at the letter. Okaru, who was now employed in that house, was another spectator and read the letter from her room above by reflecting it in her hand-mirror. Seeing this, Yuranosuké again began to play the fool, announcing his intention of redeeming her. His intention, indeed, was to kill her after he had ransomed her, because she had become possessed of his secret. Suspecting nothing of this, Okaru was delighted at the prospect of being redeemed, believing that she would soon see Kanpei again.

Her brother Heiyemon came for her, and, from what she said to him, divined Yuranosuké's purpose, which he resolved to fulfil himself. As he was about to kill her, he told her about Kanpei's death, whereupon, she declared that life was now empty for her and death a boon. She would kill herself.

But Yuranosuké, touched by such sincerity on the part of the brother and sister, agreed to admit Heiyemon into the conspiracy, while he and Okaru joined in stabbing to death Kudayû whom they had found under the verandah.

When Senzaki and the rest realized the object of all Yuranosuké's fooling, they were filled with admiration.

Act 8. This act shows the arrival of Honzô's wife at Kyoto with her daughter. Honzô was the man who had prevented Hangan from killing Moronao, and his daughter was engaged to the son of Yuranosuké, and had been brought to Kyoto for the marriage.

Act 9. The mother and daughter met Yuranosuké's wife and told her the object of their visit, but she, angry because Honzô had stopped her dead master from slaying Moronao, broke off the engagement. The two poor women were so overwhelmed with shame that they determined to commit suicide, when Yuranosuké's wife reappeared to tell them that the betrothal might be permitted to continue, on one condition : they must bring to her the head of Honzô.

Then, quite unexpectedly, Honzô himself appeared in the disguise of a strolling flute-player. He began by railing at Yuranosuké for the prodigal life he was leading and then made as if to attack the loyal retainer's wife. At this moment Yuranosuké's son rushed in and killed Honzô with a spear, which was precisely what he had hoped would happen; he had realized his mistake in hindering Hangan and was anxious to atone by the sacrifice of his life. Understanding this, Yuranosuké permitted the two young people to marry, and then set off alone to Edo to make final preparations.

Act 10. A merchant of upright character, named Amakawaya Gihei, who had prospered through Hangan's patronage, was entrusted by Yuranosuké with the delicate task of supplying all the weapons necessary for the enterprise. Eager to make his help effective and secret, Gihei sent his wife, Osono, back to her family, and lived meanwhile with only his son and a loyal, simple-minded apprentice.

Osono's father, Ryôchiku, was an avaricious and hard-hearted physician, formerly in the service of Kudayû, and, having a rich suitor in view for Osono, he took this opportunity to constrain Gihei to give her a letter of divorcement. Scarcely had Ryôchiku left than a posse of police raided Gihei. They told him they knew how he had supplied Yuranosuké with weapons and ordered him to confess all he knew about the plot. But the faithful merchant refused, even when they threatened to kill his son. In fact, Gihei was about to strangle the boy himself, crying, " See my heart—unfettered even by love for my son!" At this critical moment Yuranosuké emerged from a large weapon-chest and made it clear that the " police " were his fellow-conspirators. They had been putting Gihei's fidelity to the most searching test.

A knock came at the door. It was Osono, handing back her letter of divorcement and asking to be allowed to see her son. But since he had already agreed to her father's proposal, Gihei felt he could not permit her. So Osono, destined by her cruel father to marry another man, was about to leave with the intention of committing suicide, when a masked man appeared and cut off her chignon. He was one of Yuranosuké's samurai who had been ordered to make any remarriage impossible for her by depriving her of her hair, which she could not now dress in the way required. This man gave the chignon to Gihei and then set off to join his comrades in their heroic adventure.

Act 11. The forty-seven *rônin*, led by Yuranosuké, attacked Moronao's mansion on a snowy night and cut off his head. With this trophy of vengeance fulfilled, they set off for the grave of their master, Hangan.

Very soon after its performance on the puppet stage, this play was adapted for the *kabuki* theatre, and has been such a big draw ever since that it has come to be called " Kabuki Elixir," never failing to cure the worst cases of depression.

The work is so wrought with essential drama that it is now regarded as the standard test of good acting. An actor was never ranked among the greatest until he gave a convincing performance in the rôle of Yuranosuké. And Honzô, Hangan and Kanpei are also fine, outstanding parts, adding much to the dramatic quality of the play.

In contrast with the conventional five-act play, this has eleven acts. Several of these, for instance, Act 2, where Honzô snaps off the pine branch; Act 7, with the mother and daughter making their journey to Kyoto; Act 10, in the house of Amakawaya; and the final Act, with the night attack on Moronao, are rarely performed today. Apart from this, the play suffers little from the cutting which is the fate of most of the older plays. This is due both to its high intrinsic value and to the number of excellent parts it offers for performance.

KÔSHOKU ICHIDAI OTOKO

(The Life of a Satyr)

Kôshoku Ichidai Otoko was written by Ihara Saikaku in 1682, the earliest of his *ukiyo-zôshi*. *Ukiyo-zôshi* (mundane tales) fall roughly into three kinds : those constructed more or less on the lines of an ordinary novel ; those which are a collection of more or less unrelated tales ; and those where the author achieves a sort of unity by relating a group of varied adventures to some one single character. The *Ichidai Otoko* belongs to this last group, consisting of a collection of fifty-four short tales around the personality of a man named Yonosuké. In the absence of anything like a plot, a synopsis is well-nigh impossible. We can only give a brief account of Yonosuké himself, and then a brief résumé of his adventures.

We may divide the book into four parts, each reflecting a phase of the hero's life. The first four chapters deal with him from seven to ten years of age, showing his experiences as a sexually precocious child. Picturing as it does the love affair of this child with one of the maids in his home, his senior by many years, this portion is acceptable only as an extravaganza or as a study in abnormal psychology. The next nine chapters form the second part, and cover the years from eleven to nineteen, when he lived the amorous life of an impulsive, sentimental and foolish youth, whose parents had to disown him in the end. The third part, of fifteen chapters, deals with his period of wandering from twenty to thirty-four. This shows his varied adventures in a constantly changing environment and his relations with many different women. The remaining twenty-six chapters cover his life up to sixty, this last section showing him suddenly transformed at the age of thirty-four from a wanderer into a man of wealth as he is summoned home to inherit an immense patrimony. In line with his previous behaviour, he continues his riotous living, only on a larger scale.

We leave him at sixty pondering over his past and contemplating his future. He had drained the cup of worldly pleasure, and could not bring himself to enter on a religious life of meditation. So he decided to set off in quest of some entirely new amorous adventures. With seven bosom friends he set sail on the boat Yoshiiro-maru from Izu province for Nyogo no Shima, an island inhabited entirely by women, and there we lose sight of him.

Going from chapter to chapter is like unrolling a picture scroll depicting one aspect after another of amorous manners and modes. We see a harlot of Shumoku-machi in Fushimi, a prostitute at a public bath-house in Hyôgo, a fishwife of Suma, a girl in a tea-house at Yasaka in Kyoto, strolling actors at Niôdô, a harlot at Kitsuji-machi in Nara, a waitress on the Tôkaidô, a perfume-seller in Edo, an unlicensed prostitute in Osaka, a temporary concubine in Kyoto, the women of Tomo in Bingo province, fishwives at Kokura in Buzen province, a harlot at Inari-machi in Shimonoseki, a hussy in Osaka, promiscuous lodging at Ohara, a harlot at Teradomari and nuns of Sakata in Uzen province, *shaku* waitresses and *kanpyô* harlots, a professional medium, a woman grinding rice at Mito, a harlot at Oiwaké in Shinano province and some obliging nail-sellers, the maid in a mansion at Edo, a bed-fellow renewed every ten days in Kyoto, several harlots at Shimabara and fishermen's wives at Kada, Kashôji, Sano in Izumi province and elsewhere.

From these amorous adventures we obtain a realistic picture of many of the manners and customs prevailing at that time.

Yonosuké's ladies of easy virtue, as we see, are drawn from all parts, but mainly from the Three Cities (Kyoto, Edo and Osaka). They are portrayed with so much vivid detail that the work might almost be taken for a series of biographies of famous courtesans, notably, Yoshino, Mikasa, Fujinami, Hatsuné, Noaki, the two Taka-hashis, Kaoru and Yoshizaki of Shimabara in Kyoto; Yoshida, Komurasaki and Takao of Yoshiwara in Edo; Yûgiri, Mifuné, Washû and Azuma of Shinmachi in Osaka.

The author also deals at length with the different types of courte-sans and the places where they live. Among the gay quarters he mentions Shimabara, Yoshiwara, Shinmachi, Shibaya-machi in Ôtsu, Muro in Harima province, Fukuro-machi in Sakai, Yanagi-machi in Chikuzen province and Maruyama in Nagasaki.

The whole book contains fifty-four chapters, that is, one for each year of Yonosuké's life from the age of seven to sixty. Yet these chapters, apart from the person of the hero, are practically independent units, lacking all continuity of plot or character which pertains to a novel. It may well be that the chapters are fifty-four in number solely in imitation of the fifty-four books of *Genji Monogatari* and that the amorous adventures of Yonosuké are largely derived from the same work.

The book indeed is largely a realistic version of *Genji Monogatari*. The earlier novel reflects the aristocratic life of the Heian period, and Hikaru Genji is the embodiment of its ideals. The later book, however, has a much more democratic flavour and Yonosuké is the incarnation of the tastes of the merchant class. The epicurean lives of the nobles of the Heian period, passed in the pursuit of emotional, mainly amorous, pleasures, differ little in essentials from those of the later merchant class, albeit the latter tend to be more vulgar and lewd. It was almost inevitable then that *Kôshoku Ichidai Otoko* should have built itself so largely on *Genji Monogatari*, showing quite a number of analogies in the adventures portrayed.

This does not mean, of course, that the author of the later work was trying to imitate his predecessor. There is one fundamental difference between the two works, and that is, whereas *Genji Monogatari* maintains a consistent plot, Saikaku's work is little more than a collection of fifty-four more or less independent chapters. Such a difference as this can be explained both on historical grounds and also from the characteristics of the two authors.

Historically, we must consider the nature of the *kana-zôshi* and the *ukiyo-zôshi*, which form the popular fiction of the seventeenth century. The *kana-zôshi*, which flourished especially in the earlier part of the century, consist of collections of stories with plenty of incident based largely on traditions well-known throughout the whole country. Then later the *ukiyo-zôshi* came much into vogue, with their vivid descriptions of the gay life of the cities and accounts of the popular actors and courtesans. A work like *Kôshoku Ichidai Otoko* aims at combining these well-known traditions and descriptions of the life of the time, its most popular personalities and its most striking manners and customs. It is this which accounts for the nature of the work and the realism of its style.

Then there is the character of the author himself. Saikaku was a man gifted with an extraordinary memory and a very sensitive power of association, who had had wide experience of life. These qualities are revealed, not only in his *ukiyo-zōshi*, but also in his *haikai* as well as in his skill at *yakazu-haikai*.

Yakazu-haikai consists in attempting to compose as large a number of *renku* as possible in a given length of time, say, one day. It was regarded as an ascetic exercise in *renku* composition and was a form of competition for high renown. Saikaku attempted it on three occasions, on the last of which he succeeded in composing as many as 26,500 pieces in the one day, a sensational feat that has never been surpassed. The *renku* of the Danrin school to which our author belonged had its own peculiar characteristics. The verse form need not necessarily consist of the conventional seventeen or fourteen syllables and it involved the use of themes and phrases lying at hand, the sort of style in short that could be well employed only by a man of wide knowledge and with a genius for association.

But such qualities are not enough to make a man a great novelist. For that imagination and creative power are necessary, and Saikaku was lacking in those qualities. Accordingly, a work such as *Kōshoku Ichidai Otoko*, which is a loosely constructed collection of realistically written chapters, is precisely what one would expect from his particular genius.

A salient feature of this work is its remarkable realism. There had been genuine realism also in *Genji Monogatari*, which had formed the model for many writers. But their untalented imitation had practically reduced the characters in their novels to mere types of the old realism with no life of their own. Saikaku broke with the tradition of his time and depicted actual living people whom he saw around him with their personal idiosyncrasies. The characters of his women are really alive, although it must be noted that he did not as a rule indulge in a delicate portrayal of details but preferred rather to indicate character in a broad way by emphasizing peculiarities and eccentricities.

Reading such a work leaves us impressed with the comprehensiveness of his experience of life. He sees the beautiful and good, but especially the ugly and evil. He can hardly escape the accusation of vulgarity, obscenity and disorderliness from anyone accustomed to the more traditional type of novels ; and indeed he has long been

[313]

criticized for the meanness and immorality of his outlook. But even if one admits that, on social and ethical grounds, he may deserve censure, yet to him certainly belongs the credit of portraying a side of human nature hitherto hidden, and in this way making a real contribution to the general development of the novel.

———————

IHARA SAIKAKU
(1642—1693)

KÔSHOKU. ICHIDAI OTOKO
(**LIFE OF A SATYR**). Printed
in 1682.

**ILLUSTRATION TO KÔSHOKU
ICHIDAI OTOKO.**

**ILLUSTRATION TO NIPPON
EITAIGURA (TALES OF
RICHES).** Printed in 1688.

KÔSHOKU GONIN ONNA

(Five Wantons)

Kôshoku Gonin Onna from the pen of Ihara Saikaku was published in 1686. It consists of five books, one for each story, each book containing five chapters. In each case the name in the title of the book is that of the man chiefly concerned, not the woman.

There is good reason to believe that each of these five stories is derived from actual events. The affair of Onatsu and Seijûrô, which forms Book I, is traditionally said to have taken place in 1661, although there is nothing that can be called real evidence. We cannot lay too much stress on the fact that a story in Nishizawa Ippû's *Midarehagi Sanbon'yari* (Three Stories of Adultery as Revenge) refers to Onatsu's ruin in her later years, for, after all, this is only a chapter in a novel; and Chikamatsu derives his *Gojû-Nenki Utanenbutsu* (Commemoration of the Fiftieth Anniversary of the Death of Seijûrô) from a similar source. But the story in Book II of the cooper and Osen is known to have been based on an event in January 1685, although the details are obscure. With regard to Book III, there is little probability that the *uta-zaimon* (a kind of folk-song) conveys the real truth about Osan and Shige'emon The tale of Yaoya Oshichi (Book IV) is included in detail in such works as *Tenna Shôishû*, a comprehensive collection of strange stories of the Tenna era, and *Kôto Chomonshû* (Noted Stories of Edo), but the accounts differ considerably and it is difficult to say which is the more realiable. The last story, that of Oman and Gengobeé, although the event is said to have actually happened in 1663, has only come down to us in popular ballads (*kouta*).

Book I. The Tale of Seijûrô

Seijûrô, the good-looking son of Izumiya Seizaemon, a rich brewer in the then noted port of Muro in Harima province, had from his youth led a dissipated life and become attached to a courtesan named Minakawa. His father was so gravely offended that he disowned him, and this led Minakawa to commit suicide. Seijûrô would have followed her example but for the strong entreaties of his friends, who put him in charge of an acquaintance in Himeji. ୬

Through the good offices of this acquaintance, Seijûrô obtained employment as a clerk in the shop of one Tajimaya Kuemon, and, filled with remorse, the young man applied himself so diligently to his work as to win his employer's regard. Kuemon, however, had a young sister named Onatsu, aged sixteen, who fell in love with the youth, and her affection was returned. Finding scarcely any opportunity of being alone together, the young couple decided to elope to the Kamigata (Kyoto and Osaka) district. They boarded a passenger-boat at Shikama, near Himeji, but, unfortunately for them, the boat was compelled to put back to shore because one of the passengers, an official express messenger, had left his box of letters behind. This gave their pursuers a chance of overtaking them and they were taken back and imprisoned separately.

To make matters worse, a large sum of money, 700 *ryô*, was found to be missing from the Tajimaya's shop at the time of their flight, and suspicion naturally fell on them. Seijûrô was accused of instigating Onatsu to commit the theft, and was unable to produce any evidence to substantiate his plea of innocence. So, adjudged guilty, he ended his days on the scaffold at the age of twenty-five.

Kept in ignorance of his fate, the unhappy Onatsu continued to pray night and day for his release. Then, one day, she overheard some boys singing, " Since you have killed Seijûrô, why not Onatsu too ? Leave her not to mourn his death." Learning the truth thus she became distracted at her lover's death. They tried in vain to keep her confined in her home, for she was continually eluding them to go and pray at her lover's grave. On the hundredth day she attempted to commit suicide, but her family prevented her, and afterwards allowed her to enter a convent where she ended her days.

Book II. The Tale of a Cooper

A cooper fell in love with a young girl named Osen in the service of a wealthy man of Tenma in Osaka. Through the help of an old woman he was enabled to meet her and learned that she returned his affection. She promised to go with him on a secret trip to the Grand Shrine at Isé Complications arose when, on the way, they met Kyûshichi, a clerk working in her master's house, who was also in love with her. He insisted on attaching himself to them, and contended with the cooper to win her affections. So the girl and the two rivals came to Kyoto, where the cooper proved the victor. The two lovers succeeded in obtaining the permission of Osen's master to marry, and in due course they had two children.

All went well until one day Osen went to the house of a neighbour, named Kôjiya Chôzaemon, to assist him in holding a Buddhist service. She was busy doing something in the store-room, when Chôzaemon came in to get some article from a shelf above her. He dropped it and in retrieving it disarranged Osen's recently dressed hair. When his wife noticed Osen's appearance, her jealous suspicions were aroused, and she kept on all day girding at her husband. Eventually, this reached the ears of other people, and everybody began to suspect them of actual misconduct.

Osen was aroused to fury at this false accusation. " What a hateful woman she is ! " she cried, and soon the thought came, " Well, since she chooses to suspect me without cause, I'll punish her by really having an affair with her husband." She found Chôzaemon only too ready to reciprocate, and so the liaison began. Then, on the night of *hôbiki* (lot-drawing) in January, they were caught together. In her shame Osen committed suicide, while Chôzaemon was made a prisoner and put to death.

Book III. The Tale of a Calendar Merchant

A calendar merchant named Daikyôji who lived in Kyoto had a beautiful wife, Osan, who was devoted to him and diligent in all her duties. He had to leave home for some time to go to Edo on business, and, in order to give the women of his household some protection, an honest young clerk named Shige'emon was sent from Osan's people.

One of Osan's maids, a young country girl named Rin, fell in love with the clerk, and was always seeking an opportunity of being alone with him. Her mistress noticed the young girl's ardour for Shige'-emon, and thought to play her a trick. So she set to work and composed a love-letter to Shige'emon, pretending it came from Rin, who could not write. Completely taken in, the young man replied favourably and Osan managed to intercept his letter. To lead him further in this deception, she wrote again, in Rin's name, arranging a meeting. Then she made arrangements with her maids whereby she was to sleep in Rin's room, her intention being to wait for Shige'emon's arrival and then bring her maids into the room to mock at him.

Inadvertently, however, Osan dropped off to sleep while awaiting the young clerk's arrival, and woke up only to find that he had already gratified his passion on her. Having reached this pass, she felt that the secret could not possibly be kept. She told Shige'emon all about the trick she had proposed to play on him, and decided to continue the intrigue at the cost of her honour. So she arranged to take some friends, including Shige'emon, on a pilgrimage to the Ishiyama temple in Ômi province.

On the night of their arrival, the lovers stole out of the inn and feigned a double suicide by drowning in Lake Biwa. Actually, they intended to run away to Tanba province to obtain help from his aunt, and had all their travelling arrangements carefully prepared beforehand. But they found they could not stay long in Tanba, and so continued their flight to Tango province, where they entered a chapel of Monju Bosatsu (Manjusri Bodhisattva, the god of wisdom) in Kirido to pass the night. During the night, Monju appeared to them in a vision and admonished them to come to their senses. But they paid no heed to the divine command and continued to live together.

At last the husband Daikyôji heard of their whereabouts through the report of a local chestnut-dealer who used to visit Kyoto each year. A body of police went after them and apprehended them, and they were executed at Awataguchi.

Book IV. The Tale of a Greengrocer

There was a certain greengrocer named Yaoya Hachibeé living at Hongô in Edo. At the year's end a fire broke out in that neighbourhood and his house was destroyed. So the whole family, including an only daughter named Oshichi, aged sixteen, took refuge in the Kisshô-ji temple at Komagomé near by.

One evening, a youthful temple attendant named Onodera Kichisaburô was much troubled by a small thorn in his finger, and Oshichi's mother, after watching for a while his unavailing efforts to remove it with a pair of hair-tweezers, called him to her and offered to help. But, finding her eyesight not good enough, she called Oshichi to help. The contact of their hands inflamed the two young people with love, and they began to write secretly to each other.

In course of time the greengrocer's house was rebuilt and then the whole family left the temple; but, with the help of a maid, Oshichi kept up her correspondence with Kichisaburô. One day, when it was snowing heavily, the young man disguised himself as a farmer selling truffles and visited the greengrocer's. No one knew who the traveller was, but the greengrocer and his wife kindly offered him a night's shelter from the storm in a corner of their shop. It so happened that they had to visit some relatives near by to congratulate them on the birth of a child, and, in her parents' absence, Oshichi entertained Kichisaburô in an inner room.

They were overjoyed at this opportunity of meeting again, but the parents returned all too soon. So they spent the rest of the night pouring out their love in writing to each other. After this, Oshichi found separation from Kichisaburô unbearable and hit upon a way to bring them together again. Assuming that her family would once more take shelter in the Kisshô-ji temple if the house should again burn down, she set it on fire one windy night. But before the fire had taken a proper hold it was discovered and put out, and her crime was exposed. She was condemned and put to death, staining the grass of Suzu-ga-mori with her blood.

Kichisaburô was ill in bed at the time and so heard nothing until it was all over. Then he was overwhelmed with grief and tried to commit suicide. Thwarted in this he became a Buddhist priest.

Book V. The Tale of Gengobeé

A man named Gengobeé lived in Kagoshima in Satsuma province. He was a homo-sexualist, and two handsome youths whom he had dearly loved had both died. Chagrined over life's uncertainties, the unhappy man joined the priesthood and retired to a mountain to live. However, a girl named Oman who had been in love with him for some time, continued to write him love-letters in his mountain retreat. But he was in no disposition to answer.

When Oman learned that it was grief for the death of two youths that had driven him into retirement, she disguised herself as a young man and called at his hermitage. The sight of such a beautiful youth moved Gengobeé greatly and he was quite delighted to offer shelter. Though he soon learned the true sex of his visitor, his love for her did not abate and so the two continued to live together. But now they had to go out to find a living and as the man had learned something about acting while he was in Kyoto, the two supported themselves in this way.

Meanwhile, Oman's parents were in search of their absconding daughter, and were so delighted when at last they found her that they refused to interfere with her happiness and consented to her marriage with Gengobeé. In addition, they made over to her so much property that, no matter what a spendthrift her husband might prove to be, he would not be likely to exhaust it in his lifetime.

The present work differs considerably in form from the previous compositions of Saikaku. *Kôshoku Ichidai Otoko* (The Life of a Satyr) and *Shoen Ô-kagami* (A Mirror of Love) are both collections of fragmentary chapters, whereas *Kôshoku Gonin Onna* consists of five stories whose five chapters are held together by a single theme. Still, the structural form of the present work need not be taken to mark any development in Saikaku's style, for it probably followed more or less unconsciously on the special character of the theme. While the pornographic incidents in *Ichidai Otoko* have a merely topical quality, in the present work the interest lies in the progress and development of the love stories. One can read any one of the chapters in *Ichidai Otoko* separately and find in it an independen interest, but here the chapters are parts of the story. One may attribute this to the change of theme from the spasmodic activity of sensuality to the continuity of pure affection.

The other more salacious and more commercial works are but observations and presentations of particular aspects of the lives of merchants, whereas the tales of these five unhappy women are drawn from the material of human life as a whole. There is thus a much broader outlook in this than in *Ichidai Otoko*, although, as has been suggested, this is the natural outcome of the theme selected rather than the conscious intention of the author.

With the exception of the last, all these tales are of a tragic character, each ending in the death of the principal character. Yet they are not primarily intended to be tragedies. Thus, in what is perhaps the saddest tale of all, that of Onatsu and Seijûrô, it is two quite fortuitous occurrences, the express messenger mislaying the box of letters and the loss of the 700 *ryô* from the shop, that wreck the lovers' happiness d bring about the death of Seijûrô and the madness of Onatsu ut the main fascination of the work is not so much these tragic dings as the account of the beginning and unfolding of the love ffairs. The love story is the thing.

The most conspicuous example of this is the tale of the cooper nd Osen. Although this ends in the death of two lovers, yet most f the story is taken up with the story of the cooper's wooing of)sen. The tragedy that followed after their happy marriage is of a omplementary nature. There can be little doubt that the author ntended these four chapters to be regarded as love stories and not s tragedies.

The main subject of this work is the love of women, and later it ame to be called *Tôsei Onna Katagi* (The Nature of Modern Women). The author spends most of his time in giving a vivid description of is unfortunate heroines. Yet, despite Saikaku's wonderful powers f observation, his genius for catching events and persons on the ving, he is sometimes lacking in psychology, nor is his realism always onvincing. For instance, there is no attempt to explain psychologcally the action of Osen, who risked her life in committing adultery with her neighbour Kôjiya Chôzaemon merely because she was ngry at his wife's groundless jealousy and suspicion. Yet without his the story lacks all plausibility. Such psychological hiatuses re frequent in Saikaku and must be regarded as a real weakness.

NIPPON EITAIGURA

(Tales of Riches)

Nippon Eitaigura by Ihara Saikaku, published in 1688, is als known as *Daifuku Shin-Chôjakyô* (A New Way to Become Rich) ar *Honchô Eitaigura* (Our Country's Millionaires). It consists of thirt stories, divided into six books of five tales each, which tell of me chants who amassed fortunes and how they gratified their worldl desires. This was at a time when the class system was rigid an merchants and samurai lived quite separate lives. While money making was not compatible with the dignity of the samurai, there wa little else for a merchant to do. Therefore in amassing money, an also in spending it wildly, we find the main activity of the merchan and these tales acquaint us intimately with one of the most importar sections of society in those times.

There is little more to be said about the work and style of th author, and so we will content ourselves with giving a brief outlin of each story in the order in which it appears.

Book I.

Chapter 1. The temple in Mizuma village in the province c Izumi had made a practice of lending money to pilgrims in the belie that such lending would bring the borrower good luck. The limited their loans to the small sum of ten *mon* (farthings) and require that twice that amount be paid back at the end of a year, that is, on hundred per cent. But on one occasion a man from Edo name Amiya surprised them by applying for a loan of one *kan* (1,000 *mon* The priest without much consideration granted this loan, only to b troubled with qualms very soon after, and as the years went by h anxiety increased. Then, at the end of the thirteenth year, the debto who had meanwhile amassed a fortune, came back to repay th money with full interest. This amounted to the considerable sum c 8,192 *kan* and had to be carried on the backs of several horse

Gratified by the merchant's laudable honesty, the temple devoted the money to building a new tower as a memorial.

Chapter 2. A man who had inherited a fortune from a thrifty father increased it greatly by practising still greater thriftiness. One day, on returning home from a funeral, he picked up a sealed letter. He opened it to find a letter from a client to a courtesan enclosing a gold coin. As, from the letter, the woman appeared to be in a very miserable state, he went to the trouble of calling upon her in the gay quarters at Shimabara in order to give her the money. She was, however, too ill for him to see, and he, once in the place, felt reluctant to leave immediately. So he decided to take as much pleasure as that piece of money would cover. The experience so delighted him that he was led into a life of debauchery and ended with squandering his entire fortune.

Chapter 3. In the rice markets of Kitahama in Osaka quite a large quantity of rice was spilt from the sacks every day. A poor widow used to sweep this up to provide food for herself and her son. But even after they had eaten all they needed there was still some rice left, which the widow hoarded and sold secretly. At the end of twenty years she had thus been able to put by the sum of 12 *kan* 500 *mon*. This provided the son with a capital to set up as an exchange broker, at which he proved so successful as to amass a large fortune. He is said to have always treasured the broom and winnowing fan his mother had used.

Chapter 4. A draper named Mitsui Kuroemon lived at Suruga-chô in Edo. In those days drapers used to sell on credit, and that only by the bolt, but he, for the first time, sold his goods by length and insisted on cash payment at fixed prices. This was found to be so very convenient that his shop became crowded with customers and he did a roaring trade.

Chapter 5. When the owner of a wholesale bleaching store named Matsuya died suddenly in Nara, he was found to be deeply in debt. His thirty-eight-year-old widow struggled along with the business for some time in order to provide for herself and her young son. As the business still went downhill, she decided to sell it and clear out. But when she found that the house was only valued at 3 *kan*, while the total debt was 5 *kan*, she devised the following plan. She announced that the business would be sold by lottery, issuing tickets at 4 *mon* each. Since over 3,000 people bought tickets, she received 12 *kan* in all, leaving her, when the debt of 5 *kan* was paid, with a profit of 7 *kan*, with which she was able to retrieve the family fortune. The maid of a family in Nara won the lottery, and so found herself a great house-owner.

Book II.

Chapter 1. There was a certain citizen of Kyoto named Fujiichi who was honest, hard-working and exceedingly economical. In this way he had become very wealthy, and one New Year several young neighbours called on him for advice on how to succeed in life. While they were waiting for him, they heard the sound of pounding in a mortar, coming from the direction of the kitchen. This gave them hopes of receiving some New Year entertainment, and they were wondering what it would turn out to be, when Fujiichi appeared on the scene. He sat down and gave them a lot of sound advice on the various ways of saving money, concluding with the remark that one way of making a fortune was never to give meals to chance callers. So they had to leave without any refreshment. The sound they had heard had issued from the mixing of some starch to repair the covers of an account-book.

Chapter 2. Kiheiji, a soy-maker of Ôtsu in Ômi province, was a poor pedlar, satisfied to live honestly. He used to tell his wife about the ways and means whereby many of his customers made money and insisted that he was quite fortunate since he had never run into debt. But on December 29th one year his house was struck by lightning and many utensils in the kitchen were destroyed. The purchase of new ones caused him to run into debt for the first time, and this made him most unhappy.

Chapter 3. Shinroku, the son of Daikokuya Shinbeé of Kyoto, was a dissipated young man. Eventually his father disowned him and he set out for Edo. As he was passing through the village of Ono, he saw some boys crying over a black dog which had died. He persuaded them to give it him, and then out of fallen leaves and branches he made a fire and cremated it. Afterwards he raked the ashes together and, assuming the voice of a peasant from the mountains, went about hawking them as medicine made from charred wolf bones. The money he obtained from this not only paid his travelling expenses but left him with a profit of 2 *kan* 300 *mon*. With this as his capital he amassed the sum of five thousand *ryô* in about ten years.

Chapter 4. In the business of whaling the rôle of the man who leads the whole company is known as *hazashi*. There was a man named Tengu Gennai living in Taiji, a whaling centre in Kii province, who was peerless in that rôle. He laid the foundations of his fortune by inventing a method of extracting oil from the bones that had hitherto been thrown away as waste. It was his custom every January 10th to visit the Ebisu shrine at Nishinomiya in Settsu province, where, on one occasion, he learnt in a dream inspired by the god Ebisu how to pack fresh sea-bream in such a way that it could be sent long distances. Through this he increased his fortune greatly.

Chapter 5. A large wholesale rice merchant named Abumiya Sôzaemon lived in the northern town of Sakata where he employed a large number of clerks. His house was also the centre for those sales clerks from various provinces who had to visit Sakata. It came to be noticed that those among the visitors who immediately on arrival changed their clothes and went out sightseeing rarely came to anything in later life, whereas those who remained in the house and made good use of the opportunity of talking to Abumiya's clerks regarding current market quotations and so on prospered and became independent merchants. Such widespread confidence was placed in Abumiya's judgement by all that no one ever felt the least anxiety about lending him their money, although making loans to wholesale dealers is proverbially a most hazardous business.

Book III.

Chapter 1. There was a certain man who desired to set up business in Edo but lacked capital. Tortured by hunger and the frustration of his hopes he was wandering about the streets, when he noticed some carpenters returning home from building in Marunouchi. All of them carried bundles from which shavings and fragments of wood were dropping quite unknown to the men. So he obtained a handcart and followed them from Suruga-chô as far as Sujikai Bridge in Kanda, picking up what they dropped until his cart was almost full. This he sold for 250 *mon*. So he went on, each day selling the shavings that he picked up, and occupying himself on rainy days with making chopsticks out of them. Out of the small but regular profit

he man aged to make he was in time able to start as a timber merchan
At the end of forty years he had amassed the vast sum of 100,0c
ryô

Chapter 2. In the province of Bungo there lived an hone
iellow named Yorozuya San'ya who had inherited a large fortune, t
which he added by the reclamation of waste lands. But one day h
took his mother for a trip to Kyoto to see the sights, and lost h
head as he made his first acquaintance with the pleasures of city lif
On his return nothing would content him but having his hous
rebuilt in Kyoto style and his garden redesigned and improvec
Then next he had to surround himself with beautiful women in a lif
of luxurious ease; and he even went so far as to have water fror
the waterfall of Otowa in Kyoto for performing *chanoyu* (the tea
ceremony), and so in the end he squandered all his wealth.

Chapter 3. Zenzô was a small pawnbroker of Fushimi in Kyotc
One year he visited the Hatsusé shrine in Yamato province an
noticed that the curtain before the sanctuary of Kannon, the Goddes
of Mercy, had become badly worn by being raised so often. H
pretended to be very pious and won the confidence of the priests b
raising the curtain himself several times. They were quite delighte
when he offered to contribute a brand-new curtain in place of th
old worn one. This, however, was made of valuable gold brocade
which he cut up and sold, piece by piece, at a very great profit t
himself. Yet it proved to be his sole successful venture, for no
long afterwards he fell into a state of ruin.

Chapter 4. A wealthy man named Izuya at Enokojima in Osak
went bankrupt, and even though all his property passed into th
hands of his creditors, a proportion of his debts remained unpaid
He promised, however, that all should eventually be repaid, ar
returned to his native place, Ôshima Island in Izu province. There
by his diligence, he amassed another fortune and, after seventee
years' absence, returned to Osaka to settle his debts. When he coul
not trace a creditor, he took the money due and dedicated it to th
Grand Shrine at Isé as an offering. There were other creditor
whose families had died out, and the money due to them was used tc
erect a stone pillar on Mt Kôya-san. This was called Shakusen-zuk
(the Pillar of Debt) and served to help their souls to find their rest.

Chapter 5. A draper named Chûsuké who lived in Surug

province had inherited a good business from his father, which his own unbusinesslike habits quickly brought to ruin. He had many crack-brained schemes and once succeeded in getting his credulous neighbours to put up the money necessary for a journey to Nissaka in Tô:ômi province, simply on his assurance that this would certainly make him wealthy. But they realized how foolish he was when Chûsuké tried to make his fortune by tolling the Bell of Eternity at Sayo-no-Nakayama, of which tradition says that he who tolls it will enjoy great good fortune in this world though he has to go to hell in the next. In pity they helped him start in business as a bamboo-worker, his little daughter of thirteen selling what he made in the streets. One day a rich couple, returning from a pilgrimage to the Grand Shrine at Isé, encountered the young girl and were so impressed by her beauty that they took her for their son's wife. Thanks to this stroke of good fortune, Chûsuké was at last enabled to enjoy a little of that prosperity which had been his dream.

Book IV.

Chapter 1. There was a small dyeing establishment in Kyoto called Kikyôya, whose honest master and mistress, despite all their industry, could not prosper. Ever in the shadow of poverty, they enshrined, one New Year's Day, a straw doll of their own making which they called the God of Poverty, and on the night of the 7th the god himself appeared and expressed his joy at their devotion to him. Before he disappeared he uttered the words, "Willows are green and flowers crimson." Inspired by this, the dyer devised what is called "crimson dyeing," and in ten years amassed a fortune of more than one thousand *kan*.

Chapter 2. A man named Kanaya, of Hakata in Chikuzen province, made a visit to a tea-house at Maruyama in Nagasaki, where he noticed a screen belonging to one of the girls named Kachô. It was of great value, for specimens of ancient handwriting were pasted on it. This brought him back frequently to Kachô and at last he succeeded in obtaining her permission to sell it. He sold it to a daimyo for a large sum, which was afterwards used to ransom Kachô and enable her lover to marry her.

Chapter 3. Pilgrims to the Grand Shrine at Isé also used to visit the subordinate shrines and make their contributions. These were invariably of a very modest kind, but one day a merchant from

Edo named Fundôya startled everybody by scattering the great sum of 200 *kan* all the way during his pilgrimage from one to another of these shrines. Between the ages of twenty-one and fifty-five, he had accumulated a large fortune of 7,000 *ryô* to hand down to his son, and had chosen this means of showing his gratitude.

Chapter 4. A cunning fellow named Risuké, living at Tsuruga in the province of Echizen, started life as an itinerant tea-seller, but later became a tea-merchant, in which business he made large profits through selling adulterated goods. He remained unmarried, stating that he would not take a wife until he had acquired a fortune of 10,000 *ryô*. But before that had happened, he went mad and, after blurting out his misdoings, died in delirium.

Chapter 5. There was a successful shopkeeper named Hinokuchiya in the town of Sakai in Izumi province, who overheard a servant of his refuse to sell a *mon*'s worth of vinegar to a customer who came late at night. So next morning he called the servant and bade him dig up the ground in front of the gate to the depth of three feet. When he had done so, the master asked him if he had found any money. The man replied that he had found nothing but pebbles and shells, and then the master told him never again to refuse a *mon*'s worth of trade, since all the work he had just done had not yielded even that modest amount.

Book V.

Chapter 1. A poor tradesman in Nagasaki used to manufacture confetti, but, just because it was made nowhere else in the country, he was able eventually to obtain the capital to start as a haberdasher and gain a fortune of 1,000 *kan*.

Chapter 2. Yamazakiya, who began life as an oil-seller at Yodo in Yamashiro province, affords an example of prosperity achieved through versatility of effort and shrewd judgement. He went into the business of marketing the carp and other fish for which the river Yodo was noted, extending his activities so as to include in his scope the fish caught as far off as Tanba and Ômi provinces. He also did a good business in selling raw fish in slices, and later became a successful money-changer. His clerk had profited so much by association with him that, when he started on his own account in the rice trade, he soon became prosperous. Unfortunately, however, he allowed himself to be led away from his practice of always trad-

ng on a cash basis by opening a credit account with a weaver at
Nishijin. In the end, overwhelmed by unpaid accounts, he lost
all his capital.

Chapter 3. A certain farmer, Kusuké, had a genius for inven-
tion which brought him great wealth. He led a most frugal life and
when he died he left his fortune of 1,700 *kan* entirely to his son Kuno-
uké, while to his other rel...ives he left not a single article of value.
The son felt ashamed of his father's meanness, and, although he knew
he was acting against his father's dying wish, made a generous dis-
tribution among his relatives and clerks. Later, he became addicted
to pleasure and when he died he had no legacy to bequeath to his
sons but only a burden of debts.

Chapter 4. Higurashi, a wealthy man of Hitachi, had a large
number of dependants of various kinds, whom he dismissed at the
time of an official inquiry into the number of lordless men (*rônin*).
So these dependants had to take up various occupations, but the
only one among them that proved successful was the sole one who
even as a *rônin* had never given up his sword.

Chapter 5. Yorozuya, a rich man in Mimasaka province, surprised people by choosing the most jealous girl he could find as a
wife for his son. But her watchful jealousy proved an excellent
check on the young husband, who found himself leading a most
moral life, with the result that, not only was the home peaceful,
but prosperous to boot. After a while, however, following a sight-
seeing trip to Kyoto, the wife became much more tolerant in her
attitude. So her husband again began to live the same riotous life
he had led before marriage, and in the end he brought his family to
ruin.

Book VI.

Chapter 1. A man named Toshikoshiya of Tsuruga in Echizen
province had amassed a great fortune from his business as a *miso*
(bean paste) seller, which he conducted in a wretched-looking hovel.
But when his eldest son married, the son, supported by his mother,
entreated the father to build a new house more worthy of his wealth.
He yielded to them and erected a magnificent new house and shop.
But his customers were mainly the simple people of the locality who
were accustomed to the old premises and felt embarrassed to enter
such a fine new building. This fact, combined with other misfor-

tunes, proved disastrous, and within six years the son had lost the fortune that the father had acquired by forty years of strenuous efforts.

Chapter 2. There was a money-changer who did a good business near Nakabashi at Tôri-chô in Edo. He noticed among his employees a young apprentice of great ability, whom he adopted, eventually turning the business over to him. Within fifteen years the young man had raised the value of the business from 2,800 *ryô* to 30,000 *ryô*.

Chapter 3. The only son of a man named Kogatanaya of Sakai in the province of Izumi was taken seriously ill, and the doctors could do nothing for him. At last one doctor appeared who was skilful enough to effect a cure. The father's gratitude was as unstinted as his joy, and he lavished on the doctor a hundred silver coins, twenty bundles of floss silk and a pair of large saké casks. With this the doctor was able to buy himself a house, while Kogatanaya, whose fortune at the time was about forty *kan*, began to prosper still more.

Chapter 4. A poor fellow named Yozaemon, living at Yodo, once saw something round and black, of a huge size, drifting along the river Yodo when it was swollen after the early summer rains. He went after it in his boat and found it to be a valuable piece of lacquer which he was able to sell for a large sum. It did him little good, however, for he abandoned himself to a course of luxurious living and ended even poorer than before, leaving nothing behind him but his name.

Chapter 5. At Kitayama in Kyoto there lived under the same roof what were called the "Three Couples." These were the grandparents, their son and his wife, and the grandson and his wife, their ages being respectively eighty-eight and eighty-one, fifty-seven and forty-nine, twenty-six and eighteen. They were all in good health and cultivated their farm together in perfect harmony, so that all people envied them their good fortune. The neighbours used to ask the grandfather to cut them a strickle, since, according to the popular belief of the time, a strickle cut by such a man as he was bound to bring them good luck.

ANSÔ SATOMI HAKKENDEN
THE EIGHT RETAINERS OF
ATOMI). Complete set consisting
106 volumes.

TAKIZAWA BAKIN
(1767—1848)

IPPENSHA IKKU
(1765—1831)

SHIKITEI SAMBA
(1776—1822)

NANSŌ SATOMI HAKKENDEN

(The Eight Retainers of Satomi)

This exceedingly long novel, consisting of nine books with ninety-eight chapters, is from the pen of Kyokutei Bakin and was published in one hundred and six volumes. It belongs to that very popular class of Tokugawa novel known as *yomihon* (reading books) in which the subject-matter was considered of more importance than the presentation, and in which virtue was always triumphant. The work occupied the author twenty-eight years in writing, Book I appearing in 1814 and Book IX in 1841. Such a long succession of volumes does indeed speak for the perseverance of the author, especially as during these years he met with many domestic misfortunes, worst of all the affliction of blindness which came upon him before the work was finished, so that he had to dictate it to his family. Only an iron will and robust constitution enabled him to accomplish his purpose. In an appendix to the last book he gives in some detail an account of the difficulties he had encountered.

In any work of the *yomihon* type one must expect a great admixture of legend and sheer fantasy, for, in any case, it was essential that the author should show the divine forces co-operating with the human, so that justice may always be done. This present work draws considerably from such histories as *Hōjō Godaiki* (Records of the Five Generations of the Hōjō), *Kōyō Gunkan* (A Survey of the Battles in Kai) and *Satomiki* (Records of the Satomi), but it is based mainly on the Chinese novel *Chūgi Suikoden* (*Chung i shui hu ch'uan*, Riverside Traditions of Loyalists), and also takes in a great deal of purely legendary material. The author was impressed by the clear and candid style of *Chūgi Suikoden* in particular, which he even sought to surpass. Again, the eight knights of the *Nansō Satomi Hakkenden* must also have been modelled in part on the one hundred and eight heroes of this great Chinese novel.

The family names of the eight knights, all beginning with the ideograph for *inu* (dog), and the miraculous rosary-bead that each possesses suggest their birth from the inspired Fusé Himé. Also the eight knights have each in their names as well as in their rosary-beads one of the eight ideographs for benevolence, righteousness, propriety, wisdom, loyalty, sincerity, filial piety and fraternal love, and this reveals the writer's intention to colour his work—in proper *yomihon* style—with exhortations to Confucian morality. So far as the narrative and incidents generally are concerned, this intention is fully realized, but it can hardly be said that each of the eight heroes strictly expresses that one of the virtues he is intended to represent.

The spirit of the work is a mixture of the prevalent Japanese ideal of Bushido and the author's own devotion to Confucian morality. The author lightens his purpose of establishing the victory of poetic justice by means of a play of fantasy, although it cannot be said that either in this or his other works does he quite succeed in his aim.

What he is most successful at is in gathering copious material from Japanese and Chinese sources, historical, traditional, legendary and mythological, and blending it into one long story with a high degree of consistency and order. In spite of the innumerable characters and episodes, all intended to support the author's own ideal of life, the work, viewed as a story, does maintain a wonderful harmony, with a freedom from contradictions that merits praise.

The style is clear, and yet at the same time rich, although it might have been better had the author, in his desire to achieve a semi-poetical effect, not employed the rhythmical seven-and-five-syllable form in a work of such great length.

A brief synopsis of such a voluminous work is an exceedingly difficult task ; it is impossible to refer to every interesting story when there are so many. We must be content with indicating such incidents as are essential for a general understanding of the plot.

Yûki Ujitomo, lord of Shimôsa province, rose in revolt against the Shogun Ashikaga, but was defeated and his castle at Yûki captured in the 4th month, 1441. One of his generals, Satomi Suemoto, after helping his eldest son, Yoshizané, to escape with his retainers Sugikura Ujimoto and Horiuchi Sadayuki, fell fighting at his post.

Yoshizané and his party escaped to the province of Awa which was then divided into three fiefs. Prior to Yoshizané's arrival, these had been held by three daimyo, Anzai Kagetsura, Maro Nobutoki and Jin'yo Mitsuhiro, but Mitsuhiro had been treacherously slain by a vassal named Yamashita Sadakané, who had usurped his fief. Therefore, when Yoshizané arrived, seeking the help of the daimyo Kagetsura, he found him about to set out with Maro Nobutoki to attack the treacherous Sadakané. To Yoshizané came Kanamari, loyal retainer of the murdered Jin'yo Mitsuhiro, asking him to join in raising an army in the cause of justice. This he did and succeeded in defeating Sadakané and in restoring peace to Awa.

Yoshizané married and had a son Yoshinari and a daughter Fusé Himé. The girl used to cry miserably at night and so the troubled father prayed to the gods for her recovery, and was given a rosary on which the eight ideographs of benevolence, righteousness, propriety, wisdom, loyalty, sincerity, filial piety and fraternal love were engraved.

The girl then had a happy childhood, but when she was sixteen years old there was a quarrel between her family, the Satomi, and the Anzai family. Hostilities broke out and the fighting went badly for Yoshizané. One day, looking at his pet dog Yatsubusa, he jokingly said that he would give him his daughter Fusé Himé if he could kill the enemy leader. The dog went out alone, penetrated the enemy's camp and came back with the head of Kagetsura. After this the tide of battle turned and Yoshizané gained the victory.

Although Yoshizané had now become the lord of Awa, he repented his jesting words, the fulfilment of which the dog never ceased from demanding. But the young girl herself, believing that providence intended it, fled from the castle in company with the dog and hid herself with him in a cave in Tomiyama. There she set about the dog's education by chanting to him the *Hoké-kyô* (the Saddharma Pundarika Sutra). When Fusé Himé found herself pregnant she killed herself, and from the fatal wound a white smoke rose up, out of which eight rosary-beads, each containing one of the eight ideographs already mentioned, were scattered into the eight corners of the sky. These eight beads symbolize the eight knights or " dog-warriors " who later appear.

At the time of the capture of the castle of Yûki, with which the story opens, Ashikaga Mochiuji, governor-general of the Kanto district, was at feud also with the Shogun Ashikaga. His attendant Ôtsuka Shôsaku placed upon his own son Bansaku the duty of escaping with his master's treasured sword Murasamemaru, and the young man with his wife settled down in Ôtsuka, his native place, in the Toshima district of Musashi province.

Bansaku had a son named Shino, but when this boy was eleven, trouble arose because Bansaku's pet dog Yoshirô killed a cat belonging to Yayayama Hikiroku, husband of his eldest sister-in-law. This led to Bansaku's committing suicide, and his son Shino slew the dog Yoshirô. Out of the wound he had inflicted on the dog there flew a bead engraved with the character of "Filial Piety" and entered Shino's body. After that he called himself Inuzuka Shino Moritaka.

Shino became very friendly with a youth of his own age named Gakuzô, the son of Inukawa Noritô, late steward of the manor of Hôjô in Izu. He was the possessor of a rosary-bead inscribed "Righteousness" which he had received at his birth. He was then a ward of Hikiroku and was in his service. He took the name Sôsuké Yoshitô after forming his close friendship with the young Shino.

Hikiroku was trying to arrange a marriage between Shino, then eighteen, and Hamaji, but later found it more profitable to give her to another suitor Higami Kyûroku, a country official. Hikiroku engaged Aboshi Samojirô to steal the sword Murasamemaru from Shino, and to kill him to boot. Shino fled, while Aboshi Samojirô kidnapped Hamaji and ran away with the treasured sword. The girl Hamaji loved Shino deeply and, remaining faithful to him, was killed. Samojirô was also killed by the hermit Jakumaku Dôjin, who robbed him of the sword. This hermit was really Michimatsu, son of Inuyama Dôsaku, an old retainer of Nerima, and was then known as Inuyama Dôsetsu Tadatomo.

Meanwhile, Shino arrived at Koga, bearing the false sword that Samojirô had substituted for the original, and he did not find out that it was a counterfeit until he was just about to present it to Ashikaga Nariuji. Suspected of espionage, he was hunted down by Inukai Genpachi Nobumichi, the bravest warrior of that clan, who had been adopted by Inukai Kenbeé, a samurai of Koga, and who owned one of the beads, engraved "Sincerity."

Genpachi overtook Shino and engaged him in combat on the

roof of the pinnacle of Hôryû-kaku overhanging the river Toné. Both warriors fell from the roof and lay senseless in a boat which was carried downstream as far as Gyôtoko-no'ura, where they were both rescued and tended carefully by an innkeeper named Bungobeé. This Bungobeé had a son, Kobungo, more commonly known as Inuta-no Kobungo, who possessed a mysterious bead inscribed "Fraternal Love." The unrelenting search for Shino led to the house of Bungobeé, who was arrested on suspicion of harbouring him.

Kobungo's younger sister, Nui, was married to a man named Fusahachi, who suddenly divorced her and threatened to give information about Shino. Kobungo therefore killed him, precisely as Fusahachi had wished, for, feeling himself under a great obligation to Bungobeé, he desired to sacrifice his own life as a substitute for Shino. Kobungo then cut off his head, pretending that it was the head of Shino, and so obtained his father's release. He then took Genpachi and Shino to Ôtsuka to call on Inukawa Sôsuké.

Daihachi, only son of the dead Fusahachi and Nui, possessed a bead engraved "Benevolence." Taking upon himself the name Inué Shinbeé Masashi, he set out for Awa, but en route was spirited away.

In Toshima of Musashi province, Shino, Genpachi and Kobungo learned of the misfortune which had overtaken Gakuzô (Sôsuké) after Shino's departure. Kyûroku, furious at the loss of the beautiful Hamaji, had killed Hikiroku and his wife, and Gakuzô, in loyalty to his master, had slain Kyûroku, and lay in prison condemned to death. From this the three heroes rescued him.

The four warriors then set off in search of Inuyama Dôsetsu in the direction of the castle of Shirai, owned by Ôgigayatsu Sadamasa. Dôsetsu happened to meet Sadamasa as he was on his way back from hunting accompanied by many of his men. Among them were Kosugi Daichirô, who had killed Dôsetsu's master, and Kamado Saburô, who had slain his father. Dôsetsu attacked and killed both these men, and, surrounded by Sadamasa's men, was fighting for his life, when the four companions appeared, and rushed into the fray to rescue him. In the end, the five warriors managed to escape, each making his way separately to Mt Aramé-yama.

By good fortune they all met again at the house of a woman named

Otoné at the foot of the mountain, who owed her life to Dôsetsu's mother. Sadamasa soon discovered their hiding-place and sent men to surround the house and capture them. However, once more they all managed to escape.

Kobungo made his way to Asagaya in the province of Musashi, where he killed a wounded wild boar and so saved the life of Nami-shirô who was hunting it. In gratitude Namishirô took his rescuer to his own house, where his mischief-making wife brought a false charge against Kobungo before an official of the Lord Chiba Yoritané. Although he was found innocent, another retainer named Makuwari Daiki accused him of being a spy and kept him in his own house as a prisoner.

Daiki tried to get Kobungo to take part in a plot against Chiba, but in vain. The traitor then secretly sent for some assassins; but a *dengaku* (ancient rustic pantomime) actress, whom he had invited to his house, slew both her host and his hired ruffians. Thus Kobungo was able to escape, while the actress turned out to be Inusaka Keno Tanetomo, son of Awabara Tanenori killed by Daiki, who had disguised himself as a woman in order to effect his revenge.

Kobungo and Keno escaped together, but lost each other by the river Sumida, where Kobungo met his servant who told him of his father's death, and so he returned for a while to his native place and then set out on a journey to Kamakura in quest of Keno.

Meanwhile, Inukai Genpachi had set forth from Mt Aramé-yama in search of his companions, but on reaching the foot of Mt Kôshin-zan in Shimotsuké province he heard a very curious story about a ghost that haunted the mountain.

Some time before, he was told, Akaiwa Ikkaku had climbed the mountain with some friends in order to destroy a monster said to haunt it. His friends had lost heart and deserted Ikkaku, leaving him to push on all alone into the mountain depths. Next day, their numbers reinforced, the villagers climbed the mountain again and discovered Ikkaku, whom they accompanied home. Soon after-wards, Ikkaku began to show such a cruel hatred to Kakutarô, his son by a former wife, that Kamori Norikiyo, elder brother of Kakutarô's mother, had pity on the lad and brought him up in his own home up to the age of eighteen. Then, having seen him happily married to his daughter Hinaginu, he and his wife died. Ikkaku meanwhile had married Funamushi, widow of Namishirô, who proved a cruel stepmother to Kakutarô and his young wife. She seized their property and separated them, and Kakutarô had been forced to live in a dilapidated cottage in Inumura.

Having heard this story, Genpachi penetrated into the recesses of Mt Kôshin-zan under cover of night. He encountered a goblin at the stone gate of Tainaikuguri and shot it in the left eye, and then pushed on until he found himself in a cave where he was welcomed by a figure sitting by a fire. This was a ghost, the ghost of Ikkaku. He told Genpachi that when he had been left alone on the mountain years before, he had been attacked and killed by a great wild cat, and it was this cat, in the guise of Ikkaku, who had returned and had tortured Kakutarô. Genpachi had just shot at this cat, and now the ghost of Ikkaku begged him to go and save Kakutarô from his troubles and avenge his own death.

Genpachi at once descended the mountain and called on Kakutarô whose name led him to believe that he might be a fellow knight. And indeed Kakutarô had been the possessor of a bead with the ideograph " Propriety," but his wife Hinaginu had swallowed it by mistake.

Just then the false Ikkaku came to Hinaginu, accompanied by Funamushi, and bearing a bag of *matatabi* powder, a herb much liked by cats, which he had chanced to obtain. He told Hinaginu that she must give up to him the liver of the unborn child in her womb to mix with this powder for a sovereign specific for the diseas of the eye from which he was then suffering. Hinaginu felt she could not refuse and so disembowelled herself, but hardly had she done this when the mystical bead flew from her and struck Ikkaku dead.

Then Genpachi told them the story he had heard from the ghost. He pointed to the skull he was carrying, which he said was that of the real Ikkaku, whereas the man just killed was a mountain-cat. Thus Kakutarô found his father's death avenged and the monster removed from the mountain. From that time he took the name of Inumura Daikaku Masanori and set out with Genpachi to find his fellow knights.

During this, Inuzuka Shino had been staying at the house of Yorogi Mukusaku, a distant relative and the headman of a village in Kai province. There he was loved by a girl brought up by

Mukusaku, named Hamaji, who was possessed by the spirit of the dead Hamaji, but Nabiki, Mukusaku's second wife, was opposed to the match. Moreover she persuaded her paramour, Awayuki Nashirô, to kill her own husband, and then accused Shino and Hamaji of the crime before Lord Takeda. But when Takeda's deputy arrived on the scene to arrest the two lovers, he turned out to be Inuyama Dôsetsu himself who was trying to rescue Shino from danger.

Dôsetsu had come to that place in company with Inukawa Sôsuké, after his flight from Mt Aramé-yama, and had stayed on while Sôsuké had gone to visit Kobungo. Then by chance he heard of Shino's danger and was able to save him. When Lord Takeda Nobumasa heard of the heroic quality of these men he tried to invite them into his service, but they declined, contenting themselves with avenging the death of Mukusaku. The girl Hamaji was discovered to be the daughter of Satomi Yoshinari who had been carried off by an eagle at the age of two, and she was sent to Awa.

Inuta Kobungo had sailed from Kamakura, and after a stormy voyage he arrived at the islands of Ôshima and Miyaké-jima. Thence, he reached Echigo province by way of the Kinki and Hokuriku districts, and put up in the village of Ojiya in order to beg the assistance of Ishikameya Jidanda. There he chanced to be present at one of the bull-fights for which that place is noted, and he astonished people by his great courage in overcoming a particularly fierce bull.

The wicked Funamushi had also drifted to that district, and was then living as the wife of a bandit named Dôji Kôshi Shutenji. She made her way into the presence of Kobungo in the guise of a masseuse and tried to stab him, but was caught by him and handed over to Jidanda, who tied her up and left her a prisoner in the Kôshin-dô shrine on the mountain. To this shrine came Inukawa Sôsuké, seeking a rest in his search for Kobungo, and with honeyed words Funamushi persuaded him to set her free. Then she beguiled him to the den of her bandit husband Shutenji, but, fortunately, Sôsuké realized his danger in time and, with the opportune aid of Kobungo, killed all the bandits.

In recognition of their meritorious deeds they were invited by Inanoto Yorimitsu, steward to the Lord Nagao Kageharu, to stay with him; then, to their great surprise, they were made prisoners.

Yorimitsu, it turned out, was obeying the commands of the wicked mother of Kageharu. When, however, he recognized the true worth of the men, he set them free, substituting the heads of two of the bandits for theirs.

Escaping from this peril, they met Inusaka Keno by the side of Lake Suwa, and from the rosary-bead he had, bearing the character "Wisdom," they knew him for one of the "dog-knights." He was, however, engaged on a private mission, and parted company with them as they went on to the province of Kai.

Meanwhile, Inumura Daikaku and Inukai Genpachi, after travelling along the Tôkaidô Highway for three years, arrived at Senju, a suburb of the city of Edo. Here they were arrested by mistake under suspicion of complicity in a robbery committed in the house of Higaki Natsuyuki, a powerful samurai in Hokita. Their lives were in the greatest danger, when they were miraculously saved by the ghost of Fusé Himé. As they continued their way they met their fellow "dog-knights," Shino and Dôsetsu, who were watching the movements of Ôgigayatsu Sadamasa in the neighbouring castle of Isarago.

At the same time Inusaka Keno, in the guise of an acrobat, was searching the precincts of the Tenjin shrine for Komiyama Ittôda, who had killed his father. Ittôda, now assuming the name of Tatsuyama Mendayû, had become a favourite retainer of Sadamasa, and happened to be passing by Suzugamori on his way to Odawara. There Keno succeeded in waylaying him, and attacked him. During the fight Kobungo and Sôsuké appeared, and with their aid Keno slew Mendayû. Furious at this, Sadamasa himself led out a large force to Shinagawa, where he fell into an ambush laid by Genpachi, Daikaku and Dôsetsu. In the surprise, Sadamasa barely succeeded in escaping with his life to the castle of Nari. Shino, for his part, had occupied the castle of Isarago with a small force and had opened the granary to feed the poor people of the district.

Turning to the Satomi family in Awa, we find that Yoshizané had handed over the headship to his eldest son Yoshinari. With the aid of his four principal retainers, Sugikura Ujimoto, Horiuchi Sadayuki, Arakawa Kiyozumi and Tô-no Tokisuké, he occupied a very powerful position in the castle of Inamura. Hikida Motofuji was then lord of Tateyama, having dispossessed its former owner by force. Captivated by the beauty of Princess Hamaji of the Satomi family, he sought her hand in marriage, only to be refused by Yoshinari, and in revenge carried off Yoshinari's son, Yoshimichi.

With his son held by Hikida as hostage, Yoshinari, despite his large forces, could do no more than lay siege to Tateyama Castle. His father, Yoshizané, had meanwhile been attacked by the remnants of the defeated army of Anzai and Maro as he was on his way to Tomiyama, and it might have gone ill with him but for the sudden appearance of Inué Shinbeé. Shinbeé introduced himself as one of the "dog-knights," and conducted Yoshizané safely down the mountain. Then, with the old lord's permission, he set off alone to the castle of Tateyama.

Shinbeé succeeded in capturing Motofuji alive and installing himself as the new master of the castle. Yoshinari had pity on Motofuji and spared his life, but the rascal turned to the witch Myôchin to help him in recapturing the castle. Her magic deluded Yoshinari into believing that Shinbeé was engaged in a love affair with Hamaji, and this caused him to alienate himself from Shinbeé. Then Motofuji was easily able to retake the castle.

The Satomi family sent an army under Arakawa Kiyozumi, which was defeated by the magic of Myôchin, while the Princess Hamaji was kidnapped. But the divine spirit of the Princess Fusé Himé appeared and her power proved stronger, so that Hamaji was rescued.

Meanwhile Shinbeé, after leaving Inamura, set off for Edo and in the plain of Uenoga-hara he helped to save Kawagoi Takatsugu, one of Sadamasa's retainers. Then he met a miraculous white fox, which had once been a faithful nurse to Takatsugu, which told him the latest news of Awa. Accompanied by Takatsugu and a retainer of Satomi's whom he met by chance, Shinbeé sailed to the province of Kazusa. Then he marched on Tateyama where his miraculous rosary-bead helped him to break into the castle and account for both Motofuji and the sorceress Myôchin. By the light from his bead he found, in place of the latter, the corpse of a badger with eight ideographs " Even a beast has a longing for Buddhahood " inscribed on its back.

The seven " dog-knights " had gathered together in Yûki to celebrate the fiftieth anniversary of the death of those who had fallen i battle there. They were suddenly set upon by more than 350 men belonging to the lord of Yûki ; and when they were sorely beset, Shinbeé arrived on the scene from Tateyama. Thus for the first time did the eight " dog-knights " meet together, and they succeeded in defeating their numerous foes.

Lord Yûki apologized for the misdeeds of his men, and thus were the two families of Satomi and Yûki able to revive their friendship. All the eight knights returned to Awa and were received in audience by Yoshizané and Yoshinari, to whom they renewed their vows of loyalty. Each knight was granted the family name of Kanamari, and Shinbeé was dispatched to Kyoto to gain the Imperial sanction. With this he returned safely to Awa.

But Ôgigayatsu Sadamasa hated both Satomi and the eight knights. So he called together in his castle such lords as Yamanouchi, Chiba, Nagao, Takeda and Miura, and persuaded them to declare war on them. The land forces, under the leadership of Yamanouchi Akisada and Koga Nariyuki, took up their position in the districts between Ishihama and Kônodai in Musashi, while Sadamasa himself led the naval forces.

So even before Shinbeé had returned from Kyoto, the other seven knights found themselves involved in great preparations to save the castle of Satomi which was beset by land and sea. Yoshimichi was responsible for the land defence and he had the assistance of Shino, Genpachi, Sôsuké, Kobungo and, later, Shinbeé. Yoshinari placed his ships under the command of Keno, who, together with Dôsetsu and Daikaku, faced the enemy by sea. The Satomi forces won a sweeping victory and returned in triumph after occupying the castles of Isarago, Ishihama, Shinobuoka and Ôtsuka. But the Imperial Court and the shogun intervened and persuaded the enemies to come to terms. So, in order to give effect to this, the Satomi family returned the castles and prisoners they had captured. In acknowledgement of their great valour, each of the " dog-knights " was granted a castle of his own, raised to the rank of a superior retainer and given one of the eight princesses of Yoshinari to wife.

Shino's bride was the beautiful Hamaji. All the knights flourished and had children. Then, in their later days, they returned half their fiefs and went into retirement in Tomiyama, where, having acquired supernatural powers, they passed their time in peace.

DÔCHÛ HIZAKURIGÊ

(On Foot along the Tôkaidô)

Although the title *Dôchû Hizakurigé* may for convenience' sake be simply translated as " A Walking Tour," it is worth while to consider its meaning a little more fully. *Dôchû* means "journey," and *Hizakurigé* is a compound word, from *hiza* (knee), which is used to represent the leg, and *kurigé* (chestnut-coloured), which suggests " horse." This word *kurigé* came to be used not only for a journey made by horse, but by palanquin also. If we would get the full flavour of the title, therefore, we might render it as " A Tour on Shanks's Mare."

There are several works with the same title of *Dôchû Hizakurigé,* the one under discussion being the first of them. This contains eight chapters, and its more correct title is *Tôkaidôchû Hizakurigé* (On Foot along the Tôkaidô Highway). But the word *Tôkai* is omitted in the first chapter of the book, which is entitled *Ukiyo Dôchû Hizakurigé* (A Secular Walking Tour), and also from the second chapter, where we get the current brief title of *Dôchû Hizakurigé.* Its author is a certain Jippensha Ikku, who, following on the present work, produced several sequels with similar characters and in similar vein, telling of pilgrimages and visits to such places as the shrine of Konpira (Kotohira, or Kumbhira), guardian deity of seafarers, in Sanuki, the Itsukushima shrine in Aki, the Kiso highway, the Zenkô-ji temple in Nagano and the hot-spring of Kusatsu in Kôzuké. The production of these various tours occupied the author twenty-one years, and he is said to have enjoyed a far greater popularity than any other writers of his day.

Such a work as *Dôchû Hizakurigé* was precisely what the public of the time wanted. When this work and its successors were produced, that is, between 1802 and 1822, journeys for pleasure and sight-seeing were in great vogue, not only among the people of Edo, but throughout Japan. What were called *monomôdé,* pilgrimages to shrines and temples, and *yusantabi*, seeing the sights of Kyoto and other places of note, were the most popular of pastimes. The main reason for this was the great improvement that had been made in the facilities for communication, which was the outcome of the rule of the Tokugawa shogunate that every daimyo must spend alternating periods at the Shogun's court at Edo and in his fief. This inevitably meant better highways, the development of stages, inns and tea-houses, as well as the provision of good bridges, boats, palanquins and post-horses. Thus, the steep Hakoné mountains could now be crossed comfortably in palanquins, while such large and rapid rivers as the Ôi and Tenryû could be forded, either on small rafts or on the shoulders of coolies. Gone completely were the old days of benighted travellers passing troubled hours of darkness under the stars or taking rough meals in the open air.

But, moreover, along with these facilities, the pleasure of travel was not diminished by such an excess of tasteless convenience as we now experience, snatching as we do just fleeting glimpses of beautiful scenes from the windows of express trains, or passing our nights in crowded compartments. In a leisurely way, for days on end, the travellers could enjoy the wonders of the landscape, could observe the different manners and customs that attracted their attention and tickle their appetites with famous local products. Such an opportunity for enjoying this particular form of pleasure can have had no parallel in history. The times also were less strained and less competitive, and the simple pleasure of travelling added to the gaiety and interest of life. It also accorded well besides with the religious faith of the people as embodied in pilgrimages to the Thirty-three Holy Places, the Konpira shrine, the Hongan-ji temple, the Zenkô-ji temple, and the rest.

This interest in travel led to the publication of guide-books and albums of noted places, and *Hizakurigé* is only a further development, combining the character of both. It is partly a practical guide-book, since it gives accounts of roads and distances, changes of vehicles and famous local products ; and, again, it has something in common with the albums of noted places with its copious description of celebrated sights.

What gave the *Dôchû Hizakurigé* of Ikku its special character is that it has something of the picaresque novel about it, consisting as it does very largely of the adventures of two comic personages. Briefly, the story may be outlined as follows. A man named Tochimen'ya Yajirobeé was a native of Fuchû in Suruga, where the city of Shizuoka now stands. He had some fortune but had squandered it in debauchery. So he came up to Edo to live at Hatchôbori in the district of Kanda, bringing with him a companion named Hananosuké. This latter was formerly Yajirobeé's favourite strolling actor, and in Edo, he was apprenticed to a merchant, while Yajirobeé himself married with a view to settling down.

But he found the task of making a regular living too much for him. In disgust he ran away from his creditors and, taking Hananosuké with him, set out on a journey along the Tôkaidô from Shinagawa. He made a pilgrimage to the famous Isé Shrine and then saw the sights of Kyoto, this being as far as we get in the eight books of the work we are considering. The humour and comedy of the eccentric, foolish, often vulgar and sometimes mischievous activities of the two heroes on their long journey are well brought out, giving a most realistic spice to the record of places visited and the adventures en route.

Its popularity induced Ikku to continue the theme in successive *Dôchû Hizakurigé*, which came out at intervals between 1802 and 1822, and wherein the same two heroes continue their adventures in journeys to various shrines, cities, hot-springs, etc., until finally they return to Edo.

Although, for the most part, the book is concerned with the adventures and experiences of Yajirobeé and Hananosuké (who later becomes Kidahachi), the author also includes a number of comic episodes which by their nature lie outside the range of his own personal experience and observation. He draws on various sources for these, some of them being cleverly adapted from the *nô-kyôgen* (Noh comedy) of the Muromachi period, others being humorous stories current at that time. But he succeeds in blending these additions with the main theme in such a way as to make the entire work a harmonious whole.

Undoubtedly the general idea of the book owes something to earlier works. In literary history the *kokkeibon*, collections of humorous pieces, are held to be modifications of the *sharebon*, stories of the "gay quarters." *Hizakurigé* also shows a likeness to an earlier work, *Karuizawa Dôchû Sugoroku* (Record of a Gay Time on a Visit to Karuizawa), the title of which is by way of being a pun, the place-name Karuizawa suggesting *karui sawa* (gossip at tea-time) and *Dôchû Sugoroku* a form of backgammon. This book, written by Yamanoté Bakahito (Shoku Sanjin), consists of such jests and witticisms as accord with the vulgar manners, habits and speech of a citizen of Edo and his servant. For example, these two made a journey to Oiwaké in the province of Shinano, where they are shown enjoying themselves with the local ladies of easy virtue, while a country bump-kin is in an adjoining room on the spree with another harlot. Com-pared with this, *Hizakurigé* has a much wider scope, dealing mainly with the life of the people in general, but certainly it contains some-thing of the salacious element found in the *sharebon*, while the idea of a travel book written round two leading characters is certainly anticipated in *Karuizawa Dôchû Sugoroku*.

Another example is *Chikusai-Zôshi* (Diary of Chikusai), sometimes attributed to Karasumaru Mitsuhiro (1579-1638), the latter part of which deals, in the form of a travel book with unconventional and humorous touches, with a very mediocre doctor of Kyoto, named Chikusai, on a trip to Edo accompanied by a young man. Modelled on this to no small extent was the *Tôkaidô Meishoki* (Record of Noted Places along the Tôkaidô) by Asai Ryôi, the date of which is unknown. The chief purpose of this book is, as its title suggests, topographica-description, but, nevertheless, just as in the *Chikusai-Zôshi*, there are two travellers, Raku Amidabutsu and a young companion, who exchange many jests and quips. One might also mention an-other book dealing with noted places in Edo, written by Toda Mosui and entitled *Murasaki no Hitomoto*, in which again we find two lead-ing characters, Tôtôsai and Iitsu. By the time of Ikku the convention had therefore been well established of writing travel books around a couple of travelling companions who enjoy their jests and experience amusing adventures.

Nevertheless, *Dôchû Hizakurigé* is markedly different from all these predecessors in one most important respect. Despite the introduction of two leading characters with their quips and cranks, these earlier travel books use their "heroes" merely as pegs on which to hang their descriptions of famous places and popular relics. The travelling companions are devoid of any individuality. But Ikku's

Yajirobeé and Kidahachi, far from being mere puppets, are accorded the stature of heroes in a novel. All the stories and incidents are made to arise from and develop out of their particular temperaments. It is here that Ikku reveals his very real skill, and this marks the difference between his travel book and others in the same category.

The word "temperaments" is used advisedly, for it is the temperaments rather than the individual characters of the two heroes that the author reveals. They are presented as typical citizens of Edo, not of course of the highly cultured class, but the lower types, ignorant and vulgar. Temperamentally, such Edo citizens are sanguine and emotional, reacting very quickly to external stimulation, hot-tempered and all too apt to call down trouble upon themselves by their quick tongues and impetuous actions. It is in thoughtlessness of this kind that their chief fault lies. Quickly they blow hot, and just as quickly cold ; one moment they are furious with anger, the next they have regained their composure. Yajirobeé and Kidahachi show themselves in every way typical citizens of Edo, and it is their frankness and their disregard of consequences, combined with their disarming naïveté, that have endeared them to so many readers.

Not, indeed, that they are devoid of a certain shrewdness and ingenuity. But, for the most part, they employ these talents for playing foolish tricks, often making mistakes and landing themselves in amusing situations. Sometimes they manage to wriggle out of the mess of their own creating by composing a *kyôka* (comic poem), at other times they bring down more shame upon themselves. Yet, in spite of the long succession of their blunders and shames, they end their travels still cheerful and happy. This, in itself, serves well to show how typical they are of the sanguine temper of the citizens of Edo.

Also, to no small extent, these features of the two heroes of the book reveal the character of the author himself. Yet this point may have been pressed too far in the many traditions current regarding the personality of Ikku. According to these, he must have been a very free and easy sort of fellow, humorous alike in speech and conduct. One story tells how, being too poor even to buy a *kagami-mochi* (round rice-cake) for decorating his room one New Year, he drew a picture of it and stuck that on the wall of the alcove. Another New Year's Day, he was greatly distressed because he lacked the

ceremonial attire for paying the customary calls. One of his friends,
all correctly dressed, came to call on him. So he persuaded him to
take a bath, and then, quickly putting on his friend's clothes, he set
out on his own round of calls. His friend knew what an eccentric
and humorous character he was dealing with, and accepted his loss
philosophically, put on the old clothes that his host had discarded,
and returned home. There, to cap all, Ikku came to pay his New
Year call on him.

Yet we must be on our guard against too readily accepting such
traditions. For, after all, the great success of such a book was bound
to encourage the creation of legends attributing to its author the
characteristics of his heroes. Indeed, a reaction against such stories
has already set in, and there seems to be a by no means negligible
volume of evidence suggesting that Ikku, so far from having drawn
himself in his heroes, was of a very different type of character. There
is a story told by Shibai Yûchiku, who says he heard from a man
who accompanied Ikku on one of his journeys to collect material
for his book that the writer was the dullest companion imaginable
to travel with. So Minamikata Tsunekata writes, in one of his
occasional essays, that he would never have dreamt that Ikku, whom
he had met two or three times, could write such a book. Also, in
Hizakurigé Rinkô (Hizakurigé Read in Turn) Yamanaka Kyôko
has the following : —

"A very old man of Shizuoka tells me that there could be no duller
travelling companion than Ikku. He once thrust his company on Ikku,
thinking how amusing it would be to travel with one who had written a
book like *Dôchû Hizakurigé*. But when they stopped at an inn, Ikku spent
all his time writing, and even when they rested a while at a wayside tea-
house, out would come his brush. In fact, his brush seemed never to be
out of his hand, and he was continually writing on a pad of paper handker-
chiefs that he carried. He scarcely spoke a word the whole way. The old
man said it had been a terrible disappointment to him, and he could not
imagine a more tedious journey."

But it was probably this silent concentration that contributed
largely to Ikku's success as a writer. Only close attention to detail
and the observation of life's many and varied aspects could have
enabled him to present so humorously figures so representative of
Edo as his two heroes. It was rather because he was detached from
them, than through any close resemblance, that he could present
them so faithfully. A joker such as tradition has tried to make of

Ikku is not the best person to give a realistic presentation of jokeis. Such a man would be far too apt to stray into exaggeration and artificiality, faults from which *Dôchû Hizakurigé* is comparatively free. Although the work may lack profundity, there is no denying its realism and humour. Incident succeeds incident, most of them told very briefly ; and, indeed, the shorter the tales the better they are as a rule. The personalities of the actors and the surrounding circumstances are brought out with few but telling strokes of the brush. His light and easy realistic style is far better than Rijô's, better even than Sanba's.

In a work whose touch is so light there is scarcely room for much in the way of moral criticism. Yet precisely because of that, it is sometimes regarded as an immorally conceived work presenting immoral heroes. It must be realized, however, that had it been marked by any ethical tendency it would have been an entirely different piece of literature, ironical or satirical. As it is, its light and easy style, its unconventional touches, even its moral irresponsibility, are the very qualities that make it a humorous masterpiece.

UKIYO-BURO

(The World's Bath-House)

Ukiyo-buro (The World's Bath-House) is one of the masterpieces of what are termed *kokkeibon* (books of humour). Originally the title was longer, the word *Odoké-banashi* (jokes) being prefixed. The public bath has long occupied an important place in the life of the Japanese people, and those in a city like Edo were just as much social clubs as places for washing oneself. Except that the baths for men and women were kept distinct, the public bath-house had little or no privacy and reserves. Each was crowded with people first of all washing themselves together and afterwards soaking in the same large common hot-bath. In such circumstances, the visitors naturally got to know each other quite well and to talk freely. Furthermore, each bath-house had a room on the second floor, where those guests who had the leisure were in the habit of meeting together for a chat or to play *go* (checkers) or *shôgi* (chess). The present work gives a realistic picture of the ever-changing human scene in these public bath-houses.

People dropped into these places quite casually, and chance meetings would take place either in the bath or the room upstairs. In some cases, of course, those who met had never seen each other before and had little expectation of meeting again. Such people would scarcely indulge in more than a commonplace conversation, exchanging the compliments of the season, and their views, perchance, on daily life. But, as a rule, the habitués of any one bath-house would be near neighbours, and well acquainted with each other's intimate affairs.

In either case, their talk could hardly be focussed on some one developing theme, and accordingly a book like *Ukiyo-buro* lacks the evolution of incident found in an ordinary novel. It is simply a book of gossip, from which, nevertheless, we can obtain some idea of the varied sides of life and the difference in human characters.

The topics appear to have been chosen more or less at random, while the persons introduced are essential types rather than distinct individuals. So it possesses neither plot nor hero. Rather is it a faithful record of conversations on a variety of topics among people of all sorts and conditions who appear successively on the steamy stage. Following the style of the *sharebon*, it lays stress mainly on conversation. The talk is the thing, and so *Ukiyo-buro* is written in colloquial rather than literary language, while the narrative that serves to hold the conversation together is inserted between the talks in small characters in the manner of running notes.

The work is divided into four books, and was published in nine volumes between the years 1808 and 1812. Book I begins with describing a morning bath, which is partaken of by a retired employer, a man suffering from palsy, a middle-aged man and his son, a doctor, a country bath-attendant and others. Then, as the day proceeds, we are introduced to a friendly old man, a samurai from Kyushu, a citizen of Osaka, several children, a man under the influence of drink, several men playing *shôgi* upstairs, five theatrical managers and a teacher of *gidayû* (dramatic ballad).

Book II shows us the women's bath. It begins with some waitresses exchanging confidences, then the chatter of a woman and her daughter, two old women, an easy-going wife, a woman from the Osaka district, a nurse-maid and a young girl; and culminates in a ribald conversation in which a regular gossip, a young woman proud of just having been apprenticed to a house, a maid-servant and a wet-nurse take part.

Book III is a continuation of Book II. We find some geisha talking about their customers, when a concubine joins in and the general topic is "men of the world." Then two girls come in and begin talking about their parents. A good-natured housewife enters into a conversation with an older woman about their respective experiences with maid-servants; and afterwards we are given the other side of the picture when two servants begin talking about their employers. Then other sides of life are presented as a very free-spoken woman, a mother, a rustic maid-servant, a girl-student of the classics, an ex-waitress in a tea-house and the wife of a *gidayû* teacher appear on the stage and carry on the conversation from one subject to another.

Book IV takes us back to the men's bath-room. Into it enter a regular liar, a *haikai* poet, a retired employer who cannot be kept from thrusting his advice on everybody present, a dissipated young man, a buffoon, a man from the Osaka district, a young man of fashion, a semi-drunk, as well as the sufferer from the palsy already mentioned.

This idea of retailing the conversation that takes place in the public bath-houses can be traced to Itô Tanboku, who published his *Sentô Shinwa* (New Stories from the Public Bath-House) in the Hôreki era (1751-1763). But the author of the *Ukiyo-buro* does not appear to have been directly influenced by this work. Instead, he says that he took the idea from a story told by Sanshôtei Karaku, who was a famous *rakugo* (comic story) teller of that time.

There is no doubt that, so far as Book I is concerned, Shikitei Sanba, the author of this work, has been conspicuously influenced by Ikku's *Dôchû Hizakurigé*, both in his selection of absurd characters and the comic description of incidents. *Edo Sakusha Burui* (Edo Writers Classified) points this out, at the same time severely criticizing Sanba and saying that, although his work is akin to *Hizakurigé*, it is greatly inferior to it So far as Book I itself is concerned, this criticism is well justified. There Sanba is indeed imitating Ikku, who was then at the height of his popularity, and Sanba shows himself far inferior to his prototype.

But, after Book I, a distinct change can be observed. In the following books the style is much fresher and more original. The characters introduced are much more like the ordinary people of daily life, and their talk is just the sort of gossip such people would indulge in. Indeed the whole thing becomes much more realistic. It is very doubtful, however, if the author himself was conscious that he was effecting a change of attitude.

It seems reasonable to assume that, when writing Book I, in which all the characters are men, the author, consciously or unconsciously, found himself reproducing much the same spirit as pervades the popular *Hizakurigé*. But when he came to write Book II and to show women taking their baths and conversing with one another, he could not but feel that the characters and incidents of his model were entirely unsuitable for presenting the manners and customs of the women of that time, characterized as they were by gentleness and elegance. There could be no female counterparts of such base vulgar, pleasure-seeking types as Yajirobeé and Kidahachi. So perhaps, scarcely realizing it, he was driven to look to real life itself for his types, thus introducing on his stage a variety of ordinary examples of contemporary womanhood, abandoning a forced humour for an easy realism.

Having been forced to change his method in the course of writing Book II, he began to discover his own peculiar genius in the later books. As the work became more realistic, he began to develop his special genius for ironical, rather than "slap-stick," humour and continued this in his subsequent works.

He wrote several *kokkeibon* (books of humour) which can be divided into two different kinds. One of these carries on the lesson learnt in writing *Ukiyo-buro*, and in this realism is of primary importance, and satire secondary. This is well exemplified also in *Ukiyo-doko* (The World's Barber's Shop), which is a companion volume to *Ukiyo-buro*. Quite different from this type are such works as *Koko, Hyaku Baka* (A Hundred Fools, Ancient and Modern), and *Meitei Katagi* (When a Man's Drunk), both of which are primarily satiric and ironical.

In *Ukiyo-doko* the scene is laid in a barber's shop instead of the public bath. Almost as much as the bath-house, the hairdresser's shop was a centre of the social life of those days, especially among the ordinary people; and so it too affords a most suitable setting for portraying a variety of human types. The excellent realistic style which characterizes the last three books of the earlier work, is maintained here, and we are presented with a collection of brief sketches of actual life. Plot and continuity are lacking just as in *Ukiyo-buro* since here as there we are presented with a group of people having no relationship with each other except their chance appearance on the scene. They meet and soon part again, but their meeting is the occasion for a brief, realistic conversation. Such works as those of Sanba can be most aptly described, in the words of the late Dr Tsubouchi Shôyô, as an "overturned box of toys," for there is no sort of order or connection to be found in the characters and events spread before us. That a collection of short episodes need not necessarily be lacking in unity is shown by Ikku's *Hizakurige* which is comparatively strong in plot and continuity. It may be

1at a voyage or journey lends itself better to this than the very casual 1eetings characteristic of a public bath-house or a barber's shop; 1ut it may also be that Ikku had talents of a different order from 1ose of Sanba.

These *kokkeibon* are characteristic of the life in Edo at this period. t was a time when peace prevailed and the different social classes 7ere definitely marked off from each other. Traders, whether on small scale as shopkeepers, or on a larger scale as merchants, >rmed one of the lower classes. Whatever their talents or wealth, 1ey were allowed no scope beyond the sphere of commerce and 1dustry. Consequently, they lacked any honourable ambition and mployed their means and leisure usually in mere pleasure-seeking. n this age of stagnant peace, Edo culture became overripe and was haracterized mainly by the perfection of the means of enjoyment nd the epicurean zest of the Edo merchant. Such a society was the rery soil for the gay and superficial humour of the *kokkeibon*.

The literature of this period gives one good reason to doubt if his stratified and stagnant society of Edo contributed much to the eal enjoyment of life. Certainly, as compared with the unrest, nisery and tumult of the long period of civil wars, it did afford many nore opportunities for pleasure-seeking. But nothing is more edious than a life in surroundings that are crystallized, changeless nd free from the dangers of war, and tedium makes real enjoyment mpossible. In a life so dull, the least little excitement becomes a ;reat event.

This truth was well exemplified when, in the year 1821, a few ears after the publication of *Ukiyo-buro*, a couple of camels were xhibited at Ryôgoku in Edo. True, a camel was a rare beast in apan. Several had been imported at various times in the remote Jara period, but none since. Yet not even that could have accounted or the immense sensation this couple created without the utter lullness of life generally. Vast crowds went to see them, their urine vas sold as the elixir of life, and their hair and pictures were eagerly napped up as charms for ensuring domestic harmony. They were he one topic of conversation, and for some time after served as a ubject for *kyôka* (comic poems), colour prints, popular ballads, :usa-zôshi (short novels), and *rakugo* (comic stories), while they .ppeared as the most popular design on envelopes and calendars

[353]

and even cakes.

It is not surprising then that in a society such as this the ordinary people should have seized on the opportunities afforded them by the public bath-house and the barber's shop for a little diversion from the general tedium of life. These places became their unofficial clubs, and the gossip there served to spice their lives. So it was also that pilgrimages to shrines and temples and purely pleasure trips came into vogue. Travel was easy, and ordinary life was a great thing to get away from. Hence we get those amusing rascals Yajirobeé and Kidahachi on their laughter-making travels and Sanba's realistic pictures of the gossiping fun in the public bath-house and the barber's shop. Hence the succession of those books of humour like *Hanagoyomi Hasshôjin* and *Kokkei Wagôjin* of Ryû ei Rijô, *Myô chikurinwa Shichihenjin* of Baitei Kinga and many others, all of which derive their subject-matter from the epicurean life of Edo in those days.

———

UGETSU MONOGATARI

(Tales of Moonlight and Rain)

Ugetsu Monogatari is a collection of nine short ghost stories by Ueda Akinari, written in 1768, but not published until 1776. Stories of this kind have a long history in Japanese literature; the first known collection dates as far back as the Nara period. This was the *Nippon-koku Genpô Zen'aku Ryôiki* (Japanese Tales of Retributive Miracles in this World). During the succeeding Heian, Kamakura and Muromachi periods the number of such collections considerably increased, the stories being drawn from Indian and Chinese as well as Japanese sources.

One of the most famous of these was *Kii Zôdanshû*, a collection published at the end of the Muromachi period, which included a few strange and grotesque tales from the Chinese book of ghost stories called *Sentô Shinwa* (*Chien têng hsin hua*, New Night Tales). Coming nearer to modern times there is the *Otogi Bôko* (Fairy Tales), which was an adaptation made by Asai Ryôi from the same Chinese classic. Once this alien work had been transplanted in Japanese soil, many translations and adaptations of similar literature began to appear, among which may be mentioned *Kokon Kidan Hanabusa-Zôshi* (Grotesque Stories of Ancient and Modern Times), *Hitsuji-gusa* (Forgotten Fragments) and *Shigeshigé Yawa* (Wild Grasses), all by Kinro Gyôja. These three belong to almost the same period as *Ugetsu Monogatari*, and are very similar to it in their contents. Nevertheless the work we are considering is of a much higher literary quality.

Each of the nine stories contained in the work is derived and adapted from one or other of the many preceding collections among the Chinese and Japanese classics. Herewith we give a list of the stories with their respective sources : —

1. " Shiraminé," from *Hôgen Monogatari* (Story of the War of the Hôgen Era), etc.

2. "Kikka no Chigiri," from *Kokon Shôsetsu* (Tales Old and New), *Yusei Meigen* (Satirical Analects), etc.
3. "Asaji ga Yado," from *Man'yôshû* (Anthology of a Myriad Leaves), *Konjaku Monogatari* (Tales of Long Ago), *Otogi Bôko* (Fairy Tales), or, more accurately, according to modern scholarship, from the Chinese book *Sentô Shinwa* (New Night Tales)
4. "Muô no Rigyo," from *Kokon Sekkai* (Novels Old and New).
5. "Buppô-ô" and
6. "Kibitsu no Kama," from *Sentô Shinwa* (New Night Tales)
7. "Jasei no In," from *Seiko Kawa* (Fine Tales from the Lake Si Hu).
8. "Ao Zukin," from *Ujishûi Monogatari* (Supplement to the Uji Tales).
9. "Hinpuku-ron," from Rohô's *Senshin-ron* (On Mammon)

Different though these stories are in their subject-matter, they are alike in being tales of the grotesque and supernatural. Yet there is such a remarkable realism in the way in which the supernatural features are presented that it is difficult to say where the actual world ends and the unseen begins.

This is most probably due to the fact that the author himself had an unquestioning faith in the reality of the unseen world. Consequently, the reader finds himself taken along into the author's own world in such a way that his purely aesthetic appreciation of the work is not affected by the grotesque and supernatural nature of the subjects. It is this sincerity of presentation that lifts Ueda Akinari above his contemporaries in the same field and makes *Ugetsu Monogatari* a masterpiece of the grotesque school, unchallenged in Japanese literature.

We shall now give a synopsis of each story.

1. *Shiraminé* (Mount Shiraminé)

It was in the autumn of the year 1168 that Saigyô, the famous priest-poet, went to pay homage at the mausoleum of the ex-Emperor Sutoku on Mt Shiraminé in the province of Sanuki. While he was chanting sutras during the night, he heard someone calling him, using his familiar name, "En'i, En'i." He opened his eyes to find an emaciated figure standing before him, which he assumed to be that of the departed ex-Emperor. So he bowed himself low

fore it and ventured to admonish the spirit to awake from the
phere of delusion and so attain to the peace of Buddhahood. The
pirit paid no regard to him, but changed into a more horrible form,
ecoming devilish in appearance and in voice. It proceeded to
tter terrifying curses on the world and its inhabitants, and then fore-
old that the whole clan of the Heiké would soon meet its doom
nd be utterly destroyed in the sea beyond. Full of grief and pity,
aigyô offered to the troubled spirit a poem inspired by the occasion,
which it calmed down and vanished from his sight. Just then
he moon sank behind the mountain and day began to dawn.

Thirteen years after, as foretold, evil days fell on the Heiké
an, until, after a prolonged period of disasters, its members found
ntimely graves in the raging waters of the western sea.

2. *Kikka no Chigiri* (A Tryst for Chrysanthemum Time)

There was once a samurai named Hasebé Samon, who was con-
nt to live in honest poverty with his mother in the post-town
f Kako in Harima province. One day he learned that another
amurai was staying in that place, suffering from a serious illness.
'hat samurai was called Akana Sôemon. He had been the teacher
the martial arts of En'ya Kamon, deputy of Tomita in Izumo
rovince. Kamon had been treacherously killed by Amako Tsune-
isa, his former lord, and Sôemon had set forth to revenge his pupil's
eath. He visited Lord Sasaki Ujitsuna of Ômi, in order to enlist
is aid, but the man was a coward, and so Sôemon's purpose had
een frustrated. On his way back, he had fallen seriously ill.

Samon, out of the kindness of his heart, visited the sick man and
ared for him as if he were one of his own flesh and blood until he
as completely restored to health. By that time they had become as
timate as brothers. Their parting was a sad one, but Sôemon felt
mself under an obligation to set out once more for Izumo. But
e solemnly promised to be with Samon for the next Chrysanthemum
estival.

Time passed, and the appointed day arrived. Samon had no
oubt whatever that Sôemon would keep his promise, so he kept
atch for his friend from early morning, but in vain; the sun set,
d there was still no sign of him. It grew late and Samon's mother
ent to bed, yet the samurai still would not give up hope. At last,
: was about to fasten the door when he saw the figure of a man in

the darkness. The figure drew nearer, and he saw that it was none
other than his confidently awaited friend. Joyfully he ushered him in
but as they began to talk he noticed something strange about him. He
put a few questions, and then he heard the following uncanny tale

Sôemon had gone to Izumo to settle accounts with Amako
Tsunehisa, but had then been thrown into prison by his own cousin
Akana Tanji. He was still in prison when the appointed day of
meeting came, and unable to escape he was in despair at being pre
vented from keeping his promise. Remembering, however, that
a spirit could cover great distances with no regard to time, he had
determined to sacrifice his life. Thus, in spirit form, he had been
able to keep the tryst. Then, begging compassion from Samon, the
figure vanished from sight.

Samon wept aloud and awakened his mother from her sleep
She too, when she heard the story, wept the whole night through
When day came, Samon, with his mother's approval, hastened of
to Izumo to deal with Akana Tanji. He upbraided the man for
his unjust treatment of the unfortunate Sôemon and then cut him
down with a single revengeful blow.

3. *Asaji ga Yado* (The Desolate Cottage)

In the village of Mama in the province of Shimôsa lived a man
named Katsushirô. It so happened that he had to go to Kyoto of
business, leaving behind him his young and beautiful wife, Miyagi
Shortly after, war broke out and even the Kanto district was ravaged
by the fighting hordes. On leaving, Katsushirô had promised hi
wife that he would return to her in the autumn, and even when autumn
came and her husband did not return, Miyagi continued to have
faith in him. As time went on, hardships came upon her. The
other men, attracted by her charms, tried all sorts of means to win
her, but she resisted them, although this meant keeping hersel
entirely indoors. At the year's end, her maid left her, and she
remained quite alone.

Katsushirô meanwhile had indeed set out to return by autumn
But, first he was robbed of all his goods, and then he learned that
barrier had been set up on the way, through which no traveller coul
pass. So, halfway home, he was compelled to turn back to Kyoto
Then he paid a visit to Ômi province, where he fell seriously ill. Afte
a narrow escape from death, he tried hard to repair his fallen fortune

naking many journeys between Kyoto and Ômi. Once ruined, however, he found it very hard to make another start. Seven years had elapsed before he was able to return to his home.

He arrived there in the evening in the season of the early summer rain, and to his delight he found his wife and home just as he had left them. After a night of sweet reunion, Katsushirô woke up to find himself lying in a roofless, desolate house, with the moonlight streaming whitely upon him. He looked around and saw a grave mound, apparently that of his wife, on the spot where their bed had been.

The next morning neighbours told him the sorrowful news that his wife had chosen death rather than be untrue to him.

4. *Muô no Rigyo* (The Dream Carp)

About the middle of the Enchô era (923-930), there was a priest named Kôgi, belonging to the Mii-dera temple, who was a clever painter, showing especial skill in depicting the scaly beauty of the carp. This priest fell ill and died, yet since his body remained strangely warm, his family put off burying him.

After three days, he suddenly came back to life. But, amid the rejoicings of his family, he astonished them by requesting them to send a special message to a parishioner named Taira-no Suké. " I, Kôgi, have been restored from death by a miracle," the message ran, " and I know that at the present moment you are drinking and making a meal of freshly prepared pickled fish. Stop your drinking a while and come and see me at the temple here." Then he added to the messenger, " Watch Master Suké closely, and you will see it is exactly as I have said."

So it was. Taira-no Suké was engaged exactly as Kôgi had said he would be. Marvelled at the messenger's account, he did as Kôgi had bid him, hastening with the messenger to the temple. Then Kôgi astonished them all still further by telling them exactly how Bunshi the fisherman had caught a fine carp, which he had sold to Taira-no Suké, and how the latter had forthwith prepared a banquet to be partaken of with his brothers. How could he know all this, they asked. Then he told them the following story.

Feeling himself burning hot with fever, Kôgi had made his way to the shores of a lake, where he was enviously watching the carp swimming in the cool water. Then the lake god had appeared,

congratulating him on his sympathetic understanding of the carp
spirit which he had embodied so skilfully in his paintings, and presented him with a rich robe shining like the scales of a golden carp
Then he found that he had indeed been turned into a carp and was
swimming happily about in the cool lake. After a while, however
he began to feel very hungry, when he caught sight of Bunshi sitting
there with his fishing line. Knowing quite well what the sweet-
smelling bait concealed, he had been able to withstand the temptation for a while, but gradually, as his hunger increased, he found i
too much for him. After all, he thought, it would be all right, since
Bunshi knew him and he would be able to explain to him who he
was. So he swallowed bait and hook and was hauled ashore. Wrig-
gling at the end of the line, he kept on crying out, "I say, it's me
it's me," but without making the least impression on Bunshi, who
calmly unhooked him and brought him to Taira-no Suké.

There he again made repeated efforts to tell the cook who he
was, but no one seemed to hear him. The cook took up a great
knife and was just about to cut his head off, when he gave such a
great shout of fear that he woke up from his dream.

5. *Buppôsô* (The Sacred Bird)

A certain man named Muzen went with his son on a pilgrimage to
Mt. Kôya-san. He set himself to pass the whole night in chanting
prayers at the Tô-ô-dô Hall. Night was exceedingly silent on the
sacred mountain, nothing being heard save only occasional bursts
of divine song from the sacred bird, *buppôsô*.* Muzen was listening
to this, when suddenly, heralded by voices calling silence, there
appeared a man clad in an ancient noble's attire, followed by many
attendants, and began to hold a council. Muzen was invited to join
them in their deliberations, and very soon discovered that the
nobleman was Hidetsugu, the late Kanpaku (Civil Dictator), and
that all the other members of the council were men who had died
some time before. Realizing that he was in the midst of a company
of spirits, he was terrified, and still more so, when, in a state of
great excitement, the whole ghostly council sprang to their feet
crying that the hour of battle had come. Muzen could contain his
fear no longer, and then Hidetsugu declared in a terrible voice

---

* The broad-billed roller, *Eurystomus orientalis*.

" We have revealed ourselves to mere humans, we must take them with us to the hell of Ashura," whereupon some old retainers were heard to remonstrate, saying that living people should not participate in that devilry.   However, they all began to drift further and further away, making clamours all the while.   Then Muzen suddenly came to his senses and, waking up his son, began the descent of the mountain with him.

6. *Kibitsu no Kama* (The Kibi Cauldron)

There was a youth named Izawa Shôtarô belonging to a well-to-do agricultural family in the village of Niwasé in the province of Kibi (or Kibitsu).   He was to receive in marriage a beautiful young girl named Isora, daughter of Kasada Miki, a Shinto priest of that province.   It was the custom in Kibi to boil a cauldron of water at the shrine by way of divination, and when this was done, the oracle foretold that the marriage between these two young people would be unlucky.

The warning was unheeded, and for a time the young couple lived happily together.   But it was not long before the young husband fell in love with Sodé, a courtesan of Tomo.   When his parents discovered that the infatuated Shôtarô had gone so far as to ransom her and make her his mistress, they were very angry and had him locked up.   Throughout all this, the young wife Isora behaved admirably and was most anxious to patch things up.   Shô aiô deceived her with a show of penitence, and then, seizing his opportunity, ran away with Sodé and sought help from a relative of hers named Hikoroku who lived in the district of Inami in Harima province.   There they lived together in secret until Sodé died.   It was Shô arô's habit to pay daily visits to her grave, near to which he noticed another freshly made grave which was visited by a young woman.   One day he got into conversation with her, and she invited him to go with her to her home.   He did so, only to find himself confronted with his wife Isora, a terrifying figure in a sad state of emaciation.   Shôtarô was so shocked at the reproaches she hurled at him that he fell down in a faint.

He recovered consciousness to find himself in a remote and deserted chapel, and hurried back to the house of Hikoroku, to whom he told the whole story.   Hikoroku suggested consulting a soothsayer, and they were informed that the revengeful spirit of his wife was afflicting him. Already it had killed the unfortunate Sodé, and it would not be long before it would kill Shôtarô. To escape that fate it was necessary that he should shut himself up in a state of strict confinement and abstinence over a period of forty-two days.

So Shôtarô returned home, pasted red amulets on the gate and windows and started on his period of strict abstinence. Regularly each midnight, the revengeful spirit came to the door, but could not get in. It poured forth bitter reproaches, but it could do nothing against Shôtarô. Forty-one days had passed by, and only one more night of abstinence remained. The hours of darkness passed, and day seemed about to break. Leaping with joy, Shôtarô called out greetings to Hikoroku next door, for after such a long interval he was most eager to talk with him again.

Each of them opened his doors to hasten to the other, when Hikoroku heard his friend give a fearful cry. He jumped outside and found that, although the sky had seemed to be getting lighter it was still night; it was the ominous light of the full moon that had deceived them. Shôtarô was nowhere to be seen; there was nothing except a lock of his hair hanging from the eaves.

7. *Jasei no In* (Passion of a Snake)

Toyo'o was a handsome young fellow, second son of a man named Ôya-no Takesuké who lived on the headland of Miwagasaki in Kii province. One day he took shelter from the rain in a hut where he found Manago, an exceedingly beautiful girl, also seeking shelter. She afterwards showed him the way to her magnificent residence, and they soon became betrothed, Manago presenting him with a fine sword, which, however, was one of the treasures belonging to the Kumano Gongen shrine. He was accused of theft and put in prison.

Compelled to make restitution, he led the officials of the shrine to Manago's house, but instead of the splendid residence he expected to find, there was on the spot only a desolate ruin. Greatly wondering, he led them into an inner room, where they found Manago and a maid. The officials tried to arrest them, but they disappeared in a clap of thunder. However, they left behind them the other valuables that had been stolen from the shrine.

Although the officials let Toyo'o free, he felt so much ashamed that he went off to his elder sister in Yamato. There he met Manago and her maid again, and with her deceitful words she persuaded him to come and live with her once more.

One day, he and the two women were out together, admiring the cherry blossoms on Mount Yoshino, when an old man happened to pass by them as they stood gazing at the waterfall. Manago turned her face away quickly, but not quickly enough, for the old man cried out, " 'Tis you, you devil! Again misleading a man!" Whereupon Manago and her maid plunged into the depths of the fall.

Toyo'o returned to Kii where he was fortunate enough to marry Tomiko, a beautiful lady of the Court and daughter of Shôji of Shiba. But she became possessed by the spirit of the snake, and began to behave just like Manago, speaking with exactly the same tone of voice. When her father Shôji realized this, he was greatly distressed and turned for help to the priest Hôkai Oshô of the Dôjô-ji temple at Komatsubara. The priest gave him a special sacred stole and told him what he must do with it. So he gave it to Toyo'o who seized Tomiko quickly and, before she could do anything, had her well wrapped up in the stole. After waiting awhile, Toyo'o removed the stole, when Tomiko was revealed fast asleep with a white snake, about three feet in length, curled up on her breast. The priest put the snake in an iron pot, took it back to the temple and buried it securely in the ground so that it could nevermore escape.

8. *Ao Zukin* (The Blue Hood)

A high priest, Kaian Zenji, arrived one evening after sunset at the village of Tomita in Shimotsuké province, seeking a night's lodging. To his dismay, all the villagers ran away and hid themselves whenever he approached, showing extreme terror. At last, finding one a little bolder than the rest, he interrogated him and learnt that he had been mistaken for a mad priest who dwelt in a deserted temple on the neighbouring hills, and who occasionally appeared in the village to terrify them all. The villager went on to tell the following story about him.

This lunatic had once been a good and noble priest, but he had been excessively devoted to a handsome young boy who had died. The sight of the boy's dead body had driven him so mad that he refused to be parted from it; he had ended by eating the putrid flesh and gnawing the bones. Then he descended in a frenzy on the village and terrified the people so much that they felt he had become a fiend. The villagers had kept away from him, and his disciples had all left him, while the temple had become a ruin, where he lived on all alone.

Kaian thereupon went on to the temple himself and passed the night there. While he was sitting in a gloomy inner hall, lighted only by the moon shining through the cracks, the lunatic came rushing in as if searching for flesh. He seemed not to notice Kaian's presence, but went on rushing about, until at last he sank down to the ground in a state of complete exhaustion.

Next morning Kaian set the poor lunatic on a flat stone and placed a blue hood on his head. Then he gave him the following Buddhist poem:—

> The moonlight shines o'er the cove,
> The breeze whispers through the pines.
> How can our thoughts be evil
> In this long serene night?

He bade him try to reflect on the meaning of these lines, and then he left the temple.

The following year he passed through the village again, and once more ascended the mountain. He found the lunatic still seated as he left him on the flat stone in the desolate temple precincts. As he drew near he could hear him humming over to himself the lines of the poem. Kaian uttered a loud cry, and the lunatic vanished from sight, leaving nothing behind but the blue hood and some whitened bones on the stone.

9. *Hinpuku-ron* (A Discourse on Wealth)

Oka Sanai, a retainer of Gamô Ujisato, was a samurai distinguished for his valour, but he was very avaricious and had acquired a vast amount of money and treasure. One night the spirit of wealth appears at his bedside, enters on a discussion about riches, expounds the way of national administration, ends by foretelling the subjugation of the whole country by the Tokugawa clan and with the approach of dawn disappears.

———

KAJIN NO KIGÛ

(Romantic Meeting with Two Fair Ladies)

Kajin no Kigû is saturated with the author's own personal experience and opinions ; indeed, more than half of its contents may be regarded as autobiographical. Accordingly, we believe that, if we prefaced our consideration of the novel with an account of the author's life, we should arrive at a much clearer understanding of it.

The author's real name was Shiba Shirô, but he wrote under the name of Tôkai Sanshi. *Tôkai* (Eastern Sea) is the term by which the ancient Chinese alluded to Japan, and the full meaning of Shiba's *nom de plume* may thus be rendered as "a gentleman tourist from Japan," the import and peculiar aptness of which become clear when taken in conjunction with the title of the novel.

Shiba Shirô, born in December, 1852, was a loyal retainer of Lord Matsudaira, the daimyo of Aizu, who fought against the Satsuma and Nagato clans on the side of the Tokugawa Shôgunate in the struggle that ended in the Meiji Restoration. Shirô was only a boy of fourteen at that time, but had already fought as a full-fledged soldier. After the Restoration, in common with all the samurai of the defeated Aizu clan, he suffered great poverty and hardship. But he persisted with his education, studying economics and commerce with the utmost zeal. Realizing that a one-time member of the Aizu clan would never be given the opportunity to rise to any high governmental position, he resolved to serve his country in the sphere of business. Having tasted the bitterness of defeat, and feeling an unflagging sympathy with those in similar straits, he vowed never again to be a loser himself. In reading *Kajin no Kigû* this should be definitely borne in mind.

Crossing over to the United States in 1879, he entered a business college in San Francisco, but in the spring of 1881 transferred to Harvard University, where he majored in political economy. His next move was to enter the University of Pennsylvania at Philadelphia, where he continued his chosen study at the Wharton College of Finance, devoting most of his attention to the work of Kelly, the famous economist and advocate of the system of protection, and finished by receiving the degree of Bachelor of Finance. The greater portion of his expenses while in America was provided by the wealthy Iwasaki, founder of the House of Mitsubishi, as the result of an appeal made on his behalf by a number of friends, including Inukai Tsuyoshi who half a century later was to become Prime Minister. The remainder he found himself by occasional earnings from articles he contributed to Japanese and American newspapers as well as from lectures on Japan delivered to American audiences.

From the first Shiba had held that, considering the nature of the problems besetting Japan, she had no alternative but to work out her destinies as an industrial nation, a view which was to be justified by subsequent events. In fact, it was in order to play his own part in Japan's industrial development that he had specialized in the study of economics. Nevertheless, compared with the rest of the world, Japan's capacity and resources were at a very low level, and it seemed scarcely conceivable that she could take her place among the great nations of Europe and America. As a loyal subject of Japan, Shiba could not help entertaining grave misgivings for her future, fearing lest, through the superior might and the machinations of Western Powers, she might suffer the same inglorious fate that had befallen his own Aizu clan under the post-Restoration régime. He saw that to stave off such a fate it was imperative that she should enrich her national resources as quickly as possible, a work calling for national unity, the thoroughgoing co-operation of all classes, and, especially, industrial expansion. But political freedom was a condition precedent to any great industrial development. With liberty to improve their conditions and under a régime of free competition, the people could hopefully exert themselves in the development of their industries. On this point Shiba held views similar to the liberals of his day, although, in opposition to the liberals who insisted upon international free trade, he held that protection was necessary. As Shiba saw the matter, free trade was possible only when carried on between countries of equal, or balanced, national resources, but where such a wide disparity existed as between Japan and the Western Powers, the advantages would be exclusively to the stronger, the weaker being reduced to the status of a colony. Hence he insisted that, in the matter of trade with foreign countries, the policy of protecting home industries was the only one to pursue.

When Shiba returned to Japan in 1885 after his long absence abroad, he found grounds for the gravest apprehensions. The national strength was far from reassuring, political freedom was lacking, as was the capacity to rise industrially, while foreign trade was only enriching the Western Powers at the expense of Japan. He realized that if this continued the country would inevitably be reduced to the level of " a second Aizu." He recalled how many weak nations in history had been subdued or oppressed by the strong. China, Annam, India, Turkey, Egypt, Poland, Hungary, Spain, Ireland, Madagascar, all formed a striking object-lesson in the problem of national survival, and he was determined to do all he could to prevent his own country from treading the path along which those ill-fated nations had gone. Accordingly, he decided to warn his fellow-countrymen by publishing his own views on such vital matters as political freedom, a firm foreign policy and the development of the State on an industrial basis. Yet to do so he would necessarily have to criticize root and branch the present administration. Under the existing regulations, however, any such criticism was strictly forbidden, and the only way left for him was to present his views under the guise of fiction. In taking this course, he was merely following the method then in vogue among a section of the Opposition, who made great use of the political novel to air their views. The result was *Kajin no Kigû*, the first part of which was published in 1885 and the last and eighth part in 1897.

The hero of " Romantic Meeting with Two Fair Ladies " is, of course, the author himself, under the guise of Tôkai Sanshi, or " a gentleman tourist from Japan," the story opening in the spring of 1882, the year after he had removed to Philadelphia. One day, while Sanshi was viewing the Independence Hall, he met two beautiful women, and later he met them both again as he was boating on the river Delaware. One was of Spanish birth, named Yolanda, the other Irish with the name of Korlen. Yolanda's father was the leader of the Don Carlos Party, a passionate patriot who had fled the domination of Napoleon III of France and was now a political

[367]

refugee. Korlen's father was a wealthy Irish merchant, who was also an arden' patriot, devoted to the cause of Home Rule. Like their fathers, Yolanda and Korlen were also strong patriots with a burning hatred for their respective enemies, France and England.

Yolanda relates to Sanshi in detail the fall of modern Spain from power, and Korlen enlarges on England's oppression of Ireland and the Irish independence movement. Both these narratives contain the author's implied warning to Japan. Moreover, the Chinese cook employed by these two women was the impoverished scion of a once distinguished family, and harboured a seething resentment against the white race's exploitation. So when Sanshi recounted his own tragic experiences during the Meiji Restoration, he was listened to with deep sympathy by these three people, and thus did the four become comrades with one common aim in view.

Later, when visiting the grave of Benjamin Franklin, Sanshi encountered Louis Kossuth, the Hungarian patriot. In the course of their talk, Kossuth predicted that Russia was likely to be Japan's greatest enemy and went on to recount the causes of Poland's loss of independence, telling of the arrogance of powerful countries and the sufferings of the weak. He showed how national ruin follows from internal dissension, even mistaken ideas regarding liberty often leading to national disaster. Here again, of course, Sanshi is addressing a warning to his own people.

Shortly afterwards, the two women and the Chinese cook suddenly disappeared and Sanshi had many anxious moments, until he learned that they had secretly embarked on the first vessel bound for Europe on hearing that Yolanda's father had been taken prisoner in Spain, in the hope of rescuing him. Much worried regarding their personal safety, Sanshi visited Fannie Parnell in order to obtain news of them. She had, however, received no tidings of them, and shortly after, on July 20, 1882, she died.

One evening Sanshi paid a visit to Mrs Parnell's grave, carefully avoiding the public eye, since he wished to read out a memorial addressed to her spirit. As he was doing so his eyes fell on a shadowy figure whom he discovered to be Korlen. Thus strangely reunited, they talked about what had happened in Spain. She described how the party reached their destination safely and tricked the governor of the prison, in which Yolanda's father was confined, into releasing him. But while escaping to France by sea great storm had struck their boat, and all four were thrown overboard. Korlen herself had been rescued after struggling for some time in the water, but she believed that the other three were all drowned. Sanshi was greatly distressed by this, for he had been secretly in love with Yolanda.

Before long an extraordinary piece of news reached the two friends. Arabi Pasha had stirred up a revolt in Egypt, but what surprised them both was the report that the Pasha's chief of staff was an elderly Spanish general, who was accompanied by a beautiful woman, apparently his daughter. Afterwards, Mademoiselle Kossuth, daughter of Louis Kossuth, delivered to Sanshi a gold ring that Yolanda had asked her to forward to him, thus confirming the fact that Yolanda and her father were still alive, and that the old refugee was indeed serving as the Pasha's chief of staff. Moreover, from Mademoiselle Kossuth Sanshi and Korlen heard all about her father's lifetime of patriotic activity and how Hungary had come to be a subject nation, all this, again, being for the edification of the author's fellow-countrymen. He actually makes the Hungarian lady compare, in a very pointed fashion, the activities of the Japanese Government with the methods pursued by Austria's rulers, describing Prime Minister Itô as the Metternich of Japan. In receiving the good news about Yolanda and her father, Korlen set out for Egypt. Sanshi was eager to accompany her, but just at that time he received the news of his father's death and had to return to his own country.

On arriving in Japan, Sanshi managed to get a die-hard Cabinet Minister (Tani Kanjô, the Minister of Agriculture and Commerce in the Itô Cabinet) to recognize his abilities and appoint him as his private secretary. This is a historical fact, as is also the further one that Sanshi accompanied the Minister to Europe. On board the ship Sanshi fell in with that same Chinese cook who had gone to Spain with Yolanda and Korlen, and from him learned how Korlen was faring and also of the situation created in Egypt by the white race's aggression. The aged Chinese patriot was now on his way to Annam to assist the natives in their fight against the French invaders. The two talked long about the situation in Asia and decided that all Asia must unite in order to check the aggressive inroads of the Western peoples. At Ceylon Sanshi and his chief were able to meet Arabi Pasha, and the description of that meeting, most eloquently written, is one of the high lights of the novel. Through the mouth of Arabi Pasha the author gives expression, with all the persuasive logic at his command, to his ardent conviction that one must ever be on guard against the imperialism of the white race, whose aggressiveness is camouflaged with the Christian principles of peace and brotherhood.

Their arrival in Egypt afforded Sanshi an opportunity of meeting with Yolanda quite unexpectedly. Her father, he learned, had departed for the Sudan before the quelling of Arabi Pasha's revolt in order to aid the "false prophet," the Mahdi, in his investment of the British and Egyptian forces under General Gordon which were maintaining the puppet Khedive's authority at Khartum. Yolanda meanwhile had remained in Cairo, where she had been abducted by a son of the Khedive and subjected to all sorts of cruelties. She had finally managed to escape and was hiding in a safe retreat at the time of her encounter with Sanshi. Yet the agents of the Khedive's philandering son were still searching for her and hence it was dangerous, if not impossible, for her to come out of hiding. Sanshi would have been only too glad to take her with him, if only he had not been en route for Europe in an official capacity. But he was able to give her money to pay her passage to America where he promised to meet her later.

One of the objects of his chief's trip to Europe was to attend the lectures of Dr Lorenz von Stein on political science at Vienna, for the great Austrian authority was then acting in an advisory capacity to the Japanese Government. His chief's sojourn in Austria gave Sanshi the opportunity of making a tour of inspection to Turkey and to visit Greece and Italy. At Turin he called on Kossuth, who again warned him against Russian ambitions in the Far East.

On the ship from England to America Sanshi was surprised to find Korlen. It seemed that she had left America in order to join Yolanda in Egypt, but had only reached Paris when her presence was discovered by the prison governor whom she and Yolanda had tricked in Spain. She had just managed to elude capture, but the watchfulness of the authorities made it hopeless for her to try to reach her friend. They narrated to each other their experiences since they had last met, and dwelt long on the subject of their mutual friends, Yolanda, Mademoiselle Kossuth, the Chinese cook and the rest.

When Sanshi and the Cabinet Minister returned to Japan in 1888, they both resigned their positions. Attaching to themselves a group of die-hard nationalists, they took the lead in opposition to the Government, showing conspicuous courage and enterprise. As a result of the efforts of numerous public-spirited men, a national legislature, the Diet, was convened, to which Sanshi was elected. There he displayed great activity as one of the leading members of the Oppoisition.

The rest of the novel is taken up with the many public events in which Sanshi was concerned up to the year 1896. Indeed, from 1888 on, the two beautiful women, Yolanda and Korlen, cease to have any part in the story, which henceforth is occupied with Sanshi's political career.

When the last part of the novel appeared in 1897, Sanshi, that is to say, Shiba, received the post of Vice-Minister of Agriculture and Commerce in a Ministry formed by his political friends. After that, Shiba was re-elected several times to the House of Representatives, and once held the office of Councillor to the Foreign Office. He died at Atami, the famous hot-spring resort, in September, 1922, at the age of seventy-one.

Kajin no Kigû is the most powerfully written of the many political novels that appeared in the early Meiji era, and its influence has been deep and wide. Even in the literary sphere it has affected later compositions in various ways. For instance, when Sanshi employed the word *Kajin* (a beauty) in his book, it was quite a novelty, but the word passed into the current language from this time. Still, what created the greatest impression on his readers were, first, his revelatory portrayal, accomplished with wide insight and understanding, of Japan's place in the international sphere, and, secondly, his ardent prophetic utterances, based on apt examples supplied by history, which brought about a general awakening among the Japanese people of their sense of a national destiny.

There were other political novels produced about the same time, which, although to a lesser degree, exercised great influence on the development of Japan, among which may be mentioned *Setchû-bai* (Plum Blossoms in the Snow) and *Kakan-ô* (The Nightingale among the Flowers) by Suehiro Tetchô, and *Shin Nippon* (New Japan) by Ozaki Yukio.

KONJIKI YASHA

(The Gold Demon)

Konjiki Yasha is a novel of monumental scope and proportions by Ozaki Kôyô (1867-1903) which was originally published as a serial in the *Yomiuri Shinbun*, the first instalment appearing during the month of January, 1897, after which instalments appeared with daily regularity over a period of six years until 1903, when the author's untimely death brought it to an abrupt close, without a dénouement. All this time it was widely appreciated, as it is still today much talked of as the most popular work of modern Japan, and is a subject for frequent adaptations both for the stage and the screen. The hero of the story is Hazama Kan'ichi, and Shigisawa Miya the heroine. Kan'ichi lost his mother in early childhood, and then, after some years of poverty and hardship, was bereaved of his father when still only fourteen years of age. Being thus left a homeless orphan, he was given a home by Miya's father, Shigisawa Ryûzô, who felt himself under an obligation to the boy's father for some act of kindness. He more than repaid this by looking after Kan'ichi for the next ten years. Not only did he see him through the middle school and the high school, but he promised to give him, on his graduation, his only daughter Miya in marriage and to make him his heir. Kan'ichi's feelings of deep gratitude to Ryûzô for his showing such great kindness to him had always caused him to try to repay him by the closest application to his studies, while his love for Miya was so great that he would not have hesitated to lay down his life for her. The prospect thus opened to him by Ryûzô caused him to look forward to a future with her with the most ardent hopes and expectations.

Miya was a girl of such surpassing beauty that, wherever she went, everyone admired her ; the professors at the musical academy she was attending, including even the principal himself, were all loud in their praises of her loveliness. Such universal admiration could scarcely have any other effect than arousing her vanity. So, although she was not unmindful of the love she and Kan'ichi had for each other, she could not resist the feeling that a girl so fascinating was bound to receive proposals of marriage from someone more handsome than he and, almost certainly, considerably richer. Although she had never clearly defined the matter in her own mind, money was proving to have a much greater appeal to her than love.

Then, exactly as she had imagined, the young and wealthy suitor appeared on the scene in the person of Tomiyama Tadatsugu, heir to the millions of the famous head of the Tomiyama Bank, and fresh from a tour of the world. He met Miya at a party and, falling in love with her at first sight, sent her a proposal of marriage. Thus, Miya had to come to a decision regarding her feelings for Kan'ichi. Torn between love and riches, she was at a loss which to choose, but finally her worship of the gold demon triumphed over the call of her heart and she decided to accept Tadatsugu. Her parents could not help feeling that this course would be to her happiness and comfort. Dazzled also by the prospect of such a wealthy son-in-law, they gave their consent. They were not, indeed, indifferent to the pledge they had already made to Kan'ichi, and greatly regretted having to disappoint him, but, for his daughter's sake, Miya's father earnestly entreated Kan'ichi to assent to breaking off his betrothal to her, promising him in return to finance his university education and also to send him abroad for further studies so as to afford him every opportunity of becoming an expert in his chosen field of study.

Kan'ichi was stunned by this unexpected blow. He was already under such a debt of gratitude to Ryûzô that he felt he ought not to refuse to accede to his wishes. But he could just as soon think of parting with life itself as parting from Miya. The only way to avert this calamity was, he felt, to see her and find out exactly what her real feelings were. Even though her parents, blinded by the allurement of great wealth, should, as he considered might well be the case, be trying to force her into marrying the millionaire playboy Tomiyama, they were not likely to succeed so long as she remained loyal to him, for, judging her love by his own, he believed that her feelings towards him could not possibly have changed.

So, in order to learn Miya's own ideas on the matter, Kan'ichi departed forthwith for Atami, the popular seaside hot-spring resort within two hours' ride of Tokyo, where she and her mother happened to be spending a few days. He took Miya out for a walk along the beach. It was an evening in mid-January, and there, with the full moon shedding its soft beams on the rippling sea, he besought her to tell him her true feelings. When she did so and he realized that she had transferred her affections to Tomiyama, indignation rose in his heart at this betrayal of his love. He warned her that by rejecting love and becoming the slave of riches she was inviting untold misery for the future. Tears of grief and indignation filling his eyes, he tried to convince her that love was infinitely more valuable than wealth, but in vain. He begged her to reconsider her decision, or—that evening's meeting must be their last.

"Oh where," he cried in his anguish, "where shall I be looking on that moon this same night a year from now! On this same night the year after! On this same night ten years hence! For the rest of my life will I bear in my heart the memory of this painful night. On this same night a year from now my tears will throw a veil of shadow across the face of the moon. And, when you see that shadow, remember that somewhere on this earth I shall be hating you and weeping as I am doing now this night!"

Miya could not help being deeply stirred; she threw herself on her knees and clung to him tightly, weeping frantically. But the worship of the gold demon had taken root in her soul and could not be eradicated. She had continued to hold on to the wild, ambiguous hope that, though loving Kan'ichi, she could still marry Tomiyama and enjoy material and social success. But the wish for such success was incompatible with Kan'ichi's love, and when at last he realized that all his pleading with her was futile, he vowed he would never see her again, and, freeing himself from the kneeling, clinging figure, left the spot in a rage.

This incident is the best-remembered by all readers of "The Gold Demon" and the most dramatic in the whole story.

From that moment Kan'ichi's character underwent a complete transformation. Leaving the house of his benefactor, Shigisawa, he obtained a situation as clerk to Wanibuchi Tadayuki, a money-lender notorious for his avarice, his deceitfulness and his cunning. He did this with a deliberate motive. Money, as he now bitterly saw it, was the one omnipotent force that rules mankind. He was determined therefore to amass a huge fortune and then, with the power thus obtained, wreak vengeance on Miya for her faithless desertion of him. And the business of money-lending seemed to him to offer the greatest possibilities for achieving his end. He did not realize how utterly senseless his whole scheme was, since wealth could do nothing to restore a love that had been desecrated, or return to him a maiden Miya. But so completely preoccupied was he with the one idea of revenge that he could think of nothing else. Nothing else mattered to him, so outraged had he been by Miya's treachery, so shaken to the very core of his being.

For four years he put his whole heart and soul into his chosen profession, using every means, no matter how foul, to squeeze the fruits of usury out of his unfortunate victims. During that time his once innocent and sympathetic nature became cruel and calculating, his gay and cheerful qualities gave way to a gloomy, obstinate savagery. Nor was he unaware of the change he had undergone; he deliberately cultivated a wanton ruthlessness and tyranny in the hope that it might appease the anger and disappointment that always rankled in his heart. Accordingly, when his master Wanibuchi was burned to death in his house through the act of an outraged debtor, he had no compunction about taking over the business and arousing an even deeper scorn and enmity from the people as a despicable "loan shark" than his base employer had done.

Miya, meanwhile, through her marriage with Tomiyama Tadatsugu, had at her command a huge fortune and was able to indulge herself in every sort of splendour and luxury that money makes possible. But that was all she gained; she obtained no inward satisfaction. True, her one object in marrying Tomiyama had been to live the sumptuous life that only the heir to millions could offer. She had no thought of her husband's affections, so long as her extravagant desires were amply satisfied. If he showered her with attentions, well and good; but, if he did not, then it was even better, since it left her free from the necessity of making any response. Then, the time came when she felt satiated with extravagance of living, and her husband's demonstrations of affection became an annoyance. Her thoughts turned to the past; she began to conjure up memories of her love for Kan'ichi, and felt a wistful longing that only grew more intense with the passing of the days.

Then, four years after their parting at Atami, at the house of a certain Viscount Tazumi, to which she and her husband had been invited, Miya came face to face with Kan'ichi who happened to be there on business. From that time her love for Kan'ichi waxed stronger and stronger, and she could not think of him without remorse for having betrayed his love. She realized that she was the cause of his having sunk to the level of a universally despised usurer, and an eager desire to entreat his forgiveness overwhelmed her. She poured forth all her feelings in a letter. But Kan'ichi tore it up without even opening it. Again and again she wrote to him, but all her letters went the way of the first, unread, torn to fragments and thrown into the waste-paper basket. Unable to endure his silence any longer, she actually went to see him in secret, but Kan'ichi, bitter hatred smouldering in his heart, would not give her a chance to utter one pleading word; after he had subjected her to the savage outpourings of his long-pent-up wrath, he forced her out of his house.

Prior to this Kan'ichi had become acquainted with a woman named Akagashi Mitsué, a money-lender like himself. She was a married woman, but that did not prevent her making advances to him. It did not matter that Kan'ichi detested her and avoided her as much as possible, even at times snubbing and humiliating her; she refused to be discouraged by such treatment and only persisted the more with her attentions. It so happened that, just at the time when Miya had gone to seek Kan'ichi's forgiveness, Mitsué came as usual to plague him with her amorous advances. The glance she had of Miya, younger and more beautiful than herself, evoked Mitsué's jealousy and made her even more persistent in pursuing him.

Later Kan'ichi was informed by his bosom friend, Arao Jôsuké, that Miya was anything but happy in her married life. A feeling of pity for her awoke within him, but he was yet far from being in the frame of mind to forgive her. Yet he brooded over her unhappiness and made himself miserable, while his dislike for Mitsué grew more and more intense. Then one day, just before dawn, he had a most vivid dream in which he saw Miya and Mitsué fighting for possession of him. Mitsué flashed out a short sword and attempted to stab Miya, only to be deprived of the weapon and have it turned against herself with fatal results. Then Miya next essayed to stab herself, but just before plunging it into her throat she turned to him and entreated him to assure her he had forgiven her. In the dream he let himself be persuaded, and they clung together for a moment in a passionate embrace. Suddenly, Miya thrust him aside and jumped over a precipice into the mountain stream below and killed herself. As he lifted her lifeless body in his arms, he was filled with an overpowering emotion which left him with the clear conviction that, out of respect for his beloved's remorse and suicide, he ought at once to change his manner of living, abandon the un-savoury business of money-lending and lead a decent human life with honour and dignity.

From the time of that vivid dream Kan'ichi found it possible to think of Miya with greater calm. Now when he received letters from her entreating his forgiveness, he no longer tore them up unread; he did at least read them through.

This is a brief outline of the plot of " The Gold Demon," so far as the author had taken it when he was cut off by death. As it stands, it is not clear how the spiritual changes in the leading characters would continue to develop. Yet one may hazard the conjecture that the author had envisaged some such course of events as that indicated in the dream episode.

From his youth until his death in 1903, the author, Ozaki Kôyô, was honoured as one of the leading novelists of the country. " The Gold Demon," by reason of its magnificent conception, its polished prose, and its value as a commentary on contemporary life and thought, is regarded as his greatest work.

The story brings out two important points. The leading theme of the novel is that in the struggle between love and the worship of money, love eventually proves the victor. Since the conclusion of the war with China (1894-5), Japan had rapidly become a capital-istic nation and the people worshippers of mammon, secure in the belief that money is the open-sesame to human happiness. Ozaki Kôyô, however, believed, and in this novel attempts to show, that, no matter how potent money appears to be, its power over human life is after all evanescent; while love, although apparently weak in comparison, possesses in actual fact the quality of permanence. The other important point to be mentioned is that, in the person of his heroine Miya, the author seeks to portray the modern woman of the Meiji era. In an age so strongly under the influence of mammon worship, it is hardly to be expected that women would not be affected. In the earlier, feudalistic days, when once a woman was married she usually reconciled herself to whatever disappointment she might meet with later, and thrust from her mind all thought of any former love. When Miya, after her temporary surrender to the dazzling allurements of riches, awakens to her folly, however, her thoughts return to her former lover and she remains faithful to him. In her the author suggests the mental agony, the introspection, the strength of character, of the women of the Meiji era. For that reason, "The Gold Demon" is valuable as an aid towards understanding, not only the general characteristics of the times in which it was written, but in particular a certain social phase of modern Japan.

ÔDA ROHAN
(1867—1947)

OZAKI KÔYÔ
(1867—1903)

GUCHI ICHIYÔ
(1872—1896)

IZUMI KYÔKA
(1873—1939)

GOJÛ NO TÔ

(The Pagoda)

The novel, *Gojû no Tô*, is not only the finest piece of work of the author, Kôda Rohan, but must be regarded as one of the most representative works of the Meiji era. Like so many other novels at that time it was first published serially in the daily newspaper, the *Kokkai*, in 1891-2, making a deep impression.

No specific reference is made in the novel to the period in which it is set, but from the form of the dialogue and the customs and manners presented one gathers that the scene is laid in the Edo period when the Tokugawa Shogunate was in power. The hero is a journeyman carpenter by the name of Jûbeé, the other important characters being Jûbeé's main antagonist, a master-builder named Kawagoé-no Genta; Seikichi, who is apprenticed to Genta; and Rôen Shônin, chief priest of the Kannô-ji temple of Yanaka in Edo.

Jûbeé was a particularly good carpenter. Not only was he skilful in using his tools, but he was quite capable of designing even a largish building in first-rate style. But he was lacking in practical initiative, and had such a stupid expression that he was nicknamed *Nossori* (Clumsy) by his fellow-workers who failed to realize his capacity. So it was his fate to have to waste his energies on simple little odd jobs that led nowhere, and in so doing he grew quite advanced in years.

Then it happened that Rôen Shônin of the Kannô-ji temple at Yanaka decided on the erection of a five-storied pagoda to serve as a sancturay for invoking those Buddhist tutelary deities who watch over the peace of the country and the tranquillity of its people, and he entrusted its building to Kawagoé-no Genta. So far as position went Genta was Jûbeé's superior, in fact he was his *oyakata* or boss. Since Genta was a really capable master-builder, he was fully aware of Jûbeé's skill as a carpenter, and had always treated him considerately. Yet not even he had any idea of Jûbeé's remarkable gifts as a builder and architect.

〔 379 〕

When Genta began to speak to Jûbeé about his plans for th erection of this pagoda, the journeyman experienced a great thril Now indeed, he felt, had come his opportunity to display his geniu and inscribe his name on the scroll of fame. Should he let thi chance slip by, he might never have one again. Yet, in order to tak advantage of it, he could scarcely help making an enemy of Gentæ to whom he was indebted for many past kindnesses. Like ever true Japanese he suffered tortures because of his profound sense c obligation, and when his wife reproached him for contemplatin; anything against Genta, he was on the verge of abandoning hi ambitious plan. Yet, try as he would, he could not prove traitc to his inspiration. So, in the end, he went directly to the priest Rôen Shônin, and urged him to entrust the work of erecting th pagoda to him. That aged churchman possessed a very great wis dom and understanding, and he could see from Jûbeé's words, hi whole attitude, and his ardent determination, that he was dealin, with a genius who had never yet been given the chance of provin; his worth. So he replied that, providing Genta could be persuade to agree to the proposal, he would be glad to let Jûbeé undertak the work.

Greatly encouraged by this, Jûbeé asked Genta to surrender th contract to him. Genta was utterly amazed at the suggestion for he had not the least confidence in the journeyman's ability t undertake so large a task on his own responsibility, while Seikich and his fellow apprentices resented it because they regarded it as ai attempt to do their master out of the job. Nevertheless, Gent was kind enough to listen to what Jûbeé had to say, and could nc help feeling pity for a man who harboured such a fanatical confidenc in his own abilities. He even offered to let Jûbeé become joint con tractor with himself, and, further, when the fervent carpenter refuse to accept any such compromise, he went so far as to yield up th principal rôle in the task to Jûbeé, himself to act merely as assistant Jûbeé was deeply touched by such great generosity, but he coul not bring himself to give any one a share in the work. Finally Genta agreed to give up the entire work to him, save that he wishe to be allowed at least to offer him advice based on his own wide experience and to make a few suggestions on fundamental point: But it was precisely here that Jûbeé had far greater confidence i himself than in Genta, and so he flatly rejected the proviso. This proved too much for Genta's magnanimity, and for the first time he showed himself really angry.

"Very well," he said, "have it your own way. But, mark this. If you fail, I'll see to it that you suffer the consequences."

Thus it was that the contract for building the five-storied pagoda fell into Jûbeé's hands. But so soon as he began the work he found himself beset with tremendous difficulties. In the designing, indeed, it was just as Jûbeé had foretold. He was able to draft the plans for a pagoda whose beauty and magnificence were equal to any edifice that had been erected by the master-builders of the past or present. But in order to give these plans concrete expression he had need of the labour of his former co-workers. They, however, regarded him as a madman and were often unwilling to follow his instructions. To make matters worse, Genta's apprentice, Seikichi, full of hatred for what he chose to regard as Jûbeé's treachery to his master, attacked him while he was at work and inflicted serious injuries on him. Nevertheless, Jûbeé managed to overcome all the troubles that befell him by dint of his dogged will and determination, and, in the end, he succeeded in erecting his magnificent structure. The author indulges in figurative language in describing (in Chapter XXXI) the grandeur of the pagoda. It was, he says, "like the form of the great god Indra rising on the top of a rock, body erect, to the massive height of some two hundred feet, with its feet stamping and its eyes sending forth thunderbolts as if upon a host of demons at bay."

Jûbeé felt that he had endured all that a man could possibly be called to endure in bringing this fine building to completion. But one great ordeal in the shape of Nature's fury had still to be suffered, for, on the day before the completion ceremony, a terrible storm swept the Edo district. Jûbeé was resolved to protect his beloved work of art even at the cost of his life. So he mounted to the topmost floor of the pagoda, and waged a silent battle against the raging storm throughout the night, determined that he would perish if so much as a single board or a single nail were torn away by the violence of the elements. For if the pagoda should show the least weakness anywhere, that would reflect on his skill as a builder; and, in face of what had happened between him and Genta, his conscience would no longer permit him to trouble the earth. But Nature's ordeal left him undefeated, for the pagoda passed through the storm un-scathed. And so, without any further untoward incident, the ceremony of dedication was duly performed by Rôen Shônin.

The storm, which the five-storied pagoda had so nobly withstood, had wrought heavy damage elsewhere; in fact, not one house or temple in Edo but had suffered. When this was realized, then all Jûbeé's former co-workers, and even Genta himself, acknowledged that now indeed it was clear that he was a real genius. The people of Edo also, when they heard about it, flocked in their hundreds of thousands to gaze on this new pagoda which alone had stood unscathed in the great storm, and, marvelling, paid their tributes to the achievement of this hitherto unknown master.

The central theme of this novel is the glorification of human genius and the power of man's will, together with the conviction that art is imperishable and immortal. When one considers the actual state of things in Japan at that time and the condition of its literature, one will the more easily understand why such a work as *Gojû no Tô* was greeted with so much approval by contemporary critics and the intelligentsia. For it appeared just in the midst of that critical period between 1887 and 1892 when Japan was essaying her first appearance on the world's stage. People had come to realize that, in such circumstances, constructive genius and industrial capacity were essential. Turning to the field of literature in particular, we find that the writers of the Meiji era up to that time had practically limited themselves to making translations and adaptations of European works. In the field of fiction there had been no original or creative activity. But the enlightening effect of Western fiction and the growing awareness of their country's literary traditions had by about the year 1887 begun to awaken Japanese writers to the possibilities of a greater independence and originality.

Tsubouchi Shôyô led the way in the realm of theory with his *Shôsetsu Shinzui* (Essentials of Fiction), and gave expression to the principles propounded in a number of novels. He was followed by a succession of new authors and new works, the most notable being: Futabatei Shimei, with his most modern of realistic novels, *Ukigumo* (Drifting Clouds), Yazaki Saganoya, with his *Hatsukoi* (Puppy Love), Yamada Bimyô, author of *Musashino* (The Plain of Musashi) and

Kochô (The Butterfly), Ozaki Kôyô, whose early period gave us *Iro Zangé* (Confession of Love), *Kyara Makura* (Pillow of Aloes), and *Sannin Zuma* (Three Wives), and Mori Ôgai, distinguished author of *Maihimé* (The Ballet Girl), *Fumizukai* (The Letter Carrier) and *Utakata no Ki* (The Record of a Bubble). It was a time when creative genius and fanatical devotion to art were hailed as of prime necessity, and it was precisely then that *Gojû no Tô* was published. It was most cordially accepted as giving clear and artistic expression to one aspect of that ideal which Japan in general and Japanese literature in particular were urgently demanding. When the critics and the intelligentsia acclaimed this novel, they were, in a word, greeting the artistic fulfilment of the ideal of young Japan.

One of the qualities that has given *Gojû no Tô* a permanent place in our literature is its prose style, with the splendour of its classical diction, its virile spirit and its exuberant poetic fancy and imagery. The description of the violent tempest, for example, has come to be admired as the finest piece of prose of that type in the fiction of the Meiji era. Also the character of Jûbeé, the hero of the story, is of a kind rarely found in Japanese literature previously. One critic has compared him with the hero of Ibsen's *Brand*, declaring that the author himself possessed a strain of the superman's philosophy of " all or nothing."

At the time when he wrote *Gojû no Tô*, the author was living near the Tennô-ji temple at Yanaka, which, like the temple in the novel, also boasts of an imposing five-storied pagoda, surviving to this day. It is said that the inspiration for his novel grew out of his gazing night and day at this pagoda from his study.

Rohan is the pen-name of Kôda Shigeyuki, who was born in July, 1867, at Kanda in the old city of Edo. His father, a samurai, was one of the officials of the Tokugawa Shogunate who were in charge of the ceremonies, receptions, inquiries and other duties. The family possessed an artistic heritage, for in his mother's veins flowed the blood of many artists. His two younger sisters, Kôda Nobuko and Andô Kôko, have also achieved artistic fame, in their case as musicians.

Born as he was just when Japan was in the throes of the Meiji Restoration and its birth as a modern nation, both the system and the methods of education available for the youthful Rohan were of the crudest sort. But Rohan, even as a boy, had a very strong determination and set himself to study the outstanding Chinese and Japanese classics as well as the ponderous tomes of Buddhist sutras. His earliest ambition, it would seem, was to become a historian or a scholar, but, to his great dissatisfaction, circumstances did not permit of his entering college. Partly to divert his mind from this moody restlessness and partly because he had no high opinion of the work of those authors who were then in the literary limelight, he began to write a novel, *Rodandan* (Round as a Dew-drop), a queer sort of love story in a vein of symbolism. It proved to be a success, and so he went on writing one novel after another. His *Fûryû-butsu* (Romantic Saint), *Isana-tori* (Whale-hunting), and *Hitofuri-ken* (The Superb Swordsman) were all well received as works of real merit; but it was with the publication of the *Gojû no Tô* that he came to be reckoned a first-class novelist. Along with Ozaki Kôyô, he was acclaimed as one of the most brilliant stars in the galaxy of modern talents.

His great contemporary Kôyô delighted in telling a love story and excelled in framing tragic plots and in the delineation of feminine psychology. Rohan, on the other hand, was at his best in portraying male characters and liked nothing better than to chant the praise of human resolution, while most of his stories contain elements of profound mystical and philosophical teaching. Unlike Kôyô's tragical conceptions, his plots are designed rather along the lines of that comic attitude to which Meredith has given special significance. Like Meredith, Rohan was persuaded that his duty as a novelist lay in remedying social evils through the medium of "thoughtful laughter." One of the things, however, at which those Europeans who are familiar with his works have especially marvelled is the dexterous manner in which he weaves profound Buddhist thought into his stories, this, indeed, being one of his distinctive qualities.

In 1887 he began to issue in serial form his work, *Fûryû Mijinzô* (Vignettes from Life : A Folio of Imaginary Portraits), which may be compared to Balzac's *Comédie Humaine*. After it had been running for a number of years, its publication was discontinued, and the story remains incomplete. Consisting of more than a dozen of individual portraits, it was an attempt to depict in the form of a novel a phase of the contemporary social history of Japan from the beginning of the Meiji era, a very bold undertaking indeed, and one that was greeted with great expectations by his readers as indicating, in some of the pieces especially, a change from Rohan the Romanticist to Rohan the Realist.

From 1897 his heyday as a novelist began to decline, and he came to concern himself more thereafter with scholarly research, his original passion which he had never lost. As the result of these studies he published a good many pieces in the form of miscellanies, which were likewise widely and appreciatively received.

The year before the outbreak of the Russo-Japanese War (1903) saw the publication of Rohan's final work as a novelist, *Sora Utsu Nami* (Raging Billows). But, with the outbreak of the war, there was a feeling among some of the leading intelligentsia that, at such a time of national strain and stress, it smacked of frivolity to be either writing or reading novels, and so Rohan voluntarily withdrew this novel from circulation. With this as the turning-point, Rohan's interest thereupon shifted from fiction to poetry. He planned a lengthy work under the title of *Kokoro no Ato* (The Trail of the Spirit), a narrative poem of a lyrical character, and published the first part of it which he called *Shutsuro* (Leaving the Hermitage). It received little consideration from the professional poets, but the general public received it very favourably.

Rohan's scholarly labours, which had extended over a long period of years, at last received official recognition by his appointment in 1908 as lecturer in Japanese literature at the Kyoto Imperial University and, later, by the award of a doctorate of literature by the same university.

In his later years his taste turned towards things historical, and he produced a series of historical novels. In this sphere he introduced a novelty of style, strikingly similar to the form of Andr Maurois's "biographical novel." One of these, *Unmei* (Destiny), treats of the tragic conflict occurring between the reigns of the second and third emperors of the Ming Dynasty of China, the story being laid out on a scale so magnificent as to constitute a unique achievement.

Rohan's many activities extended to the sphere of the drama, his work here being represented by *Nawa Nagatoshi** and several other

---

* Nawa Nagatoshi played a distinguished part under the Emperor Go-Daigo (1289-1319) in the struggle between the Court and the Ashikaga Clan which resulted in the founding of the Ashikaga Shogunate.

plays. His travel sketches also possess a special interest in that they reveal in a natural, unadorned state his character and point of view.

At the time of writing (October, 1941) Rohan enjoys excellent health and general respect as a veteran master of Japanese literature since its new awakening in the Meiji era. Two of his works have been translated into English, *The Pagoda*, which was translated by Sakaé Shioya in 1909, and *Leaving the Hermitage*, by Jirô Nagura in 1925.

KÔYA HIJIRI

(The Kôya Mendicant*)

Izumi Kyôka (1873-1939), the author of this novel, was the out-standing disciple of Ozaki Kôyô, the distinguished author of *Konjiki Yasha* (The Gold Demon). Kyôka's fi·st works of fiction were in the realistic style for which his master was noted, but later he adopted the mystical treatment peculiar to the Romantic school, in which he came to occupy a unique position among the writers of modern Japan. *Kôya Hijiri*, published in 1900, is a representative work in his later style.

The novel is presented in the form of a story of his youth which Shûchô, abbot of the Rikumin-ji temple on Mount Kôya, recounted to the author when the two happened to be lodged at the same inn in the course of a visit to the northern districts. Mount Kôya in the province of Kii is famous as the monastic retreat where the Buddhist priest Kûkai (better known by his posthumous name of Kôbô Daishi) founded the Shingon sect, and which has since become as sacred to that sect as Assisi to the Franciscans. Those monks who are sent out to preach throughout the country for the purpose of raising contributions are known as the *hijiri* of Mount Kôya. The tale deals with an episode in the early life of one of these.

One day in midsummer the monk Shûchô, then barely twenty years of age, set out from the province of Hida (Gifu prefecture) for the adjoining one of Shinano (Nagano prefecture). Since Hida is situated in the midst of the mountainous districts of central Japan, one could reach Shinano only by means of a precipitous mountain path through a thick forest. While following this trail the young monk lost his way, and found himself in a maze of densely growing trees and undergrowth where there was not the least sign of human

---

* *Hijiri* is literally "sage" ; the *hijri* of Mt Kôya were members of a mendicant order of itinerant evangelists, much the same as the Franciscan friars of the Middle Ages.

presence and where, even in broad daylight, the brooding blackness of night held sway. Only after surmounting great difficulties, cruelly bitten by innumerable leeches, was he able to grope his way about sunset towards a solitary house in the heart of the mountains.

In this house lived a beautiful young woman, apparently of about twenty-eight years of age, and her husband, a poor idiot scarcely capable of coherent speech or any rational activity, with a faithful old man-servant. The woman cast a sympathetic gaze on the exhausted figure of the young monk, and willingly acceded to his request to be allowed to pass the night there. She led him to a brook at the foot of a cliff behind the house to wash the stains of travel from his tired body and cleanse the sores which the blood-sucking leeches had made. Pouring the pure, refreshing waters of the mountain stream over his body, she washed him with a tender soothing touch. Being a monk, Shûchô had never previously come into such close contact with a woman, and the pleasure of having his body washed by this beautiful young woman gave him the sensation of being enveloped in a cloud of heavily scented petals. Then, to his astonishment, she proceeded to undress herself, revealing a dainty white body, smooth as glossy silk, and began to bathe in the clear waters of the brook. The moon was just appearing from behind the mountain range, and he felt something unearthly in the sight of her sublime form as she stood on a rock with the moonlight playing around her, dipping her hands now and then in the murmuring waters of the brook below.

Suddenly, from somewhere a tiny monkey appeared and leaped upon her bare shoulder.

" Little brute ! " she cried, " Can't you see I have a visitor ? " and struck the little creature gently on its head as it stole a look at her face from under her upraised arm.

Then a huge bat as large as a crow swooped down and hovered around waiting for a chance to alight on her also, while a mammoth toad crept up out of the shadows to leap playfully about her shapely feet. She spoke to each of these strange visitants in turn, reproving them, but in not unkindly tones.

Then she brought her guest back to the house, where they supped. After supper, the old man-servant brought out of the stable a spirited horse which he was to take in to the village market over the long night road.   As soon as the horse caught sight of the woman it stopped in its tracks ; no matter how hard the servant tugged at the reins, it refused to move forward.   Then the woman stepped down into the yard, and going up to the horse began to stroke its mane. Next, she undressed and, flinging her kimono over the horse's eyes, crept between its fore and hind legs and, face upward, swung to the opposite side.   She then retrieved her kimono and slipped it on, and the old servant, taking advantage of this moment, pulled again at the reins, and the horse started to trot briskly along.

The young monk, a witness of this strange rite, realized that the woman possessed some mysterious, occult power over these animals. Then, at midnight another remarkable incident occurred.   The whole household lay deep in slumber, utter stillness reigning in the woods around, when a loud commotion suddenly began to rage outside. Out of the confusion, individual sounds could be distinguished, the bleating of sheep, the noisy mooing of cows, and a furious fluttering, vaguely recognizable as the beating of the wings of some gigantic bird, while the sound of mincing steps approaching seemed to be those of some two-legged creature, wearing, it seemed, straw sandals. Then as if the house had become surrounded by a multitude of beasts, the weird chorus of snorts and howls and the thunderous flapping of wings rose louder and louder in a frightful, blood-curdling crescendo.   It was as if all the bestial horrors of hell were being enacted there, just outside the thin wooden door, in the pale light of the moon.

The young monk Shûchô, wide awake and rigid with fear and expectancy, lay holding his breath.   He could hear the woman in the next room moaning in her sleep as if under the oppression of a terrible nightmare.   She was talking in her sleep, and twice he heard her exclaim, in a stifled but authoritative tones, " Can't you under-stand, I have a guest here to-night ? "   And twice he heard her roll over on her bed.   The house, meanwhile, was violently shaken, as if quaking under the reverberations of the thunderous noise outside.   Making a desperate effort at concentration, Shûchô chanted a Buddhist incantation in a subdued voice, and soon afterwards the midnight air settled back to its former stillness.

When morning came, Shûchô brushed aside all the attempts of his hostess to detain him, and left the house, tramped down the mountain road and about noon arrived at the outskirts of a village. Then he realized that, although he had torn himself from the woman's presence with a feeling of great relief, he could not shake off the spell she had cast over him. He began to recall her great kindness to him throughout, how tenderly she had bathed his tired body in the running brook, and how she had exerted herself to make him comfortable though he had been a passing stranger seeking a night's shelter ; and as he thought of these things he could not resist the feeling that henceforth it would be dull indeed to continue as an itinerant monk and study for the priesthood. Even to wear the fine purple robes of an abbot and rule over a monastery now seemed to him to lack all attraction, compared with the happiness that might be his if he returned to the woman's house and spent the rest of his life with her ! He went slowly on his way, plagued with doubts and uncertainty, wondering if he could possibly decide to make so radical a break with his past.

At this point he met the old man-servant coming back from the village where he had gone the previous night to sell the horse. He entered into conversation with him and thus first learned the truth about the woman who had so charmed him.

She was the daughter of a physician who had formerly resided in a village at the foot of the mountain. Thirteen years earlier a youth had been brought to her father's surgery for an operation. The sight of his suffering had awakend her sympathy, and she did all she could to comfort him. But while performing a delicate operation her father had made a grave blunder, as a result of which the youth had become a cripple and idiot. Partly out of compassion and partly from a desire to do something to make amends for the blunder of her father, the girl had married the youth and had gone to live with him in that solitary house on the mountain.

For thirteen years she had lived apart from the community, but, in its stead, she had acquired a strange occult power over men, making them her slaves as long as she willed, and then, when she was tired of them, by a magic spell transforming them into beasts.

Such was the true character of the woman as revealed by the old man-servant. The horse, he said, which he had led from the stable the night before was one of those who had been enamoured of her and then transformed into his present shape. The young monk, thus illuminated, recalled with horror the strange incidents at the brook and the terrible midnight commotion. He thought of that poor little monkey, the huge bat that had hovered around her, and also the clamorous cries of the sheep and cattle and other creatures that had surrounded her house in the ghostly moonlight, and he shuddered to think of the fate that might have been in store for him. Now he realized how foolish, how shameful and terrible it had been for him to have felt the lure to return to such an enchantress. Greatly shaken in spirit, he hastened to resume his way to the village before him.

This brief summary of *Kôya Hijiri* may, perhaps, suggest something of the weird, but also mystical and supernatural, quality of the novel. Such scenes as that where the beautiful sorceress, naked in the moonlight, lingers by the banks of the secluded mountain stream, with all manner of beasts hovering about her, are rendered with a wealth of picturesque effect, giving the story a truly artistic charm.

But its chief significance lies in its symbolic rendering of human passion. The transformation of those who pursue the sorceress with their desires into various animals is clearly intended to show the bestial nature of such men's sexual attitude towards women. On the other hand, the sorceress's nightmare sufferings as she is nightly surrounded by clamouring beasts suggest that, although she has triumphantly exerted her power over them, her conscience is tormented by the realization of her own sin in having by her charms brought them to such bestial degeneracy.

And the young monk himself stands for the type of human being who has succeeded in escaping from the hell of passion into which these others have fallen.

For these reasons *Kôya Hijiri* merits particular consideration as an important work in the symbolist literature of modern Japan.

TAKÉ KURABÉ

(Comparing Heights)

Také Kurabé, published in 1896, is the work of (Miss) Higuchi Ichiyô (1872-1896), who died at the early age of twenty-four. Yet the work she had done in that brief spell of life was such that she ranks with Lady Murasaki, the writer of Japan's classical masterpiece, *Genji Monogatari* (The Tale of Genji). In particular, this present work is regarded as one of the finest novels of the Meiji era (1868-1911).

In the north-eastern corner of Tokyo lies the district known as the Yoshiwara, the chief pleasure-centre of the city since the early days of the Tokugawa Shogunate. The fair denizens of this quarter are the *yûjo* or *oiran*, whose name can best be rendered as "courtesan" or the Greek "hetaira," and who, since the central purpose of the quarter is pleasure, are here treated with extraordinarily high respect. This class of women, certainly their higher types, presented during the feudal régime a very special quality of feminine culture, a culture which to a diminishing degree still lingered on in the Yoshiwara during the Meiji era up to the time when the author of *Také Kurabé* was living.

At the entrance to the Yoshiwara stood the Ômon, the Great Gate, passing through which one came upon a world apart, a world of other standards and a different spirit. There men and women indulged in merry-making to the music of the *samisen* and the light rhythm of drums. It was a world of pleasure-seeking and promiscuous love-making, which had produced its own peculiar attitude of mind. This spirit was expressed in the vernacular by the words *hari* and *ikiji*, which signify a kind of vanity and pride in emulation, a headstrong refusal to accept defeat in any form, and a desire to avoid at all costs incurring the contempt of others. In many cases, this spirit assumed the form of taking pride in helping the weak and crushing the strong. It was this spirit, with its complexity of motives and impulsions, that set the standard in the Yoshiwara. Moreover, it was an infectious spirit, for, not only within the confines of this district, but also in the surrounding districts, great store came to be set by *hari* and *ikiji*.

Také Kurabé, set in this milieu, depicts the attachments, the calf-love, of the boys and girls living in a street called Daionjimaé, at the entrance to the Yoshiwara. The leading characters are a four-teen-year-old girl named Midori, brought up at a house of courtesans called Daikokuya, Shinnyo, a youth of fifteen in the service of the Ryûgé-ji Temple, and Shôtarô, aged thirteen, of the firm of Tanakaya.

Midori's elder sister Ômaki happened to be the reigning beauty of Daikokuya, and through her Midori was able to secure the finery in which to deck herself and provoke the assiduous attentions of all those in her little world. Also, having money to spend freely, she was able to buy presents, such as sets of coloured rubber balls, sometimes even dolls and larger toys, for her twenty girl-classmates at school, and in consequence she was regarded as a queen among them, and herself assumed queenly airs. She was naturally stub-born, and this inevitably made her haughty and self-centred. She was also on remarkably easy and friendly terms with the boys of the neighbourhood, whom she scarcely regarded as being of a different sex. Doubtless, the peculiar environment in which she was brought up was largely responsible for this aspect of her character. It was an environment in which courtesans were dominant and the object of general admiration, among women just as much as men. The great prospects open to a girl who entered that profession, with its possibilities of love affairs and even marriage with men of wealth and high position, caused the dwellers in the environs of the Yoshi-wara to regard with envy the parents of pretty daughters who might some day become courtesans. Accordingly, reared in such an at-mosphere, Midori had no fear of men, nor any aversion to the profession of prostitute, but confidently went her own wilful way.

The boy Shôtarô possessed a fair complexion and great charm of manner. His mother had died when he was very young, and his father had returned to live in his ancestoral home in a distant prov-ince, so that the boy had been left to be brought up by his ma-ternal grandmother. Lacking proper control, he too was of the wilful sort, especially since he came of a family connected with the money-lending business and always had plenty of money at his disposal. Spending this liberally among his boy companions, he was accepted by them as their leader.

Shinnyo was of a different type. He was the adopted heir of the Abbot of Ryûgé-ji temple, and was a thoughtful and discreet boy, very fond of study. Conscious of the fact that some day he would succeed to a dignified ecclesiastical office, he was wont to assume a somewhat aloof attitude. Both he and Shôtarô were devoted to the girl Midori, although Midori herself, at least in the beginning, had no feeling towards either of them that could be described as love. She regarded them simply as friends.

After a while Shinnyo began to avoid the girl more and more, as his friends were whispering among themselves that he was hoping to marry her some day. Not that he objected to this. Indeed, he was secretly elated, but, from bashfulness, he found himself affecting an air of indifference so as to conceal his love. But Midori, still a girl, could not understand the true meaning of the barrier he was setting up between them; her proud and sensitive spirit took offence at his attitude, and the more aloof he showed himself the greater was her resentment.

This was then the situation at the time of the festival of the Senzoku shrine on the night of August 20th. This festival was one of the gay annual celebrations held in the district, and it was always the occasion for rivalry between two troups of young people, the Main Street group and the Side Street group, who vied with each other in decorating their streets with elaborate festoons. The Main Street group was fortunate in having many boys of well-to-do families, and so, having much more money to spend, was invariably successful in these competitions. Shôtarô was the leader of the Main Street group, and therefore was the chief object of the hatred of the Side Street boys, smarting under the sting of defeat.

The leader of the Side Street group was a boy named Chôkichi, who had a great respect for the more reserved Shinnyo of the Ryûgé-ji temple. So this year he asked him to become a supporter of his group. Shinnyo did not like this sort of rivalry and had always avoided taking any part in it, but, in the circumstances, he felt it would be hardly manly to refuse. Moreover, he also disliked the way in which the Main Street boys vaunted their superiority.

Once again, the Side Street group was defeated in the competition. Chôkichi, too hot-headed to bear this defeat, determined to vent his anger on Shôtarô, and so, having rallied his companions, he led them to the place where the Main Street group was gathered together. But Shôtarô was not there, and the Side Street boys, looking for someone on whom to have vengeance, seized hold of a boy named Sangorô and beat him up.

Midori, who happened to be there at the time, could not bear to stand by and see the helpless boy treated in this fashion. She dashed to his defence and abused his maltreators roundly for their brutality. But they, so far from feeling ashamed of what they had done, even turned on her, calling her insulting names and even flinging an old straw sandal at her, which cut her face slightly. The proud and masterful Midori resented this bitterly. She had always been accustomed to the respect and attentions of those around her, and had never thought it possible that she would be insulted by a young rough like Chôkichi, for whom she had nothing but contempt. She jumped to the conclusion that Shinnyo was responsible for what had happened, not indeed openly, but manoeuvring the whole cowardly affair from behind the scenes; whereas Shinnyo knew nothing whatever about it. Midori became more indignant than ever with Shinnyo after this, and at the same time she grew much more friendly and intimate with Shôtarô.

Yet, despite herself, Midori's feelings underwent a change. It was because of her headstrong refusal to suffer a slight and her native pride and vanity, together with her complete unconsciousness of sex in her dealings with these boys, that she had at first resented the apparent cooling off of Shinnyo's friendship. But as the woman in her developed, her affection for Shinnyo grew in spite of herself, although her indignation still remained. Meanwhile Shinnyo, although he now avoided her even more assiduously than before, had become increasingly fond of her. Despite the growth of this mutual affection, it remained unspoken on both sides; but Midori, all the same, ceased associating with Shôtarô and kept more closely to her home.

In due course, at the end of that year, it was decided that Shinnyo should enter a Buddhist college and assume the robe of a priest. This meant that he would have to renounce all worldly love. So, one day, he secretly left a single spray of artificial narcissus within the gate of Midori's house as his final gift to his love. Midori found it and, although it never occurred to her that the flower might have come from Shinnyo, she picked it up. Placing it in a vase she gazed on it contemplatively. How lonely it seemed, and yet how neatly, cleverly made !

The reader may, and not without reason, judge the plot of *Také Kurabé* to be somewhat trite. But the plot is the least part of it, for the author has concentrated her main efforts on the delineation of the character of these young boys and girls, their feelings and ways of thinking, and with remarkable success, especially in her portrayal of the character of her heroine. The development of Midori's headstrong pride and vanity, shaped as it is by her environment and becoming still more pronounced as she grows older, is drawn with minutely delicate care. So also is her gradual transformation from a tomboy in easy comradeship with boys to the young woman conscious of her sex, and now in characteristically feminine fashion showing herself gentle and meek. Throughout her mental processes, every nuance of her thoughts in all their varied changes, as she is confronted continually with new situations that tax her emotions, is described with grace and skill. It is in this that Higuchi Ichiyô is without a peer among Japan's modern novelists, and in this that the most distinctive feature of her work lies.

Another quality that lends distinction to her work is that the charm of the story is heightened by a pervading sense of pathos. Not only in *Také Kurabé* but in all her works is this quality to be found. For she tends to regard all human relations as peculiarly transitory and solitary. This gives her writing a note of tender lyricism, derived in the main from the pessimism that accompanies a fatalistic outlook on life. Among European writers of a similar tendency Turgeniev seems to be her closest counterpart. It is probable that this attitude to life was shaped by her own circumstances, for Higuchi Ichiyô was herself brought up in poverty, endured great hardships in gaining a livelihood, and came perforce to regard human existence as essentially sad and lonely.

A third distinctive quality of the novel lies in its revelation of interesting manners and customs of its age. This quality might be regarded as extraneous, or at least merely incidental, to the consideration of the novel as a work of art but for the skill and realism with which the revelation is made. The tale is set in the gay Yoshiwara and its environs, whose peculiarities of speech, dress, habits and way of life are a purely local manifestation to be found nowhere else but in the Yoshiwara in the middle of the Meiji era, that is, from about 1887 to 1896. And it is only the fact that the author once lived there in the street called Daionjimaé, which makes possible such a presentation as she has given. She drew all her portraits from life, the three chief characters, Midori, Shinnyo and Shôtarô, it is said, having their living counterparts. Her novel bears the stamp of authenticity and certainly provides excellent material for understanding the manners and customs of a very distinctive district of Tokyo at a certain time. For these reasons, *Také Kurabé* has won a secure place among the masterpieces of modern Japanese literature.

JŪSAN'YA

(The Thirteenth Night)

Jûsan'ya is also from the pen of (Miss) Higuchi Ichiyô, being published in 1896, the same year as *Také Kurabé*. The stories rank equally high, but their subject-matter differs greatly. Whereas *Také Kurabé* is concerned with the loves and attachments among boys and girls brought up in the singular environment of the Yoshiwara and its neighbourhood, *Jûsan'ya* portrays the tragedy of married life in an ordinary, respectable home of about the same period, between 1887-98.

The story falls into two parts. The first part tells us the story of the heroine's unhappy married life with her husband. Her name was Oseki, and although she was of very humble parentage, her beauty so attracted the fancy of a high government official, named Harada Isamu, that he married her in the spring of her seventeenth year. Her parents were naturally elated and took the greatest pride in their daughter's highly successful marriage, while her younger brother, thanks to Harada's influence, was able to obtain a good situation in a government office. The attitude of Oseki's whole family towards her husband was one of profound gratitude. Unfortunately, however, Oseki's married life was not as happy as her parents and brother supposed. She was a faithful and dutiful wife to Harada for seven years, and was the mother of a boy of six, and yet, for some unaccountable reason, he always treated her with great cruelty and made her life one long misery. Nevertheless, to the members of her family she appeared throughout only in the guise of a most dutiful wife, a true example of this country's ideal wife and mother. She said not a word of her husband's continual maltreatment, for she knew that if she were to tell her parents it would only cause them grief and anxiety.

Yet, in spite of all her unselfish intentions, the breaking point arrived when Oseki felt she could no longer endure her husband's cruelties. One night she went to her parents' home, and, with the tears streaming from her eyes, she revealed to them the tragic circumstances of her life with Harada.

"During the first six months of our married life," she said, " my husband treated me kindly enough. It was from the time our child was born that he became an altogether different person. The mere thought of his cruelty to me makes me shudder. I felt as if I had been cast into a horrible valley of darkness, where not a single ray of light could ever break through. When he first began to abuse me I could only suppose that he was doing it in jest, but I soon learnt that he was in deadly earnest and that he had ceased to love me. The very deliberation of his cruelty and the many different forms it took has convinced me that he was hoping to break my spirit in the end so that I should leave him of my own accord."

Then, feeling that she must justify her own conduct to her parents, she continued,

"I am not the sort to get jealous if my husband should have an affair with a geisha or keep a mistress. That is often the way with men, especially with a vigorous man like my husband. Truly, I did not permit it to worry me very much when I learnt that he was keeping a mistress. Whenever he goes out, to see no matter whom, I always help him to get ready, trying to avoid giving him any cause of offence whatever. Yet he finds fault with everything I do. If he had had the decency to point out where I was wrong, I might have been able to correct my errors. Instead, he claims that everything I do is wrong, and that the unpleasant state of things in our home is all due to my wrong attitude and behaviour. The truth is that he has not the least affection for me, and is nothing but a cruel and heartless brute."

Oseki's father had not been able to listen unmoved to his daughter's sad tale. Still, he saw clearly that, if she were to secure a divorce from her husband, she would have to give up what was after all a fine life, at least, materially and socially, and spend the rest of her days sharing the poverty of her parents. So he pointed out to her the many advantages of her situation, despite all her trials, hoping in this way to dissuade her from taking the drastic step she contemplated. "One sees many elegant ladies," he said, " who outwardly appear to be quite happy and contented. They are not always so. You feel bitter about your own case because you think that you are the only woman who is suffering. It would be much wiser for you to take it all philosophically as part of a woman's lot in life."

Then he went on to remind her that her brother was under a great obligation to her husband. "I know how trying it must be for you, but you are doing this partly for your parents' sake, and partly also for your brother's. Besides you must think of your child. You have stood it all this time, so I am sure that you will still be able to continue to bear it." Finally, with all a father's sympathy, he said to her, "Alas, whichever way you go, there will be tears for you, and I prefer, therefore, that you weep your tears bravely as the wife of Harada. We all understand what you are suffering, your father, your mother, and your brother, and we shall all share it and weep with you."

Oseki had come to her father firmly resolved to secure a divorce at all costs, but the sympathetic exhortation of her father moved her so much that she resigned herself to her fate.

"I realize now," she said, "that it was indeed selfish of me to want to leave my husband. If I had only repressed my own feelings, things would perhaps have gone much more smoothly. I am sorry that my thoughtlessness should have been a worry to my father and mother."

In this repentant mood she set out disconsolately to return to her husband's house.

The second part begins with Oseki's unexpected encounter on her way home with her former sweetheart, now a rickshaw man.

As she stepped out of her parents' house Oseki hailed a passing rickshaw, but it had taken her only as far as a lonely spot in Ueno Park, when it was suddenly halted, and the rickshaw man bade her dismount, saying that he would not want any fare for the ride so far. Oseki, amazed, reproached him for wishing to leave her stranded in such an isolated spot at night. But the man only replied that he had developed a sudden distaste for pulling a rickshaw, and told her to get down. Oseki begged him to keep on, at least, until they met another rickshaw to which she could transfer. At last, the man seemed to realize that he had been unreasonable in trying to force her to dismount at such an unlikely place and resumed his way with a muttered apology.

But, during the argument Oseki had happened to catch a good look at his profile, and it struck her that he was not unlike the friend of her girlhood, Kôsaka Rokunosuké, for whom she had once entertained a tender feeling. " Aren't you. . . . ? " she exclaimed, forgetting herself. Then, as the man turned round in surprise and looked her full in the face, she could see his features distinctly. There was no mistake about it, and she slid out of the rickshaw. The man now recognized her, and was greatly embarrassed and ashamed to have been discovered as having fallen so low as to become a rickshaw man.

This Rokunosuké was the only son of the proprietor of a smart little tobacco shop near where Oseki used to live. As a youth he had been regarded as an agreeable and intelligent fellow; he and Oseki had really been child-sweethearts, though neither had ever breathed a word of it to the other. When Oseki, under her parents' direction, had married Harada, Rokunosuké had been so bitterly disappointed that it had changed his whole life. He had fallen into evil company, and not even when his anxious mother had found a bride for him in the hope that marriage might induce him to settle down, did he make the least change for the better.

He went from bad to worse until het was completely ruined; his family was broken up, his wife returning to her own parents, his mother to relatives in the country. He fell so low as to become a rickshaw man, living in a room on the second floor of a poor lodging-house. He passed his days in a world that looked utterly black to him; he had lost all ambition and did not care how he lived. Sometimes, when the mood was on him, he would go out and pull a rickshaw; more often he would idle away his time in his cheap upstairs room for days on end. A fit of melancholy would sometimes seize him even in the middle of a job, and then he would suddenly hate what he was doing and would turn round to his passenger, bidding him alight and refusing any fare. He had in truth lost all interest in life, and just went on hopelessly and drearily from day to day. To that extent had his disappointment over Oseki's marrying someone else broken his heart.

When Oseki saw his condition, she was able to realize how great must have been his disappointment. Rokunosuké began to apologize for having tried to force her to alight, and now invited her to get in again and let him take her to her destination. But this she declined to do, preferring to walk with him for a while. So they strolled about the park side by side, exchanging reminiscences of their childhood days. Oseki felt a deep compassion for this once happy and vigorous youth now changed for love of her into a gloomy and shiftless rickshaw man. At last they reached the gateway of the park, beyond which lay the gay quarter of the city. There they parted, the one turning to the right, the other to the left, she to resume her unhappy life with her brutal husband, he to the desolation of his poor upstairs room.

As it happened, the night on which the heroine and her fallen lover had so strangely met was the night of the thirteenth of September, the night of the moon-viewing, an annual festival which has been observed in this country from the most ancient times. It is from this that the story receives its title of *Jûsan'ya*, "The Thirteenth Night."

The novel possesses two outstanding features. One is a characteristic that it shares with *Také Kurabé* by the same author, the sense of pathos that pervades the whole work. The case of the man who loses all ambition because of his disappointment in a love affair of his boyhood and drifts into a wretched aimless life in a poverty-stricken little lodging-house is pathetic enough. But equally pathetic is the fate of the girl he had loved, married to the high official Harada, surrounded by every material comfort, with every outward sign of happiness, and yet the victim of a most unhappy marriage, suffering a bitter inward grief. All is expressive of the author's pessimistic view that human life must by its very nature be a sad and pitiful thing.

The other outstanding feature is, perhaps, more important. It is that the heroine of the present novel is a perfect example of the enduring patience of the women of Japan. Her own inclination is to leave her brutal husband, but in changing her mind and deciding to go back once more to the maltreatment that awaits her, or the admonition of her father, she embodies to a very high degree the quality of fortitude characteristic of the Japanese woman. The women of the feudal age, mainly under the influence of the spirit of Bushido, were schooled in the virtue of absolute submission to their husbands, and as a result cultivated a high degree of fortitude, which, by inheritance, still forms an outstanding trait of the Japanese woman of today. Nor is this a quality to be found in the women alone, although there it is most definitely emphasized and developed ; it may be taken as a national characteristic of the Japanese generally. For the cultural development of the race owes much to its capacity of age-long perseverance.

MAIHIMÉ

(The Ballet Girl)

Mori Ôgai, the author of this short story, was a man of remarkable versatility. Born the son of a physician, he was educated for the same profession, and rendered great services to the government in that capacity, making some important contributions to medical science. But, although he did not specialize in literature, he had a natural bent for authorship, and his literary output is of such high quality as to place him among the foremost of modern novelists in this country. He was not only well read in European literature, but was also conversant with Japanese and Chinese classics. Indeed, his talents and interests seem to have been as varied as some of the great figures of the Renaissance. German culture in particular appealed to him, and there his interest went far beyond the bounds of literature to include drama and painting, in which he showed discrimination and taste of a high order. Those who were best acquainted with his wide range of gifts often referred to him as " the Goethe of Japan," and certainly in the matter of versatility he bore a close resemblance to the sage of Weimar. He himself, it would appear, actually set out to emulate Goethe for whom he had an unbounded admiration.

He was born in January, 1863, at Tsuwano-machi in the province of Iwami, now part of Shimané prefecture, his family being in the service of the lord of Tsuwano in the capacity of hereditary physicians. From all accounts, there was nothing at all remarkable in either his father or his mother, but Ôgai, even as a little child, revealed himself a prodigy. At five he entered the school founded by Lord Tsuwano, where he studied the Chinese classics and also Dutch, which was then the only European language that Japanese in the provinces had any opportunity of learning. Then in 1872 he set out for Tokyo with his father. Already at this early age Ôgai had shown his talent for literature, and he would almost certainly have decided to study literature, had he been allowed to follow his own inclination, but, as the profession of medicine was a family heritage, his father felt that he owed it to his ancestors to educate the boy as a physician in order to carry on the tradition.

After having acquired a thorough grounding in the German language, Ôgai next year entered the Medical College, where he graduated in 1881. He was only nineteen years old at the time, and although in Europe or America to graduate at nineteen or thereabouts may not be a rare feat, it was, especially under the educational system of those days, remarkable in Japan, where, even for a brilliant student, it was next to impossible to graduate until at least twenty.

Immediately upon graduation Ôgai became a member of the Army Medical Bureau, where he devoted all his efforts, by the order of the authorities, to a study of the system of hygiene practised in the Prussian army. Sent to Germany to make an exclusive study of hygiene, in order that he might become an expert on this subject, he carried on his studies for five years, from 1884 to 1888, at Leipzig, D esden, Munich and Berlin under such famous scholars as August W. von Hofmann, Max von Pettenkofer and Robert Koch. But his thirst for knowledge could not be limited to the study of hygiene, and so he enlarged the field of his studies to include as much of literature, philosophy, drama and painting as his time and means permitted. The result was that his five years in Germany enabled him to round off his studies, not only as a medical scientist but also as a man of letters. Both in literature and philosophy he had made himself familiar with the most recent work and thought of nineteenth-century Europe and thus acquired those elements essential to culture which were lacking in the realm of letters in his country at that time.

It was during just those five years of Ôgai's sojourn abroad that the literature of Japan had begun to take on anything of a modern form. In 1885, only a year after he had departed for Germany, there occurred a memorable event in the development of Japanese literature, the publication of Tsubouchi Shôyô's *Shôsetsu Shinzui* (The Essentials of Fiction), the most lucid, the most daring, the most powerful, demand for a revolution in Japanese fiction that had stirred the Meiji literary world. It rejected those romances which had extolled the morality of the samurai class with the glamour of romantic imagination, and proclaimed instead the need for a new type of novel based on realistic presentation. Nor was Tsubouchi satisfied with theorizing on the reform of fiction, but, by way of practical demonstration, he published his *Tôsei Shosei Katagi* (Scenes from Modern Student Life), written on the lines that he declared the modern novel ought to follow. Stimulated by his argument and example, the literature of Japan started on a new modern trend, as is evidenced by the writing of *Ukigumo* (Drifting Clouds) by Futabatei Shimei and other works referred to in the chapter on *Gojû no Tô* (pp 382-3). Such writers as Ozaki Kôyô and Kôda Rohan, however, who were destined to follow Tsubouchi as the leading literary figures of the age to come, were only just beginning to write and had not yet revealed their real power. Thus it happened that, just at the time when the minds of contemporary intellectuals, spurred by the revolutionary views of Tsubouchi, were at the very height of their quest for something new and still more new, Ôgai returned to Japan, bringing with him a wealth of knowledge and appreciation of the most recent Continental, especially German, literature. It was, therefore, only natural that the rôle of critic and guide of the new literary movement should be thrust upon him, although he himself had never sought such a rôle. But having once accepted the responsibility, he acquitted himself valiantly, as was shown, for example, by his editorship of the critical review *Shigarami-Sôshi* (Wattling Magazine). But Tsubouchi had built up most of his arguments on the basis of the traditions of English literature prior to the nineteenth century, whereas Ogai's sphere of knowledge and interests was markedly different from this. Consequently, after the publication of Ôgai's literary dicta, a controversy arose between the two leaders regarding the essential elements of fiction. For about half a year, 1891-92, they argued in the main around the question whether a novel should be essentially subjective or objective, and ended without reaching a final decision. One thing, however, became quite clear, that the logic of circumstances was forcing Tsubouchi to yield his position as leading critic to his encyclopaedic opponent. One great benefit which had its origin in this literary feud between two such able men was that it deepened the knowledge of those engaged in literature and had an epoch-making effect upon the progress of modern Japanese fiction.

Apart from giving literary criticism the benefit of his erudition, Ôgai also translated into Japanese a large number of European novels, plays and poems, which he intended to serve as working models for elevating the standard of creative literature in his own country. But the plenitude of his natural endowments finally led him to enter into the sphere of creative literature itself. In quick succession Ôgai published three short stories, *Maihimé* (The Ballet Girl), *Fumizukai* (The Letter Carrier), and *Utakata no Ki* (The Record of a bubble), all based on material and experience accumulated during his long residence in Germany, and these three stories alone would have been enough to give him immortality in the world of letters.

Maihimé (The Ballet Girl), whose publication created quite a sensation, appeared in the January 1890 issue of the *Kokumin no Tomo* (The Nation's Friend), then the foremost critical magazine edited by the famous journalist Tokutomi Sohô.

Its main theme is the tragic love affair between Ôta Toyotarô, a Japanese engaged in research work abroad, and a German-born ballet-dancer named Alice, with Berlin as the setting. It is told in the first person, and is in the form of a record of happenings which Ôta tearfully recalls and sets down on paper on board the ship which is bearing him back to Japan.

Although the hero Ôta is not an exact likeness of the author himself, there is a very close resemblance between the two. Ôta is presented as brilliant from childhood, as graduating from college at nineteen, and then immediately entering a government office. In these respects he is an exact portrayal of Ôgai, and the respects in which he differs are, on the whole, trifling—the author specialized in medical science, while the hero of the story has taken up jurisprudence; and, again, while Ôgai went to Germany to study hygiene, the hero is sent to study various systems of government.

Before going to Germany, Ôta had been a man of petty ambitions, his two great aims in life being to achieve the ordinary routine success of a bureaucrat and to assure to his widowed mother a comfortable old age. Life in Germany, however, hastened the release of a new sense of "self" that had so far been dormant. His chief in the Home Office had encouraged him to become a law machine, a facile expert with all the ramifications of his subject at his fingers' ends, who would be able to meet all the demands of the authorities with clocklike precision. And until yesterday, so to speak, he had looked at the matter exactly in that way, quite content to become the tool of bureaucracy. But the longer he savoured the life of Germany, the less did he fancy a destiny as a mere cog in a machine. Against the express wishes and requirements of his chief he began to explore avenues that would enlarge his mind and experience. His mind, indeed, had broken through the trammels of bureaucracy and was demanding freedom. At last, his reports to the Home Office began to prove unsatisfactory, and malicious statements regarding Ôta's conduct abroad also reached his chief. These were to the effect that the young man kept himself aloof from his fellow-countrymen in Berlin, and that, although he put on airs of smug respectability, he was clandestinely associating on intimate terms with German girl of questionable character. Actually, these slanderous inuendoes were almost entirely prompted by jealousy. Certainly Ôta was rarely in the company of his fellow-countrymen, but that was not because he was proud or haughty, but because he had no liking for the sort of life they led. Nor was he a man of sufficient hypocrisy to lead a secret licentious life. That slander was completely unjustified. And when they spoke of a girl of " questionable character," his defamers were putting an altogether wrong construction on his relations with Alice, the ballet girl. Alice was a girl of great beauty which was well matched by the purity of her soul. It was her mother whose character was " questionable " in that she was quite ready to profit from her daughter's beauty since it enabled her to lead an idle and luxurious life. She had often brought Alice to the very depths of despair, and it was when she had been driven to the last extremity that Ôta had saved her. He had come upon the girl in her sad predicament quite by chance, but the circumstances were such as would bring about an attachment. This very quickly ripened into a genuine love for each other, which, however, was only misinterpreted and became food for scandal among Ôta's jealous fellow-countrymen.

Unfortunately, Ôta's chief believed the scandal and discharged him from the government service. Driven to choose between returning home and being loyal to Alice, Ôta was at last won over by Alice's love, and decided to stay on in Berlin. He lived with her, earning a living by acting as foreign correspondent for Japanese newspapers. The report of his mother's death reached him and was a great grief to him, but this new life of freedom, for which his spirit had been unconsciously yearning for years, sufficed to restore his composure. Moreover, he was expecting to become a father, and this made him doubly happy.

About this time a Japanese Cabinet Minister, Count Amakata, arrived at Berlin, and among his entourage was a friend of Ôta's named Aizawa Kenkichi. Aizawa felt it a pity that a man of Ôta's intellectual calibre should be left neglected in a foreign land, and recommended him strongly to Count Amakata, who arranged for Ôta to undertake a number of studies and researches. Ôta, grateful for his friend's kindly assistance, did all he could to aid the Minister in translating various documents and correspondence and in accompanying the statesman to Russia as interpreter. Count Amakata could not help recognizing the young man's ability and, like Aizawa, became convinced that his talents could be more usefully employed at home.

Although Ôta had both ability and sagacity, he was not a man of iron determination. He now found himself wavering between two irreconcilable courses ; he did not desire to part from Alice, and yet he promised both Count Amakata and his friend Aizawa that he would accompany them to Japan. When, at last, the time came when he must break the sad news to Alice that he must leave her, he passed such a terrible night, going through such excruciating mental agony that he could not endure it and fainted away.

While he lay in bed delirious, his friend Aizawa told Alice as gently as he could of Ôta's decision to return. When she realized the full import of his words, she was so astounded and dismayed that her mind became unhinged. Yet, most pitiable thing of all, in spite of her own calamity, Alice still found the strength of will to grope through the dark confusion of her mind to the bedside of the man she loved and, without a complaint, to expend her own too feeble strength on nursing him.

It took Ôta a long time to recover, and when the time for parting came, Alice's mind had given way beyond all hope of recovery.

So it came about that, on the ship carrying him to his distant home, Ôta sat all alone in his cabin, writing of what he had left behind. Thanks to his friend Aizawa and the generosity of Count

〔 409 〕

Amakata, every arrangement had been made to ensure that poor Alice should not suffer from material want. But his grief overwhelmed him as he saw again before his eyes the vision of the woman he loved, bereft of reason and hope, and hugging to her breast a baby's dress in vague anticipation of motherhood, weeping distractedly.

Of this story Mori Ôgai once said, " I have attempted to portray a Japanese who was living in Berlin at the same time as I, who came to grips with the kind of situation described in the story." He then went on to say, " There are a good many European works of fiction with similar plots." He was obviously seeking to convey the impression that in writing " The Ballet Girl " he had done no more than combine these two factors, an actual occurrence and a plot in accordance with European literary traditions. Yet this alone would not have sufficed to produce the intense pathos, the tragic sincerity, revealed in *Maihimé*. People were not long in surmising that Ôgai himself had suffered a painful love affair similar to that of Ôta and Alice in his story. This was most likely the truth, and he is said to have cherished to the end of his days the conviction that his own Alice was the one and only woman for him.

There are many qualities in " The Ballet Girl " to account for the immense popular approval that greeted it. Its presentation of a special type of young Japanese intellectual, its youthful yearning for freedom, the charm of its romantic sentimentalism, its hero's love affair with a European at a time when admiration for Europe was at its height, its exotic atmosphere with its descriptions of life in a foreign country : all these elements were new to the fiction of the time, and were something which the youth of the country was particularly ready for. Nevertheless, there can be no denying that its most impressive quality was the author's artistic skill in presenting an actual, deep emotion. It would be no exaggeration to say that readers of *Maihimé* learnt for the first time the nature of the technique of modern craftsmanship. Ôgai's prose style too is unique, and, combining as it does a wealth of classical beauty and modern sensitiveness, it constitutes a most attractive quality in his work.

After the publication of " The Ballet Girl," Ôgai long continued in the capacity of critic, translator and original to contribute, as few others have done, to the development of Japanese literature. Moulding as he did the modern fiction of this country so as to become as fully modern as possible, his achievements are held in extraordinarily high respect by our men of letters at the present day.

Following his return from abroad, Ôgai also won distinction as an army surgeon. He rose in succession to be a professor of the Army Medical College and the Military Staff College with the rank of surgeon-colonel and, finally, surgeon-lieutenant-general. He received a doctorate in medicine, and soon afterwards one in literature. On his retirement from the army, he held the dual position of chief librarian of the Imperial Household Department and curator of the Imperial Museum. He died in July, 1922, at the age of fifty-nine.

SHIMA CHIDORI TSUKI NO SHIRANAMI*

(Strolling Thieves)

This play by Furukawa Mokuami (1816-1893) was first produced in 1881, with such famous actors as Danjûrô, Kikugorô and Sadanji in the leading rôles. It met with enormous success at the time and is even to-day a popular favourite, being still billed from time to time as part of the *kabuki* repertoire. The author's activity covered the later, declining years of Tokugawa feudalism and the transitional period of the Meiji era, and he was accounted the foremost dramatist of his day. Hence his inclusion here among the representative authors of modern Japan.

Throughout his career Mokuami's distinguishing gift was the power of depicting particular aspects of life with great fidelity and understanding. His works fall into two classes according to whether they deal with the last phase of feudalism or the new world of Meiji. The former class is called *kizewamono*, and the latter *zangirimono*. The word *zangiri* (hair-cut) refers to the change in the fashion of hair-dressing that came about during the Meiji era. Men of the old régime were accustomed to wear their hair long in the *magé* (chignon) style, but with the Restoration in 1868 and the consequent increase of intercourse with Europe and America, that style lost favour and was abolished because it was contemptuously referred to by foreigners as a "pigtail," and the simple style of short hair, called *zangiri*, took its place. The *zangirimono* are those plays by Mokuami whose scenes are laid in the first fifteen years or so of the Meiji era. There are about a dozen of these, *Shima Chidori Tsuki no Shiranami* being considered the masterpiece among them.

The play consists of five acts and nine scenes. The principal

---

*This title is a poetic play on words—*Shima Chidori* (island plovers), suggests "migratory"; *Tsuki no* (of the moonlight) suggests "nocturnal" ; " *Shiranami* (white-capped waves) is a poetic term for "thieves." So "The migrant plovers flying over white-capped waves in the moonlight" means "men who come from the provinces to the city and rob people at night."

characters are Akashi-no Shimazô and Matsushima-no Senta, with Mochizuki Akira almost as important. Akashi-no Shimazô was the son of a fisherman of Akashino'ura, a region along the south coast of Harima province (Hyôgo prefecture), with a craze for gambling, who in consequence of a theft had to leave his native place for Tokyo, capital of the new régime, to look for a job. Unable to find any honest work, he again took to stealing and was caught and landed in jail. While serving his sentence, Shimazô became friendly with a fellow prisoner, Matsushima-no Senta, with whom he entered into a pledge to share everything to the death as brothers. Senta was the son of a peasant family in the suburbs of Sendai who, like Shimazô, had committed a theft in boyhood, had come to Tokyo to seek a job in vain, and, resorting to robbery, had ended up in prison.

Soon after their release from prison, the two broke into the Fukushimaya Pawnshop run by one Seibeé and got away with a thousand yen in cash. But Seibeé put up such a stout resistance that Shimazô had to draw his short sword, wounding him in the leg. Then they divided the loot equally between them and parted to return to their families, Shimazô to Akashino'ura and Senta to Sendai, for Shimazô had an aged father, a younger sister and his own motherless child, and Senta his poverty-stricken parents, and the two robbers were mindful of these family ties and obligations.

When Shimazô arrived at his native place, very well dressed on the strength of the stolen money, and offered the remainder of the money to his father, the old man's suspicions were aroused. He came to the conclusion that Shimazô could have acquired so much money only by dishonest means and refused to accept it. With tears in his eyes he besought his son to lead an honest life, and then, just when the old man's distress was beginning to have some effect, Shimazô's little son came bursting into the house, full of happiness at his father's return. Shimazô noticed that the little fellow was limping, and when he learned the cause of it, he was for the first time filled with a fear of retribution for his crimes and the desire to reform. For, on that very night when he and Senta had broken into the Fukushimaya Pawnshop, indeed at the very moment when he wounded Seibeé in the leg, it so happened that a large kitchen knife, lying on a shelf here in his father's house, had fallen down on his son Iwamatsu, who was sleeping beneath it, and had inflicted a deep wound on his leg, severing the ligaments. The awful certainty with which the sin of the father had been visited upon the child effected his complete reformation.

Shimazô resolved that he must acquire by honest means the amount of money he had stolen, and then make restitution to the pawnbroker, and hand himself over to the police in order to pay the penalty of having broken the law. Informing his family of the decision he had made, he went back to Tokyo, where he started a retail *saké* shop at Kagurazaka, and devoted himself to building up an honest business.

In the meantime, his friend Senta had had a very different experience. From an old acquaintance whom he met on the way to his home he had learned that both of his parents were already dead, and so he had decided to remain at a place called Shirakawa, where he had taken a fancy to an itinerant geisha, named Oteru. He did not stay long, however, for he came under the notice of the police and only just managed to slip out of their hands. So he returned to Tokyo and resumed his old game of stealing for living.

Quite by chance Senta discovered that his one-time love, the geisha Oteru, had now become the wife of a wealthy money-lender named Mochizuki Akira, and that they were living in a splendid mansion at Kagurazaka. This Akira had formerly been a retainer of the Tokugawa Shogunate, but, anticipating its fall and the coming political changes, he had set about feathering his nest by extorting money from wealthy citizens on the pretence that it was to be used for the government's military purposes. Although he was detected in this and arrested, he was released from prison on the fall of the Shogunate at the Meiji Restoration ; and had made a new start in the money-lending business. Senta thought it would be easy to make capital of his past relations with Oteru. Akira, however, did not prove an easy victim ; he showed that he still possessed the grit and determination of a samurai of the old régime, and summarily put the would-be extortionist to rout. Senta nursed a bitter grudge on this account, and began to plan to break into Akira's mansion and murder him and Oteru.

But, since he could scarcely carry out such an attempt by himself, he began to ponder on what help he might possibly enlist. It was then that he came across Shimazô again at his *saké* shop in Kagura-zaka, and made an appointment for a secret meeting. Late one night in front of the *torii* gate at the Memorial Shrine in Kudan, the two old associates met and Senta revealed his intentions to Shimazô, asking for his assistance. Shimazô, however, was now thoroughly reformed character, and not only did he refuse to listen to the proposal, but he went on to warn Senta against undertaking such a rash enterprise. This angered Senta, who drew out a sword and in blind fury struck at his friend for going back on the pledge he had once made. Shimazô dexterously avoided the blow and seized hold of Senta's hand in order to dispossess him of the weapon. Soon the two were locked in a desperate struggle, but in the end Shimazô knocked the sword out of the assailant's hand, overpowered him and pinned him to the ground. Then, kneeling over the prostrate Senta, Shimazô earnestly pleaded with him to abandon his evil ways, urging him to give up this life of thieving and begin a new and honest life. " We will both," he said, " go and give ourselves up to the police and submit to whatever the law decrees. That is the manly thing to do." It might well be, he continued, that such voluntary submission on their part would serve as an example to other thieves to go straight, and thus they would be indirectly serving the State. So kindly, so sincerely, did he plead that Senta, as if awakening from a bad dream, for the first time realized how evil his life had been.

Full of remorse, he apologized to Shimazô from the bottom of his heart for the wrong he had tried to do him. Then to prove his sincerity he picked up the sword that had been knocked out of his hand in the struggle and tried to kill himself with it. Shimazô managed to stop him and to persuade him that such an action was only futile and foolish. As for the plan of breaking into Akira's mansion to kill him and his wife, that, of course, had passed clean out of his mind.

Shimazô was filled with joy that he had made a new man of Senta, and was ready to go with him at once to the police to make a full confession. But an obstacle still remained in that there was still the thousand yen to be returned which they had stolen from Seibeé. They knew, moreover, that the loss of this money had ruined the unfortunate man's pawnbroking business, while the wound in the leg inflicted by Shimazô had crippled him. ust when they were at their wit's end what to do, who should appear from behind a tree near by but Akira and offer to provide the necessary amount? It happened that he had been returning home late when he had espied the two men talking, and, feeling somewhat apprehensive, had hidden behind the tree and so had overheard all that had passed between them. When he had first heard Senta's murderous proposition he had been greatly alarmed, and felt quite sure that, if they had attacked him unawares, they would certainly have killed him. But when he heard Shimazô's admonition to Senta and Senta's complete repentance and found that the only obstacle to their turning over a new leaf was the want of a thousand yen, he expressed himself as only too glad to furnish them with it. Chivalry and kindly feeling had perhaps prompted this generous offer, but certainly also a feeling of gratitude for his own escape.

Thanking Akira for his generosity, Shimazô and Senta, once blood brothers in crime, set out in the highest spirits to pay their debt to Seibeé, to society and to the gods. And as they went, the crowing of a cock heralding the dawn was heard and through the darkness the first faint streaks of a new day began to appear.

Such is the summary of *Shima Chidori Tsuki no Shiranami*. Apart from its interest as a drama, it has three salient features. The first is of a historical nature. The three chief characters in this play, not only Shimazô and Senta but also Akira, are connected with the business of robbery in one form or another. This, indeed, is a notable feature of many of Mokuami's plays. So frequently were his principal characters robbers and burglars that he was given the nick-name of Shiranami Sakusha, " Maker of Robbery Yarns." But the reason for this is not so much in Mokuami's personal predilection, as in the circumstances of the times in which he lived, bridging as he did the late feudal period and the beginning of the Meiji era. As the feudal régime approached its end and the Tokugawa influence declined, administration of the law became more and more lax. Pickpockets, thieves and burglars were everywhere and unrestrained. Even the advent of the Meiji era saw but little improvement ; the very vastness of the social changes involved for a while only the increasing instability and lawlessness. Therefore, in this respect, Mokuami's plays are an apt commentary on the times in which they are set.

The second characteristic deserving attention is that the play is obviously written to point a moral. The dramatist makes it clear that he believes in the essential goodness of men, and would blame their environment for the evil they do. t is only right to expect that they should return to the virtues that belong to them by nature ; they ought to be admonished for their evil ways and encouraged to follow the path of righteousness. Holding such a view of man, Mokuami considered that it was an important function of literature to make a moral appeal. In " Strolling Thieves " both Shimazô and Senta repent of their evil-doing, and become good, honest men ; it is the dramatic presentation of such a reformation that gives a special interest to this play.

Thirdly, the play definitely suggests that the Meiji era in which it was laid had the promise and brightness of the dawn. The end of the play shows a new day beginning as the reformed thieves set forth to return the stolen money and give themselves up to justice. his symbolizes the spirit of the Mei'i era, during the twenty years or so following the Imperial Restoration. The kaleidoscopic confusion of Japanese life began to take a more ordered form and, under the influence of the more advanced culture of the European nations, larger and more enlightened ideas prevailed, with the result that the general attitude of the people was one of unlimited hopes and expectations. There was an atmosphere of confidence towards life and readiness to face the future ; the nation felt that it was marching forward to the dawn. In giving expression to this spirit lies the play's cultural significance. It also accounts for the play's favourable reception and the great popularity it has achieved.

KIRI HITOHA

(A Fallen Paulownia Leaf)

This drama is from the pen of Tsubouchi Shôyô (1859-1935), and its production in 1896 marked an epoch in the Japanese drama of the Meiji era.

It is a long historical play in seven acts and fifteen scenes, having for its subject the events immediately preceding the famous Osaka Winter Campaign of the year 1614. Toyotomi Hideyoshi, the great military leader who had seized the reins of power in the latter part of the sixteenth century, had died in 1598, naming his young son Hideyori as his successor and Tokugawa Iyeyasu as the child's guardian and adviser. Within little more than a decade after Hideyoshi's death, the majority of the samurai throughout the country were siding with Iyeyasu, while the power of the youthful Hideyori had declined. Iyeyasu determined to take advantage of the changing situation and overthrow Hideyori in order to make himself in name as well as in fact the supreme military ruler of Japan. The discord between the two factions came to a head with the Tokugawa forces taking the offensive against the Toyotomis in the two campaigns which are known as the Osaka Winter Campaign of 1614 and the Osaka Summer Campaign of 1615. The Toyotomi forces were defeated on both occasions, and with the capture of Osaka in 1615 and the death of Hideyori the whole country passed under the rule of the Tokugawas.

The play has as its background the discord between the two rival houses and the events attending the fall of the Toyotomis and the rise of the Tokugawas. The plot is concerned with the origin and development of the dissension within the ranks of the Toyotomi forces at Osaka that contributed so largely to the fatal result. Two memorable characters, Lady Yodogimi and Katagiri Katsumoto, stand out conspicuously in the dissension as opposing protagonists, with Lady Yodogimi's arrogance and Katsumoto's devotion constituting the warp and the woof of the drama. A certain number of episodes are built up on this out of the author's fertile imagination, and the result is a tragic presentation of the manner in which the House of Toyotomi went to its doom.

Lady Yodogimi, the mother of young Hideyori, was a woman of great beauty and pride, reminiscent of Cleopatra. As might have been expected of the widow of the Great Hideyoshi, who had fed her vanity with all the pomp and splendour with which he had surrounded her, she still maintained a magnificent style of living and, even in the face of imminent defeat and ruin, continued to conduct herself as if the sixty-odd provinces of the country were her private personal possessions. The steady rise to power of the Tokugawa family filled her with overmastering jealousy, and her distrust and suspicion of those in her service grew into an obsession. Katsumoto, on the other hand, was the man whom Hideyoshi had trusted so completely as to make him tutor and guardian of young Hideyori, and well he merited the trust reposed in him, being a high-minded warrior and the very paragon of loyalty.

After Hideyoshi's death, Katsumoto had become the power behind the Toyotomis, and on him fell the responsibility of preventing the encroachment of the swelling Tokugawa influence. But although he was a samurai of the utmost integrity, he was by nature a temporizer, lacking or wavering in decision, and so he frequently played into the hands of his enemies. Worst of all, since it was he who actually wielded the power, his failures afforded an excellent opportunity to the more ambitious of the Toyotomi party to insinuate themselves into Lady Yodogimi's good graces as a preliminary to dislodging him from his high position. Chief among these intriguers were Ôno Dôken and his son Shurinosuké. Since Shurinosuké was also Lady Yodogimi's lover the odds were heavily against Katsumoto, who was gradually neglected and avoided by the Lady. Not only was he troubled with enemies within, but the Tokugawa party was watching for an opportunity to intensify the internal dissension and to alienate him from his own party, realizing that the House of Toyotomi could not be defeated until Katsumoto's influence had been undermined. Thus plotted against from within and without, Katsumoto was in a dangerous position ; but, fully conscious of his obligations to his dead master

Hideyoshi, he loyally devoted his whole energies to retrieving the diminishing fortunes of the Toyotomis.

The curtain rises just as the Tokugawa intrigue is finally enmeshing Katsumoto in its toils. The House of Toyotomi had just erected a huge statue of Buddha at the Hôkô-ji temple in Kyoto, and also a great bell in the belfry attached thereto. The inscription on the bell contained a phrase consisting of four Chinese characters, "Kokka Ankô," meaning "Tranquillity to the State". It so happened that the second and fourth characters, *ka* and *kô*, were the characters denoting *iyé* and *yasu*, with which the name "Iyeyasu", is written. This was excuse enough for the Tokugawas to take offence, affecting to interpret the division o the name Iyeyasu in this manner as a curse directed against the Tokugawa leader.

As soon as he heard of the matter, Katsumoto realized the need for decisive action and set off personally to Sunpu (now the city of Shizuoka) where Iyeyasu then resided, to put the matter right. But since the "curse" was a deliberately trumped-up charge, it was not likely that he could achieve anything, no matter how many explanations and disclaimers he made. Iyeyasu utterly refused to listen to any protestations of innocence, and put forward three alternative demands as the only means of settling the affair. These demands were, 1. The House of Toyotomi must abandon Osaka astle, then regarded as the strongest fortress in the country, and move out to an adjoining province, or, 2. Make yearly visit to Edo to do homage as vassals of the House of Tokugawa, or, s Send Lady Yodogimi to Edo as a permanent hostage.

These alternatives were all equally unreasonable and unacceptable. Yet Katsumoto realized that there was no chance of victory for the Toyotomi if it came to an open outbreak of hostilities, and so to get out of a very difficult quandary he agreed to comply with the last of the three demands. But, in doing so, he was merely seeking to gain time, having ideas of his own about the way the demand would be met. He was calculating that before Lady Yodogimi could reside as a hostage in Edo, a house would have to be built for her and that three or four years, at least, could be wasted over such matters as a long and careful investigation for a suitable site, and in the transport of the right sort of choice wood all the way from Osaka. By that time, Iyeyasu would be well over seventy perhaps dead, and then the demand might, in more favourable circumstances, be quashed or consigned to merciful oblivion. That was the thought he had in his mind as he set off to Osaka in order to reveal it to Lady Yodogimi and win her approval.

But, unfortunately, he had chosen exactly as the Tokugawas had hoped he would, and they took good care to see that the news of Katsumoto's capitulation in the matter of Lady Yodogimi should reach Osaka before he did. The proud Yodogimi was furious with anger, and the Ônos, father and son, together with other ambitious men who were jealous of Katsumoto, seized the oppor_ tunity to denounce him. In the most flagrant terms they con_ demned h'm for yielding to so impossible a demand as the surrender of his liege-mistress as a hostage; and all on his own responsibility without so much as consulting her. It was even being bandied about that he was a traitor and in collusion with the Tokugawas, when the unfortunate Katsumoto himself arrived on the scene. He was summoned immediately to appear before Lady Yodogimi and was subjected to a stiff cross-examination, in which he was bound to admit that he had agreed to the Tokugawa demand for Yodogimi as a hostage. He could not, however, explain his reasons for doing so, for, if he were to reveal his secret intentions and the Tokugawa party heard of it, then, not only would all his efforts and scheming be useless, but the situation would be made even worse. He did his best to persuade Yodogimi to give him an interview alone, so that he might explain the situation to her in confidence. It could hardly be expected, however, that Yodogimi, in any case strongly suspicious of him and now harbouring a definite aversion towards him for having turned traitor, would consent to such an interview; and, in any case, those who had now ob_ tained her ear would never have permitted him the opportunity to speak to her alone. So black, indeed, did things look against him that even those who had previously trusted him now felt that he had betrayed their cause. The loyal but hot-tempered Ishikawa Izunokami demanded an interview with him on his way back from the castle, when he urged him to wipe out the stain on his name by committing *harakiri*; and because Katsumoto refused to act on this advice, the angry nobleman in a violent rage humiliated him by kicking him like a dog. But Katsumoto was willing to endure any personal indignities, because he knew full well that he was the mainstay of the Toyotomi party and that his life was therefore of the utmost value to them.

Meanwhile a grand council had been summoned in the castle, and, with one exception, all were unanimous that the death penalty should be pronounced on Katsumoto as a traitor. The exception was Kimura Nagatonokami, a young lord who had enough intelligence to realize that they must be misjudging Katsumoto and had the courage to say so. He called attention to Katsumoto's honourable record of loyal service, and declared his intention of seeking him out to learn what were those secret intentions which he was convinced lay behind Katsumoto's apparent surrender to the Tokugawas, and which, for obvious reasons, could not be made public. So he set out on his lone mission to Katsumoto's mansion.

There Katsumoto, who had every confidence in young Nagato's sagacity, revealed to him the true motives that had prompted him in making his decision. Nagato was able to appreciate fully the delicacy of the situation and expressed his complete concurrence with what the other had done. But meanwhile events had been happening to render all his efforts abortive; the faction hostile to Katsumoto did not intend to lose this golden opportunity of getting rid of him and had persuaded Lady Yodogimi to sign an order summoning him forthwith to the castle, their intention being to encompass his death before Lord Nagato could make his report to their liege-mistress. Katsumoto saw through the scheme, and decided to set off at once with his loyal retainers to his own castle at Ibaraki, near Osaka, not because he feared death, but because he regarded it as utter folly to sacrifice his life for so useless a purpose. On his way there he arranged to meet ord Nagato again, and told him that it was certain that, now he had been driven away from any possibility of rendering active assistance to the Toyotomi cause, the Tokugawa forces would soon be making an attack on Osaka. He gave the young lord specific instructions regarding the steps to be taken if war should break out, thus delegating to one whom he trusted the grave responsibilities which intrigues within and without had made it impossible to fulfil himself. Then the two brave soldiers parted, promising to meet each other again in the next world.

Such is the outline of the main plot of *Kiri Hitoha*. Of the various episodes woven into the play, two deserve special mention. One is the dream episode, in which Lady Yodogimi, while dreaming that she was one of a merry party with her dead husband, Hideyoshi, among the cherry-blossoms on Mount Yoshino, finds herself suddenly transported to the dreary graveyard where Hidetsugu lies buried among his ancestors. This Hidetsugu had been appointed by Hideyoshi as his successor, but this had conflicted with the ambitions of Lady Yodogimi for her own son, and she had falsely accused him of a serious offence, with the result that he had been violently put to death on Hideyoshi's orders. Here, beside Hidetsugu's grave, Yodogomi is tormented by the ghost of the murdered man and also by those of his kin, the whole dream episode being intended to show how Lady Yodogimi was being tortured by her conscience for past wrong-doing. The other episode is concerned with the pitiful love affair between Katsumoto's beautiful daughter Kagerô and Ginnojô, the rather feeble-minded son of her father's chief political foe, which ends in their both committing suicide, the young man by drowning. The introduction of such episodes as these gives a highly tragi-romantic character to the play.

There are good reasons for calling this an epoch-making work. In the first place, it is a historical drama in the real sense of the word, whereas previously there had been nothing to deserve such a title. True, many plays had been written, those of Chikamatsu Monzaemon, for example, around material taken from historical sources ; but practically none of them had done more than borrow the names of characters and the bare outline of events, without attaching any importance to the achievement of historical truth through the framing of plots, character delineation, and the presentation of the peculiar aspects of life and thought in different ages. For all these, so essential to any real historical drama, the authors had drawn simply on their own imagination. Compared with such works, *Kiri Hitoha* is the first play to render truly the actual facts of history.

But, and this forms a second reason for the play's high place in general estimation, it possesses something more than simple historical authenticity. It is invested throughout with the author's penetrating insight into the logic of events, those destinies which men bring inevitably upon themselves and their age by their own acts and deeds.

Thirdly, the characters of this play, particularly the central figure of Katagiri Katsumoto, are presented as quite ordinary individuals subject to indecisive resolves and makeshift schemes; whereas, in plays previously written around historical figures, the characters had invariably been presented on the heroic scale as men of quick decision, magnificent alike in word and action. In *Kiri Hitoha* all such shoddy mummery is cast aside, and we see real people only too much like ourselves. This is in itself enough to entitle the play to be called epoch-making.

This play has additional interest in that the influence of Shakespeare can be seen in it. The reason is not far to seek. Tsubouchi Shôyô, the author, was a great admirer of and authority on the great dramatist. He was not only the first to introduce Shakespeare to Japanese readers, but even dedicated his whole life to the task of translating his complete works. So eminently successful was he in rendering them into his own language in a form worthy of the original that he stands out as Japan's foremost Shakespearean scholar. This accounts for the Shakespearean echoes to be found in his own original dramas; for the fact that Lady Yodogimi, the heroine of *Kiri Hitoha*, bears a marked resemblance to Lady Macbeth, while the unfortunate girl Kagerô has in her something of the peculiar pathos of Shakespeare's Ophelia. Yet, despite the signs of such influence, *Kiri Hitoha* remains on the whole a peculiarly Japanese play, in the manner of treamtent as well as in its emotional quality.

WAKANASHÛ

(Collection of Young Herbs)

Shimazaki Haruki's father, Masaki, was a nationalist scholar, hereditary inn-keeper and post-master in a mountain village on the Nakasendô, the mountain highway along which feudal lords, government officials and merchants passed between Edo and Kyoto, staying for the night in his house. The new age which followed the Meiji Restoration brought economical difficulties to Shimazaki's inn as well as to the district. The railway was built several miles west of the village and the old highway became a local path. No travellers passed along the highway, the inn once so busy was deserted, and the Shimazaki family was gradually reduced to poverty. Shimazaki did his best for the district, and for Shinto principles. But everything went contrary to his hopes ; Japan was changing, and to his nationalist eyes deteriorating, very rapidly under Western influence ; and he died in despair.

Haruki, better known by his pen-name Tôson, was born in 1872 in this tragic atmosphere. The boy was nine years old when he was sent to his sister's family in Tokyo. There he studied English against his father's wish, in 1891 graduated from a Christian missionary college, and found a post as teacher of English in a girls' school. There he became acquainted with Kitamura Tôkoku, the pioneer of the new literary movement, and engaged in the publication of a literary monthly, *Bungakukai* (The Literary Circle). This period of his life was one of spiritual struggles. He resigned his post as teacher, parted from his missionary friends, and for some time led a wandering life.

What he sought was a new life of spiritual growth, of more sweetness and light. A new age in the political and mechanical sides of life had begun, but the force of habit and convention was very strong. The whole literature of the Meiji era was the record of bitter struggle of the old and new thoughts and moral attitudes.

For the first time in the East literature concerned itself with the hard, real problems of social and individual life—no longer was literature a mere escape from life, to nature, to fantasy or to unashamed sensualism. Young Japanese poets who saw the opening of the Diet in 1890 could not realize how strong was the force of the people's mental habits; they launched forth their new romantic idealism which was soon to founder in the sea of old customs and ideas. Kitamura Tôkoku exhausted his strength in the struggle, and died in 1894. Tôson might have met a similar fate if two years later he had not gone to Sendai, a city two hundred miles northeast of Tokyo, to take up a post in a college. Here he spent a year of tranquillity and wrote poems on his own passions and yearning remembered in calmness. A poem entitled *Kusamakura* (Wandering) tells of his inner life when he arrived at Sendai in 1896. It begins :—

" Over the evening waves cries a sanderling : though I am not the bird, yet I am beating my wings of thought towards the lonesome open sea ! "

Af er recollecting his sad, solitary wandering, he tells us how he came to Sendai.

" ... So was I like a fallen leaf of autumn driven on by the wind. Beckoned on by yellow morning clouds, I passed Shirakawa by night.

" I love the pathless wilderness,—is it because I have not yet found my way wi hin me ? I wandered about with troubled mind and came to Miyagi plain at Sendai.

" O Miyagi plain, home of my heart. To me, perplexed and passionate, dear was that wild plain with withered grass and faint sunshine.

" To my solitary ears the north wind sounded like a lyre ; to my sad eye colourless stones seemed like flowers.

" Ah ! whom shall I tell of the sights of so lonesome a plain on a winter's day, whom but those who have tasted and known the sadness of a companionless life ? "

He goes on to sing of the sad sights of human life and nature. At last the solitude grows unbearable to him; he wanders to the seashore, as desolate as the plain. There the poet somehow feels spring coming; and expects to see green shoots budding on the sands in spite of the falling snow.   The poem concludes with the lines—

> " Climbing up a great rock which towered by the shore I gazed forward.   Spring was coming on the Aurorean clouds. ' Twas dawn with the sound of tide afar ! "

This poem may be understood as the expression of the poet's feelings at the time of his arrival at Sendai.   In the preface to *Tôson Shishû* (Tôson's Poems), published in 1904, the author tells us about the time :—

> " The age of new poetry came at last !   It was like a beauti-ful dawn.   Imagination, wakened from a long sleep and reju-venated, enriched the language of the people.   Traditions came back to life again.   Nature was clothed in new colours.
>
> " Most of the new poets were young and sincere.   Their art was crude and incomplete, but without guile or affectation. Youth enkindled them, and enthusiasm lighted up their faces. The fresh and overflowing current of thought made many a young man forgetful of sleep and food ; the agony and sorrow of the new age drove some to madness !   Forgetful of my own inability, I joined the company of new poets.
>
> " Poetry is said to originate from emotion recollected in tranquillity, yet my poems are indeed confessions of hard struggle.
>
> " Who can be contented with old life ?   Everyone strives to make his own way ; it is a duty of a young man.
>
> " Life is Force :   Force is Expression :   Expression is Word. A new word is new life."

Tôson's poems are deeply sincere, and natural expressions of himself and of that newly awakened age.   They are intensely personal, yet at the same time national, and are now regarded as the very fountainhead of the new Japanese poetry.

The first edition of the *Wakanashû* (published by Shunyô'dô, August, 1897) contains fifty-one poems ; the " Selected Poems of Tôson " (published by Iwanami, 1927) contains forty-six poems ; the final revised edition (published by Shinchôsha, April, 1936) contains thirty-five.   Below is given a prose version of one of his early works.

Oyô

I have passed along most of the dream-paths which girls do tread. Looking back on my life's ascending way, on the landscape I gaze.

By the calmly-flowing river Edo I was born ; under the cherry blossoms on its banks, I grew to maidenhood.

Sea-gulls floated on that wide stream, white violets bloomed amid the tender young grass by a rivulet :—there many a dream I dreamt !

I served at the court ' above the ninefold-violet cloud ' ; and of a spring night stood in the moonlight before the royal apartments.

The palace, adorned with clouds and waves, loomed in the mist, or glittered in the sun ; of an evening spring rain wet the balustrade of the jewelled pavilion.

Wi h my eyes I saw grea personages in splendour ; and scented the perfumed dresses of ladies in high favour.

I saw men eclipsing in glory those around them, as the morning star that ascends the dawning sky eclipses the lesser lights.

I saw the last of distinguished men, who like the declining sun fade away in the twilight of their fame.

In spring I would hide myself under the flowery shade of the quiet royal garden to weep for one : in autumn would I lean on the casement, and gaze at the evening clouds, longing for my distant friend.

My only sister died, and I left the royal court to come back to the river Edo today. Oh, solitary autumnal sight !

The frost-bitten yellow leaves are scattered from the cherry trees ; the quiet stream Edo flows on never to return—and I walk slowly remembering the past.

To think that I waste myself unknowingly, I am overpowered by youth, and sitting on the grass by the bank, I smile and weep.

This poem may be called a Japanese ballad of the eternal feminine. Tôson has written at the same time six poems of a similar type representing six different female characters, poems which show the budding genius of the great novelist.

The chief verse-form Tôson uses is the stanza of four lines of twelve syllables, with a minor pause after the seventh syllable in each line, a very popular form in Japan which may be called the "common metre " of the Japanese poetry. Tôson gave it freshness and new charm by making it capable of subtle variations. The second and third stanzas of *Oyô* will be read as follows :—

| ︠ ⌣ ⌣ ⌣ ⌣ | ﹏ ⌣ ⌣ | ⌣ ⌣ ︴ | ﹏ ─︤ |

Mi zu shi zu ka na ru E do gawa no
12(7) 21 16(8) 15(7) 50 22 34(10) 14(3) 28(3) 57(6) 44(48)

Naga re no kishi ni uma ré idé
(4)46 (4)11 (5)46 (22)43 (13)26 (18)21(11) 10(8) 58(58)

Ki shi no sa ku ra no ha na ka gé ni
(8)11 (8)24 (8)28(7) 6(9) 17(6) 10(5) 50(6) 6(4) 21(21(7) 7(5) 25(7) 36(61)

Wa ré wa oto meto na ri ni keri
13(12) 26(14) 33(7) 36(6) 50 (7)7(6) 12(8) 27(12) 33(118)

Miya ko dori uku ô kawa ni
28(9) 53(8) 46(10) 34(16) 29(12) 49 57 (48)

Naga reté so so gu kawa zoi no
46(6) 31(6) (5)15 (5)9 46(11) 42(6) 41 60 (48)

Shiro sumi ré sa ku wa ka ku sa ni
6(2)40(10) 24(2) 36(11) 7(9) 38(9) 15(2) 9 15(18) 25(4) 37 (42)

Yu mé ô kari shi waga mi ka na
11(3) 12 42(9) 35(14) 34(84) 11(1)11 15(58) 6(7) 51

The signs—and⌣indicate the length of the syllables, the figures indicating the duration of time measured by oscillographic recording (unit of measurement : one-hundredth of a second), while the figures in brackets show the duration of the pause.

At the period when these poems were written, the old style of recitation was still in use ; if they are spoken, in the modern manner, the cadence of the verse above may be indicated as :—

Mi zu shi zu ka na ru E do gawa no
15(8) 9 19(27) 10(10) 24(8) 7(2) 12(19) 7(4) 16 43 (10) 22(45)
━━━170━━━ ━━━147━━

Naga reno kishini umaré idé
26(7) 42(27) 40(22) 45(15) 22(79)
━━━162━━━ ━━161━━

Kishi no saku rano hana kageni
28(3) 9(27) 11(2) 22(7) 23(6) 28 (8)
━━━109━━ ━━━140━━

Waré wa oto mé to nari ni ké ri
6(4) 13 43(9) 8(10) 8(8) 26(6) 8(2) 26(5) 13 (86)
━━━109━━ ━━━172━━

Miya ko dori uku ô kawani
16(13) 18(4) 35(7) 22(15) 26(10) 48 (15)
━━━130━━ ━━━135━━

Na ga ré té so so gu kawa zoino
16(3) 8(3) 8(9) 16(9) 5(4) 11(8) 20(14) 23(4) 53 (60)
——————134—————— ————140————

Shiro sumi ré sa ku wa ka kusani
22(11) 21 16(10) 8(8) 22 6(6) 13(14) 32 (54)
——————118—————— ————125————

Yu mé ô kari shi wagami kana
8 9 17(8) 20(8) 22(26) 40(9) 18 (7)
——————117—————— ——67——

MIDAREGAMI

(Dishevelled Hair)

The Meiji era (1868–1911) was that of ardent renovation under Western influence in eves department of life. *Kajin no Kigû* (Romantic Meeting with Two Fair Ladies) may be taken as a representative of the political novels in vogue just before the promulgation of the constitution (1889) and the opening of the Diet (1890). By 1890 there was a sudden change in mental attitude; a period of introspection began when eyes were turned inward, and the theme of novels was private, emotional life; *Maihimé* (The Ballet Girl) of 1890 marked the beginning of a romantic movement, and a little later there was a sudden burst of lyrical poetry.

Stimulated by this lyrical revival evinced by *Wakanashû* (1897) and other works of this period, there were repeated experiments in rejuvenating the traditional *haiku* and *tanka*. In January 1900 Yosano Hiroshi (1873–1935) founded a club of new poets named Shinshisha (Coterie of New Poets), and from April on published a monthly magazine called *Myôjô* (the Morning Star), supported by such eminent scholars and poets as Mori Ôgai, Ueda Bin, Susukida Kyûkin, Kanbara Yûmei, and Ishikawa Takuboku, which ran to the hundredth number before it ceased to appear in 1908, dying away when the romantic movement gave place to naturalism.

What Yosano did at the beginning of the movement was to make an attack on the conventional sentiments, diction and style of the old schools, and give bold encouragement to straightforward expression of what was seen by the eye or felt in the heart.

> Painters would have used
> For picture of those bamboos
> But thin blue pigment;
> And the sunset at Saga—
> Was it not also as cold?
> —

O wind of Autumn !
Shall I give you a name that
Is fitting to you ?
O maid of unsettled mind
Wearing dishevelled hair !

The conscious use of colour symbolism and personification was a new technique taught by European poetry, and the expressions were fresh and new to the readers of those days.

In 1897 a girl of nineteen, who read Yosano's poems published n the *Yomiuri*, thought it would be easy and pleasant to compose *tanka*. The girl was Ôtori Akiko, born at Sakai near Osaka in December 1878 the daughter of the proprietor of a cake-shop. In spite of the pressure of her parents, who wished to bring her up as an ordinary home-keeping woman, she was an ardent student of history and literature.

When Yosano started the literary monthly *Myôjô*, she sent him her poems, which were much admired and published in the magazine, Greatly encouraged she continued to send more and more poems, which were more and more exclusively passionate love poems. Miss Ôtori and Yosano married in the autumn of 1901. *Midaregami* (Dishevelled Hair), published a few months previous to the marriage, was a small book of 6 by 3 inches, containing four hundred verses by the poetess.

Of an evening
Into the cherry flower's shade
Stole a baby fox,
When, thrilling its flossy hair,
O'er Saga Plain rang out a bell.

—

Strolling past Gion
To Kiyomizu, I feel,
With cherry and moon,
That every person I meet
Is beautiful to gaze on.

—

Nineteen years has she ;
From her comb flows rippling **down**
Her raven-black hair :
How beautiful is the pride

Of the spring-time of her youth !
—

In purple colour
Upon the slender grasses
    Did the shadows fall
When on the breezy spring moo
Combing my hair I was seated.
—

Dreaming one Spring night
I thought I heard someone pluck
    A string of my lyre,
But ' twas the snap of a hair
As pillowed on arm I lay.
—

No Camellias,
Neither plum-blossom for me,
    No white flowers, pray ;
In peach-blossom do I find
Hue that rebukes not my sin.
—

I did not know why,
But I somehow felt as though
    You awaited me,
And came in a flowery moor
In the light of the new moon.
—

If out in the field
I happen to gather some sprays
    Of wild plum-blossoms
Then consoled I shall soon be ;
We part only for a while.
—

In my life there breaks
A violet-coloured dawn,
    A dawning of love ;
Wafted on by breezes soft
A bird is couched on the sea.
—

Sutras are bitter,
On this sweet evening of Spring
    Accept songs, I pray,
O, twenty-five Bodhisattvas

In the Holy of Holies.

—

Without even once
Touching the so soft bosom
Wherein hot blood throbs—
Do you not feel lonesome, you
Preachers of Ways and Doctrines?

Her *tanka* are the records of moments of greatest interest in her life,—not so much perhaps the events of her life as fancies and conceptions which moved her and were her whole life for the moment.

The lingering traditions of the feudal ages forbade a girl, especially one of common birth, so freely to express her heart. Yet she dared to do so, sometimes very boldly and always most charmingly, in spite of all traditions, and moral and spiritual dogmas. Older people were scandalized, but neither blame nor abuse could stop the flow of her spontaneous song; and other young men and women followed her suit in expressing themselves with equal freedom, enlivening the monthly *Myôjô* by such *tanka* for several years. Most of these poems may be but cheap and rubbishy sentimentalism, yet we cannot forget that her little book of verse, breaking the spell of tradition, awoke a new spirit in Japanese poetry.

Mrs Yosano continued to write poems until death took her away in May 1942. So prolific was she that twenty-one volumes of *tanka* were published in twenty-eight years. The "Collected Tanka of Akiko," 3 vols., published by Shinchôsha in 1919–20, contains about 4,800 poems selected from the fifteen books from *Midaregami* to *Akiko Shinshû* (New Poems by Akiko). In this edition she revised early poems, and omitted some. The *Midaregami* of this edition contains 325 poems. The "Collected Edition of Yosano Akiko" was published by Kaizôsha in 1933.

INDEX

INDEX

[437]

[440]

[441]